ENCOUNTERS
THAT CHANGED THE
WORLD

For Laura

ENCOUNTERS
THAT CHANGED THE
WORLD

by Rodney Castleden

Futura

A *Futura* Book

First published by Futura in 2009

Copyright © Omnipress 2009

ISBN: 978-0-7088-0164-2

Produced by Omnipress Ltd, United Kingdom

Printed in INDIA

Photo credits: Getty Images

Futura
An imprint of Little, Brown Book Group
100 Victoria Embankment
London EC4Y 0DY
An Hachette UK company

CONTENTS

IV: ENCOUNTERS WITH LOVE

V: ENCOUNTERS BY CHANCE

VI: POLITICAL ENCOUNTERS

VII: HOSTILE ENCOUNTERS

VIII: CREATIVE ENCOUNTERS: FROM ANTIQUITY TO 1900

IX: CREATIVE ENCOUNTERS: THE TWENTIETH CENTURY

INTRODUCTION

WE ALL HAVE encounters that change the way we think, the way we see the world, and ultimately the way we behave. It is one of the characteristics that make us human beings. A lot of these encounters are commonplace, like the encounters we have with our teachers at school, and most of us can remember moments when a teacher somehow, by telling us or showing us something, made us see things differently. For me it was encounters with my two English masters, A. H. Collins and Charles Pelham, which had the most profound effect. Then there are encounters with friends, co-workers, husbands, wives and lovers, building over the course of months, years and decades to change us piecemeal in all sorts of ways. And there are fleeting encounters with strangers, maybe a brief conversation, maybe no more than a fragment of someone's conversation overheard as they pass. Two sixteen-year-old boys passed me in the street recently, their heads bowed, talking quietly and reflectively to each other. One, thinking hard, said, 'I – would – walk 400 miles to have the chance to go out with Karen Chambers.' I walked on and they walked on, so that was the sum total of the encounter, but I walked on with the thought that romance and medieval courtly love were after all alive and well on Blatchington Hill. Somehow it gave hope for the future. All these different encounters, significant and insignificant alike, are woven into the fabric of our lives, changing us sometimes subtly and gradually, sometimes with dramatic suddenness, into different people.

This book is inevitably about encounters experienced by people who have made their mark, famous people whose lives are a matter of record. Among the big names are Roman emperors and American presidents, great artists and great writers. Their significant encounters were, equally inevitably, with other well-known figures. Yet it is interesting to see that there are some significant encounters that are with relatively unknown people; even bystanders, people who happen to be in the right place at the right time, can play their part in the unfolding of history. A classic example of this is the anonymous French infantryman who shot and killed Nelson at Trafalgar; it is still not certain who he was.

Some encounters look full of promise, as if they should lead on to something momentous, yet they don't. One of these was the meeting of two remarkable 19th century writers, Algernon Swinburne and Guy de Maupassant. There might have been a sensational and scandalous relationship springing from this encounter. Swinburne was evidently interested in seducing the young Maupassant and showed him some pornographic photographs in an attempt to interest him – but it was to no avail. Nor did the meeting lead to any further meeting of minds, or any meeting at all, though Maupassant did later on write a version of the encounter as a kind of literary curiosity. But, as I hope this book shows, the unpredictability of human encounters is what gives them their peculiar interest.

Some encounters are life-changing meetings between generations, an older person handing on knowledge and experience to a younger person, acting as a role model, encouraging and cultivating a nascent talent. Examples of these include Socrates and Plato, Charles Lyell and Charles Darwin, Sigmund Freud and Carl Jung, T. S. Eliot and Michael Tippett. Some of these relationships have a positive and creative appearance, and yet when you look at them closely they turn out to have been destructive. The relationship between the middle-aged composer Frederick Delius and the young Philip Heseltine looks like a classic case of positive mentoring, an experienced older man helping a young man find himself – yet in the end it all went badly wrong. Did Delius give fatally bad advice? I rather think he did. There are other cross-generation encounters that look as though they were completely sterile and unproductive, and yet on examination they generated a creative result, like the fifty-seven-year-old Michelangelo's long infatuation with a young man who did not return his affection – Tommaso Cavalieri. Michelangelo's love led to an outpouring of poetry and may have influenced the subject matter of his sculpture too.

History is by its nature very incomplete; some events are documented, many are not. This effect is exaggerated by today's celebrity culture. We circulate an ever-increasing amount of information about an ever-decreasing percentage of the population. The Bloomsbury group of artists and writers, for example, has generated a biographical literature that far exceeds the modest output of its subjects. The English writer Lytton Strachey, who was part of the Bloomsbury set, was a man of moderate achievement – he wrote half a dozen biographical books, including *Eminent Victorians* and *Queen Victoria* – yet he appears as a major character in a film, his role in *Carrington* played by Jonathan Pryce, and in various incarnations in at least four different novels. He has been the subject of at least six full-length biographies. Interest in Strachey seems to stem mainly from the fact that he belonged to the same social circle as Virginia Woolf and Duncan Grant. His celebrity is mainly borrowed. Strachey's *Letters* have recently been published. We may perhaps feel that we now know more than we need to know about Lytton Strachey.

So it is that, in many situations, we know a great deal about an encounter from one participant's point of view and much less from the other's. We know Michelangelo was in love with Cavalieri, because art historians and biographers have carefully researched the artist's life, but we know next to nothing about Cavalieri's thoughts regarding Michelangelo. An extreme example of this is the friendship of Socrates and Plato. Because Plato wrote and Socrates did not, we know a great deal about what Plato thought of Socrates. Because of the documentary void, we sometimes forget that we know absolutely nothing about what Socrates thought of Plato. We think of Plato as being Socrates' greatest pupil, and perhaps Socrates did too, or did he see the young Plato as just another pupil?

There are many reports, across the centuries, of people's encounters with God. This is the not the place to debate whether these are encounters between people and a supernatural force outside themselves or encounters between different layers within their own minds – the conscious and the unconscious. Often these encounters are intensely personal, private experiences that powerfully influence, often transform, individual lives. Sometimes these encounters affect whole communities; Joan of Arc's heavenly voices led her into battle, where she helped a disinherited dauphin to the French throne. Occasionally profound spiritual experiences remake communities and lead to the emergence of a new religion; it certainly happened to Moses, Jesus and Mohammed.

Many of the encounters described in this book are multiple encounters. It is much easier to understand the poet William Wordsworth if we explore his encounters with the poor, with the French Revolution, with landscape, with other writers, such as Coleridge, Lamb and Keats, with his lover Annette Vallon and with his sister Dorothy. It is the sum of these encounters that make up Wordsworth's life: the sequence of encounters is his biography. In a similar way, Queen Victoria's relationship with Prince Albert is easier to understand in the context of her love (and hate) relationships with several other people, such as her mother, Sir John Conroy, Lord Melbourne, Lord Palmerston, Gladstone, Disraeli and John Brown. Victoria's personal life becomes much easier to understand in terms of a series of loves. Many episodes in history are really a succession of encounters; the encounter between King Edwin and the Christian missionary Paulinus followed on from St Augustine's encounter with pagans in southern England, and that in turn followed Pope Gregory's encounter with a group of English slave boys in Rome.

It is striking how many encounters happen quite by chance. The novelist Kingsley Amis once commented that initially he had found the otherwise excellent novels of his friend Antony Powell slightly lacking in credibility because the same characters kept bumping into one another by chance in a wide variety of situations. It was Amis's main criticism of Powell's novel sequence *A Dance to the Music of Time*. But as he got to know Powell better, he realised that those chance meetings really did happen, especially in Powell's Eton-and-Balliol social class. The poet John Keats met Coleridge by chance while walking on Hampstead Heath. He also on another occasion – unimaginably - met Wordsworth in a fog on Hampstead Heath. Michael Tippett met T. S Eliot by chance, when they both (separately and independently) visited someone else's house, and the chance meeting led on to Tippett himself writing the words for his own operas.

The importance of chance in the unfolding of events is disconcerting, as it means that many of the things that happen to us might just as easily not have happened. In fact, a lot of history might easily not have happened. If his driver had not accidentally taken the wrong turning in a street in Sarajevo, the archduke would not have been assassinated, and the First World War might not have happened.

Another striking feature is the fact that many of the encounters described in this book have such a powerful emotional charge. The encounters that have the biggest creative results generate strong, wrenching passions. Often the passion is two-sided, like the intense relationship between Freud and Jung, or between Elizabeth Barrett and Robert Browning. But sometimes it is strikingly one-sided, as in the relationship between Michelangelo and Cavalieri. And with Dante and Beatrice it is even more extreme. Beatrice had no idea whatever of Dante's feelings for her, and she died in her twenties without knowing that he was already turning her into a literary icon that would ensure her immortality; she was to all intents and purposes completely outside the encounter!

One encounter that has inspired an enormous amount of media comment and speculation in recent years is the political and personal relationship between the British prime minister Tony Blair and his chancellor Gordon Brown. Exactly what happened in the way of deals and promises of handing over power is still not known. Were there promises? Or hints of promises? Or conditional promises? Both men will very likely one day write comprehensive autobiographies, so there is the chance that what really happened may emerge. But even those immediately involved in such exchanges only see part of the situation, not all of it, and I suspect that neither Gordon Brown nor Tony Blair fully understood one another, or what they were doing to one another psychologically. It may well be that the whole truth will never be known about that unusually tense political encounter.

I
ENCOUNTERS WITH GOD

MOSES AND THE
BURNING BUSH

(CIRCA 1270 BC)

THE MAGISTERIAL, RESOLUTELY serious figure of Moses strides solemnly through the early books of the Old Testament. He is such a familiar figure to most of us that it is hard to see him as he really was. It is hard too to visualise the astonishing magnitude or appreciate the sheer audacity of what he did. It was, or looks very much like, what the Greeks would later call hubris; the Greeks would concoct the myth of Prometheus to illustrate what could happen to mortals who seize from the gods what is theirs. Who was this Moses? Certainly he was a Hebrew prophet and lawgiver who lived in the bronze age, but we sometimes overlook the fact that he actually created a world religion as a result of his claim to personal direct communion with God.

We are told that he was born in Egypt of Levite parents, during the time when the people of Israel were slave workers, captives in Egypt. In the bronze age, taking people as booty in time of war was a very widespread practice; both men and women were carried off to do various kinds of work. During the Trojan War, which took place perhaps a generation after Moses, around 1250 BC, men were evidently taken as slaves; this is mentioned in the poems of the Greek Epic Cycle. Women were routinely taken away to do work in textile manufacture, as we know from the archive tablets found at some of the Greek centres, and they were referred to as 'women of Lesbos' or 'women of Chios' according to the places round the Aegean where they had been captured. So the captivity of the Israelites and their transfer to Egypt to work was a perfectly normal practice in those times. It would be wrong to see the Israelites as a people singled out for special discriminatory treatment;

they were persecuted no more than any other conquered people of the late bronze age.

We are told that as a baby Moses ('Mosheh' in Hebrew) was nearly killed in a general slaughter of male Jewish children ordered by the Egyptian Pharaoh. He was rescued by being concealed by his mother in a chest in bulrushes by the bank of the River Nile. He was found in the bulrushes by one of Pharaoh's daughters and given a privileged upbringing. Whether this slaughter of children really took place has to be questioned, because it has its precise parallel in the New Testament in the Massacre of the Innocents, which the infant Jesus narrowly escapes. Jesus, as Moses' spiritual successor, is said to have gone through the same experience of narrow escape. Repeated stories, or stories with close parallels, like this should always excite suspicion when it comes to the realities of history. Either the earlier story or the later story, or both, may be untrue. Interestingly, the first century Alexandrian scholar Philo took the line that the story of Moses was pure legend: a collection of fables designed to showcase the Ten Commandments.

Then we read that when he grew up Moses killed an Egyptian who was bullying an Israelite and had to run away in order to avoid punishment. Moses went to live in Midian with the priest Jethro and married one of Jethro's daughters. He became the father of Gershom and Eliezer.

Then came the moment which changed not only his life but the lives of all the Israelites. While tending Jethro's flocks as they grazed on Mount Horeb, Moses had a momentous encounter with God, who spoke to him out of a burning bush. The bush was apparently on fire, yet not consumed by the flames. The word used in the Hebrew specifically means brambles, but it is very close in form to the word Sinai, and some scholars think the reference to the burning bush is due to a copyist's mistake. It may be that originally the reference was to an encounter with God on Sinai. But how could Sinai have been on fire yet not consumed?

For the moment, before trying to answer this question, we should return to the story as we have it. Yahweh saw Moses approaching the bush and told him first to take off his sandals because he was treading on holy ground. Moses hid his face. When Moses asked him who he was, Yahweh replied that he was the God of the Patriarchs, Abraham,

Isaac and Jacob, and revealed that his name was Yahweh. In antiquity the name was believed to derive from a Hebrew word meaning 'I am that I am' or 'He who is', which was suitably mysterious and awe-inspiring. But modern Bible scholars think 'Yahweh' is more likely to come from 'hawah' - 'blow' or 'fall' – and so mean 'He who blows or makes things fall'. This would fit in with Yahweh as a storm-god. The principal deity of the Hittites at this time was a Weather-god, in some places called Teshub. A treaty between Hattusilis III the Hittite high king and Ramesses II the Egyptian Pharaoh was explicitly to make 'eternal the relations which the Sun-god of Egypt and the Weather-god of Hatti have established for the land of Egypt and the land of Hatti.'

Whatever it meant, the new god made his name known to Moses at the burning bush – Yahweh, often later rendered 'Jehovah'. He also appointed Moses as the leader of the Israelites and commanded him to bring the people of Israel out of Egypt. Moses was also to tell the elders of the Israelites that Yahweh would rescue them and lead them to Canaan, a territory evocatively described as a 'land of milk and honey'. The newly named god was aware that the Egyptians were oppressing the Israelites, was displeased by this, and demonstrated his displeasure by visiting upon them a series of terrible plagues, culminating in the death of the first-born.

Following this encounter with Yahweh, Moses was invested with supernatural powers in order to help him carry out his mission. Yahweh apparently understood that neither the Israelites nor the Egyptians would take Moses' account of his encounter at face value; he had to prove that he had a powerful god on his side. These supernatural powers included the ability to turn a staff into a snake, turn his hand temporarily leprous, and turn water into blood. Yahweh presented Moses with a staff, as if it were a staff of office, like a bishop's crozier.

Moses was alarmed by his encounter with God and reluctant to take on the role God was giving him. He argued that he lacked eloquence and that someone else should be sent instead. Yahweh reacted angrily to this, telling him to use Aaron as his assistant; Aaron was more eloquent and already on his way to meet Moses. So Aaron was assigned a divine mission by Moses, just as Moses had just been assigned his mission by Yahweh.

The place where this encounter took place was by ancient tradition Mount Serbal. But in the fourth century this site was replaced by St Catherine's Monastery, at the foot of Mount St Catherine. A bush found growing there (a bramble) was transplanted a few yards, into the protection of the courtyard of the monastery. Its original location was marked by a chapel, with a silver star marking the spot where the bush emerged from the ground. The monks there believe that this was the original bush seen by Moses; people entering the chapel are expected to take off their shoes, just as Moses was.

The situation is made more complicated still because of a modern shift in popular beliefs towards the Bedouin tradition. Nowadays it is Jebel Musa (Mount Moses) that is believed to be the biblical Mount Sinai. This is next to Mount St Catherine. But the three locations, Mount Serbal, Mount St Catherine and Jebel Musa, are close together near the southern tip of the Sinai peninsula. Modern scholars do not believe that the biblical Sinai can have been in the south at all, most preferring a location in the north, perhaps in the Hijaz area or near Petra.

By this stage Moses had become the leader of the people of Israel and in about 1270 BC he led them out of captivity, eastwards into the Sinai peninsula, and from there into Kadesh and Moab. When the Egyptians tried to pursue them to get them back they were drowned in the Red Sea.

While the people of Israel were wandering across Sinai, Moses ascended Mount Sinai and there he had another momentous encounter with Yahweh. This time Yahweh gave him the Ten Commandments, a brief and simplified law code – a far simpler one than was then in operation in the Hittite Empire, for instance. Moses came down from the mountain and presented his people with the new commandments. When he did this, in effect mediating between the Israelites and Yahweh, Moses became the founder of the Jewish religion.

After Moses led the Israelites to freedom from the town of Ramesses on the Nile delta, they underwent a long period of apparently aimless wandering. This was interpreted by Moses and his people as a period of testing and proving by their new god. Eventually Moses led them towards the borders of what was seen as 'the promised land', the land of Israel that ever afterwards was claimed by them and their successors right down to the present day as God-given. This continuing belief lies behind many of the territorial struggles that have gone on in Israel/Palestine over the last hundred years.

At Mount Nebo, to the north-east of the Dead Sea, Moses died and it was left to his successor, Joshua, to lead the Israelites across the River Jordan into the Promised Land of Canaan. This part of the story is supported by archaeological evidence. In the hills north of Jerusalem there was a marked increase in settlement around 1200 BC, and unlike earlier settlements in the area the new settlements were free of pig bones – in other words they were Jewish settlements.

Stories were later invented to flesh out the biography of Moses. He was said to have initiated the worship of snakes and bulls, though we know these practices were widespread in the eastern Mediterranean region in the bronze age; the Minoans had both snake and bull cults 200-400 years earlier. It is difficult to know whether there is any truth in these peripheral stories. But there is no doubt that Moses was the founder of Israelite nationhood, that it was Moses who welded the many tribes together into one nation. He was also, in a quite extraordinary way, the founder of the Israelites' religion. He introduced the Israelites to their new god, Yahweh and acted as their sole mediator with him. He was clearly a great charismatic leader, able to persuade his people that he could not only speak with God but was the sole interlocutor – they had to deal with God through him.

The creation of the Ten Commandments was perhaps less of an achievement. It represents a very simplified and incomplete code of ethical conduct, even for the time. Even so, in its simplicity and brevity, it became a memorable banner for the new religion – and has remained so ever since. The Ten Commandments have all the power of a corporate logo.

The question remains, what Moses actually saw in the burning bush. It is perhaps easiest to understand in theological terms. What Moses was seeing was the sun, with its unending burning heat that never dies; the sun has often been identified with God, in many cultures. Some theologians see the fire as God's uncreated energy; Moses was being given a privileged glimpse of something divine that mortals cannot usually see. This is a theological explanation. In the Eastern Orthodox

Church there is a preference for using the phrase 'the unburnt bush' and it is seen as foreshadowing the virgin birth of Jesus. Mary the mother of Jesus is viewed as having given birth to Jesus without suffering any 'harm', in the sense of loss of virginity, in the process. This is seen as a later parallel to the bush burning without being burnt.

There are other explanations. Benny Shanon of the Hebrew University of Jerusalem suggests that Moses could have been under the influence of hallucinogenic substance when he 'saw' the burning bush and 'heard' the voice of God. Entheogens found in the dry areas of the Sinai peninsula and also the Negev Desert in the southern part of Israel were often used for religious purposes by the Israelites. This would have been completely in line with practices in other bronze age cultures in the eastern Mediterranean. The Minoans on Crete were using opium to produce altered states and enhance religious experiences. The plant used to produce Moses' experience was perhaps Peganum harmala, which has been used by the Bedouin in modern times, though not identified with any plant mentioned in the Bible. Another possibility is acacia, which is mentioned in the Bible. Some species of acacia produced effects that can make people 'see music'. So Moses may have deliberately consumed the leaves of an hallucinogenic plant in order to enhance a mystical experience – which we know was a contemporary practice – and therefore met God while he was in an intoxicated, altered state.

There is yet another explanation for the burning bush, if 'burning Sinai' is what was really intended. A mountain that burns yet is not consumed is a volcano. There are no volcanoes in the Sinai peninsula that are known to have been active in the last 3,000 years or so, but there are three active volcanoes in northern Saudi Arabia, within 200 miles of Sinai. The likeliest candidate is Jebel Bedr, a black volcanic cone. The Exodus may have taken the Israelites from Ramesses in Egypt south-eastwards across the Sinai peninsula to Jebel Bedr in Saudi Arabia, before turning north to reach the promised land. The eruption column rising from Jebel Bedr could have been what attracted the Israelites towards it – and explain the 'burning pillar of fire' described in the *Book of Exodus* as guiding the Israelites through the wilderness.

21

BUDDHA SITTING BENEATH THE PIPPALA TREE

(528 BC)

THE FOUNDER OF Buddhism was a prince living in the north of the Indian subcontinent. He was Siddhartha, the son of Suddhodana the rajah. His people were the Sakyas, a warrior tribe living in the little kingdom of Kapilavastu 150km north of Benares. His mother was Queen Maya. Prince Siddhartha was born in about 563 BC. It was a significant moment in history, when Nebuchadnezzar II of Babylon died leaving the long-imprisoned king of Judah still captive in Babylon, and the Athenian general Pisistratus seized power in Athens. Cyrus the Great ruled the Persian Empire. Taoism was founded by the Chinese philosopher Laotse at just that moment and Confucius would be born in China in just another ten years time.

Soon after the prince's birth wise men predicted that he would become a Buddha. His father was alarmed at this, as he wanted his son to lead a full life, not the life of an ascetic, and succeed him as a ruler. He resolved to make court life so pleasant for his son that he would not want to relinquish it: accordingly he lavished every luxury on the boy. At the age of sixteen Prince Siddhartha married Princess Yasodhara and the king gave them as a wedding present three palaces, one for each season.

The young prince and his bride passed their days in happiness and luxury. At first he lived the conventional and very comfortable life of a prince. But he became disillusioned with palace life and wanted to see the world outside the palace. He made four visits beyond the palace walls and saw four things that made him want to change his life. On the first three trips he saw sickness, old age and death. This made him question his own life – how could he enjoy his own trouble-free life when others were suffering so much? On the fourth outing he saw a wandering monk who had given up all of his belongings to end the suffering he saw everywhere. The prince thought about what he had seen and decided he wanted to be just like the wandering monk. When he was twenty-nine he put the luxurious life of the court behind him, abandoning his wife and possessions, his kingdom and his friends, to lead the life of an ascetic. He cut off his hair to show that he had renounced the world and began to call himself Gautama. He wore ragged clothes and wandered about in search of an end to suffering.

For six years following this he led a life of extreme deprivation and austerity, a level of self-denial that amounted to self-torture. He meditated and had only roots, leaves and fruit to eat, but still enlightenment did not come. He considered what he had done. Neither his luxurious life in the palace nor his life as an ascetic in the forest had led him along the path to freedom. Excesses in either direction were evidently destructive. After that the prince started eating nourishing food again and built up his strength. At the end of this period he achieved self-enlightenment.

The prince's encounter with God, his achievement of enlightenment, happened one night in 528 BC, while he was sitting meditating under the Bodhi (Awakening) tree, a pippala tree on the banks of the Niranjana river in Bihar. The place would come to be known as Bodhgaya. There was a full moon, which is for many people a time of heightened mental and creative activity, though often they do not like to acknowledge it for fear of ridicule. He was determined to attain a state of enlightenment, and swore not to leave the spot until he had found an end to suffering.

During the crucial night he was visited by Mara, an evil spirit, who tried to tempt him into giving up his quest by sending his alluring daughters to tempt him into carnal pleasure. Then Mara tried other ways of distracting him: bolts of lightning, wind and torrential rain. When these onslaughts of extreme weather had no effect, he sent armies of demons and flaming rocks. But the prince resisted all of these attacks and as they ended he realised how to remove the cause of suffering. He had gained wisdom. He understood everything as it truly is. He had awakened to a higher reality in which he was able to remember his past lives and acquire supernormal knowledge.

Buddha discovered three great truths. The first is that nothing is lost in the universe; things may change, transform, metamorphose, but nothing is ever destroyed. The second is that everything is in a state of continuous change. The third is that change happens due to cause and effect connections; whatever happens has a consequence.

This was the enlightenment, the moment of profound insight when Prince Siddhartha became known as Buddha. The Tibetans call him Shakyamuni, which means 'the sage of the Shakya clan', but he is almost universally called Buddha, 'the enlightened one' or 'the one who is fully awake'. In this new persona, he went to the Deer Park close to Benares and shared his wisdom with five holy men. They immediately understood what had happened and became his disciples, forming the very first Buddhist community, in effect an order of monks. In his lifetime a parallel order of nuns was also formed. From the moment of his enlightenment on Buddha travelled from place to place with his disciples, spreading his teaching, a process that went on for over forty years. There was spiritual teaching, and there was also ordinary humanitarian work, helping people of every kind along the way. They lived simply, sleeping wherever they could and relying on the generosity of strangers for food.

Buddha died in about 486 BC at the age of about eighty at Kusinagara in Oudh. There was always a danger that enthusiastic followers might deify him during his lifetime, but he insisted all along that he was an ordinary mortal. His followers accepted this, but accorded him the status of an extraordinary man, which he certainly was.

At one time it was commonly believed that the life of the Buddha was pure myth, but it now seems that it represents an historical reality, although the reported miracles probably belong to a still earlier period. Monuments raised by Asoka after his conversion to Buddhism can still be seen. There was enormous excitement in the nineteenth century when a monument containing five vessels was discovered in Nepal. One contained some bone and carried the inscription, 'Of the brothers Sukiti, jointly with their sisters, this is the receptacle of the relics of Buddha, the holy one of the Sakyas.' But it appears that the bones belong to the time of Asoka, which was 200 years after Buddha's death, and so are unlikely to belong to Buddha himself.

Buddha achieved enlightenment, but he freely admitted that others had become buddhas before him and others would achieve the same level of enlightenment after him. It is questionable whether Buddha invented a completely new religion. It is more likely that he was promoting a revolutionary transformation of an existing Brahmin faith. The key ideas of the Buddhist religion are that human existence is wretched, that non-existence or 'nirvana' is the ideal state, and that nirvana can only be achieved by the rules of Buddhism. Death does not bring nirvana, because souls transmigrate after death, and the unholy are condemned to transmigrate through many existences.

Buddhism became a very popular religion, spreading rapidly through India, especially following the conversion of King Asoka. By the third century BC it dominated the whole of the Indian subcontinent. Later it declined, especially during persecutions by Brahmanism in the seventh and eighth centuries AD and the ensuing invasion by Islam. Buddhism had nevertheless flourished by spreading to China, Sri Lanka, Burma, Thailand and Japan.

Through his revelation beneath the banyan tree, Buddha founded one of the great world religions. Because of the distinct beliefs and practices involved, Buddha's new religion had a major effect on the cultural development on south-eastern and eastern Asia. It is hard to imagine what the cultures of the east would have been like without Buddhism, without that strange mystical encounter by moonlight under the pippala tree on the banks of the Niranjana.

WITNESSING THE RESURRECTION OF JESUS

(33)

WHAT WE KNOW about Jesus comes almost exclusively from five short books known as the Gospels and the Acts of the Apostles. The Gospels of St Matthew and St Luke tell us that Jesus was the first-born son of Mary, the wife of Joseph, a carpenter. He was born in a stable in Bethlehem because Mary and Joseph were on their way to Nazareth, Joseph's home town, for a Roman population census and there was no room for them at the inn. The circumstantial evidence suggests that this happened in 6, 7 or 8 BC.

The information contained in these sources is very limited, covering a total of only fifty days in Jesus' life. There is insufficient material to write a 'Life of Christ', although that has not deterred countless well-meaning authors from trying, inevitably fleshing the story out with their own projections.

What is very clear is that Jesus made a profound impression on his followers. The particular personal quality responsible for this impression was described as his grace: a ready sympathy, an understanding, a tenderness, and a way of meeting people as if they were already of importance to him. The grace of Jesus has been described as 'a deep-seated adequacy, bestowing itself on others and enriching them'. Another quality that impressed people was his authority, which enabled him to interpret scriptures and even to forgive sins.

After the custom of the time, Jesus followed his father's trade as a carpenter, but as a youth he developed a sense of religious mission. After baptism by his cousin John the Baptist, he spent forty days in the wilderness, wrestling with all kinds of temptations. After this rite of passage, which may be likened to the night Buddha spent under the pippala tree, Jesus gathered a group of disciples and organised two missionary journeys round Galilee. This culminated in a huge religious rally, where it was said he miraculously fed five thousand people.

There were many other religious sages and teachers at that time. Jesus drew attention to himself by flouting social conventions. He was very ready to mix with socially unacceptable people such as publicans, tax collectors and sinners. He was ready to perform miracles on the Sabbath. He drove the money-lenders out of the temple in Jerusalem. The overall emphasis of his mission was always on inclusiveness – he preached to Jews and non-Jews – and on love, humility and charity.

During his missionary journeys, Jesus revealed himself to his followers as the Messiah, the promised saviour who would release the Jews from subjection. He also made cryptic references to an expectation that he would soon suffer death but be resurrected from the dead. One great puzzle is that Jesus never directly claimed to be the Messiah, and never claimed to be the Son of God. These claims were made on his behalf. This can be interpreted in more than one way. It may have been part of his technique as a spiritual guide to create an atmosphere of mystery about himself, a mystique; or it may have been a teaching method to lead his disciples to draw their own conclusions. Another alternative is that Jesus did not know that he was the Messiah, or did not believe that he was, but that his disciples decided either before or after his death that that is what he must have been.

Jesus referred to God in a conventional way, seeming on the face of things to have no special original view of God. His God was the Jewish God who had been worshipped for the previous six or eight centuries and Jesus did not make a point of teaching about him in particular – a point that has often been overlooked in the past two thousand years. But the ancient Hebrew God, the Yahweh of Moses, had distinct archetypal roles incorporated into his image that appear not to have interested Jesus. The ancient God was the lord of animals, the lord of the harvest, the lord of wisdom, the lord of war, the lord of vengeance. What Jesus did was unusual. Instead of discussing or overtly reinterpreting the ancient Hebrew God, or appearing to re-cast him in a new role, Jesus repeatedly referred obliquely to God in his own idiosyncratic way, almost off-handedly, emphasising the Fatherhood of God. Jesus in fact used the word Father as a substitute for God almost all the time. This evidently sprang from his knowledge that he was in some sense the Son to this Father. Many Christians of later generations have seized on this to argue that Jesus was the unique and only Son of God, and that this fact entitled him to unique reverence. But it may be that Jesus simply wanted people to see their lives – everybody's lives – in terms of sonship to the Father-god.

Jesus' relationship with God presupposed a continuing son-father relationship. This was different from Moses' relationship with God. Moses, back in the bronze age, went up a mountain to have special set-piece meetings with God – summit conferences, in fact – and then came down to share with his people what he had acquired. King Minos of Crete was also a bronze age figure, and the later Greeks told a story about him which may have been an oral tradition from the bronze age; he lived at Knossos, his capital city, but every nine years he went up Mount Ida where he was received by Zeus, his father. In these encounters, Zeus gave Minos the laws he was to impose on his people. This Minoan practice was very similar to the Mosaic practice – and belongs to the same period.

What Jesus was doing was reinforcing a later idea of God living among us all the time.

The earthly career of Jesus came to an end with a visit to Jerusalem in AD 33. The Gospel of St Mark describes Jesus entering Jerusalem in triumph, but it is likely that he arrived in the run-up to a religious festival, the Passover, at the same time as a crowd of other provincial pilgrims in a joyful holiday mood. The 'Hosannas' were almost certainly not for him. At his famous Last Supper with the disciples, the Passover meal, Jesus hinted (again obliquely and mysteriously) that he would be betrayed by one of them. Judas Iscariot, one of the disciples, immediately afterwards went to the authorities and his betrayal led to the arrest of Jesus within a few hours in the Garden of Gethsemane.

Jesus was subjected to a hurried trial and condemned to death for blasphemy by a Jewish council. Then he was taken before the Roman procurator to have the sentence confirmed. Pontius Pilate is unlikely to have been interested in the blasphemy charge and he instead seems to have condemned Jesus to death for causing a civil disturbance. The story was probably tampered with in antiquity in order to incriminate the Jews; if the Sanhedrin had found him guilty of blasphemy the sentence would have been stoning. Instead the sentence was crucifixion.

Pilate was surprised when he was told that Jesus was dead after hanging on the cross for only a few hours, but gave his consent for the body to be taken down for burial.

'On the third day', in other words two days later, the disciples had various indications that Jesus had risen from the dead. There has been a great deal of discussion over the centuries as to what really happened that first Easter Morning, but the gospel accounts invite us to believe that Jesus physically came back to life in the tomb, and walked out into the garden to greet Mary Magdalene, who had arrived to anoint his body.

Some Christians today believe that Jesus remained physically dead, but that the disciples were overwhelmed by his spiritual presence; it was as if Jesus had come back to life. Another possibility is that Jesus was not actually dead but unconscious when taken down from the cross, and revived later, maybe even that the crucifixion was somehow stage-managed so that Jesus would survive the ordeal. A serious problem with this 'Passover Plot' explanation is that the disciples had a few sightings of Jesus during the first few days following the crucifixion, and then nothing more. The implication is that he just walked away and started a new life somewhere else, taking no interest in the new religion he had launched, and that leaves far too many questions hanging in the air.

Whatever happened, and it seems unlikely that anything further will ever be discovered about it, the followers who had scattered in dismay and despair immediately after his shameful execution as a common criminal were reunited in Jerusalem a few weeks later. There were about 120 of them and for some reason they were fired with a common conviction that Jesus was alive, had been seen by several people, and would shortly return as the Messiah. They adopted an attitude that had been gradually evolving during Jesus' lifetime, an attitude of faith.

How we interpret the gospel accounts depends very much on our own mindset: in effect whether we are prepared to believe in supernatural explanations of events, whether we believe in a God who is ready to bend the laws of nature in order to convey a special message to mankind. Perhaps, rather than exploring our own values and predispositions, it is safer to set those aside for a while and explore the values of the first century, a time when resurrection and reincarnation were part of the general belief system, a time of miracles and magic and divine intervention. The resurrection of Jesus was an event that conformed to the beliefs of those days. The prophets Elijah and Elisha were both reported to have raised people from the dead. Jesus himself raised Jairus' daughter and his friend Lazarus from the dead. People were ready to believe such things were possible: uncommon, but possible.

There is something about the meeting between Mary Magdalene and the newly resurrected Jesus that strikes our ears as strange, something that should remind us that the first century mindset was very different from our own. When Mary met Jesus in the garden at dawn that first Easter morning, she thought he was the gardener. She did not recognise him. In other words, it is quite possible that the person she met was not Jesus at all; perhaps he really was the gardener. Some days or weeks later, two of the disciples were walking along the road to Emmaus when they were overtaken by a man who walked with them. They did not recognise him at all. It was only later that 'their eyes were opened and they knew him'. Again, from the narrative it is clear that this man did not even look like Jesus, yet the disciples decided he was the resurrected Jesus. Not many years before people thought John the Baptist might be Elijah risen from the dead, when they could not have known what Elijah looked like.

This was a culture in which people could evidently 'rise from the dead' in the form of a completely different person. There were also precedents for people rising from the dead after three days. A Hebrew tablet from several decades before the time of Jesus has been found, bearing an inscribed message in which the Archangel Gabriel addresses a suffering 'Prince of Princes' in the following terms: 'In three days you shall live; I, Gabriel, command you.' Indeed, this text may be where the 'third day' of the gospels came from.

The ascension of Jesus into heaven at some point after the resurrection is mentioned in several of the bible texts. In some places the ascension happened straight away, but in others it was over a month later. According to the Gnostics it took place as much as eighteen months afterwards. Invoking an ascension was an essential part of assuming a resurrection. It was necessary to explain the relatively small number of sightings of Jesus after the resurrection and Jesus's absence during the years that followed. One can almost hear the sceptics' response to the early Christians as they tried to promote the doctrine of the resurrection: 'If he rose from the dead, where is he now?' And the disciples replied by describing the ascension.

Nor was this the end of the early Christians' encounters with God. The early Christians, the disciples who had known Jesus in life, seem to have gone on sensing that their leader was still among them – a common side-effect of bereavement. The book of the Acts of the Apostles describes a scene where Jesus' disciples, the whole community of about 120 people, were gathered together in an upper room when they experienced, collectively, the Holy Spirit descending on them. Tradition has it that the room was the one where Jesus ate the Last Supper. At nine o'clock in the morning, the biblical account tells us, 'suddenly there came a sound from heaven like a rushing mighty wind, and it filled the house where they were sitting. And divided tongues that looked like flames appeared to them, and the tongues hovered over each of them. They were all filled with the Holy Ghost, and began to speak with other tongues, as the Spirit gave them utterance.'

Suddenly they were miraculously able to speak in languages other than their own – languages they had not learned. Some witnesses thought they were drunk, but some visitors to Jerusalem from other parts of the Roman Empire recognised them as foreign languages and understood what they were saying. Many early converts to Christianity experienced the same gift. The event confirmed that although Jesus

31

might have ascended into heaven, the disciples were not alone; God was still with them. In fact before Jesus ascended into Heaven he had said he would send them a helper; at the time they did not understand what he meant, but now they knew.

The Christian feast of Pentecost, literally 'the fiftieth day' after Easter Day in the Church calendar, is celebrated ten days after Ascension Day. It is both historically and symbolically connected to the Jewish festival of Shavuot, the fiftieth day after the Exodus, when Moses received the Ten Commandments. There is a general recognition that the visitation by tongues of fire marked the beginning of the Christian Church.

The disciples seem to have persuaded one another, perhaps by the kind of intense group hysteria seen in some modern revivalist meetings, that Jesus had risen from the dead, ascended into heaven, and sent them a holy spirit as a guide. They were so convinced that the divine spiritual presence of Jesus was still with them that they committed the rest of their lives to preaching the Christian message. Many of them risked martyrdom in order to do that.

CONSTANTINE AND THE FLAMING CROSS

(312)

THE ROMAN EMPEROR Constantine came to power not in Rome but in Britain, in the fortified city of York, then known as Eboracum. In the year 306 York had been the imperial capital of Constantius, the emperor in the West, and he made it his headquarters for the campaign against the barbarians who lived beyond Hadrian's Wall. Constantius successfully quelled the barbarians, but then died in York – of old age. His son, Flavius Valerius Aurelius Constantinus (Constantine), had assisted his father in the war against the Picts, and had been named by his father as his successor. Constantine accordingly put on his father's purple imperial robe and in response to this symbolic act the troops compliantly hailed him as emperor. This probably happened in the principia, the focal building of the fortress, and the remains of it can still be seen in the crypt of York Minster.

Constantine was at this time thirty-three years old, and a mature soldier with a distinguished military record. He had fought in the emperor Diocletian's expedition to Egypt in 296, and he had fought under the emperor Galerius in the Persian war; he had also fought for his father in Britain. But this did not guarantee his succession, and there was already another emperor still living, Galerius. He did not wish to quarrel with Constantine, and he acknowledged him as a caesar (leader) but not as an augustus (co-emperor) nor as an imperator (emperor). With the Roman Empire divided in two and more and more unresolved claims to the two imperial thrones, the situation became increasingly complicated until in 308 there were no fewer than six emperors: Galerius, Licinius and Maximin in the East and Maximian, his son

Maxentius and Constantine in the West. Maxentius drove his father out of Rome and following this Maximian committed suicide. Maxentius has been presented to us as an unworthy candidate, who was frittering his time away seducing the wives of senators.

Maxentius threatened Gaul with a large army and this prompted Constantine to make a move against him in 312, marching his army across the Alps to Rome. The two armies met just outside Rome on the Milvian Plain. The battle that followed was to decide not only Constantine's future but the future of Rome and the future of Christianity. Maxentius had a large army, and Constantine appealed for help from the gods. His appeal was answered by the appearance in the noon-day sky of a flaming cross. It was described as being like a long spear overlaid with gold, with a cross bar. Christian interpreters later elaborated it further to make it into a *chi-rho* cross, an important Christian symbol. Afterwards, that same night, Constantine had a dream in which he was visited by God, who said to him, naturally in Latin, 'In hoc signo vinces' ('By this sign you shall conquer').

It is impossible to tell now whether there really was a flaming cross in the sky or whether Constantine was experiencing a projection from within his own mind. In his essay on UFOs, Jung comments that people who rigorously suppress or deny the contents of their unconscious minds on a regular basis are particularly susceptible to unprompted celestial visions of this kind. They represent the unconscious mind asserting itself. In some cultures these projections are interpreted as alien spacecraft or flying saucers, in others as angels. The ruthless soldier and aspiring emperor may well have had a profound psychic experience that bore no relation to what was actually happening in the sky.

But there is another possible explanation. Occasionally there are meteorological conditions that can produce unusual light effects. In the intensely hot dry summer of 1976 I too saw a strange light near the sun at noon. It was a vertical bar of very bright light, coloured like a short rainbow. I realised what it was – a short section of a solar halo, visible where a patch of thin high cloud passed across one arc of the halo. It occurred to me when I saw it that if there had by chance been a thin strand of low cloud passing across this vertical bar it would have looked something like Constantine's cross. So, perhaps what Constantine saw was a natural meteorological effect.

Constantine took the advice given by God in his dream at face value, and made his troops paint crosses on their shields. When they went into battle the next day, they carried these images of the cross; a Christian battle standard was carried in front of them as well.

Maxentius partly destroyed the Milvian Bridge with the intention of hindering Constantine. When Maxentius needed to retreat, he ordered a makeshift wooden bridge to be built alongside it. While he and his soldiers retreated across it during the battle, the bridge collapsed underneath them and Maxentius and many of his troops were drowned. Constantine's army was victorious, not only in the Battle of the Milvian Bridge but in the civil war as a whole. With the deaths of Galerius in 311 and Maximin in 313, Constantine became the sole ruler of the West and Licinius sole ruler of the East.

The vision of the flaming cross and the dream of the voice of God led directly to Constantine's conversion to Christianity. In 313, Constantine issued a joint edict with Licinius, the Edict of Milan, which gave civil rights to Christians throughout the empire and guaranteed them religious toleration – in itself a landmark in the development of western civilisation. In 323, Constantine defeated Licinius and had him put to death. This made Constantine the sole ruler of the Roman Empire – East and West – and he chose to make the ancient city of Byzantium his capital, renaming it Constantinople in 330.

The long-term significance of the Milvian Bridge episode was enormous, as Constantine became the first Christian emperor, and Christianity became the official religion of the Empire in 324. Rather surprisingly, Constantine himself was baptised only shortly before his death. After 300 years as a minority religious cult, struggling for recognition and indeed survival against the claims of many other beliefs, Christianity was firmly established as a world religion, though significantly changed in nature.

In York itself, the career of the first Christian emperor was also commemorated in a significant way. The exact place where Constantine made his claim to be emperor was remembered long after his reign was over. In 627, three hundred years later, two hundred years after the fall of the Roman Empire, King Edwin of Northumbria built his first church in York. This church dedicated to St Peter was very deliberately built on the ruins of the Roman principia. King Edwin was newly converted to Christianity from paganism, and wanted to establish his link with Constantine, the first Christian emperor. The seventh century church that he built was the first York Minster, the forerunner of the cathedral that dominates the city of York today – and stands on the same spot.

But any presentation of the Emperor Constantine as a benign, meek and mild figure would be wrong. He was aggressive and violent, ruthlessly exterminating all opposition. He even had his eldest son Crispus and his wife Fausta executed on treason charges. He planned to divide the empire among his three sons by Fausta: Constantius, Constantine and Constans. But – ever the warrior - Constantine 'the Great' fought a war against Constans and lost his life in the process in 337. It does not from any perspective look like a Christian life, yet the vision and the dream did have the effect of establishing Christianity as the official religion in the Roman world in the middle of the fourth century – and for many centuries afterwards.

ST AUGUSTINE'S ENCOUNTER WITH PAGANISM IN ENGLAND

(600)

A FRENCH MONK named Gotselin came to live in England in 1053, settling at Canterbury in 1090. While he was there he wrote a *Life of St Augustine*. He included a story, which has often been dismissed as a fable, about Augustine's visit to Cerne Abbas in Dorset to deal with pagan idolaters. He tried to correct what he saw as their evil ways, and they chased him away. 'But God's messenger according to the precept of the Lord and the example of the apostles, having shaken the dust from his feet, cast upon them a judgement they richly deserved ... by divine justice any way of things that were dreadful to the figure of Helia.'

We know from later accounts that a god called Hele or Helith was worshipped in that area, and the name was attached to the chalk hill figure now more usually known as the Cerne Giant. This is a huge figure of a naked warrior, waving a club above his head and wearing only a girdle. He is fifty-five metres high from the soles of his feet to the crown of his head. Notoriously, he sports a huge erect phallus seven metres long. It has been assumed by a lot of people that because of its blatant nudity it cannot be very old – an intolerant medieval church would not have allowed it – but there is evidence that it was there in AD 600. St Augustine saw it.

St Augustine's encounter with pagan idol-worshippers at Cerne Abbas must have taken place between 600 and 603. The formal foundation of Cerne Abbey did not come until 987. There was a later tradition that King Canute had rebuilt the abbey and this may be a folklore version of the refounding in 987 of an earlier religious house. The thirteenth century seal that shows the appearance of the west front of the abbey church also shows the abbey's two founders, Aethelmaer (the 987 founder) and St Augustine.

In fact there was said to have been a small religious house consisting of three monks and a hermitage on the abbey site in the ninth century. Egbert's son gave a second smaller house in the Cerne valley and later a third grant of land, again in the Cerne valley.

St Edwold, a brother of the murdered King Edmund of East Anglia, fled to Dorset in about 870 as a refugee and lived the life of a hermit in the Cerne valley. It is possible that Edwold's hermitage stood beside St Augustine's Well, a feeder of the River Cerne, and the source of quite a lot of folklore. St Augustine's Well was a pre-Christian sacred spring. When Edwold died he was buried at his hermitage and a struggle broke out at once between Sherborne and Cerne for custody of the saint's remains. Cerne won, and Edwold's remains were transferred to the abbey.

The legendary founder of the earlier religious house was Augustine, the sixth century missionary sent by Pope Gregory to convert England to Christianity, and who died in 604. The medieval legend has Augustine travelling from Kent across to Dorset to suppress idol-worshippers at Cerne. It contains hidden references to the Cerne Giant, the hill figure at Cerne Abbas, and these references imply that the Giant's existence was well known in Canterbury and elsewhere in England.

The 'legend' of St Augustine and the idol-worshippers was undoubtedly garbled by several re-tellings before it was written down, but it is by no means as fanciful as most historians have assumed.

In the sixth century, just before Augustine's arrival, there were centres of pagan worship in Dorset. The dark age historian Gildas, writing in about 540, mentions in his book *The Ruin of Britain* that 'the devilish monstrosities' of pagan cult images were still to be seen in his day 'both within and without the deserted enclosures.' He probably meant the deserted temple enclosures created in the iron age. There was one of these, a small rectangular earthwork, standing on the hilltop immediately above the Cerne Giant. It is still there and known as The Trendle. Gildas lived in Dorset, and he may have had in mind wooden idols he had seen in the Trendle, 'within the deserted enclosure', or the Cerne Giant, 'without'. Either way, we have documentary evidence from sixth century Dorset, from sixty years before Augustine's arrival, that pagan cult images were visible in the landscape.

At about the time when the story says he visited Cerne, Augustine was in the area. In 603, the year before his death, he held two disastrous conferences with delegates of the Celtic church on the margins of their territory. These conferences with Welsh Christian priests took place at Aust, on the 'English' shore of the Bristol Channel. Augustine was within fifty or sixty miles of Cerne Abbas at the time of the visit in the story; he could easily have visited Cerne on his way to or from Aust.

The medieval chronicler William of Malmesbury tells us what happened. Augustine was mocked by the villagers, who drove him and his followers away with cows' tails fastened to their clothes. Augustine accepted this abuse and shouted to his companions, 'cerno deum qui et nobis retribuet gratiam et furentibus illis emendationem unfundet animam.' This strange statement, which is eye- and ear-catching in a number of ways, translates as, 'I see God, who will give us grace and these people a change of heart.'

If Augustine was driven northwards out of Cerne (probably the direction he had come from), he would indeed have seen a god, if not his own: he would have seen the Cerne Giant. Augustine was punning, in the style of the time, on the name of the place. He used the word cerno. William of Malmesbury thought the name of the place came second, as a result of the saint's remark. He believed that what Augustine actually shouted was 'Cerno Hel!' – Hel meaning God in Hebrew, and that the place came to be known as Cernel in consequence. This is revealing, because it reveals two ideas: that William knew of the existence of the Cerne Giant and that it was known as Helia, Helis, Helith, Hele, Heil or Hel. It also shows that Augustine could easily have encountered, centuries before the time when William was writing, a landscape image impressive enough to be an unmistakable deity.

As a punishment for their treatment of Augustine, the people of Cerne were 'sent a shameful token' by Augustine's God: their children were from then on to be born with tails. At this threat they repented and asked Augustine to come back and remove his curse, which he did. He also commanded a crystal fountain to break out (St Augustine's Well), which he used to baptise converts.

In a later version of the story, written in the 13th century, Walter of Coventry names the pagan god worshipped at Cerne as Helith. A very similar account written in 1297 by Walter de Hemingford was probably paraphrased from Walter of Coventry's account or copied from a common source. It begins, 'In the district of Dorset . . . where the god Helith was worshipped.' In the *Golden Legend*, written rather earlier in the 13th century by the Dominican monk Jacobus de Voragine, there is the same story again but instead of Cerne it is set 'in a certain town inhabited by wicked people'. They worship an idol called Heil or Hele.

This recurring name was thought by many antiquarians to have been the Saxon name of the Cerne Giant, and they thought it was connected to the Old English word *Heoloth* (Hell) or the Germanic Saxon word *helig* (holy). Either would seem reasonable, though it is likelier still that when the Saxons arrived the Cerne Giant was already named Helith. Probably the pagan cult relating to the Cerne Giant was strong enough to persist into the Christian period, in spite of the efforts of Augustine, Edwold, Aelfric and the 'mynster-menn'.

But then there is the matter of the idol itself, which some medieval sources seem to say was thrown down or broken in pieces by Augustine. There is independent evidence that the native Britons were worshipping idols at this time. Not long after Augustine arrived in England, landing in Thanet in 577, he wrote to the pope telling him of the idolatry problem in England and seeking advice. The medieval sources show Augustine in a draconian mould, afflicting unbelievers with curses and smashing up their idols. But Pope Gregory sent him and his companion, Abbot Mellitus, a letter giving specific instruction. Gregory had decided 'upon mature deliberation on the matter of the English that the temples of the idols in that nation ought not to be destroyed.' So Augustine anxiously reported seeing offensive images that he felt should be destroyed; he got his detailed reply from Gregory in June 601. This is quoted in full in Bede; unfortunately Augustine's letter has not survived.

Gregory's reason for reprieving the pagan temples in England was that the missionaries could take them over gradually for Christian worship. If people saw Augustine and his followers tearing down their temples they would set their hearts against Christianity, whereas if they saw their temples respected and continuing in use they might be won round. In the same enlightened way, Gregory suggested that the pagans' animal sacrifices might be adapted to Christian use by persuading people that they were killing the animals to eat in a sacred meal in God's praise. These are pointers to what happened when Augustine and other Christian missionaries went to Cerne and had to decide how to deal with the pagan practices that still went on at the ancient sanctuary – the huge chalk figure, the earthwork above it and the precinct beside it that included the sacred spring.

The story of Augustine breaking in pieces the pagan idol was a misunderstanding of what happened at Cerne, where a major pagan sanctuary was divided in two. If Edwold's hermitage stood to the north of the sacred spring, the Christian foundation would have stood between the spring and the Giant.

The medieval texts have been repeatedly quoted in translation but two crucial points in the original Latin have been overlooked. One is the use in the 10th century account by Gotselin of the word *typus*. This has invariably been translated as 'idol', following the translation of Gotselin by Jerome Porter in 1632, but if Gotselin had meant idol, he would have used the perfectly acceptable word *idolum*, which was in common use throughout the middle ages. Indeed Gregory used the word *idolum* three times in his letter to Mellitus and Augustine. The monks of Canterbury used it again in their epitaph for Augustine. That Gotselin chose the word *typus* instead shows that he meant something else. Typus is better translated as 'figure on a wall', which actually fits the image of the Cerne Giant better. We think of an idol as a three-dimensional object, a sculpture in the round, whereas what was meant was something relatively flat on a wall. The correct use of the word *typus* was familiar to Gotselin and his medieval readers from its use in Cicero's *Letters to Atticus*. Cicero is ordering very specific kinds of artwork from Atticus, specific things for specific rooms. He says, 'In addition I give you a commission for bas-reliefs which can be inserted into the plaster walls of the hall.' This is very revealing. Typus is not just a figure on a wall, but a very special kind of figure on a wall, a bas-relief. One of the peculiarities of the Cerne Giant is that it is modelled in low relief, the green spaces between the white chalk lines standing slightly proud, slightly convex, out of the hillside.

But if Augustine encountered the hill figure at Cerne, how did he 'throw it over' as all the accounts say? The Latin word in each text, clearly copied from one to another, is *injecit*. This can indeed mean 'threw over', but it can also have the legal meaning 'took hold of, seized, took possession of'. This last meaning would make more sense in relation to a hill figure. It would also fit well with the idea of Augustine and his missionary team setting up a permanent mission close beside the Cerne Giant and the idea of an early Christian settlement on what would later become Cerne Abbey.

So, quite unexpectedly, this close encounter with some obscure medieval Latin texts can bring us much closer to a dramatic encounter between Christians and pagans in Dorset in 600. And it brings into high relief an even more remarkable encounter between a mighty pagan god, the chalk figure leaping naked along the hillside, and a crusty and disapproving saint.

MOHAMMED'S REVELATION OF THE WORD OF ALLAH

(610)

MOHAMMED WAS BORN in 567 or 569, and was the nephew of the chief of a small tribe. His mother Aminah died while he was still very young – his father too was dead - and the orphan was brought up initially by his grandfather and then by his uncle, Abu Talib.

As a young man, Mohammed seems to have visited the desert to pick up the customs of the Bedouins. He also accompanied traders from Mecca to Syria and perhaps Egypt and Mesopotamia. After these travels, Mohammed was gradually drawn towards a life of religious contemplation, though it is not clear what prompted this development. His life as a caravan conductor probably came to an end when he married Khadija, a wealthy widow who was fifteen years older than him. With Khadija he had six children.

Mohammed acquired a reputation for practical wisdom, although his formal education was not exceptional. At the time when Mohammed decided that he was to become the mouthpiece of God, the paganism of northern Arabia had fallen under the Christianising influence of the Byzantine empire. The south of Arabia had fallen under successive influences – Jewish, Abyssinian, Persian. Arabia in Mohammed's day was a religious melting-pot.

A story is told of Mohammed going off in search of 'the religion of Abraham'.

Mohammed's claim to be God's mouthpiece was a claim to autocratic power, so he was extremely cautious about the way he asserted that claim. For three years he and his followers formed a secret society and before that there was a period of preparation which involved a divine revelation in a cave on Mount Hira (Jabal al-Nour) near Mecca. It is interesting how the pattern of going up a mountain to meet God repeats in the history of religion; King Minos went up a mountain to confer with Zeus, and Moses went up a mountain to receive commandments from Yahweh. Now Mohammed went up a mountain to have truths revealed to him by his god. The ancient Minoan belief system was based on both peak sanctuaries and cave sanctuaries, and profound religious experiences were believed to be had in both locations; two of the most important Minoan sanctuaries were caves near mountain tops.

Mohammed acquired a routine of solitary meditation for several weeks each year in the cave on Mount Hira. The Islamic tradition is that during one of these visits to Mount Hira, in 610, the archangel Gabriel started communicating with him and that the first verses to be recited were the Koran 96: 1-5. Again, according to an Islamic tradition, Mohammed was deeply disturbed when he had the initial revelations, and even considered throwing himself off the mountain. But he was stopped by the spirit, which told him he had been chosen as God's messenger. On returning home, he was reassured by his wife. Another tradition maintains that Mohammed was neither surprised nor frightened by the revelation. But the initial revelation seems to have been followed by a pause of three years, and in that time Mohammed devoted himself to prayer and contemplation. When the revelations started again, he was commanded to start preaching.

The earliest revelations to Mohammed took the form of pages which were to be revealed only to his nearest relatives; these solemn utterances were cast in the form of rhymes. From an early stage the production of written communication was set aside in favour of oral communication. The prophet would speak in a trance and his followers would write down the utterances as he spoke. The dictated revelations would eventually form the text of the Koran. In the Koran, Mohammed is not addressed directly by name, but by a series of appellations which make his role clearer: prophet, messenger, servant of God, announcer, warner, reminder, witness, bearer of good tidings, light-giving lamp.

Western academics have analysed the text of the Koran to test for variations in the 'voice'. They found none, and this strongly suggests that the Koran is the voice of the Prophet alone.

The early work of dictation while in a trance was done in private, virtually in secret, within the family. But by the time Mohammed made his first appearance as a preacher in public – in Mecca in 616 – he was already the leader of a united community of committed followers. As he became more successful, some of his followers were persecuted and he found a refuge for them in Axum, in Abyssinia. The Abyssinian king and his advisers took the side of the refugees, apparently regarding them as persecuted Christians – completely misunderstanding who and what they were. They were, even so, being supported and this significant diplomatic victory infuriated the Meccan leaders, who blockaded Mohammed in one quarter of the city.

Mohammed responded with a conciliatory 'revelation', to the effect that the Meccan goddess should be recognised as well as Allah. Mohammed later extricated himself from this by declaring the revelation to be a fabrication of the Devil.

Shortly after this both his uncle and guardian Abu Talib and his wife Khadija died, leaving Mohammed isolated and unprotected. He fled to the oasis of Taif and from there negotiated with various wealthy Meccans for protection. Mohammed was glad to have an invitation to go to Yathrib (later to be called Medina) as dictator. The citizens there suffered from feuding and needed a strong and impartial outsider to come and act as an arbitrator. So, he went into exile or hejira ('flight') and the date of the hejira, 16 July 622, is taken as the beginning of the Mohammedan era.

The Meccan authorities were alarmed at the prospect of a regime hostile to them being in control in Medina, which lay on an important caravan route. Plans were accordingly laid to have Mohammed killed. The Prophet, as he came to be known, took refuge temporarily in a cave, delaying his arrival until 20 September, the Jewish Day of Atonement, in 622.

Mohammed's power grew and grew from this point on. In the next ten turbulent years, he consolidated what he had achieved and one of the world's major religions was established. Islam is founded on the holy book, the Koran, which contains the fruits of the Prophet's repeated communions with Allah. These encounters with God led to Mohammed being held in exceptionally high regard by his followers through succeeding centuries. They see him as the last and greatest law-bearer in a series of prophets, restoring the uncorrupted original faith of Adam, Abraham, Moses, Noah and Jesus, a fundamentally and un-compromisingly monotheistic faith.

KING EDWIN, PAULINUS AND COIFI

(627)

POPE GREGORY'S INITIATIVE to convert England to Christianity began with the mission of St Augustine in 597. Gregory the Great's interest in England and the English began in 573 with a chance encounter with a group of English boys in the Roman slave market. He just happened to see them in the street and was fascinated by their fair skin and fair hair. When he asked who they were, he was told that they were Angles (English) and he commented, 'Non Angli, sed angeli' – Not English, but angels. That encounter triggered Gregory's mission to convert England to Christianity.

Augustine was a reluctant and in many ways highly unsuitable missionary to send to England; he seems never to have believed that he could succeed. There were village communities in southern England that were determined to hang on to their pagan practices. There were Christian communities in Wales, but Augustine managed to antagonise their priests by demanding their deference. He managed to alienate potential allies. After Augustine died in 604, his supporters and successors went on with the work of conversion, but it was a slow process.

It was thirty years before the missionary Paulinus managed to infiltrate the court of King Edwin of Northumbria. He preached to the king in 627 and he must have thought he was dreaming when he heard the king's reply. Edwin said that he was both willing and bound to accept the faith that Paulinus taught. He would need to discuss the matter with his chiefs and advisers, the ealdormen. If they were agreeable to the idea, they might all be baptised together. Paulinus readily agreed to a debate.

At Edwin's council meeting the king asked each of his elders in turn what they thought about the new religion and the new style of worship that went with it. Coifi, the chief pagan priest, was the first to speak. His words were surprising. 'Notice carefully, King, this doctrine which is being expounded to us. I frankly admit that, for my part, I have found that the religion which we have hitherto held has no virtue nor profit in it. None of your followers has devoted himself more earnestly than I have to the worship of our gods, but nevertheless there are many who receive greater benefits and greater honour from you than I do and are more successful in all their undertakings. If the gods had any power they would have helped me more readily, seeing that I have always served them with greater zeal. So it follows that if, on examination, these new doctrines which have now been explained to us are found to be better and more effectual, let us accept them without any delay.'

Coifi's speech was remarkable. He was confessing to a complete loss of faith in the official established religion of the kingdom, a confession that in later centuries would have meant a heresy charge and possible execution. More than that, he was admitting that he had no confidence in the religion of which he was the chief priest. Coifi was a man in spiritual crisis. But he was also expressing dissatisfaction with his secular career. It is not clear what sort of advancement he had expected from King Edwin, but he evidently had not received it and was disappointed to see others advanced instead of himself. There is an implication that the king was already favouring Christians in some way and this was a nudge to Coifi and the other elders to convert in haste.

This is to an extent confirmed by what happened next at the council meeting. One of Edwin's elders spoke. He agreed with what Coifi had said and added, 'This is how the present life of man on Earth appears to me in comparison with that time which is unknown to us. You are sitting feasting with your ealdormen [earls] and thegns [retainers and servants] in winter time; the fire is burning on the hearth in the middle of the hall and all inside is warm, while outside the wintry storms of rain and snow are raging; and a sparrow flies swiftly through the hall. It enters in at one door and quickly flies out through the other. For the few moments it is inside, the storm and wintry tempest cannot touch it, but after the briefest moment of calm, it flits from your sight, out into the wintry storm again. So this life of man appears but for a moment; what follows or indeed what went before, we know not at all. If this new doctrine brings us more certain information, it seems right that we should accept it.'

This beautiful metaphor of human life and the great unknowns that surround it was a far more spiritual response to the situation than Coifi's. Then other elders spoke, all supporting Edwin's proposed conversion. Coifi spoke again, saying that he would like to listen more carefully to what Paulinus had to say about the Christian God. Edwin asked Paulinus to say more, and when he had spoken, Coifi spoke even more enthusiastically than before. 'For a long time now I have realised our religion is worthless; for the more diligently I searched for the truth in our religion, the less I found it. Now I confess openly that the truth shines out clearly in this teaching which can bestow on us the gift of life, salvation and eternal happiness. Therefore I advise your majesty that we should immediately abandon and commit to the flames the temples and the altars which we have held sacred without reaping any benefit.'

Then King Edwin announced in public that he had accepted the gospel preached by Paulinus. He asked Coifi who was going to desecrate the altars and shrines of the old religion. Coifi answered, 'I will, for through the wisdom the true God has given me no-one can more suitably destroy those things which I foolishly worshipped, and set an example to everyone.'

Coifi asked the king to provide him with weapons and a stallion – both by custom forbidden to a high priest – and he set off at once to destroy the pagan high shrine of Northumbria. This stood at Goodmanham, now a small hamlet near Market Weighton. There is nothing there to indicate that it was once a major cult centre – only a cluster of ancient holy wells and springs. There is no sign of the shrine or its idols – but then we know that Coifi systematically destroyed them in 627. The ordinary people who saw him that day thought he had gone mad. As he approached the shrine armed with sword and spear, Coifi hurled his spear into it, desecrating it, then urged his companions to set the whole complex on fire. It was destroyed completely and utterly – nothing whatever remains of it – and the Church of All Hallows was built on its site.

As a result of this almost mythic encounter between Paulinus, Coifi and Edwin - the Christian missionary, the pagan high priest and the king of Northumbria – the king, his courtiers and the whole kingdom of Northumbria were converted to Christianity. Edwin was like some other Anglo-Saxon kings of his day in that he saw political advantages in conversion. He was able to set himself up as God's agent on Earth in his kingdom, which enhanced his kingly status. He was also able to deploy Christian priests, who could read and write, as civil servants. The ealdormen were under pressure to go along with the king's conversion. They too needed to become Christians in order to stay close to the power centre. But many of the ordinary people of Northumbria were unhappy about the change, preferring to keep to their old ways and old beliefs. This became evident when Edwin died: the kingdom reverted to paganism. It was just the same in East Anglia, where King Redwald had converted to Christianity, but there was a reversion on his death. Redwald is thought to be the king who was treated to the spectacular (and pagan) ship burial at Sutton Hoo.

The encounter between the old and the new religions was a long and complicated one. The pious pro-Christian versions told by the historians of later centuries were inevitably simplified versions of what happened. The ealdormen who spoke in support of King Edwin's conversion were represented as divinely inspired; in fact they were probably being politically astute. They understood that Edwin was already more than halfway to conversion and that he was already favouring Christians – and they were desperate to be on the winning side. And Coifi too was prepared to make a complete nonsense of his life so far, even to the extent of destroying his own holiest shrine, in order to please his king.

ST BONIFACE AND THOR'S OAK AT GIESMAR

(723)

BRIXWORTH CHURCH, ON a ridge a few miles to the north of Northampton, is one of the finest Saxon buildings still standing. The Reverend C. F. Watkins, the vicar of Brixworth from 1832 to 1873, began an ambitious scheme of restoration. He removed as much as he dared of the later additions, stripping the fabric of the church back to its Saxon state. The result is a marvellous achievement – one that would not be possible today, where the heritage industry subscribes to a 'culturally correct' policy of leaving in place almost any alteration to a building because it is part of its history. Luckily, Watkins was unencumbered by heritage bureaucrats. Thanks to his vision, we can encounter the Anglo-Saxon world close up, and see the great building for what it was when it was first raised in 680: a Saxon tribute to the architecture and ideals of ancient Rome.

Before the major restoration, some work was done in 1809 in the Lady or Verdun Chapel to remove a bump on the inner face of the south wall, and this led to a major discovery. When the whitewash and plaster were removed, it turned out that the projection was caused by a stone reliquary, which slightly over-filled a cavity in the fabric of the wall. The reliquary was carved in the fourteenth century and it consists of an upper stone with four gables (the lid) and a cube-shaped lower stone (the relic container). When the lid was lifted off, the lower stone was found to have a cylindrical hollow containing a wooden box. Inside the box was a human throat bone and a slip of paper. Unfortunately the piece of paper disintegrated when handled, but it had some writing on it including the initials 'T. B.' These are thought to be the initials of Thomas Bassenden, the chantry priest at Brixworth in the 1530s. This sets the scene for the secretion of what was clearly a saint's relic at a time when Cromwell's men were going round Britain destroying saints' relics. This one was rescued from its impending encounter with destruction. Thomas Bassenden had pushed the reliquary into the makeshift hole in the wall and then plastered over it; the projection implies that all this was done in great haste.

But whose throat bone was it? In the early 1500s, there were altars in the church dedicated to Saints John, Catherine, Edward and Boniface, so it must be one of those four. Historical records reveal that in the middle ages there was a Guild of St Boniface at Brixworth and also a three-day fair held annually on St Boniface's feast day, 5 June and the days immediately before and after. The bone most likely belongs to him, and was the focus of a local cult.

The church itself has an unusual design. Running round the outside of the apse is a ring crypt, a horseshoe-shaped corridor now open to the sky but originally covered with a stone vaulted roof. There are only half a dozen churches in Europe with this feature, and all of them were designed to provide access for pilgrims to a special vault directly under the altar, where a major saint's relics were placed for special veneration. Pilgrims would come through the church, pass through a door and down four steps into the ring crypt, walk round to peer in at the relic in its mysterious candle-lit vault, and have a sense of being in the presence of the saint. After their mystical encounter they continued round the ring crypt to come back up into the church by way of another flight of steps and a second door.

The presence of the ring crypt corroborates the idea of a St Boniface cult at Brixworth in the middle ages. When the foundations of the apse were excavated by Watkins, he found that the original Saxon apse had been semicircular in plan, not rectangular like its fifteenth century replacement. He also found that there was a gap in the original apse wall at the east end, exactly where he would have expected an access doorway to the relic crypt, though he did not include this in his reconstruction. It is also odd that Watkins decided to rebuild the apse in a polygonal shape, which it had never been at any stage.

Who was this Boniface? Oddly, he was not born at Brixworth, nor did he die there. No-one knows what the connection may have been. St Boniface was born with the name Winfrith in about 680, at Crediton in Devon, just when Brixworth Church was being built. He joined a religious house at Nursling near Southampton, where he became a scholar and teacher, writing a Latin grammar and book on the scansion of poetry. He earned the trust of King Ine of Wessex and was sent on an important mission to negotiate with Archbishop Bertwald of Canterbury.

Winfrith enjoyed his sheltered monastic life at Nursling, with the comfortable prospect of a career as an abbot and perhaps a bishop ahead of him. And he enjoyed the company of other clerics; he probably met and conversed with St Aldhelm, the great scholar and bishop of Sherborne. But he wanted to encounter pagan Europe, to become a missionary. The 'pilgrimage for Christ' was a popular idea in the Church at the time, and for many people it meant little more than a purposeful separation from home, friends and family. He agonised over the decision, because it meant giving up what he had, and taking up instead a life of travel, hardship and danger. Eventually he made the decision, was given permission by his abbot, Wimbert, and in 716 with a group of friends he travelled to London, where they boarded a ship that took them across the North Sea to Frisia (northern Holland).

Winfrith arrived at a bad moment. Willibrord was already there, attempting to convert the pagan leaders of the area, and having a very difficult time. Two years earlier the Frisian leader, Duke Radbod, had rebelled against the encroachment by the Franks on his territory and launched an attack on Willibrord's headquarters at Utrecht. Radbod was unimpressed by the Christian missionaries. He asked one of them what had become of the kings, his ancestors, who had not believed in Christ, and the missionary told him they were suffering the torments of Hell. Radbod saw the folly and injustice of this and said that he would rather be with his ancestors; what was the point of going to Heaven with a few poor people? Winfrith found Frisia too turbulent and chaotic to deal with. With no experience behind him, he had little choice but to return home to Nursling.

Two years later, he set off again but this time not to Frisia. Instead he went to Rome. Pope Gregory II received him warily; Winfrith was a completely unknown figure. But after a series of conversations with him the pope finally sent him to Germany. The instruction was 'to make a report on the savage peoples of Germany. . . to discover whether their untutored hearts and minds are ready to receive the seed of the divine Word.' But Gregory also instructed Winfrith to 'teach' (convert to Christianity) any pagans. He also honoured Winfrith by giving him a new name, Boniface, which meant Good-doer. This was well-meant, but Winfrith often had to explain who he was, signing letters with both names, 'Boniface, also known as Winfrith'.

Winfrith was a prolific letter writer, and a surprisingly large number of his letters have survived. He travelled extensively, and in doing so met a great many people, but many of his encounters were in writing, which makes it possible for us, even after all these centuries have passed, to eavesdrop on those meetings of minds. He wrote to men and women of every station: four popes and four kings, four archbishops, thirty bishops, perhaps a dozen abbots and abbesses, several nuns, numerous priests and over twenty laymen. Some letters were on mundane matters, others on points of theology, others were full of human warmth: and they inspired a warm response from others. Take this moving letter from the nun Leoba, which shows an extraordinary and unexpected level of intimacy with Winfrith:

'Most reverend Winfrith, most dear to me in Christ and bound to me by ties of kinship, I, Leoba, least of God's servants, wish enduring health and prosperity. I beg you graciously to bear in mind your ancient friendship for my father, Dynne, formed long ago in the West country. It is now eight years since he was called away from this world, and I ask your prayers for his soul. . . I am the only daughter of my parents and, unworthy though I am, I wish that I might regard you as a brother; for there is no other man in my kinship in whom I have such trust as in you. I have ventured to send you this little gift, not that it deserves even a kindly glance from you but that you may

have a reminder of my insignificance and not let me be forgotten on account of our wide separation. May the bond of our true affection be knit ever more closely. . .'

When he was about seventy, Winfrith received a very long and friendly letter from King Ethelbert of Kent, thanking him sincerely for his prayer and then adding a request.

'I cannot easily state in words what joy and comfort it brought me. . . so precious a gift. . . so sudden and without expectation. There is one other favour I want to ask and which, from all I hear, will not be very difficult for you to grant, namely to send me a pair of falcons of such cleverness and courage that they will without hesitation attack cranes. We ask you to procure these birds and send them to us since there are very few hawks of this kind in our country – that is, in Kent.'

Winfrith was a great present-giver.

Winfrith left Rome in 719, crossing Bavaria to head for Thuringia, where he spoke to the princes and other leaders of each tribe. He moved on north-westwards to revisit Frisia, where he joined forces with Willibrord and stayed with him for two years.

Willibrord was impressed by Winfrith and wanted Winfrith to succeed him as bishop, but Winfrith refused because he had promised the pope he would work in Germany. So he returned to central Germany, this time armed with all the skills that Willibrord had taught him, and there he succeeded in converting huge numbers of pagans to Christianity – thousands of them.

After accomplishing this, Winfrith sent one of his associates, a man called Bynnan, to report to the pope. Bynnan eventually came back with a summons to Rome. What the pope wanted to do now was to examine Winfrith's doctrine closely, to be sure that what he was teaching was orthodox. When he was convinced, he consecrated Winfrith as bishop. But there were already signs of friction. The pope was very concerned about correct procedures – correct from the Roman point of view – and

Winfrith had been schooled in the reformed English church. But, naturally, as the years passed and Winfrith aged, he too became inflexible and wanted to impose uniform rules that disregarded local variations in practice. There were to be some abrasive exchanges between Winfrith and successive popes.

Eventually, in 723, Winfrith left Rome for the north again, heading once more for the heart of Germany. He seems to have had an instinct that converting Germany to Christianity, and so completing a continuous corridor of Christian communities from the Mediterranean to the North Sea, would add greatly to the strength and durability of the Church. He was right, and he was to play a major part in making it come about.

In central Germany, he found his way to a major pagan shrine at Geismar, the scene of a great encounter. It was a hilltop sacred to the god Thor. On it was a huge and ancient oak tree that was specially sacred to Thor. The place was the focus of the local community and its faith. Winfrith approached it with an axe and began to fell it, to the dismay of the local inhabitants. While he was attacking it a thunderstorm broke and a bolt of lightning hit the tree, completely shattering it. The tree fell apart into four main pieces and crashed to the ground in the storm. From the boughs of the fallen tree, Winfrith built an oratory on the spot and dedicated it to St Peter. The local pagans were so shaken by this event that many were converted at once; others heard about it in the weeks and months that followed. It looked like a head-on clash between the Christian priest and Thor himself. The thunderbolt – presumably released by the Christian God – had destroyed the thunder-god's sanctuary. It was a miracle which demonstrated that Winfrith's God was more powerful than Thor.

Although it sounds like a piece of folklore, this event actually happened, and it was one of the major incidents in Winfrith's missionary career, giving enormous impetus to his mission. He went on working as a missionary until he was murdered, perhaps by robbers, in Frisia in 754.

Winfrith's many encounters in the eighth century, some face-to-face, some by letter, resulted in the conversion of a large swathe of Western

Europe, consolidating the Christian church and guaranteeing its survival and success. He also worked towards uniformity of belief and worship, standardising church services, and even prescribing music – the church music now well-known as Gregorian chants. Winfrith even had a special Gregorian chant composed in his honour after he was murdered: Exsultabo in Jerusalem, I shall rejoice in the heavenly city.

JOAN OF ARC
AND HER VOICES

(1425)

JOAN OF ARC was an unusually devout peasant girl who was born at Domremy in Champagne in 1412. Her father, Jacques d'Arc, was a poor peasant farmer, though not destitute. He had five children and Joan was the youngest. Like most children in medieval Europe, she never learned to read or write but she was skilled at sewing and spinning. The picture of her as a simple-minded child spending her days alone in the meadows with the sheep and cattle is a long way from the historical truth. The one thing that marked her out as an unusual girl was her gravity and piety. She was often seen kneeling in church, completely absorbed in prayer.

There was a local village custom of singing and dancing round a special tree, which was known as the Fairy Tree. Like the other village children she danced round the tree, but she discontinued this pursuit when she was twelve years old. At her trial, ostensibly for witchcraft, her accusers tried to make something of this innocent folk custom, but the questioning led nowhere. Joan had, when very young, danced round the tree – but she had also woven wreaths for the statue of Our Lady.

In the summer of 1425, when she was thirteen, Joan first heard her voices. At first what she experienced was like a person speaking quite close to her, but there was a blaze of light as well. In later encounters she discerned the appearance of those beings who were speaking to her. Then she was able to identify them as St Michael, who arrived accompanied by other angels, as well as St Margaret and St Catherine.

Joan was always unwilling to talk about her voices. She never said anything about them to her confessor. Even at her trial, when her life was in peril, she refused to give descriptions of the saints' appearance or to explain how she recognised them. But she was adamant that she had seen them. 'I saw them with these very eyes, as well as I see you,' she told her cold-hearted judges.

The voices spoke to her repeatedly and by May 1428, when she was sixteen they left her in no doubt that she must go to the king to help him. The voices became insistent, urging her to go and present herself to Robert Baudricourt, who was Charles VII's commander in the neighbouring town of Vaucouleurs. Joan went to Baudricourt, but he was rude and dismissive, telling the cousin who accompanied her, Durand Lassois, to 'take her home to her father and give her a good whipping.'

Joan might have given up at that point, but the military predicament of Charles VII worsened and his supporters became more desperate. By the end of 1428 his cause appeared virtually lost. Joan's voices became more urgent, even menacing in tone. In frustration she answered them back. What could she do? She was just a poor girl who could neither ride a horse nor fight. But the voices went on at her relentlessly: God commands it.

In January 1429 she went again to Vaucouleurs. Baudricourt was still dismissive, but increasingly impressed by Joan's persistence. Then, on 17 February, she announced that the French had suffered a great defeat outside the town of Orleans. Nobody knew about this defeat (at the Battle of the Herrings) until a few days later. When news came through, Joan's credibility suddenly improved. She was taken to Chinon to meet the king. At her own request she went in men's clothing, for her own protection, and in the company of three men-at-arms. In the all-male environment of the army camp, she always slept fully dressed to protect her chastity.

Admitted to the presence of the king in the great hall of Chinon, which still stands although in ruins, she addressed him at once, in spite of the fact that he had tried to test her by disguising himself. There was from the start always a faction at court opposed to Joan. The King himself went along with Joan's mission, if rather half-heartedly. She shared some sign with Charles, which inclined him to believe in her. It is thought by historians that Charles harboured a secret doubt about his own legitimacy, and that Joan told him something that released him from this doubt.

After being approved by Charles, she was sent to Poitiers to be grilled by a committee of bishops and academics. The minutes of this meeting have not survived, but the answers she gave to their theological questions reassured them that there was nothing heretical about her. This in itself indicates that the witchcraft allegations thrown at her in her trial had no basis – even according to the values of the day. If she had been a witch, the bishops and doctors would not have wanted her associated with Charles's cause in any way.

After this interrogation, Joan went back to Chinon to prepare for the military campaign. The king offered her a sword. Instead she begged for a search to be made for an ancient sword that she believed lay buried behind the altar in the chapel of St Catherine de Fierbois. An ancient sword was duly found exactly where she described; her voices had told her it was there. Then a standard was made for her bearing the words 'Jesus, Maria' and an image of God the Father with kneeling angels. Before the armed struggle began, Joan appealed directly to the King of England to withdraw his troops from French soil. The English commanders were, not surprisingly, furious to receive this impudent demand from a French peasant girl, but she ordered a rapid movement of troops and succeeded in entering Orleans in April. Her presence there did much to raise morale. The fight was on to regain the kingdom for Charles.

Charles VII was finally crowned king on 17 July 1429, with Joan standing by with her battle standard.

What did Joan really see and hear? Some historians have argued that Joan was lying, while others say that she was coached by priests, but these explanations ring false. A common modern approach is to explain Joan's visionary experiences in terms of hysterical exaltation fostered by the style of preaching she was exposed to in church. There were also certain prophecies in the air at that time, prophecies regarding a maiden from the oak wood, near the Fairy Tree, who was going to save France by means of a miracle. So it may have been a state of religious and patriotic exaltation that produced the visions. But how did she know about the hidden sword?

II

ENCOUNTERS
WITH ALIENS

THE ROSWELL INCIDENT

(1947)

OVER THE PAST half century, ever since the end of the Second World War, thousands of people have reported seeing objects in the sky – hovering or flying objects that they could not account for. When the sightings have been analysed, most have been explained in fairly mundane terms. Some turned out to be meteorites, planets or stars; some turned out to be weather balloons or aircraft; some turned out to be marsh gas or unusual cloud formations. Some have remained unexplained, literally unidentified.

The Unidentified Flying Object, or UFO, is commonly a disc or cigar shape, and early on it was realised that the cigar might be a foreshortened view of a disc. Sightings have in some cases been backed up by still or movie photography, or by radar. Any idea that they might be ordinary aircraft or experimental aircraft of some kind has been rightly set aside on the grounds that the UFOs move in an entirely different way. They accelerate and decelerate much more rapidly than planes and are capable of far more advanced aerobatics. They can hover, motionless, like a helicopter. They can move straight up and down. They can dart off at remarkably high speeds, like jet planes. They can also change direction at speed in a far more agile way than any aircraft.

The main reason why people are so interested in UFOs is that they represent a possible point of contact with a civilisation outside the solar system. A recurring idea is that they might be visiting spacecraft from outside the solar system, from some planet orbiting a distant star. They therefore offer the tantalising possibility of meeting intelligent creatures from another world. They also offer a possible threat to the future of mankind, because there is no way of knowing what the intentions of these visitors might be.

Most of the sightings belong, probably significantly, to the time of the Cold War, when fears of conquest by an alien civilisation gripped both East and West. There was an assumption that the Unidentified Flying Objects were alien aircraft of some kind. Because of their odd behaviour, their ability to hover, their extreme speed, their ability to change direction in an instant, they were evidently of some advanced design. This led on to the idea that the craft did not come from the 'other side' in the Cold War but from some extraterrestrial civilisation.

If UFO sightings only began in 1948, it would be tempting to interpret them as paranoid delusions, projections brought on by Cold War panic. But there were occasional sightings long before that. An ancient Egyptian papyrus describes a mysterious disembodied 'circle of fire' that appeared in about 1500 BC. Then there was the prophet Ezekiel's vision of a strange wheeled vehicle arriving from the sky and landing in what is now Iraq in 592 BC. This had celestial occupants, each of which had four faces and four wings. The four faces were those of a man, a lion, an ox and an eagle, and these were to become the four symbolic identities later allocated to the writers of the four canonical gospels. In the iron age world inhabited by the prophet Ezekiel, these heavenly visitors were naturally interpreted as cherubim or seraphim – angels. If the same creatures had visited the Earth in the late twentieth century, there is no doubt that they would have been viewed as extra-terrestrials, as aliens. What we see is conditioned by what we are.

The Roman writer Julius Obsequens in the 4th century AD compiled a *Book of Prodigies*. One of these prodigies was a sighting in 216 BC of 'things like ships' in the sky; at Arpi, east of Rome, a round shield was seen floating in the sky. Again in 99 BC 'a round object like a globe or round shield travelled across the sky from west to east'. The round shields of those times were, significantly, saucer-shaped.

In AD 393 a bright globe suddenly became visible in the night sky near Venus. A peculiarity of this sighting was the clustering of other globes round the initial globe. They jostled one another into different formations, including one resembling a long flame of sword. A similar set of moving lights was seen for several hours by an entire Japanese army in 1235. General Yoritsume ordered a full investigation into the event. The report has a familiar, modern ring to it. The general was told that the whole incident could be explained entirely in terms of natural processes; 'it is only the wind making the stars sway.' From this we can see how right we are to be sceptical of official reports!

The reported sightings continued through the middle ages and on into the Age of Reason. In 1733, Mr Cracker of Fleet in Dorset saw a UFO on a bright sunny day. This object looked startlingly like a modern aircraft, from Mr Cracker's description, though of course he had never seen one. He described 'something in the sky. . . darting. . .the colour like burnished or new washed silver.' In one respect it outperformed a modern aircraft – in its speed. It shot off at high speed, 'like a star falling in the night'; in other words it moved as fast as a meteorite, and this capacity for amazing speeds is something that crops up again and again in UFO reports. Mr Cracker noted that his sighting was corroborated by at least two other people watching from another vantage point.

In 1878 a Texan farmer saw a dark disc-shaped object travelling high in the sky 'at a wonderful speed'; he described it (for the first time) as a 'saucer'. The post-Second World War period, and the Cold War in particular, was certainly the time when sightings were commonest. The most famous UFO encounter is the Roswell incident, which was interpreted by some people at the time as a UFO crash landing.

Perhaps by coincidence, the Roswell incident happened on 2 July 1947, only days after the highly publicised Arnold UFO sighting. At 9.50 pm, Mr and Mrs Wilmot were sitting on their front porch when a large glowing object travelled at high speed across the sky from the south-east and headed towards Corona to the north-west. They saw it for only forty or fifty seconds, but that was long enough for them to identify it as oval in shape. From what happened later it would appear that the craft changed direction during its descent, flying north-west over Roswell, then turning to fly west after about 50 miles, taking it over Socorro to crash in the Plains of San Agustin 50 miles west of Socorro. The following morning, a civil engineer called Barney Barnett, was working in the desert 250 miles west of Roswell when he saw the sun glinting on some metal on the ground. He thought it was a crashed aircraft, and went to have a look. What he found was a metallic disc about thirty feet in diameter. 'I tried to get close to see what the bodies were like. They were all dead as far as I could see and there were bodies inside and outside the vehicle. The ones outside had been tossed out by impact. They were like humans but they were not humans. The heads were round, the eyes were small, and they had no hair. The eyes were oddly spaced. They were quite small by our standards and their heads were larger in proportion to their bodies than ours. Their clothing seemed to be one-piece and grey in colour. You couldn't see any zippers, belts, or buttons.'

While he was examining it, a small group of people arrived, claiming to be an archaeological research team from the University of Pennsylvania. Barnett later told his friends, 'I noticed that they were standing around looking at some dead bodies that had fallen to the ground . . . the machine was kind of a metallic disc. It was not all that big. It seemed to be made of a metal that looked like stainless steel. The machine had been split open by explosion or impact.' The apparent discovery of bodies of humanoid aliens was sensational.

Shortly afterwards, an army jeep arrived and all the civilians were ordered to leave the site. Barnett said, 'We were told to leave the area and not talk to anyone whatever about what we had seen . . . that it was our patriotic duty to remain silent.' This was the first indication that the Roswell incident was going to be covered up. Even so, when the officers returned to the Roswell base, an official press statement authorised by Colonel William Blanchard was released, confirming that wreckage of a flying disk had been recovered. Strangely, no-one was ever able to trace any member of the team of archaeologists who visited the scene; their testimony has never been heard. Were they perhaps not archaeologists at all?

Mack Brazel had a ranch seventy-five miles north-west of Roswell, about halfway between Roswell and the crash site. There, he found widely scattered wreckage including pieces of metallic foil the morning after hearing an explosion in the night. The unidentified wreckage, scattered over an area three-quarters of a mile long by several hundred feet wide, consisted of various types of debris. Brazel wondered whether this material had something to do with the flying saucers people had seen in the neighbourhood recently, told the sheriff and the sheriff referred him to the army air force base just outside Roswell. Troops converged on Brazel's ranch, cordoned it off and searched it. Major Jesse Marcel, a staff intelligence officer of the 509th Bomb Group Intelligence Office at the Army Air Forces base at Roswell Field, said he had seen nothing like it before. 'There was all kinds of stuff: small beams [with an I-shaped cross section] about three eighths or a half inch square with some sort of hieroglyphics on them that nobody could decipher. These looked something like balsa wood and were of about the same weight, except that they were not wood at all. They were very hard, although flexible, and would not burn. There was a great deal of unusual parchment-like substance which was brown in colour and extremely strong, and a great number of small pieces of a metal like tinfoil, except that it wasn't tinfoil.'

Shortly after that, Major Marcel was ordered to load the debris of the disc onto a B-29 and fly it to Wright Field (now Wright-Patterson Air Forces Base) at Dayton, Ohio, for examination. On arrival at an intermediate stop at Carswell Army Air Forces Base, Fort Worth, Texas (headquarters of the Eighth Air Force), General Roger Ramey took over and ordered Marcel and others on the plane not to talk to reporters. A second press statement was issued, stating that the wreckage was the remains of a weather balloon and its attached tinfoil radar target, and this was prominently displayed at the press conference. Meanwhile, the wreckage of the metal disc arrived at Wright Field under armed guard; Marcel returned to Roswell and Brazel was held incommunicado for nearly a week while the crash site was stripped of every scrap of debris.

By 7 July, local radio stations were picking up the story, which naturally grew when the authorities attempted to stifle it. A news broadcast from Albuquerque describing this fantastic story was interrupted and the radio station in question was warned not to continue the broadcast: 'Attention Albuquerque: cease transmission. Repeat: cease transmission. National security item. Do not transmit. Stand by.'

General Ramey, from Fort Worth in the neighbouring state of Texas, went on the radio to explain that the Roswell incident was a case of mistaken identification and that the army knew of no flying saucers. The army held a press conference at which they claimed the wreckage was from a weather balloon. Mack Brazel was convinced that what he found was not from a weather balloon. Marcel too was convinced that the material had nothing to do with a weather balloon or radar target. His testimony should not be dismissed, owing to his background in aviation: he had served as bombardier, waist-gunner and pilot and been awarded five medals for shooting down enemy aircraft in the Second World War. Perhaps significantly, following the Roswell incident he was promoted to Lieutenant Colonel and assigned to a Special Weapons Programme. He was certain that no bodies were found among the debris at the Brazel ranch, and that whatever the object was it must have exploded above ground level. Brazel's son collected some fragments, but when two years later he mentioned in a bar that he had them he had a visit from the military, who demanded that he hand the pieces over. If the remains really were those a weather balloon, it seems unlikely that the army would have been so concerned to remove all trace of it.

The wreckage of the saucer was taken in strict secrecy from Wright Field to Muroc Air Force base in California, where it was inspected by President Eisenhower. As for the bodies of the aliens – a now-notorious film was made of what is supposed to be an autopsy of one of the alien corpses. Opinions differ as to the authenticity of the film, but there is a growing presumption that it was a hoax.

It is not certain that the wreckage found at the two sites belonged to the same craft that had somehow managed to remain airborne for over 100 miles before crashing on the Plains. It is possible that two entirely separate accidents happened on the same night within 150 miles of each other. It has also been suggested that there was a collision between two craft, perhaps two flying saucers, one of them crashing at Roswell, the other making it to the Plains of San Agustin before crashing. The quality of evidence varies between the two crash sites. The material gathered at the Brazel ranch was real enough, as it was displayed at a press conference and photographed there. There is far less evidence to substantiate Barnett's story, and as already mentioned even the archaeologists are untraceable. The Barnett story should nevertheless not be entirely dismissed.

How much of the entire incident at Roswell was a hoax? It is possible that the metal disc part was a hoax, but was there a genuine UFO crash, which the US military tried very hard to keep secret? Or was this a crash of something else, an unstable experimental craft that was being developed by the US Air Force, which they did not want the general public – or the Russians – to know about? Experiments certainly were being carried out on planes of different shapes and designs, and it is now known that some were circular. This might explain some of the sightings of flying saucers.

If a genuine UFO crashed on the Plain, it may be that the military planted the debris at the Brazel ranch in order to distract media attention from the real crash site away to the west. The display of hardware from the Brazel ranch at a press conference and the weather balloon explanation would have been enough to satisfy public curiosity, while the military spirited away the debris from the San Agustin site for secret investigation at a military air base. It was a carefully stage-managed piece of counter-intelligence.

But what of the dead aliens? It is just possible that they were the human crew of an all-too-terrestrial craft. One of the photographs of a badly incinerated corpse inside the Roswell saucer has a pair of wire-frame spectacles, half-concealed behind the corpse's shoulder. This seems to suggest that the victims were not aliens at all. What then of the bizarre fake autopsy? It is just possible that this film was an elaborately staged hoax commissioned by the military in order to put people off the scent – another piece of counter-intelligence. In a way, it would matter little whether people believed that the film proved the existence of flying saucers and aliens, or that it was an elaborate hoax; the purpose of diverting them from the military reality behind Roswell, the harsh reality of the Cold War, would be achieved. But nagging doubts remain. Ten out of thirty of the original witnesses involved in the discovery or subsequent cover-up identified the object as extra-terrestrial.

BETTY AND BARNEY HILL ABDUCTED BY ALIENS

(1961)

IN UFOLOGY, A 'close encounter' is an event in which someone witnesses an unidentified flying object. The phrase and the system of definitions that go with it were devised by the astronomer and UFO researcher J. Allen Hynek. He put forward a classification of three types of encounters in a 1972 book, *The UFO Experience*. A sighting of an un-identified flying object is classified as a close encounter of the first kind. A close encounter of the second kind involves some physical effect from the encounter in addition to the sighting, such as heat, damage to the landscape, fear instilled in animals, electronic interference with television, radio or car engines, loss of time (a memory gap). A close encounter of the third kind involves a sighting of animated beings, which might be living things or robots. Hynek himself was uncomfortable and sceptical about this class of encounter, but included it because such things were mentioned in a small number of reported UFO sightings.

Other researchers subsequently added two additional categories. A close encounter of the fourth kind is an encounter with a UFO in which a human being is abducted by the UFO or its occupants. A close encounter of the fifth kind is a joint, bilateral contact event; in other words, there is two-way communication between the witness and the occupants of the UFO. The classification does not mean that any of these encounters has an objectively verifiable reality, only that these are the sorts of encounters that have been claimed, or can be envisaged.

In September 1961, Barney and Betty Hill had a close encounter of the fourth kind when returning home in Portsmouth, New Hampshire after a holiday in Canada. As they drove along, they became aware of a bright moving light following them erratically. After a time it appeared in front of them, so Barney stopped the car and got out to observe the object through binoculars. He could see up to ten figures in shiny black uniforms moving about inside the spacecraft behind a double row of windows. Betty could not see the figures; she only heard her husband repeat, 'I don't believe it!' The UFO was by this time only 100 feet away and seventy feet up. Barney shouted, 'They are going to capture us!' and jumped back into the car. He drove off and, though they could no longer see the UFO, they guessed it was right above them. They heard a sound like a tuning fork, felt drowsy, and then realised they had lost two hours.

The Hills reported their experience, or what they could remember of it, to the nearest air base. About ten days later, Betty began to have nightmares in which she recalled some of the things that happened in the missing two hours. She saw a group of up to eleven men dressed in uniforms and military caps standing in the road, barring their way. The men assured them they would not be harmed and led them into the flying saucer. There the aliens took samples of Betty's hair, fingernails and scrapings of skin cells. Although they were released unharmed, the Hills experienced intense anxiety feelings, for which they needed psychiatric help. The psychiatrist, Dr Benjamin Simon, used a time-regression therapy technique, and under hypnosis a remarkable story emerged. The Hills' stories matched very closely, corroborating each other. One remarkable detail was the star map the leader of the aliens showed Betty when she asked where he came from. Betty was able to redraw this map under hypnosis. It was only some years afterwards that new astronomical information revealed that there was a cluster of stars close to a binary star called Zeta Reticuli; it closely matched the star map drawn by Betty Hill. Zeta Reticuli is not visible in the night sky north of the tropics, and so Betty could not have seen it for herself.

It all sounds like a genuine enough story, but Dr Simon remained convinced that the Hills were suffering from a fantasy. The reason why Barney's account corroborated Betty's was simply that Betty had already described to Barney in detail everything she had experienced in her dreams or hallucinations; he consequently knew her experiences as well as she did. The couple convinced themselves and each other that they had been abducted by aliens.

Many of the close encounter stories suffer from a fundamental lack of credibility. It is not at all unlikely that highly intelligent life forms and advanced civilisations exist on planets revolving round other stars in this and other galaxies. Carl Sagan gave an optimistic estimate that within the Milky Way, our own local galaxy, there might be as many as a million civilisations. But they would need to have developed a very remarkable technology in order to travel close to the speed of light in order to get here. And that raises a crucial question. Why on earth would members of a sophisticated advanced civilisation developing many light-years away invest hundreds of years of their time, and large quantities of whatever they use for money, to travel to the Earth to get a few samples of nail-clippings from Mrs Betty Hill of Portsmouth, New Hampshire? It seems a very unlikely project. Another reason for being sceptical is that as Carl Sagan has said the accounts of the spaceships and their occupants are 'stodgy in their unimaginativeness.' The aliens are a bit too much like human beings, and their spaceships are a bit too much like the ones drawn in children's comics – a probable source of the material for some of the fantasising. Some of the encounters utterly defy belief, yet they are fascinating even so.

A plumber called Joe Simonton in Wisconsin heard a noise in his yard. When he looked out he saw a silvery globe floating a few inches off the ground. When he approached, the hatch opened and he saw three individuals inside. They were young, five feet tall with dark hair. One gave Simonton a silver-coloured jug, indicating that he wanted it filled, so Simonton filled it with water. He watched one of the aliens cooking and used sign language to indicated that he wanted some; he was given two biscuits. He ate one. When analysed, the other was found to contain flour, sugar and fat. After the picnic, the UFO took off at a forty-five degree angle. This story has much of the flavour of old English folk tales of encounters with fairies.

71

So, then, are UFO stories explained away as weather phenomena or fantasies? Is there no hard proof that UFOs really exist, that they really are alien craft from outer space? There are some alleged UFO crashes and it has been alleged that the authorities have deliberately concealed these events from the public to avoid spreading alarm and hysteria. This is where the conspiracy comes in.

It was the 1947 sighting by Kenneth Arnold, a civilian pilot, that introduced the modern wave of UFOs and ufology. Arnold was flying near Mount Rainier when he was aware of two flashes of light. When he looked to see where the flashes had come from he saw nine shining objects coming from the direction of Mount Baker, swerving round the mountains. From their positions in relation to the mountains, Arnold estimated their speed at 1600 mph, which was three times faster than any plane could fly at that time. Arnold described the objects as 'flat like a pie pan and so shiny they reflected the sun like a mirror.' They moved oddly, 'like speedboats on rough water. . . like a saucer would if you skipped it across the water.' Just ten days later another pilot, Captain E. J. Smith of United Airlines, saw a formation of five similar objects just after taking off from Boise in Idaho. He and his co-pilot Ralph Stevens watched the saucers until, after a minute or so, they whizzed off at an astounding speed and were replaced by another four unidentified objects. Possibly this was the same group of objects that Arnold had seen just over a week earlier.

The Arnold sighting turned out to be the start of the modern age of flying saucers. It was reported globally and it prompted the US Air Force to launch a formal investigation. Dr Allen Hyneck divided the sightings into categories. There were sightings over 500 feet away, comprising 'nocturnal lights', 'daylight discs' and 'radar visuals'. Then there were sightings at shorter distances, comprising close encounters of the first kind.

The best example of the nocturnal lights sightings appeared at Lubbock, Texas in August and September 1951, when a huge wing-shaped UFO with blue lights on the rear edge was seen by hundreds of people. Observers thought it was much larger than a B-36 aircraft. One man, Carl Hart, photographed the wing and his photograph clearly showed the regular pattern of tail-lights. The air force investigators were unable to explain the phenomenon, but confirmed the genuineness of Hart's photograph. Although some lights can be explained away as due to natural atmospheric conditions, this distinctive V-formation can only have been artificial. The reports came in thick and fast, and independently, from widely spaced locations; they cannot have been made with any knowledge of the other reports coming in at the same time. There is no possibility that these sightings were a hoax.

Another sighting, fascinating for an entirely different reason, was at Leary in Georgia in January 1969. The witness this time was President Jimmy Carter, who was outdoors, waiting to address a meeting. President Carter later said, 'I am convinced that UFOs exist because I've seen one. It was a very peculiar aberration, but about twenty people saw it . . . It was the darnedest thing I've ever seen. It was big; it was very bright; it changed colours; and it was about the size of the moon. We watched it for ten minutes, but none of us could figure out what it was.'

Many of the photograph-supported sightings turned out to be hoaxes. Scores of amateur photographers rigged up dustbin lids or saucepan lids on wires. Other sightings are more sinister. Towards the end of 1978 Frederick Valentich was flying a small plane across the Bass Strait between Australia and Tasmania. He used his radio to ask Melbourne to check for confirmation of a large aircraft with four bright lights, but he was told that there were no reported aircraft in the area. Over the radio he reported the approach of the unidentified object. 'It's approaching from due east of me. It seems to be playing some sort of game, flying at a speed I cannot estimate . . . It is flying past. It has a long shape . . . coming for me right now . . . It has a green light and sort of metallic look on the outside. The thing is orbiting on top of me.'

At this point, Valentich's engine began to falter and cough. He called, 'Proceeding King Island. Unknown aircraft now hovering on top of me.' A loud metallic sound lasting seventeen seconds was heard over the radio, and then communications went dead. No trace of Valentich or his plane was ever found. It is possible that he simply developed engine trouble, ditched in the sea and did not survive the crash, but because of the strange craft hovering over his plane his father believed he had been abducted by aliens.

There have been other reports of UFOs 'buzzing' aircraft. In 1975, over Mexico City, Carlos Antonio de los Santos Montiel was approaching the city in a light aircraft, a Piper PA-24, when he found his plane vibrating for no reason. Beyond the right wing tip he saw a black disc ten or twelve feet in diameter, then to the left he saw another. Most alarming of all, de los Santos saw a third disc coming at him from dead ahead. This third disc scraped the underside of the plane. Then he found that the plane's controls had stopped working, yet the plane carried on flying smoothly at 120 mph. When the discs let him go, the plane's controls resumed and he was able to radio to the tower at Mexico City airport. By this stage he was in tears. His story was believed, because the airport controllers had been tracking the three objects on their radar screens throughout the incident. One of the controllers described the objects' bizarre behaviour. 'The objects made a 270-degree turn at 518 mph in an arc of only three miles. In my seventeen years as an air traffic controller I've never seen anything like that.'

One of the earliest reports of a close encounter of the first kind was in July 1948. At 2.45 am near Montgomery, Alabama, two airline pilots, Clarence Chiles and John Whitted, saw what they thought was a jet fighter streaking towards them 'with terrific speed'. It was about 100 feet long, cigar-shaped with no protruding fins. An intense dark blue glow came from the side of the object and ran the entire length of its fuselage; the exhaust was a red-orange flame. There was no doubt in the two pilots' minds that this was a spaceship. They even saw rows of portholes along the side of it. When the UFO disappeared into some cloud, Chiles visited the cabin to see what the passengers had made of the experience. Only one of them was awake: Clarence McKelvie. He had seen a brilliant light flashing past the window. 'It looked like a cigar with a cherry flame going out the back. There was a row of windows. It disappeared very quickly.'

Scientists have been quick to offer everyday rational explanations for flying saucers, and a great many of the sightings can indeed be explained in terms of unusual atmospheric conditions, weather balloons and aircraft. It seems very likely that some of them are psychic in origin. The psychologist Carl Gustav Jung wrote a very perceptive essay on the subject and he noticed that a great many of the sightings are reported by people whose testimony we would think was irreproachable, such as pilots and law enforcement officers. Jung's explanation is that these people are trained to function totally in the world of the everyday, and large areas of their minds are left under-exercised. Every so often the unconscious mind asserts itself, projecting an archetype into the conscious mind. What people are 'seeing' is therefore a projection of their unconscious mind. This, and the fact that the images fall within a fairly narrow range of shapes and behaviour patterns, fits well with both the range of reports and with Jung's view of modern man's neglect of the unconscious mind.

The same idea has been developed by Jacques Vallee, who has shown that sightings of UFOs seem to permeate ancient as well as modern writings, playing a significant role in the creation of myths. The strange otherworldly experiences that accompany UFO sightings certainly accord well with the idea of a 'paranormal' element.

Jung pointed out that it is no accident that what people very often see is a disc. The circular shape symbolises the universal, the whole - a powerful archetype. Why would there be a surge of UFO sightings in the 1940s and 1950s? Jung suggested that the idea of a visitation by a superior civilisation, whether benign or not, was significant in a world that had been wrecked by two world wars; the shining disc was a symbol of human hopes and fears in an uncertain world. The psychic approach has been fruitful. Those who reported being abducted by aliens were hypnotised, and their stories contained large numbers of common elements. The 'victim' sees a shining light, is guided to the spacecraft in a semi-conscious or 'out-of-body' state, and has an experience outside time in which he or she is examined by aliens. The really significant thing is that the same sequence of events is described by hypnosis subjects who have not witnessed a close encounter but are asked to imagine one. It is as if we are all programmed to project the same images of extra-terrestrials in much the same way, when prompted to imagine them.

The extra-terrestrials seen at Flatwoods, West Virginia, in 1952 were unusually repellent. A group of children saw what looked like a meteorite land on a hilltop one night in September and went to look at it together with some adults, one of whom was a soldier. They saw a ball as big as a house, making a hissing, throbbing sound. One of the group shone a torch at what looked like animal eyes up in a tree and they all saw a huge figure perhaps fifteen feet tall. It had a blood-red face and glowing greenish-orange eyes. The monster – there is no other way to describe it – floated slowly towards them, and they ran down the hill, terrified. Afterwards, two parallel skid-marks and a large circle of flattened grass were found on the site, and an unusual smell.

A more typical sighting of extra-terrestrials was the one by Jennie Roestenberg and her two children at Ranton near Shrewsbury in October 1954. They saw a disc-shaped, aluminium-coloured saucer hovering in the sky over their house. Mrs Roestenberg could make out two aliens through transparent windows in the side of the saucer. She could see them clearly. The aliens were very pale, with shoulder-length hair (which was very unusual in the 1950s) and very high foreheads. All of their features were concentrated in the lower half of their faces. They were wearing turquoise ski-suits and transparent helmets. As the saucer hovered, the humanoid aliens looked down 'sternly, not in an unkindly fashion, but almost sadly, compassionately.'

The details of this encounter are telling. It is, in all but name, a visitation by angels, and that is how the experience would have been reported in an earlier century. Encounters of this type suggest that the witnesses are projecting a need to believe that there is something out there watching over them. The accounts are a cry for faith. No wonder there was a surge of such encounters in the 20th century, a century of faithlessness.

CROP CIRCLES

(1970s)

CROP CIRCLES ARE a distinctively, though not exclusively, southern English phenomenon, consisting of patterns marked by the flattening of cereal crops. The earliest were simple discs of flattened corn; the more recent ones are more complex. When the crop circles first appeared in large numbers in the 1970s, opinion was divided about their origin. Some people were ready to believe that they were evidence of alien intelligence, that they were UFO landing sites. Those believing that crop circles are made by aliens see them as messages. The aliens are believed to be attempting to communicate with us by using ancient Sumerian symbols or symbolic representations of alien DNA.

There was a highly publicised incident in 1966. A sugar cane farmer in the small town of Tully in Queensland, Australia reported seeing a saucer-shaped craft rising about forty feet up from a swamp before flying away. When he went to have a look at the place where the saucer had landed, he saw that the reeds were intricately twisted into spirals, clockwise, on the surface of the water. The twisted and plaited reeds were able to support a significant amount of weight.

The association between crop circles and UFOs has become very strong in people's minds, but other explanations are available. Some cerealogists (or croppies) believe they are natural phenomena, produced perhaps by vortexes, descending and rotating pockets of air. Other meteorological theories invoke ball lightning or various effects of heat and wind. Tornadoes have been proposed, though these seem particularly unlikely causes as they move along as well rotating, so they should leave a meandering snail-trail of damage across the landscape. There were even theories that some kind of secret weapon such as a 'microwave cannon' might be responsible. But the simplest explanation was always that people were making them for fun.

The geographical distribution of crop circles always looked suspicious. Although the circle appeared in the middle of a cornfield, there was invariably an access corridor of some kind through the corn that would allow a human hoaxer in. The circles appear in unfenced areas, areas where there is either public right of access or at any rate lenient laws of trespass. The circles are invariably positioned so that they were highly visible from a nearby road. Many are found close to university campuses, suggesting a connection with student leisure activity. It must also be suspicious that they multiplied in the 1970s and 1980s, as the media gave a lot of publicity to a series of crop circles that appeared in Hampshire and Wiltshire. Altogether, 12,000 circles have been reported world-wide, most from Britain, but also as far afield as Canada, the USA, Japan and the Russian Federation.

Farmers understandably complain that trespassers are destroying a proportion of their crops, but the circles have a tourist value which farmers are sometimes able to exploit. When a crop circle appeared close to Stonehenge in 1966, the farmer charged an admission fee at the field gate and was able to clear £30,000 in four weeks. The crop's agricultural value was only £150. The association of (some) crop circles with stone circles, megalithic tombs and other ancient sites has led to a New Age interest in them, and a range of theories associating circle formation with mysterious earth energies. Some circles are alleged to give off certain earth energy that can be detected by dowsing.

Although the simple circles just might have had some natural explanation – though they were usually too sharp edged for that to be credible – the more recent complex designs must be man-made. In fact, in 1991 the two leading hoaxers, Doug Bower and David Chorley, owned up to creating about 250 crop circles. They had the idea while drinking at a pub near Winchester in 1976. Drawing on the 1966 Tully Saucer Nests, they made crop circles using lengths of rope and four-foot planks. Their early efforts did not create as much interest as they would have liked, so they chose a conspicuous location for one of their 1981 efforts – Matterley Bowl near Winchester. This natural amphitheatre has a road running round its edge, which gave outstanding views of the circle to passing traffic.

Chorley died in 1996 and Doug Bower has said that he, Bower, only owned up to making crop circles because his wife had become suspicious of his unexplained absences. After he told his wife, he decided to go public with his admission. A recent study concluded that eighty percent of British crop circles were not only man-made but could be proved to be man-made, because for example they had post-holes at their centres or lines of footprints leading to and from them. By implication the remaining twenty percent might also be man-made but their makers had been cleverer at covering their tracks.

In 1992, two Hungarian youths became the first people to be charged with crop damage as a result of making a circle; the judge found against them, but also decided that ninety-nine percent of the damage had been done as a result of trampling by the thousands of visitors who went to see their circle.

Appearing frequently as they did in the 1970s and 1980s, the most popular explanation was aliens who were trying to communicate with the human race. If the same phenomenon had appeared in the middle ages, people would have been keen to attribute it to the Devil or to a mythic race of giants, just as Stonehenge was the Giants' Dance. And there is a 17th century pamphlet with a woodcut which seems to show a crop circle in the making; its title is *The Mowing-Devil: or, Strange News out of Hartford-shire.* The illustration shows the Devil using a scythe to cut concentric circles in a field of oats. That was in 1678. At any time in any culture there is always a default explanation available for the unexplained – God, Satan, giants, extraterrestrials.

This leads on to the slightly unsettling awareness that crop circles were not, after all, invented by hoaxers in the 1970s. There were circles before that. In 1880 John Capron investigated the phenomenon when he saw it for himself. 'The storms about this part of Surrey have been lately local and violent, and the effects produced in some instances curious. Visiting a neighbour's farm, we found a field of standing wheat considerably knocked about, not as an entirety, but in patches forming, as viewed from a distance, circular spots . . . I could not trace locally any circumstances accounting for the peculiar forms of the patches in the field, nor indicating whether it was wind or rain, or both combined, which had caused them, beyond the general evidence everywhere of heavy rainfall. They were suggestive to me of some cyclonic wind action.'

So, while an enormous number of crop circles are man-made hoaxes, there are some that seem to have some other origin. It is hard to see how isolated occurrences like the ones that appeared in a field in Surrey in 1880 could be hoaxes. But do they represent encounters with aliens?

III
GREAT
FRIENDSHIPS

PLATO AND
SOCRATES

(399 BC)

THE ANCIENT GREEK philosopher Socrates was born in Athens in 469 BC and executed for corrupting the young in 399 BC. He had no formal disciples, founded no school of philosophy, and as far as we know he wrote nothing down – and yet he was a profoundly influential figure. One of the people he influenced was Plato, a man forty years younger than himself and who was about twenty-seven years old at the time of Socrates' death. Plato was a friend and pupil of Socrates and it is mainly through Plato's writings that we know about Socrates.

In fact, so little is known about Socrates from any other contemporary sources that we really cannot be sure what Socrates was like. Plato idolised Socrates, held him and his teachings up as models, and there must be a suspicion that his hero-worship distorted his representation of his master. Plato was a great philosopher in his own right, yet again and again in his writings he hides behind the persona of Socrates to say what he thinks. Plato is a ventriloquist, and Socrates is the dummy. There is, all the time in Plato, the sense that he is putting words and ideas into Socrates' mouth. This unusual situation – knowing about the one man only through the testimony of the other – has come to be known as the Socratic problem.

Socrates certainly existed, as there is corroboration from writers other than Plato. Xenophon, Aristotle and Aristophanes all referred to Socrates, giving us a bit more evidence of the sort of man he was. But a difficulty in seeing the historical Socrates is that nearly all the texts that were written about him are philosophical or dramatic. Listening to what Aristophanes has to say about Socrates is rather like watching a Spitting

Image sketch featuring Norman Tebbitt or Margaret Thatcher. In his play *The Clouds*, Aristophanes shows Socrates as a clown teaching his students how to bluff and cheat their way out of debt: how to argue for profit. But Aristophanes nearly always caricatures people, so we need not think of the historical Socrates as clownish. The sort of abuse of philosophy shown in Aristophanes is exactly what Socrates denounced – and that was the joke!

There is virtually nothing contemporary with Socrates in the way of a purely historical treatment. Those who have left us with character sketches or caricatures of Socrates were well-disposed towards him. We have no testimony from the Athenians who prosecuted and condemned him to death, so we have only one side of the story. Plato's *Apology* portrays Socrates' defence at his trial. Many scholars suspect that because of Plato's enormous respect for Socrates he left out some of the evidence that was produced for the prosecution. The *Apology* is obviously not a word-for-word transcript of the trial, but it is likely to be fairly accurate. Plato produced his account not long after the trial, and it would have been read by many Athenians who were present at the trial; he would have lost credibility as a commentator and philosopher if he had distorted the account of the trial by failing to disclose a key element in the prosecution case. The account cannot therefore have been excessively sympathetic to Socrates.

So, arriving at an honest appraisal of Socrates and his work, including his influence on Plato, is a challenge. No doubt some of the views Plato attributes to Socrates are genuinely Socratic in origin, but it is very difficult to be sure where Socrates' views end and Plato's begin.

The fact that Socrates talked but did not write implies that he belonged to the ancient tradition of teaching, in which ideas were passed on orally. The story of the Trojan War, which happened in the years around 1250 BC, was passed on in poems that were chanted or sung by bards for 500 years before they were written down by scribes for the first time. By Socrates' day, many things were being written down, but perhaps in that respect Socrates was a reactionary; other personality traits also imply that he was stubborn and perverse.

Plato gives us details of Socrates' family. His father was Sophroniscus and his mother was a midwife called Phaenarete. There was a tradition that Socrates was ugly, snub-nosed and had a paunch, yet he married a very young wife, Xanthippe. She was a shrew, but they had three sons, Sophroniscus, Lamprocles and Menexenus. One of his friends, Crito, thought Socrates let his family down at the end of his life; Socrates could have left Athens before his execution, and probably the authorities were hoping that he would go into voluntary exile. It would have spared them the embarrassment of killing him, but he stubbornly stayed and died – abandoning his sons. It was also clear that Socrates' uncompromising tone at his trial antagonised the jurors; if he had made some concessions, he might have lived.

Socrates appears to have had no occupation other than discussing philosophy. Aristophanes shows him being paid for teaching, but both Plato and Xenophon report that Socrates specifically denied taking payment for teaching. It may that the tradition that he worked as a stonemason like his father was true; he must have earned a living somehow. Like other Athenian men, he did military service, serving in three campaigns, Potidaea (432-29 BC), Delium (424 BC) and Amphipolis (422 BC). He was conspicuously brave, saving the life of the young Alcibiades at the Battle of Potidaea, and Plato reports the general Laches as commenting on Socrates' exceptional service at the Battle of Delium. As a warrior, Socrates was courageous and showed remarkable physical endurance, indifference to fatigue and adverse weather. He stayed out of Athenian politics entirely, devoting all his mental energies to philosophy.

Plato recounts in detail the philosophy of Socrates, which evidently proceeded by way of a conversational dialogue, exploring issues through questions and answers – in particular asking for definitions of key concepts like justice and piety. The dialogue method was designed to trick unfortunate interlocutors into contradicting themselves in order to expose fallacies. It is a very distinctive way of thinking, and one that has been followed and imitated ever since. Plato paid his mentor the greatest tribute of all by recording what he said, so that succeeding generations could know.

Plato was also in Athens at the time of Socrates' trial. The charge of corrupting the young may have had its origins in Socrates' philosophical dialogues with young men, conversations in which he challenged all their basic assumptions in order to arrive at more honest definitions of totem concepts. This fundamental questioning was seen by some citizens as subversive. It was indeed the sort of method that could lead to a generation of young Athenians questioning whether a war was a righteous and just war, and so – potentially - lead to a refusal to fight. In the 20th century, the spread and improvement of secondary education led on to exactly such questioning in the USA, for example, regarding the Vietnam War and more recently in the UK regarding the Iraq War.

Both Xenophon and Plato wrote about Socrates' one-day trial in 399 BC, but of the two only Plato actually attended the trial. It made a huge impression on Plato because it led directly to the death of his friend, who was condemned to take poison. The traumatic event also stood as a lifelong warning to Plato to mind his step. All his life, Plato wrapped up what he had to say in various ways. He used stories and allegories, like the Atlantis legend; and all the time he hid behind Socrates – partly out of veneration for the dead mentor, partly for safety. So the trial and death of his friend Socrates had a profound effect on Plato, and made his writings even harder to interpret.

Socrates was allowed visitors in his condemned cell, including his family and friends. He said goodbye to his family and asked them to leave, but several of his pupils stayed with him while he drank the hemlock and died. But Plato himself was not there. He could not conceivably have had something more important to do that day, and it seems he stayed away out of fear. He understood now what sort of state Athens was, and realised that he, as a philosopher, was in danger; his association with Socrates might put him in significant danger, and so might his writings. It is generally assumed that he stayed away out of fear. That would have been quickly followed by shame at his own cowardice. Other friends had seen it through to the bitter end, while he had not. This may have prompted Plato to write the definitive account of the death of Socrates. He wrote it in four dialogues, the *Euthyphro*, the *Apology*, the *Crito* and the *Phaedo*. It was a kind of funeral tribute, a valediction, and a kind of apology in the modern sense. It also to some extent vindicated Plato himself, and probably made him feel better about letting Socrates down.

The death of Socrates had a profound effect on Plato. As a youth he had thought of going into politics, but this revelation of the nature of the Athenian state made him steer away from it. It was also at this time that he began to write. Maybe, if Socrates had lived on, maybe if Socrates had died a natural death fifteen years later, Plato might have adopted his teaching method – and written nothing down himself. As it was, the death of his friend jolted him into writing, and ostensibly writing down the philosophy of Socrates. The writings of Plato became one of the foundation stones of Western philosophy. One commentator has said that all subsequent Western philosophy consists of no more than 'footnotes to Plato'. His importance can scarcely be exaggerated. Plato had another key role to play, as the teacher of another great philosopher, Aristotle.

ELIZABETH I AND SIR WALTER RALEIGH

(1581)

Sir Walter Raleigh (1552–1618) was not only one of Queen Elizabeth I's favourites, he was by far the most famous and most glamorous of her favourites. He was born in a West Country farmhouse and brought up as a country gentleman, though his father, also called Walter, was not a wealthy man. Elizabeth's favourite was the son of his third marriage, to Catherine, the daughter of Sir Philip Champernown. She was also the widow of Otho Gilbert and one of her sons by the earlier marriage was Humphrey, the Humphrey Gilbert who became Walter Raleigh's mentor during his youth. Early on, Walter set his sights on the favour of Queen Elizabeth I; it was the path to power and fortune, and Humphrey did all he could to help him progress along it.

Walter Raleigh went to Oxford in 1568 but, like many other upper class young men of his time, he did not take a degree. In fact within the year he had joined a company of volunteers to fight alongside the French Huguenots; his military career had begun. Ten years later his half-brother Humphrey obtained a six-year patent allowing him to take possession of 'any heathen lands not possessed by any Christian prince'. It was in effect a pirates' licence and Humphrey was engaged in a characteristic Devon gentleman's activity – the life of a maritime adventurer. In 1578, Humphrey Gilbert led a piratical expedition against the Spaniards, but was beaten back. Raleigh went with him as captain of the *Falcon*.

The failure of Gilbert's enterprises drove Raleigh to seek his fortune at court. He became a hanger-on in the retinue of the Earl of Leicester, the queen's favourite, and then attached himself to the Earl of Oxford, who was Lord Burghley's son-in-law. He calculatingly put himself at the sides of grandees, men who were in powerful positions at court. In 1580 he became a captain of a company of foot soldiers in Munster, playing an active role in suppressing the Desmond rebellion. He was also active in the massacre of Spanish and Italian adventurers at Smerwick; he was committed to a strategy of ruthless suppression of the Irish and in letters he recommended the assassination of Irish leaders. When his company was disbanded, he was sent home.

His return to England after these escapades marks the beginning of his glittering career as a court favourite. He cut a dash. In an age when courtiers were dandies and peacocks, Raleigh outshone them all. He invested a huge amount of his estate in lavish court clothes. His theatrical behaviour also drew attention to him. The well-known story that he threw his cloak across a puddle so that the queen could step across without getting her feet wet is probably true; it is the sort of thing he did in order to attract attention to himself. It is not unlike the modern TV celebrity cult, where C- and D-list celebrities will undergo almost any humiliation in order to remain in the public eye, including being thrown into pits of mud and having maggots poured over them. The craving for celebrity is not new. Raleigh was a D-list celebrity trying very hard to get onto the A-list. He looked magnificent. He was tall, good-looking, witty and he cultivated charming 'caressing' manners. How could the susceptible and easily-flattered queen not be pleased with him?

Once he became Elizabeth's favourite, rewards poured onto him that were far beyond what he deserved for his service in Ireland. In 1582 he was given a reward of £600 and the command of a company of soldiers. This command was a sinecure, as he was able to appoint a deputy to take care of the company, and this released him to spend more time at court. The queen granted him Durham House in the Strand as a town house. She gave him two beneficial leases which she had acquired from All Souls College, Oxford; these he sold on profitably. She also granted him a patent to grant licences to tavern keepers, which sounds un-inspiring, but actually brought him an income of £2,000 a year. And it did not end there. In 1584, the queen granted him a licence for exporting woollen cloths. This was England's leading export at the time, and therefore a very lucrative monopoly. It made him very rich, but also very unpopular with the wool merchants. In fact the lengthening portfolio of sinecures and monopolies was making Raleigh generally unpopular.

Elizabeth knighted Raleigh in 1584 and after that made him Warden of the Stannaries, the Cornish tin mines. Raleigh seems to have treated this favour rather differently, perhaps because it was closer to home, a key part of the local West Country economy. He used his new role as Warden to update work practices and was fair in his treatment of the work force. In 1586, the queen granted him 40,000 acres of forfeited Desmond land on the Blackwater in Ireland. He was assigned the task of generating English colonies in America, and he introduced potato cultivation. He is credited with introducing tobacco to England, but this is uncertain. King James I hated Raleigh and he hated smoking to the extent of writing a diatribe against it: but that does not mean that Raleigh was responsible for introducing tobacco to England.

In 1587, after the exposure of the Babington Plot, Raleigh was granted part of Babington's estate.

Raleigh's partnership with Humphrey Gilbert continued. Gilbert's patent was to run out in 1584, and in view of that Raleigh provided some of the capital for Gilbert's Newfoundland expedition out of his own well-lined pocket. Gilbert perished during the expedition and the patent was renewed in Raleigh's favour. Then he launched a series of colonisation ventures, which led to his association with the settlement of Virginia, named in honour of England's virgin queen. Raleigh instigated voyages of exploration. He sent two ships to Florida, and they systematically explored the eastern seaboard of North America as far as North Carolina. A region was named Virginia and a party of settlers was sent out under Sir Richard Grenville to colonise Roanoake Island. Grenville turned out to be far more interested in piracy; the settlers antagonised the native North Americans and deserted as soon as they got the chance, accepting rescue by Drake when he visited the coast in 1586. By 1589 Raleigh was resigning his rights to a company of merchants. The English colonisation of North America had begun under Raleigh and the queen was doubtless flattered to have a huge if empty colony named in her honour.

It seemed the queen was besotted with Sir Walter Raleigh, that there was nothing she would not give him. He was certainly at the height of his favour by the mid-1580s. But he was not alone. Elizabeth I was a cautious queen, cautious with powerful men in particular. She had never forgotten what her too-powerful father, Henry VIII, had done with his power over her mother, Anne Boleyn. There was always an association in her mind of love and power with death. She tried not to allow one favourite to influence her unduly, which would give him too much power. Only once, near the end of her reign, did she lose her grip. She allowed the young Earl of Essex too many liberties, too much favour – because she was in love with him – and he turned traitor.

When Essex appeared at court, Raleigh's eclipse began – the long and humiliating decline that ended in his execution by James I in 1618. But already by the Armada year of 1588 he was overshadowed by Essex. He received a challenge from Essex which nevertheless did not lead to an encounter. In 1589 he returned to Ireland where he was able to renew his acquaintance with the poet Edmund Spenser. Raleigh was able to use his influence to obtain a pension for Spenser and help from the queen to publish the first three books of Spenser's great poem The Faerie Queen. The exact reason for Raleigh's fall from favour is not known. He may have said or done something that was considered inappropriate – the queen was quick to take offence – or it may simply be that out of habit the queen was favouring someone else in order to curb Raleigh's increasing power and influence. Raleigh's arrogance won him lots of enemies at court, and it may be that a whispering campaign against him was started.

In 1589 Raleigh went with an expedition to the Portuguese coast, which was intended to provoke a revolt against Philip II. But this expedition was a failure. Another voyage, to the Azores, was planned for 1591, but at the last moment he was forbidden to sail – a typical caprice on the queen's part – and he was replaced by Sir Richard Grenville, who died in action.

The following year, Raleigh was at sea again on an expedition to intercept and plunder Spanish merchant vessels. But he was recalled by the queen. This time it was not a caprice. Raleigh had transgressed. Elizabeth had about her ladies in waiting whom for some reason she seems to have thought of as Vestal virgins. She discovered that Raleigh had had sex with one of them, Elizabeth 'Bess' Throgmorton. The queen was furious. On his arrival back in England he was arrested and thrown into the Tower along with Bess Throgmorton. To try to extricate himself, Raleigh put on what now looks like a fantastic display of despair at his fall from favour. An anonymous letter writer wrote, 'S.W.R., as it seemeth, have been too inward with one of Her Majesty's maids. All think the Tower will be his dwelling, like hermit poor in pensive place, where he may spend his endless days in doubt. It is affirmed that they are married; but the queen is most fiercely incensed and, as the bruit goes, threateneth the most bitter punishment to both the offenders. S.W.R. will lose, it is thought, all his places and preferments at court, with the queen's favour; such will be the end of his speedy rising, and now he must fall as low as he was high, at the which many will rejoice.' That was true. Raleigh's arrogance was legendary and there were many who would have been pleased to see him brought low.

From the Tower, Raleigh wrote a letter to the Queen's chief minister, Sir Robert Cecil, denying, probably untruthfully, that he had secretly married Bess. 'My heart was never broken till this day, that I hear the queen goes away so far off – whom I have followed so many years with so great love and desire, in so many journeys, and am now left behind, in a prison all alone. . .'

But the whole point was that Raleigh was not alone. He had with him either a mistress or a forbidden wife. It was a tactless thing to write, and may indicate how disturbed his mind was at the unexpected turn of events. He wrote the letter to Cecil, expecting him to show it to Elizabeth, which he almost certainly did, but the contents would not have pleased Her Majesty. As it turned out, Raleigh's leadership skills were urgently needed and he was released from the Tower almost at once. A captured treasure ship, the *Madre de Dios*, had been brought into Dartmouth and there was an orgy of riotous looting. From the West Country Sir John Hawkins wrote in desperation to Burghley that they needed Raleigh in Dartmouth to control the looters: 'Sir Walter Raleigh is the especial man.'

In June 1597, Raleigh was received again at court by the queen. He had been excluded, disgraced, for five years. Elizabeth would never forget that he had deceived her, but she was impressed at his zeal in working his way back into favour, not least by his efforts on the El Dorado expedition and the Cadiz campaign. A courtier who saw his return to court wrote that the queen received him 'very graciously, and gave him full authority to execute his place as captain of the guard, which he immediately undertook.' Elizabeth was keen to reinstate Raleigh at court; she had been unnerved by many recent events, and felt safer with Raleigh at her side than with others. 'In the evening he [Raleigh] rode abroad with the queen and had private conference with her; and now he comes boldly to the Privy Chamber, as he was wont.'

Until the rise of the Earl of Essex, which began in 1587, there were always several favourites, not one. The Earl of Leicester had been Elizabeth's leading favourite for a long time, but when he became old and sick Raleigh became the dominant favourite. But her treatment of Raleigh was different from the way she treated Leicester or Essex. She was ready to heap wealth on Raleigh, and privileges and monopolies with grand-sounding titles, but she never gave him any high office of any kind. She never admitted him to her Council. She gave him the post of Captain of the Guard. This was lucrative and grand-sounding, but it gave him no real power. Perhaps Elizabeth sensed that he was a shallow, fundamentally unreliable self-seeker, a fortune-hunter; perhaps, deep down, she did not trust him.

Raleigh was a kind of trophy courtier, a piece of beefcake to decorate her court. Elizabeth was very conscious of her appearance and commissioned some remarkably elaborate court costumes. She needed to look like Gloriana on the glamorous stage-set that was the Elizabethan court. Raleigh looked wonderful, and Elizabeth was astute enough to know that having her grandee toy-boy, 'the especial man',

RICHARD SAVAGE AND SAMUEL JOHNSON

(1730s)

SAMUEL JOHNSON WAS the son of a bookseller. He was educated at Lichfield Grammar School, went briefly to Oxford but had to leave when he ran out of money. He could not find work as a teacher and drifted into a writing career. In 1735 he married a widow more than twenty years older than himself, Elizabeth Porter, and two years later moved to London. He struggled to make a living in journalism, but gradually built a reputation. In 1747 a syndicate of printers commissioned him to compile a *Dictionary of the English Language*. This huge task took him eight years, even with six people to help him, all working in his house. The *Dictionary* is one reason we remember Dr Johnson; it was a great achievement. The other reason why we remember him is that he had a biographer, James Boswell, whose *Life of Johnson* (1791) did an enormous amount to publicise – and immortalise – Johnson's achievement and personality.

Johnson's wife died in 1752. He replaced her with a black slave, or rather ex-slave, from Jamaica; Francis Barber brought his wife and children to join Johnson's household. This gave Johnson a kind of family, and in return Johnson made Barber his heir. In spite of the success of the *Dictionary*, Johnson was always short of cash, but his situation was improved by the award of a government pension.

It was in 1763 that Johnson met James Boswell. The two men set off on a three-month tour of the Scottish Highlands and the Hebrides. As he became more famous, he led London's literary society, a kind of 18th century John Mortimer. He was the friend of the painter Joshua Reynolds, the politician Edmund Burke, the actor David Garrick and the dramatist Oliver Goldsmith. He also made friends with Henry

Thrale, a brewer and an MP, and became a near-permanent fixture in their home.

The life, work and personality of Dr Johnson are well documented. But the obscure minor poet Richard Savage is a virtual unknown, and there is something of a mystery surrounding his unlikely friendship with Samuel Johnson. Again, everyone knows that Samuel Johnson had a great friend in James Boswell, the man who wrote his biography – but this other friendship is far less well-known. Boswell knew about Savage, but found it difficult to write about him: 'a man of whom it is difficult to speak impartially, without wondering that he was for some time the intimate companion of Johnson; for his character was marked by profligacy, insolence, and ingratitude.'

Richard Savage was born in Holborn in 1698, the illegitimate son of Lady Macclesfield and Lord Rivers. He became a writer, producing two Spanish dramas and a tragedy called *Sir Thomas Overbury*, which was produced at Drury Lane in 1723. The play is a heavy pseudo-Shakespearean melodrama. Savage met the young Scots poet James Thomson, who arrived in London from Edinburgh in 1725, determined to make his way as a man of letters. Thomson sought out other writers, and along the way met Richard Savage, whose poems he admired. He, and others, admired the way Savage expanded the small landscape of pain within a man's mouth, a toothache, to the wide hostile landscape outside.

Now veers the Wind full East; and keen, and sore,
In cutting Influence aches in ev'ry Pore!
How weak thy Fabrick, Man! – A Puff, thus blown,
Staggers thy Strength, and echoes to thy Groan.

Richard Savage became a friend of the essayist Richard Steele. He met the poet Alexander Pope but found, as Thomson did, that Pope was expending his talents on translations of the classics. The dissolute Savage frequented coffee-houses and green rooms and was known for picking up actresses.

Savage was involved in a brawl at Robinson's Coffee-house at

Charing Cross. A maidservant was wounded in the head and a man called James Sinclair was stabbed to death – with a wound nine inches deep in the belly. Savage, James Gregory and William Merchant were arrested for wounding and murder. Because Savage claimed to be Earl Rivers' son, the three were not chained but allowed to walk in the open Press Yard. At the trial it emerged that because of Savage's claim to belong to the upper class he and his cronies expected to bully the staff and other habitués of the coffee house; the staff, on the other hand, had not been prepared to put up with this swagger. The brawl was a kind of class skirmish, a natural extension of Richard Savage's obsession with being part of the aristocracy.

There was great public interest in the trial. Alexander Pope was in the public gallery, taking notes. He observed that the witness accounts conflicted. Johnson did not describe either the trial or the murder in detail, as it must have been obvious that, regardless of whether Savage or one of the others drew swords first, Savage was still guilty of killing Sinclair. Sinclair himself said, before he died, that he was stabbed before he had been given a chance to draw; he said he had been stabbed 'cowardly'. Savage was duly found guilty at the Old Bailey and sentenced to be hanged at Tyburn. The case was much publicised and he was given a Royal Pardon when Lady Hertford, a well-known patroness of poets, and one of his relatives, Lord Tyrconnel, interceded on his behalf. Savage was pardoned in February 1728. Afterwards, Savage always asserted that his mother had unaccountably pressed for the execution to go ahead, wanting her son to perish, and that it was only the intervention of Queen Caroline that saved his life.

Richard Savage naturally became a minor celebrity after cheating the hangman, but he let the notoriety go to his head. He straight away applied for the position of Poet Laureate. This initiative was a failure, so he named himself 'Volunteer Laureate' to the Queen and on the strength of this he managed to scrounge an annuity of £50 a year until the queen's death in 1737.

Savage found himself fending off poverty, and also a lawsuit. One scheme was to retire to the country where he would rewrite *Sir Thomas*

Overbury. Pope and his friends raised £50 a year for him and in 1739 Savage set off for Wales. He settled in Swansea, and paid court to a famous Llanelli beauty, Bridget Jones. Running low on money, Savage went to Bristol, the revisions to the play still unfinished and informed his friends that he planned to return to London. Their response was to stop the allowance. In 1743 Savage was arrested for debt and confined in the Newgate Prison in Bristol. He was attended personally by the gaoler, Dagge. Savage died suddenly in his cell, at the age of only forty-five, in August 1743. Dagge paid for Savage's burial in St Peter's churchyard, close to the south door of the church. Savage seems to have fascinated even his gaoler. He had neither wife nor offspring.

One of the young literati whom Savage encountered in the late 1730s was Samuel Johnson, and it was Johnson who wrote a biography of Savage the year after Savage's death. By doing so, Johnson acquired a certain notoriety or celebrity himself. One anecdote often circulated about Johnson during his later life was that he and Savage had walked round the streets and squares of London all night, simply because they were too poor to pay for food or lodgings; they were instead kept going by their conversation. The starving writers, one young, one middle-aged, made an appealing image worthy of Hogarth. Johnson roman-ticised it, but there is another, far more chilling, aspect to it which Johnson includes in London:

> *Prepare for death, if here at Night you roam,*
> *And sign your Will before you sup from home . . .*
> *Some frolic drunkard, reeling from a feast,*
> *Provokes a broil, and stabs you for a jest.*

This is no fantasy on Johnson's part. As he well knew, this is exactly what the frolic drunkard Richard Savage did on the night of 7 December 1727.

But an interesting point is that no-one ever actually saw Johnson and Savage walking like this. In fact no-one ever saw them together at all. And the night-walk story was told in different versions by different people.

However they happened, the nocturnal conversations with Savage transformed Johnson. Johnson, the younger man, was spell-bound by Savage's personality. Savage was poor, neglected, brilliant, eccentric, entertaining. And the older man had mixed with all the leading writers of his time – Pope, Steele, Colley Cibber, James Thomson. It was perhaps real, perhaps a literary device, but Johnson put Richard Savage's night-walking at the centre of his story. It was a powerful image: the rejected poet moving rootlessly through a heedless and nightmarish cityscape.

Johnson was not interested in what a modern biographer would call research. There was no fact-checking. He was content to accept at face value the story told by Savage that his mother had worked towards having his death sentence carried out. Johnson repeated the story in his biography, even though Lady Macclesfield was still alive. She was, in 1743, a rich and reclusive widow in her late seventies, living in Bond Street. She had lost her title through divorce and had become known as Mrs Anne Brett.

It seems that although she had produced illegitimate children, two of them, both had died in infancy. She may therefore not have been Richard Savage's mother after all. But in support of Savage's (and Johnson's) accusations against Mrs Brett, she did not take any action against either the booklet published in 1727 or the Johnson biography published in 1744. Boswell thought that indicated that the accusations levelled against her must be true. But this is not necessarily the case. Mrs Brett had led a life full of trouble, scandal and domestic unhappiness. She had been through some high-profile litigation and perhaps just did not want any more of it. Her inaction cannot be taken as an admission that Savage's allegation is true; it may be simply that she thought that as a convicted murderer Savage had no credibility, that the whole thing was a nonsensical confabulation and as such not worth answering with a libel action. Johnson knew, from information already published in the earlier booklet, that Savage's mother had settled a pension of £50 a year on her son. But this action did not fit the image of the vengeful and unnatural mother that he (and Savage) wanted to cultivate. Here Johnson was unscrupulous. He concealed some facts in order to sustain the image of the poor persecuted outcast poet.

What Johnson did was to turn an encounter – his friendship with Savage – into a powerful novella. It appeared to be a work of non-fiction. It was a work of non-fiction to the extent that it was about a real person and the tone was factual. But it was also strongly selective and tendentious, written with a view to portraying both the subject and incidentally the author in a particular Hogarthian light. As such it was the very first modern biography, a very distinct art form whose traps and stratagems continue to imperil even the wariest reader.

HUME AND ROUSSEAU

(1765)

THE SCOTTISH PHILOSOPHER David Hume was born in Edinburgh in
1711 and initially took up law. But he suffered from bouts of depression
and tried his hand at commerce, working as a clerk in a Bristol
counting-house. In 1734 he went to Anjou, where he spent three years
studying and began work on his first major book, *A Treatise on Human
Nature*. This was the first great work of scepticism in the Age of the
Enlightenment; he argued that principles of justice and political
obligation were artificial and challenged both the natural law and the
social contract theories of Hobbes, Hooker and Rousseau. He was
disappointed with the poor reception of this important work – 'it fell
dead-born from the press', he said. He was further hampered in his
attempt to find suitable work by his atheism, which prevented his being
considered for professorships in logic and moral philosophy at Glasgow
and Edinburgh. He had to fall back on tutoring an insane nobleman.

Hume produced a new, shortened version of his book on human
nature, which he called *Enquiry concerning Human Understanding*. This
did produce a reaction. It stirred Immanuel Kant and provoked the
Idealists to counter Hume's scepticism. He wrote *Dialogues concerning
Natural Religion*, but sensed that it would prevent him from gaining
academic appointments, so he wisely refrained from publishing it until
after he had been given the post of Keeper of the Advocates' Library in
Edinburgh.

Hume became famous with the publication of *Political Discourses* in
1752 and an exhaustive *History of England* completed in 1762. The
History gave him financial independence. But Hume still felt that his
work was under-appreciated. 'The banks of the Thames are inhabited
by barbarians,' he said. 'Not one Englishman in fifty if he heard I had
broke my neck tonight would be sorry.' The English did not like him; he

was a Scot, not a Whig, and not a Christian. The last straw for Hume was the moment in June 1763 when the Earl of Bute, the Scottish Prime Minister, who as a fellow-Scot just might have favoured him, gave the post of Historiographer Royal for Scotland to someone else – William Robertson. Hume decided that it was time to get out. So the invitation from Lord Hertford the British ambassador in Paris to become his secretary was almost irresistible.

From 1763 to 1765 he was in Paris. The French literati and courtiers welcomed him enthusiastically, and made much of his warm, well-balanced personality, his sheer moderateness. When Horace Walpole visited Paris, he was astonished at how highly the French valued David Hume. He wrote in his *Journal*, 'It is incredible the homage they pay him'. Hume was happier than he had ever been. 'I can only say that I eat nothing but ambrosia, drink nothing but nectar, breathe nothing but incense, and tread on nothing but flowers.' Everyone he met treated him to 'a long and elaborate harangue in my praise.' In the Paris salon Hume encountered a huge number of French writers, critics, scientists and artists as well as philosophers. He met the editors of the *Encyclopedia*, Jean d'Alembert and Denis Diderot. Diderot wrote to Hume, 'I flatter myself that I am, like you, citizen of the great city of the world.' Hume also became a close friend of Baron d'Holbach, a contributor to the *Encyclopedia* and another passionate atheist. These new friends would become significant in Hume's eventual quarrel with Rousseau, but for the moment all was sunny and optimistic.

So, in Paris, David Hume turned from being significantly neglected and under-appreciated to being fully appreciated for the first time. One of the people he met in Paris was a philosopher who was at the bottom of the same Wheel of Fortune – Jean-Jacques Rousseau. It was the beautiful and intelligent salon hostess Madame de Boufflers who brought Hume and Rousseau together. In her salon, with its four enormous mirrors, the boy Mozart had once performed. Hume was cultivated by Madame de Boufflers, who flirted with him. When the time came for Hume to return to England, she pressed him to take Rousseau with him.

Rousseau was in fear of his life. He had been a refugee for over three years, and had been forced to move on several times. He had written *The Social Contract,* a widely condemned radical tract. He had also written *Emile,* a treatise on natural education in which he recommended that the clergy should be excluded from the education of the young. This was regarded as seditious. In Paris a warrant for Rousseau's arrest was issued and his books were burned.

Rousseau later wrote about this time in *The Confessions,* the first modern autobiography, saying that a 'cry of unparalleled fury' went up across Europe: he was 'an infidel, an atheist, a lunatic, a madman, a wild beast.' Forced to leave France, Rousseau went to a remote village in Switzerland in the hope of finding refuge, but the local priest whipped up hatred against him. He was reviled as a heretic in the street; stones were thrown at his windows.

Rousseau, in need of rescue, and Hume his rescuer met for the first time in Paris in December 1765. They had exchanged a few letters, startling for their outpourings of mutual admiration. Rousseau wrote to Hume, 'Your great views, your astonishing impartiality, your genius, would lift you far above the rest of mankind if you were less attached to them by the goodness of your heart. . .' Hume wrote to a third party, 'I find him mild, and gentle and modest and good humoured . . . His modesty seems not to be good manners but ignorance of his own excellence.'

Hume apparently made friends with Rousseau and when he returned to London in 1766 he took Rousseau with him. But even before Hume left Paris, several of his new Paris friends tried to warn him about Rousseau. Grimm, Diderot and d'Alembert all spoke of Rousseau from bitter personal experience; they had had a falling-out with him some years before and severed relations with him. Baron d'Holbach tried to warn Hume off the night before the departure for England. 'You don't know your man. I'll tell you plainly: you're nursing a viper in your bosom.'

By this time, David Hume had but ten years to live – he died in 1776 – and that final phase was dominated by his encounter with Rousseau, which began in an appearance of friendship and ended in a bitter quarrel. Hume saw himself as a moderate and equable man, and his friend the moral philosopher Adam Smith took the same view: Hume was as 'perfectly wise and virtuous a man as perhaps the nature of human frailty will permit.'

To begin with, when the two men arrived in London, things went well, except that Hume was suddenly (once again) out of the limelight that he had enjoyed for two years in Paris. He had become merely the minder of the real celebrity, the great French philosopher and novelist, Jean Jacques Rousseau. Others noticed the contrast too, seeing how irritating it must be for Hume to be plunged back into obscurity in this humiliating way. Rousseau played to the gallery, dressed in his Armenian costume (gown and tasselled cap) and accompanied by a dog called Sultan. Hume tried to make light of it, insisting that he was still very fond of Rousseau: 'I think I could pass all my life in his company without any danger of our quarrelling.' Baron d'Holbach was glad he had not yet had reason to regret his actions, but had not forgotten how Rousseau had treated his Paris friends.

Hume found Rousseau a place to live in the Strand, but Rousseau was not happy in the bustle of the city, which was in the middle of a building boom and full of smoke and noise. He moved out, first to Chiswick and then to an empty country house belonging to Richard Davenport: Wootton Hall in Staffordshire. Before he went, on 19 March 1766, he called on Hume; it was the last time they met. Rousseau thought in terms of conspiracies. He thought his letters were being intercepted and he decided Hume was at the centre of the plot. In June he turned on his rescuer. 'You have badly concealed yourself. I understand you, Sir, and you well know it. You brought me to England, apparently to procure a refuge for me, and in reality to dishonour me. You applied yourself to this noble endeavour with a zeal worthy of your heart and with an art worthy of your talents.'

Hume was angry and frightened by this unexpected and unjustified onslaught. He had thought he was doing Rousseau a favour, and had not expected to be attacked. He wrote to Davenport to express his disappointment at 'the monstrous ingratitude, ferocity, and frenzy of the man'. The root of Hume's fear was the knowledge that Rousseau was writing his autobiography. It is possible that on the journey from Paris to London Rousseau may even have shown him some of the earlier pages. Even if he had not seen any of it, he knew from Rousseau's other work what a powerfully persuasive writer he was. If Rousseau denounced Hume in his *Confessions*, Hume would be destroyed when they were published.

It had taken a long hard struggle for Hume to build his reputation; now he saw the prospect of that reputation being smashed in the eyes of posterity. His stock was high in France, and it was in France that Hume stood to lose most.

Hume took the initiative, first denouncing Rousseau to his friends in Paris, who would not have been at all surprised. He did not contact Madame Boufflers, who he knew would be sympathetic to Rousseau; he must also have felt betrayed by Madame Boufflers, who had got him into this mess in the first place. Hume's attack on Rousseau was the talk of Paris society, and of course Rousseau was provoked into calling Hume 'a black knave'. Hume foolishly required Rousseau to identify the accuser and give him full details of the alleged plot. Rousseau's flowery and brilliantly effective way with words gave him the withering if meaningless answer, 'That accuser, Sir, is the only man in the world whose testimony I should admit against you: it is yourself.' He listed all the incidents in the plot, showing how the devious Hume had masterminded it; the plot somehow involved George III. The document, sent in July 1766, was mad yet powerfully dramatic. Rousseau claimed that during the journey from Paris to London, he heard Hume muttering in his sleep, '*Je tiens J. J. Rousseau*', meaning: I have got J. J. Rousseau. Rousseau was able to pile on the terror which these sinister words inspired in his anxious soul.

Hume was horrified when he read this diatribe. He knew he could not answer it, partly because some of it was insane, partly because he did not have Rousseau's command of language. All he could do was to go through the document, writing 'lye' in the margin each time he came to another untruthful statement. Then he published a *Concise and*

Genuine Account of the Dispute between Mr Hume and Mr Rousseau. It might have been better if he had not, but Hume was desperate to salvage his reputation, knowing what mincemeat Rousseau would make of him in his *Confessions*. Paris enjoyed this scandalous literary fist-fight. Many were willing to join in, including Voltaire, who was one of many who were pleased to have an opportunity to take a swipe at Rousseau. The press published doggerel and cartoons on the subject.

With the benefit of hindsight, David Hume was over-optimistic in his view that he and Rousseau were going to be friends for ever. It is difficult to see how they could have been when they were so different as people. About the only thing they had in common was a hatred for the Church and its influence, but even in this they differed; as Rousseau professed a belief in God and in the afterlife; in almost every other way they were diametric opposites.

Hume was a man of intellect, of doubt and reason; Rousseau was a man of imagination, of certainty and feeling. Hume was moderate and cautious; Rousseau was wild and adventurous. Hume liked clarity; Rousseau liked paradox and mystification. Hume was gregarious, a man who appreciated the civilised life; Rousseau was a loner who deplored civilisation and instead admired the noble savage, the life close to nature. One of Hume's biographers wrote 'the annals of literature seldom furnish us with two contemporary writers of the first rank who cancel one another out with almost mathematical precision.' We think of the two philosophers as two great figures in the movement called the Enlightenment, yet they could not have been more different from one another. What Hume was watching, as he read Rousseau's accusations with mounting horror, was the birth of Romanticism, the wild, gothic force of unreason that would culminate in the excesses of the French Revolution.

But what of the strange journey from Paris to London – that seminal encounter between the two very different minds? What went on? It is clear now that Hume had not wanted to accompany Rousseau to London. He was pressed to do so by Madame de Boufflers, who had flirted with him to make him do it for her, but he hoped even then someone else would do it. While he was telling his French friends how much he loved Rousseau, Hume was also telling his cousin John Home how irritated he was by 'the philosopher who allows himself to be ruled equally by his dog and his mistress.' When Rousseau took off for Staffordshire, Hume knew that he would be unhappy there. He wrote to Hugh Blair, 'He will be entirely without occupation, without company, and almost without amusement of any kind. He has read very little during the course of his life and has now totally renounced all reading. He has seen very little and has no curiosity. He has reflected, properly speaking, and studied very little . . . his sensibility rises to a pitch beyond what I have seen any example of, but it still gives him a more acute feeling of pain than of pleasure. He is like a man . . . stripped of his skin.'

Perhaps it was these conflicting signals from Hume that made Rousseau begin to think Hume was up to something. Hume's negative assessment of Rousseau was in reality very unfair. Rousseau was widely read, occupied himself with music and botany, and he went on botanical expeditions to the Peak District with the Duchess of Portland. It was not Rousseau who was finished – he still had *The Confessions* to write – but Hume, whose creative life was all but over.

But what of the conspiracy? Was it all insane imaginings on Rousseau's side? The truth is that Hume did launch an investigation into Rousseau's financial situation behind Rousseau's back. He commissioned various people in France to make inquiries, but concealing from each one that he had asked others. Madame de Boufflers and Baron d'Holbach were sent on the same errand. Madame de Boufflers demanded to know why Hume was doing this; was he going to become Rousseau's denouncer, after being his protector? That is exactly what Hume was setting out to do. He admitted that he wanted to prove that Rousseau's claim to poverty was fraudulent. There was no plot masterminded by Hume, but he was trying to find out things about Rousseau behind his back, and he was saying some fairly unpleasant things about him. From Paris Horace Walpole wrote a hoax letter which pretended to be from the King of Prussia. The letter promised Rousseau refuge: 'If you want new misfortunes, I am a king and can make you as miserable as you wish.' The joke followed Rousseau to Staffordshire. Hume made out that he knew nothing of the letter, but he was evidently present at two dinners where the joke was first launched. He did know about it.

Rousseau's attack on Hume was not entirely insane after all; the two men had reacted badly to one another. Rousseau, curiously, exposed and ignited an inner self in David Hume that was imaginative, volatile, passionate, unreasoning, uncivilised, savage. They were simply two people who should never have met.

GOETHE AND
SCHILLER

(1798)

DURING THE LAST decade of his life, the German poet, philosopher and dramatist Johann Christoph Friedrich von Schiller (known to everyone as Fritz) struck up a friendship with the other great German writer of his age, Johann Wolfgang Goethe. Schiller (1759-1805) wrote to Goethe, who was ten years older and had become a well-known and powerfully influential figure, offering him his friendship. The two men discussed general ideas on aesthetics, and also their specific works in progress. Schiller encouraged Goethe to complete works that Goethe had thought of leaving as sketches. The collaboration between the two men led to a phase in German literature known as *Weimar Classicism.*

Schiller and Goethe worked together on *Xenien,* a collection of stinging epigrams aimed at their hostile critics. They took the title (which was originally Greek) from the Roman poet Martial, who used it for a collection of poems intended to accompany presents. The choice of title was therefore itself bitingly sarcastic. *Xenien* caused a sensation, and gave offence to many in Germany but, like many other writers before and since, Goethe and Schiller were frustrated by negative reviews. The targets were not just hostile critics, though; any people they regarded as enemies of their aesthetic agenda came within their range.

As a boy, Schiller had a patchy education, but he greatly admired one teacher, Pastor Moser, and had ideas of becoming a cleric. He even dressed in black robes and played at preaching. In 1773 he went to the Karlsschule Stuttgart, a military academy, where he studied medicine. Schiller suffered several illnesses, which he tried to treat himself. While still at school, Schiller read Rousseau and Goethe, and wrote his first play, *The Robbers*. This was a precocious drama of sibling rivalry and social hypocrisy, highlighting republican and revolutionary ideals. It was the first European melodrama. The play astonished its audience and Schiller himself became a sensation; later, Schiller was to be made an honorary member of the French Republic on the strength of this influential early play. After the play was performed in Mannheim in 1781, when Schiller was still only twenty-two, he was arrested and banned from publishing anything further.

Unable to live under this repressive régime, Schiller left Stuttgart in 1783, passing from there to Leipzig to Dresden to Weimar. In 1789, as revolution broke out in France, he became Professor of History and Philosophy at Jena. There, following his Stuttgart experience, he wrote only works of history. In 1799 he returned to Weimar, where Goethe persuaded him to resume writing plays.

Schiller and Goethe founded the Weimar Theatre, which became not only Germany's leading theatre but the hub of a renaissance in German drama. Schiller died in Weimar at the age of only forty-five, from tuberculosis. Schiller's coffin is in Weimar's ducal vault. After recent DNA analysis, the skull in the coffin has been shown not to be Schiller's, which raises a number of interesting questions.

Schiller's thought was a development from the philosophy of Immanuel Kant and Karl Reinhold. He developed the idea of a beautiful soul, a human being whose emotions have been tempered by reason, so that duty and inclination are in harmony. Aesthetics were central in his thinking, because the Good was also the Beautiful. Schiller was also concerned with questions about human liberty. This underlay his research on the Thirty Years War and permeated his dramas as well, such as the *Wallenstein trilogy* and *Don Carlos*. There were other historical dramas too: *Mary Stuart*, *The Maid of Orleans* and *William Tell*.

One of Schiller's major works was his *Aesthetic Letters*, which expressed disillusionment with the French Revolution, and in particular its descent into violence and its failure to put ideals into practice. He concluded that the French were inadequate to the moment. Schiller homed in on a dialectical interplay between *Formtrieb* (formal drive) and

Sinnestrieb (sensuous drive), and this led to a whole range of developments in aesthetic theory.

Developing a friendship with Schiller was life-changing for Goethe. It opened an important and extremely productive new phase of his life. He wrote *The German Refugees,* which was thought to be tedious, and *Roman Elegies,* which was thought to be scandalous. The two men produced a journal, but Schiller lost interest in it and after three years it was wound up. The collaboration between Schiller and Goethe was closer, of longer duration and on a higher level than any comparable literary friendship in the history of the world. As well as meeting and having conversations, they corresponded with each other over a ten-year period, exchanging more than a thousand letters about each other's works, and about their contemporaries' works.

Both men profited from the friendship. As Goethe redrafted and completed the novel he had begun twenty years before, *Wilhelm Meister's Apprentice* (1796), Schiller supplied him with a continuous critical commentary. As soon as this major piece was finished, the re-energised Goethe launched into an epic poem in hexameters in the Homeric manner, set in Germany and reflecting on contemporary wars and the French Revolution. This became Hermann and Dorothea (1797). It was a great publishing success and made Goethe more money than any of his other works. But it was at this time that he and Schiller wrote their *Xenien,* which made both of them unpopular. Then Goethe launched into his great verse play *Faust,* which he worked on for five years.

This re-energising that Goethe experienced as a result of his friendship with Schiller was associated with a shift in Goethe's mindset. After he made his 1786 journey to Italy, Goethe had come to believe that Weimar was a city where Classical culture might be revived, and in a very literal way. That was the thinking that lay behind the building of a hunting lodge in the ducal park in the style of a Roman villa. It also lay behind Goethe's direction of the rebuilding of the ducal palace, which had been destroyed by fire in 1774. The new palace was given a full-scale neo-classical style interior which itself had great architectural influence. But Goethe could no longer pretend that the world was continuing in the same way after the French Revolution, nor after his encounter with the revolutionary Schiller. And now he was physically cut off from visiting Italy by Napoleon. Goethe had to recognise that the world was not and could not be a Classical world, though he went on believing in the ancient ideals, launching a new periodical, *The Propylaea*, in 1798 to promote those ideals.

He thought Classical ideals were the only true ones, and the way the world was going was the wrong way. But this did not get in the way of Goethe's being on friendly terms with Romantic theorists like August and Friedrich Schlegel, or the Romantic painter Caspar David Friedrich, or the idealist philosophers Fichte, Schelling and Hegel. Goethe developed an Olympian view of the world, looking down on it and shaking his head like Zeus at the folly of what goes on below; this strongly influenced the way *Faust* developed. The character of Faust became something of a 'wrong-headed' idealist philosopher.

Goethe's last conventional drama, *The Natural Daughter*, was completed and produced in 1803. The French Revolution was the enemy of beauty; the ideals of the Classical world were no longer to be found in the European courts but in middle-class culture. Goethe was finding it harder and harder to write for the stage, in spite of the fact that he and Schiller had created their own theatre. His lack of productivity was to an extent covered up by Schiller's prolific output. Goethe managed the Weimar Theatre from 1791, rebuilding it to his own design in 1798. After that he mounted first or early performances of seven Schiller plays in six years.

But the flowering of Schiller's and Goethe's contribution to Weimar's cultural life had reached its highest point by 1803, when outside influences crashed in. It was then that the Napoleonic reorganisation of Germany began to take effect. The University of Jena lost many of its distinguished academics, including Schelling, to newer and richer universities. In 1805 both Goethe and Schiller fell seriously ill. Schiller died. Goethe made a physical recovery but the most productive part of his creative life was over. He felt he had lost 'the half of my existence'. After that, Goethe tidied up and concluded various projects, and sent off to the publisher the completed manuscript of *Faust, Part One*. The completed *Part Two* followed in 1808.

Meanwhile, Europe fell apart around Goethe. In the autumn of 1806, Napoleon defeated the Prussians at the Battle of Jena. Weimar, twelve miles away from the battlefield, was sacked. Goethe's house was spared in the general destruction, thanks to a specific instruction from Napoleon, who greatly admired the author of Werther. Working on a new and ambitious novel, *Elective Affinities*, raised Goethe's spirits. In 1808 he met Napoleon at the Congress of Erfurt; Napoleon made him a knight of the Legion of Honour. Perhaps mollified by these treats, Goethe became reconciled to Napoleon's rule.

Goethe lived on until 1832. Appropriately, there is a fine bronze monument in Weimar to Schiller and Goethe. It is unusual in being a double statue, the two men standing confidently side by side, intellectual and artistic equals. Goethe has his hand on the younger man's shoulder and they are looking in slightly different directions.

CHARLES DARWIN AND CHARLES LYELL

(1830)

TODAY, EVERYONE HAS heard of Charles Darwin, but few have heard of Charles Lyell. But in the middle of the 19th century it was very much the other way round. Lyell was pre-eminently the great man of British science, and he deserves to be better remembered today than he is; posterity is kind to some and unkind to many.

Charles Lyell, born at the end of the 18th century, was eight years old at the time of Trafalgar and eighteen at the time of Waterloo. Lyell's father was a Scots laird whose interests were divided between science and literature; he was a botanist, but also published a well-known English translation of *Dante's Inferno*. The son too had range, and started out as a lawyer, but his special field was to be geology. His *Principles of Geology* first appeared in 1830–33 and went through many editions; it was the standard work on geology and physical geography for the rest of the 19th century.

The first edition of his great work still reads well, partly because of his sharp eye for detail, his argument from case studies and for his uniformitarian approach; he believed that what we can see in the geological record is evidence that the world has always been much the same (in terms of processes) as it is today. That first edition had the broad sweep of one man's vision, with all the ideas and examples integrated into a convincing whole. During the twelve subsequent editions, new material was added to bring the piece up to date, and the book gradually lost its coherence, turning into a hotch-potch of undigested information and ideas. But it was the brilliant first edition that inspired Charles Darwin.

Lyell's grasp of earth sciences was both firm and broad. He recognised that the rock layers contained evidence of the earth's history and that that history included the emergence of the human race. This was where geology, anthropology and archaeology met. Although Lyell probably never used the word 'interdisciplinary', he was always open to those insights that frequently emerge at the boundaries of disciplines. In 1863 he produced another definitive book, *Antiquity of Man*. He was Professor of Geology at King's College, London, from 1831, President of the Geological Society of London from 1835, President of the British Association for the Advancement of Science from 1864. He was knighted in 1848 and created a baronet in 1864.

But perhaps the thing that is most intriguing about Lyell is his mentoring of Charles Darwin. When, as a very inexperienced young naturalist, Darwin set sail on HMS *Beagle*, he took with him Lyell's book *Principles of Geology*. His Cambridge professor, Revd John Henslow, had recommended the book to him. The first volume had only just been published. 'By all means read it for the facts,' Henslow said, 'but on no account believe the wild theories.' Henslow can hardly have suspected what a remarkable train of thought he was setting in motion, what wild theories he was letting loose.

In his startling new book, Lyell argued that the geological past can best be understood in terms of the natural processes we can still observe in the environment today. Rivers have always eroded away the rock in some places and deposited layers of silt in others; glaciers have always advanced in some decades and retreated in others. He also argued that change in the landscape is slow and steady. This 'gradualism' was a reaction to the more popular alternative, the 'catastrophism' of the eighteenth century. He argued that natural laws are constant and eternal, forcing processes that have operated in the past at about the same intensity as in the present. These views were not exactly revolutionary – James Hutton had advanced them at the end of the eighteenth century. What Lyell did was set out the case study evidence for the truth of these new assumptions, giving a consistent and matter-of-fact view of a world in a state of slow and very gradual change.

Darwin's encounter with Lyell through *Principles of Geology, Volume 1* was momentous, and particularly so because Darwin was reading the book as he sailed from place to place round the world seeing evidence that Lyell was right. Lyell had in effect given him a map – an intellectual map – of the world that would help him navigate his own ideas. Darwin was impressionable, open to new experience, new ideas. As his own ideas began to form regarding the evolution of species, he was not always sure which were his own ideas and which were Lyell's. 'I really think my books come half out of Lyell's brain,' Darwin later wrote. 'I see through his eyes.'

Darwin devoured the book, brilliantly grounded as it was in field-work; it seemed to place the study of geology on a new, sensible, scientific footing. Darwin did not, however, get his idea of evolution from Lyell. Lyell believed that living species were fixed and not related by common descent. What Lyell gave Darwin was a stage on which evolution might occur, the sense of the long time scale that evolution might require, the sense that almost anything might be accomplished by means of slow, unspectacular forces operating across immense periods of time. 'I am tempted to extend Lyell's methods even farther than he does,' Darwin reflected.

In 1832, Lyell published the second volume of *Principles of Geology*, and Darwin received a copy of it while he was still on the *Beagle* voyage that same year. Much of the second volume was devoted to attacking the views of Lamarck, using Cuvier's arguments. Darwin himself admitted that his good friend at Edinburgh University where he studied medicine, Robert Grant, had expounded Lamarckian theory to Darwin many times. Darwin remarked in his *Autobiography* that he may have been predisposed to consider evolution from having heard Lamarck praised so much by Grant. The specific idea that Darwin drew from Lamarck was a view of evolution as a branching process. But as time passed, Darwin absorbed this branching idea and grafted case studies collected on his *Beagle* voyage onto it; then he came to see it as his own. This often happens in science – a kind of creative memory that is inherently self-centred. Certainly Lamarck, via Grant and Lyell, prepared the way for Darwin's ideas on evolution.

Lamarck's earlier try at a theory of evolution was influential on Darwin in another way too. It had provoked a response from the Church. In 1802, a book called *Natural Theology* had been written by

William Paley. This was a retort that the evidence of design in the natural world was an argument for the existence of God. Then, in 1833-36 a succession of theologians and scientists argued the same view in the *Bridgewater Treatises*. This was very much bringing the clash between Lamarckian evolution and Christianity into Darwin's own time, and the abrasiveness of that encounter must have had a powerful effect on Darwin's hesitancy about publicising his own views on evolution.

Lamarck gave Darwin another nudge by his failure to provide a mechanism for change. Why would one species evolve into another? Lamarck left Darwin with a need to explain the process of adaptation. Later, when he had made his own ideas known, Darwin was attacked for simply restating Lamarck's theory. Interestingly, he responded by saying that he had derived neither a single fact nor an idea from Lamarck's work. He may have believed that, but Lamarck had profoundly influenced his thinking by a number of routes, not least indirectly through the second volume of Lyell's *Principles of Geology* and the conversations with Grant.

Darwin was far more conscious that he had derived ideas from his grandfather, Erasmus Darwin, who had written a book discussing a view on the transmutation of species – and Charles Darwin certainly read this when he was in his teens. Yet, in spite of this, when Darwin started out as a young naturalist he firmly believed that the species were static and unchanging. The mind works in all sorts of strange ways, and it may be that his grandfather's idea of transmutation was smouldering in his unconscious mind, behind the consciously held view, awaiting ignition. Later, Darwin affirmed that he first encountered the idea that species could be transformed in his grandfather's writings.

When Darwin returned to England, he began corresponding with Lyell, trying ideas out on him, and Lyell encouraged Darwin to develop his ideas on evolution. Many of their letters have survived. On the next page is one of the earliest letters Lyell wrote to Darwin, from Bloomsbury on 26 December, 1836.

My dear Sir,–

I have read your paper with the greatest pleasure, and should like to point out several passages which require explanation, and must have a word or two altered, but it would be impossible in a letter. I have made notes on them, and hope you will call here before you read the paper. Will you come up on Monday, January 2, and come and dine with us at half-past five o'clock, or come at five, and I will go over the paper before dinner? No one dines with us but Mr and Mrs Horner and one daughter, and Mr Horner will be glad to renew his acquaintance with you.

We dine early, because we have one of our small early tea parties, and one or two are to be here, to whom I should like to introduce you, besides a few whom you know already. If you cannot get here to dinner, you must if possible join the evening party.

The idea of the Pampas going up, at the rate of an inch in a century, while the Western Coast and Andes rise many feet and unequally, has long been a dream of mine. What a splendid field you have to write upon!

I have spent the last week entirely in comparing recent shells with fossil Eocene species, identified by Deshayes. When some great principle is at stake, all the dryness of minute specific comparisons vanishes, but I heartily long for some one here with a collection of shells, and leisure to talk on these matters with. Lonsdale is overpowered with work. Don't accept any official scientific place, if you can avoid it, and tell no one that I gave you this advice, as they would all cry out against me as the preacher of anti-patriotic principles. I fought against the calamity of being President as long as I could. All has gone on smoothly, and it has not cost me more time than I anticipated; but my question is, whether the time annihilated by learned bodies ('par les affaires administratives') is balanced by any good they do. . . . At least, work as I did, exclusively for yourself and for science for many years, and do not prematurely incur the honour or penalty of official dignities. There are people who may be profitably employed in such duties, because they would not work if not so engaged.

Whenever you come up, you must be here on Wednesday, and if you like to dine at the club do so. There is no vacancy, but you stand the first of those who are knocking at the door for admission.
Yours very truly,
Charles Lyell

The letter shows Lyell at his best; the urbane and conscientious friend and critic, offering positive and detailed advice on the crafting of a learned paper, offering what sounds like good advice on scientific research and career-building, offering time, and above all offering friendship. It also shows his awareness of the importance of a social life as a medium for scientific dialogue. But it also shows him saying one thing in private and another in public, and this was something that would increasingly irritate Darwin. Lyell would not take risks in any public forum.

Lyell was a careful career-builder. His path to the knighthood and the baronetcy must not be littered with embarrassing scandals. He encouraged Darwin in private, but he confessed that he had difficulty in accepting 'the descent of man from the brutes', as he put it, and was extremely cautious in his public statements on the issue. He suggested vaguely that new species might be 'called into being', without committing himself to saying where they might come from. He did not want to offend the Church, or the British benefice-granting establishment generally. He wanted to be professionally and socially acceptable. Darwin was amused at the amount of time Lyell and his wife spent agonising over their invitations to dinner parties – which to accept and which to turn down – but it was all part of the same drive not to offend the people who might be of most use. And of course it worked. It was Lyell who got the knighthood and the baronetcy; Darwin got nothing at all.

But there was no bitterness between the two men, and the letters that passed between them show an easy flow of scientific ideas and social chat. The following extract of a letter from Darwin to Lyell in 1838 shows Darwin at his ebullient best.

My dear Lyell,

Very many thanks for the present of your Elements, which I received, (& I believe the very first copy distributed) together with your note.– I have read it through every word & am full of admiration of it.– as I now see no geologist I must talk to you about it. There is no pleasure in reading a book if one cannot have a good talk over it.– I repeat I am full of admiration at it.– it is as clear as daylight,–in fact I felt in many parts some mortification at thinking how geologists have laboured & struggled at proving what seems, as you have put it, so evidently probable. There was also much new to me, & I have to copy out some fifty notes & references . . . You see I am in a fit of enthusiasm; & good cause I have to be, when I find, you have made such infinitely more use of my journal than I could have anticipated.– I will say no more about the book, for it is all praise.

I came up to town on Wednesday night, just two days after you went; & very much disappointed I was to find by your card you were gone.– I thought you had intended coming to town after your crag expedition, so I had made sure of seeing you, & having some geological talk. My Scotch expedition answered brilliantly.– I staid one whole day in Edinburgh, or more truly on Salisbury Craigs.– I want to hear, some day, what you think about that classical ground:–the structure was to me new & rather curious,–that is if I understand it right.– I crossed from Edinburgh in gigs & carts, (& carts without springs as I never shall forget) to Loch Leven,–was disappointed in the scenery–& reached Glen Roy on Saturday evening, one week after leaving Marlborough St.– Here I enjoyed five days of the most beautiful weather, with gorgeous sunsets, & all nature looking as happy as I felt.– I wandered over the mountains in all directions & examined that most extraordinary district.– I think without any exception,–not even the first volcanic island, the first elevated beach, or the passage of the Cordillera, was so interesting to me as this week. It is far the most remarkable area I ever examined.– I have fully convinced myself, (after some doubting at first) that the shelves are sea-beaches,–although I could not find a trace of a shell, & I think I can explain away most, if not all, the difficulties.

I found a piece of a road in another valley, not hitherto observed, which is important; & I have some curious facts about erratic blocks, one of which was perched up on a peak 2200 ft above the sea.– I am now employed in writing a paper on the subject, which I find very amusing work, excepting that I cannot anyhow condense it into reasonable limits. At some future day I hope to talk over some of the conclusions, with you which the examination of Glen Roy has led me to.

I am living very quietly, & therefore pleasantly & am crawling on slowly but steadily with my work. I have come to one conclusion, which you will think proves me to be a very sensible man, namely that whatever you say proves right; and as a proof of this I am coming into your way of only working about two hours at a spell; I then go out & do my business in the streets, return & set to work again, & thus make two separate days out of one.– The new plan answers capitally . . .

If you have a mind to be a very generous man, you will write to me & tell me some Newcastle news, as well as about the Crag . . . There is one other point, by chance, now that you are in Scotland, you might find out for me, that is the height above the sea of Loch Tay, and Loch Dochart and Tyndrum–and Loch Tula or any one of these places.– I have no idea whom to ask, or where to look.– If you should chance to meet any engineer, will you ask him.–

Pray remember me most kindly to Mrs Lyell & to Miss Lyell, when you arrive at Kinnordy. Good night, my dear Lyell–. You will think I have been drinking some strong drink to write so much nonsense.

Yours most sincerely
Chas. Darwin

Principles of Geology went through many successive editions, so there were repeated opportunities for Lyell to showcase Darwin's ideas on evolution – but he stopped short of endorsing them. Darwin felt betrayed by a friend who was in the strongest position to validate and promote his ideas. He was frustrated and angry that Lyell refused to give him wholehearted support in print, when in private conversation he was ready to give that support.

Late in his life, Sir Charles Lyell, baronet, perhaps felt secure enough in his honours to acknowledge the growing evidence in Darwin's favour. In one odd, and long-overlooked way, Lyell's ideas in the succession of species were even more ambitious than Darwin's. Lyell thought it was possible for the human race and all the familiar animal species on the Earth to become extinct – and to be replaced by dinosaurs in a new creation. He thought in terms of cycles of creation, with the human race becoming extinct and then being re-created some long time into the future. Cyclical time was a very advanced idea. And the cartoonists were laughing at Darwin!

Darwin in later life remarked acerbically that scientific men should be put to death at the age of sixty, so that their inflexible habits of mind could not interfere with the progress of the newer generations. And when he said this, he had Lyell in mind. Lyell was interfering with his progress. There was an openness between the two men that allowed Darwin to complain about Lyell's failure to support him in public, and Lyell in his turn to allow Darwin to tease him. Lyell in the end did discuss Darwin's theories at some length in his *Antiquity of Man* (1863). After he had gone this far, though still not far enough, for Darwin, Lyell asked him if 'now he might be allowed to live'; at that time Lyell was sixty-six and Darwin fifty-four. But Lyell continued to hedge when he presented his friend's evolutionary ideas and his support in print was never whole-hearted.

SIGMUND FREUD AND CARL JUNG

(1907)

FREUD WAS STRONGLY influenced by an essay of Goethe's, *Nature*, which made him decide to study medicine. This was not with any idea of becoming a general practitioner, a doctor in the ordinary sense, but with a view to doing medical research. This may explain some of the difficulties that arose later; he was far more interested in his own ideas than in the patients who were supplying him with his raw data. Sometimes, as with his Oedipus complex, he lost touch with the reality of human psychology. Anyway, driven by his literary encounter with Goethe, Freud studied medicine in Vienna.

From 1884 Joseph Breuer, an Austrian neurologist, told Freud about an experience he had had, in which hysteria was cured by using hypnosis to help the patient recall painful past experiences. The resulting recall had been a kind of healing catharsis. Freud was profoundly impressed by this and he developed Breuer's cathartic technique until it became the foundation stone of modern psychoanalysis.

In 1885 Freud moved to Paris to study under Martin Charcot, who gave him the moral support he needed to make his determined world-changing switch from treating hysteria as a neurological problem to treating it from a psychological point of view. Returning to Vienna, he developed a new psychiatric technique -- free association. He used this instead of hypnosis to find out what was under the surface of the patient's mind, and so gradually refined psycho-analysis as a method of treatment. In 1895 Freud and Breuer published *Studies in Hysteria*, but only two years later their collaboration ended in a disagreement over Freud's provocative theory of infantile sexuality. It was inevitable that Freud was going to try the patience of many friends and colleagues as

121

he developed his revolutionary new ideas. Many of them thought he was too insistent on the role of sex in the mind, and especially in the role of repressed sexual urges.

In 1900 Freud published his landmark book, *The Interpretation of Dreams*. In this he argued that dreams are disguised manifestations of repressed sexual drives. In 1902 Freud became Extraordinary Professor of Neuropathology at Vienna University. He started weekly seminars at his home, meetings of men who were thinking along similar, though not necessarily the same, lines. Conspicuous among them were Alfred Adler, Ernest Jones and Cark Gustav Jung. In 1908, the informal weekly meetings became formalised into the Vienna Psychoanalytical Society, which changed its name in 1910 to the International Psychoanalytical Association. Freud's ablest and most distinguished disciple Carl Gustav Jung became its first president.

Freud's ideas were rapidly disseminated round the world. His views were extremely doctrinaire and it was almost inevitable that, as they found their feet, several of his disciples would disagree with him so strongly that they would part company. Adler left in 1910. Jung broke with Freud in 1913. The problem was that, having found his explanation for neuroses, Freud was no longer prepared to keep an open mind. He felt threatened by Jung and on two occasions when he thought Jung's remarks revealed a death-wish against him he fainted in front of him.

Jung was born in 1875. He was nineteen years younger than Freud, just young enough to be Freud's son – and that was where some of the problems between them were rooted. Freud needed loyal disciples, and an heir and successor. He tacitly acknowledged Jung as his son and heir. Jung, for his part, was looking for a father-figure, because his own father was oppressive and dictatorial. Without intending to, the two men began to role-play. Freud played the father; Jung played the son.

Jung's clergyman father was stern and tyrannical and his parents quarrelled a good deal. The mental disturbances in the Jung household generated vivid dreams that Jung would remember and analyse in later life. After studying medicine in Basle and psychology in Paris, he worked as a physician under Eugen Bleuler at a mental clinic in Zurich, and lectured at the University of Zurich from 1905. Jung was to be an incredibly prolific writer. In one of his earliest publications he coined the word 'complex'. He wrote a study of the condition that we now call schizophrenia. As a result of these early publications, he met Freud in Vienna in 1907. They became great friends and professional associates, and regularly exchanged dreams and analysed them for one another, but Jung's ideas were bound to take him further and further from Freud's line of thinking.

It was when Jung published his new ideas on the libido and the unconscious in 1912 that the first tensions between the two men developed. Freud felt that Jung was challenging his authority; Jung became increasingly critical of Freud's insistence on the psychosexual origins of neuroses. Jung substituted his own term, libido, for a general, non-specific underlying life force. Freud remained dogmatically fixed on the sexual drive per se as the root of most psychological problems. The tension mounted. Then one day Freud refused to tell Jung one of his dreams, 'because it would undermine my authority'. Jung knew at that moment that the professional intimacy between them was at an end, and that he had to go his own way.

In 1913, Jung parted company with Freud. Jung sensed that Freud lacked a philosophical background; Jung himself was steeped in philosophy. He also saw that Freud was making a fundamental mistake in restricting analysis to the personal, when there were general processes at work. We are all steeped in history and zeitgeist; even the way in which our parents treat us and the way we are educated are socio-historical, not personal.

There was an exchange of overheated letters. Freud made the mistake of analysing some of the things Jung had said: 'Are you objective enough to consider the following slip [a slip that Jung had made in an earlier letter] without anger. "Even Adler's cronies do not regard me as one of yours."' Jung had intended to write 'theirs' and written 'yours' by mistake. What Freud was pointing out was that Jung had made a significantly revealing mistake, a slip that has come to be known as a 'Freudian slip'. Freud knew this shallow analysis would annoy and antagonise Jung, which is probably why he wrote it. He was goading Jung by patronising him. Jung replied at length, including the comment, 'Your technique of treating your pupils like patients is a blunder. In that way you produce either slavish sons or impudent puppies.' Here Jung was making another revealing Freudian slip, by showing that he thought of himself as either Freud's son or pet dog, not as an adult student. Freud was incensed at being addressed like this, composed a letter, but then did not send it. It included the comment, 'Your reaction seems out of all proportion.'

The two men were struggling to understand their own minds and emotions, and they were unable to understand the intensity of their effect on one another. It was like a tiff between teenage lovers, and all the harder to deal with because there had been no declaration or admission of love in the first place. There was a heavy irony in this situation, as the two greatest psychologists of the twentieth century ought at least to have been able to understand what was in their own minds.

A Freudian bystander would have judged that Freud was playing the father, and that Jung was reacting badly to this as he had not enjoyed his relationship with his real father, so he was playing the ultra-rebellious son. One tyrant-father was quite enough. Freud was not allowing for the dangerousness of the father-son relationship as it existed in Jung's mind. Probably this is what their colleague Ernest Jones thought, as he watched this personal and professional tragedy unfold. But the two great founders of modern psychology had said unforgivable things to each other. They went their separate ways.

As a result of this rift with Freud, Jung had a serious mental breakdown which lasted, significantly, for the duration of the First World War. Jung was sufficiently unhinged to suggest that the external struggle was a projection of his own internal conflict – that was the extent of his temporary insanity. He went on seeing patients during this period; one wonders whether he can have helped them in any significant way. He diagnosed one patient as being in the final stages of syphilis and gave him only weeks to live. The patient wisely sought a second opinion; he turned out to be manic-depressive and lived for another fifty years.

In later life, Jung was able to admit that he temporarily lost his reason between 1913 and 1918. Nietzsche had gone through a similar ordeal, also after a major quarrel with a surrogate father, the composer Richard Wagner, but had not survived, drowning in his inner world. Jung managed to use his knowledge of the unconscious mind to swim through it and turn the episode into a rebirth. He came out of the experience with a richer understanding of what it means to be insane, and went on to achieve ever-greater insights into the workings of the unconscious mind during the next four decades.

In spite of the traumatic rift with Jung – it was almost as traumatic for Freud – Freud went on to produce a string of major works: *Totem and Taboo, Beyond the Pleasure Principle, Ego and Id* and *The Future of an Illusion.* Awful though the encounter had been, both men came through it enriched.

GRIGORI RASPUTIN AND TSARINA ALEXANDRA

(1908)

GRIGORI RASPUTIN WAS born in 1869 at Prokovskoe in Siberia. He was a peasant boy and never learned to read or write, though this was no impediment to his rise to a position of unusual influence. He has often been referred to as 'the Mad Monk', but he was not a monk at the time of his fame. He joined a monastery, but left the monastic life behind when he discovered the irresistible pleasures of the flesh. Instead he adopted an itinerant lifestyle, the life of a travelling faith healer.

Rasputin claimed to possess special powers to heal the sick. He made a living from donations given by the people he healed. He supplemented this income by telling fortunes using Tarot cards. In the early years of the twentieth century, the occult was very popular among the upper classes in Europe generally. There were séances in which mediums claimed to make contact with the spirits of the dead. Many an upper class social evening had as its focus the *planchette*, a small heart-shaped pointer on castors, which in a type of séance could be made to move about on a ouija board to point to letters and spell out 'spirit messages'. Rasputin was one of many charlatans able to make a living out of this craze for the occult.

Rasputin was a tall, untidy, dirty and unsavoury-looking man. But he was also imposing, with hypnotic staring eyes and a dark beard which gave him presence. He used his charisma and deep resonant voice to accentuate his stage persona. When he arrived in St Petersburg, he made a name for himself as a mystic, and it was not long before some of the leading aristocrats started to cultivate him. Then he met the Tsar, Nicholas II, and his wife the Tsarina Alexandra. They were deeply interested in Rasputin's reputation as a faith healer because their son Alexei, the heir to the Russian throne, suffered from haemophilia. Conventional doctors were unable to offer the boy any help or treatment and the Tsarina wondered if the unconventional approach of Rasputin might be tried. When Alexei had a particularly severe episode of internal bleeding, which caused him great pain, the Tsar in desperation fatefully called on Rasputin.

This first encounter between Rasputin and the heir to the Russian throne was critical in determining his future. Somehow, with Rasputin's intervention, the bleeding stopped and the boy recovered. Rasputin became the Romanovs' family hero; they adopted him; he began to mix with the Tsarina's closest associates and friends. In time, Rasputin came to exert excessive influence over the Tsarina, to the extent that Nicholas started to resent it, but Nicholas was afraid to banish Rasputin, as he would have liked to do, because he knew that if anything happened to Alexei in Rasputin's absence, his wife would blame him for it.

The First World War broke out and Russia was soon at war with Germany. In 1915, Nicholas took the reckless step of taking direct command of his troops, as if he was a medieval king leading his troops into battle. This quixotic gesture was decisive in losing him his throne. The decision to take command came from Alexandra, and it may be assumed that she in her turn got the idea from Rasputin. While the Tsar was away at the front, the Tsarina was to be left behind in charge of the government. But she was herself German-born and the Russian people were in the thick of a bloody conflict with Germany; she was neither liked nor trusted. Rasputin's influence grew stronger, giving her more and more advice on political matters. What made matters worse was that everyone knew that this was happening, and it brought not just the Tsarina but the Romanov family generally into disrepute.

The Tsarina's obsession with Rasputin naturally led to a rumour in the palace that they were having an affair. The newly appointed prime minister, Stolypin, was convinced that Rasputin was an evil influence and he advised the Tsar to distance himself and his family from him. Some historians think the stories that Rasputin was in league with the Devil originated with Stolypin. Stolypin certainly presented the Tsar with documentary evidence of Rasputin's wild and scandalous behaviour. The Tsar was concerned, but did not want to upset Alexandra, who had become dependent on Rasputin, believing that Rasputin's presence was beneficial to Alexei's health. Rasputin was well aware that he had many enemies in St Petersburg, people who wanted him out, but he managed to persuade Alexandra that if he left her – through banishment or death – the Romanov dynasty would perish. If Alexandra had any remaining doubts, this threat quelled them. Rasputin must stay at her side.

But the ground swell of opinion was running against Rasputin – and he knew it. In a letter he wrote, 'My hour will soon come. I have no fear but you must know that the hour will be bitter. I will suffer a great martyrdom. I will forgive my torturers and will inherit the kingdom.' On the day he was assassinated he said, 'Little mother, I feel my end is near. They will kill me and then the throne won't last three months.'

But Rasputin was systematically abusing his powerful position by seducing many of his female followers, including women in the palace. Stolypin's agents assiduously compiled lists of Rasputin's misdeeds, including the names of the women. Rumour had it that the Tsarina herself was having an affair with Rasputin; it seemed possible. Then many who had previously supported him turned against him and there were several attempts to have him sent away from St Petersburg. The Tsar meanwhile was profoundly disturbed by the rumours about Rasputin and his wife. Rasputin was not only making the Romanov royal family unpopular; he was distracting the Tsar at one of the most crucial moments of his life. He was running out of time as far as saving the Russian monarchy was concerned.

Eventually, one of the many plots against Rasputin took effect. The version of Rasputin's death that was widely accepted until recently was the melodrama narrated by Prince Yusupov. Yusupov claimed that on 16 December 1916 he invited Rasputin to his house to dinner – the presence of the beautiful Princess Irina was the bait that lured Rasputin into the trap – and there Yusupov and some other aristocrats killed him. They tried to kill him in various ways (poisoning, shooting, clubbing), but Rasputin would not die until finally they drowned him in the ice-covered River Neva. It was a lurid – and highly commercial – story that the prince eventually told to the Western press. But recently evidence has emerged that British agents were involved, and it is likely that Rasputin was in reality killed by one of them. The evidence points to Lieutenant Oswald Rayner as the agent who fired the fatal bullet into Rasputin's forehead. The reason for the British intervention was that Rasputin was meddling in, and influencing, Russian foreign policy. He was advocating a Russian withdrawal from the war, which would have spelt disaster for the Allies on the Western Front.

Whether Rasputin died as a result of the shooting or was only wounded is still uncertain. Photographs of Rasputin's body taken immediately after he was taken out of the Neva show him with out-stretched arms, which some have interpreted as showing that he was struggling to untie his bonds while drowning, but the gesture could equally be a reaction to being shot. The autopsy concluded that the forehead wound was a fatal injury.

Historians have speculated about the reality of Rasputin's wickedness, and wondered whether his bad behaviour was really just a piece of political propaganda to persuade the squeamish Tsar Nicholas to get rid of him. But a secret file on Rasputin compiled by the Bolsheviks shortly after his assassination recently came to light after it was bought by the Russian cellist and conductor Mstislav Rostropovich. The 500-page secret file supplies the substance of the allegations, and in some case the specific evidence that they were well-founded. Among the papers are telegrams from the Tsarina Alexandra to Rasputin, addressing him as 'darling'. One telegram dated December 1914 reads, 'Today I shall be back in eight days. I sacrifice my husband and my heart to you. Pray and bless. Love and kisses – darling.' Even allowing for a certain floweriness of style that was common in aristocratic circles, this is fairly damning. She gives him her heart? She values him more than her husband? There is no ambiguity here. Another telegram sent about two weeks before his death read, 'You have not written anything. I have missed you terribly. Come soon.'

The secret file names many of Rasputin's mistresses and gives detailed evidence of his political influence over the Tsar. He was influencing senior appointments and persuading the Tsar to delay mobilising against Germany. The file includes some of the reports by the Ministry of the Interior's agents, who were assigned the task of spying on Rasputin. One report reads, 'Rasputin accosted women with vile suggestions.' Another agent watched him hiring three prostitutes in one day.

Obviously the secret file was put together with bias, by Bolsheviks who wanted to put both Rasputin and the Romanovs in the worst possible light. Indeed, one of the interrogators actually resigned, complaining about the bias. Even so, the evidence for Rasputin's mischief-making is overwhelming. The Tsar would probably have made enough political mistakes to ensure the abolition of the monarchy without Rasputin's help. Even so, Rasputin did a great deal to ensure that the Tsar made wrong decisions. By seducing the Tsarina, he also critically divided and undermined the Romanovs and created a fatal diversion at a time when the Tsar needed to focus his limited abilities on statecraft. Rasputin also played into the hands of the revolutionaries by making the Romanovs look ridiculous. The image of the shabby Mad Monk seducing the Tsarina and cuckolding the weak and foolish Tsar was a gift to political satirists and the enemies of monarchy. It was Rasputin who made it blindingly obvious that the monarchy had to go.

C. S. LEWIS AND
J. R. R. TOLKIEN

(1926)

CLIVE STAPLES LEWIS was born in 1898 and died in 1963. He was always referred to as C. S. Lewis, but called Jack by his friends. He was an academic, essayist and Christian apologist. He was baptised as an infant into the Church of Ireland, lost his faith during his teens, but regained it in adulthood, re-converted partly as a result of conversations with Tolkien. Today C. S. Lewis is best known for his fiction, and perhaps mainly for *The Chronicles of Narnia*. Lewis was a close friend of J. R. R. Tolkien, who was also an academic and a writer of fiction. They were leading figures at the English Faculty at Oxford University, and leading lights in an informal literary group calling itself the Inklings.

John Ronald Reuel Tolkien was born in 1892 and died in 1973. His career parallels Lewis's in some ways. He was a distinguished academic; he was Professor of Anglo-Saxon at Oxford for twenty years, and then Professor of English Language and Literature, also at Oxford. He is, even so, best known for his high fantasy books, *The Hobbit* and *The Lord of the Rings*. Other authors before Tolkien had written fantasy but the huge success of *The Hobbit* and *The Lord of the Rings* led to a great revival in this type of fiction. This was especially so after the books came out in paperback in America. Tolkien's influence has been far-reaching, and recently re-emphasised as his work has been successfully interpreted in films.

C. S. Lewis and J. R. R. Tolkien were Oxford academics, both interested in literature, both creative writers, and it was natural that they should become friends. They met and became firm friends at Oxford in 1926, calling each other Jack and Tollers. When Tolkien wrote the children's story *The Hobbit*, the two men discussed their desire to bring such stories to a wider audience. They discovered a common enthusiasm for mythical tales, which they understood had been used by societies in the past to convey their deepest spiritual truths. As boys, they had read and enjoyed such stories in collections by the brothers Grimm. Lewis had also heard some of the Celtic myths from his nurse, who had told him Irish folk tales. As university lecturers, they studied and taught the literature of medieval romance; Tolkien was familiar with the background of Norse myth. They both sensed that it was only in recent time that such tales had become relegated to 'children's stories'. They wanted to bring the whole genre of mythic tales to a much wider mainstream audience, of adults as well as children.

In the spring of 1936, Lewis praised Tolkien's *Hobbit* book, but hankered for something on a more heroic scale. They decided initially to divide the territory. After tossing a coin, they decided Lewis would deal with 'space travel' and Tolkien would take 'time travel', though things would develop rather differently. Tolkien reminded Lewis that a similar challenge had been made by Lord Byron, at Lake Geneva in 1816. He had challenged Percy Shelley and Mary Shelley to write a ghost story, and Mary had written *Frankenstein.*

Tolkien had had a sense that he would do something like this even before he met Lewis. Ever since the First World War he had been writing about a fantasy world, hundreds of pages of a cycle of myths that came from the early ages of Middle-earth. This strange pastime became a backdrop for *The Lord of the Rings*, though not *The Lord of the Rings* itself. In the preparatory years, Tolkien was in effect setting up the landscape and prehistory for *The Lord of the Rings*. Some of this material was published after Tolkien's death in *The Silmarillion.*

The young C. S. Lewis had a problem in reconciling his rational mind with his strong imagination; the two sides of his brain were pulling in different directions. He decided (rationally) that the Christian faith of his upbringing was intellectually untenable. His rational side told him that while fictional stories might be entertaining, they could not learn anything from them about things that really mattered. Tolkien helped Lewis see how reason and imagination could be integrated. One night in 1931 Tolkien, Lewis and another friend, Hugo Dyson, strolled along Addison's Walk in Magdalen College, which was Lewis's college. On this revelatory walk Tolkien showed Lewis how the two sides of the mind were reconciled in the Gospel narratives: great human story-telling, yet portraying a true event as he saw it. Suddenly Lewis sensed that the sustenance he had had from myths was a foretaste of this greater myth of Christ.

Tolkien had a profound effect on Lewis, not just by helping to convert him back to Christianity but by bringing his imagination into the centre of his life. Most of Lewis's writings were then geared to promoting the Christian message, either overtly as in *The Screwtape Letters* or covertly as in the *Narnia* books. Lewis also made a deep impression on Tolkien, who was encouraged to expand his fiction, make it more ambitious in scope. Out of that came *The Lord of the Rings*. Both came to write fictional books that propagated Christian themes by way of allegory. The idea was to sneak a Christian message past the barriers of prejudice that a secular reader might raise; it was, in a way, subversive.

The two men did not always agree, and there was a serious disagreement between them about the *Narnia* books. Lewis was proud of his first *Narnia* book, *The Lion, the Witch and the Wardrobe*, but Tolkien was unimpressed by it. He thought the Christian theme was far too obvious; Lewis was hitting the reader over the head with it. The use of Aslan the lion as a symbol for Christ was certainly obvious enough. Tolkien wove Christian themes into his own books, but tried hard to bury them so that they worked more subtly on the reader. Tolkien also thought the *Narnia* books had too many different elements, such as witches, children, talking animals; he thought that would confuse and overwhelm young readers. Tolkien was wrong about this; a later generation of children has had no difficulty in mastering the greater disparities in the *Harry Potter* books.

Lewis's attempt to weave a Christian allegory into a mythic tale was more successful in his science fiction trilogy, *Out of the Silent Planet, Perelandra* and *That Hideous Strength*. This space fantasy was directed at an adult audience.

Tolkien was unimpressed by Lewis's attempts to write popular theology. He thought this was a job better left to professional theologians, and that amateur theology was likely to misrepresent Christianity and foster heresy. Lewis broadcast some talks on this theme, and several of his friends, not just Tolkien, were embarrassed at the mistakes Lewis made. Charles Williams felt Lewis was sidestepping crucial issues and stopped listening to the talks. Tolkien expressed a lack of enthusiasm, and felt that Lewis was attracting far more attention to himself than the substance of the talks justified 'or than was good for him'.

There, perhaps we can detect a hint of jealousy. A more serious cause of friction between the two men was the type of Christianity that Lewis adopted. Tolkien was a Catholic. He helped in Lewis's conversion and was disappointed that the convert turned out to be a Protestant, and not only that but a Protestant who sometimes wrote in a distinctly anti-Catholic tone, on one occasion referring to Catholics as papists. This was upsetting for Tolkien.

For a very long time, Lewis and Tolkien met and discussed literature in the company of other male academics in what was then, in the 1930s, a strongly single-sex environment, the world of the Oxford's men's colleges. This cosy all-male society was disrupted when, after a lifetime of being a solitary bachelor, Lewis acquired a girlfriend. He launched on a romance with an American widow called Joy Gresham. Naturally, after he met Joy, Lewis spent less time with the Inklings, less time with Tolkien, and he and Tolkien grew apart. Tolkien took this badly.

What was Lewis's effect on Tolkien? When they met, Tolkien was a reticent, introspective man. Much of what he wrote was for himself only or for a small private audience. He had little confidence about releasing it to a wider audience. What Lewis did was to encourage him to finish, revise and publish his stories. At meetings of the Inklings, when Tolkien read chapters of *The Lord of the Rings*, Lewis spurred him on.

Lewis also gave Tolkien some ideas. In the space trilogy, Lewis invented the concept of Hnau, which was the embodiment of personality and rationality in animals and plants. This seems to have been borrowed by Tolkien for the Ents in *The Lord of the Rings*. Tolkien

worried more and more towards the end of his life that the Christian ethic embedded in *The Lord of the Rings* was being lost on readers. There was a revival of interest in paganism, the occult, ley lines and so on, and his work was being taken up as a platform for the new paganism. It was not at all what he had intended. Maybe his criticism of Lewis's *Narnia* books for being too overtly Christian had been wrong after all.

MICHAEL TIPPETT AND
T. S. ELIOT

(1937)

MICHAEL TIPPETT (1905-1998) was one of the great British composers of the 20th century. His was a life of many encounters: encounters with people, encounters with places, encounters with ideas.

Early on, as a student, he developed an interest in the writer Samuel Butler, and a friend suggested that he might like to meet David Ayerst, another young man with an interest in Butler. David, an historian and later a journalist with the *Guardian*, was to remain Michael's closest and most enduring friend; it was a friendship that lasted until David died, in his eighties, leaving Michael saddened and deflated. It was a friendship of opposites. Michael was a rebel, while David was an establishment man. In the Second World War Michael was a pacifist, while David joined up and rose through the ranks to become a colonel. Michael became a sage, while David became a teacher and an HMI. Michael remained a single gay man, while David was a straight married man with a family. Michael grew old disgracefully, wearing colourful clothes and courting new boyfriends in his eighties, while David calmly accepted the more usual fawn cardigan and walking stick. Perhaps because of these strong contrasts, they got on extremely well. David was responsible for introducing Michael to left-wing politics. As the decades passed, Michael the loner became increasingly glad to have a surrogate family, the Ayersts, to drop into when he felt the need for a taste of family life.

In 1932, David Ayerst introduced Michael Tippett to a gifted young painter called Wilfred Franks. This was a fateful encounter, as Michael, until then uncertain of his sexuality, fell in love with Wilfred. It proved to be the deepest, most intense emotional involvement of Tippett's life.

It is no coincidence that Tippett wrote his *First String Quartet* just as their relationship began. Franks was a Trotskyist and a pacifist; Tippett picked up both Franks's extreme left-wing political commitment and his pacifism. In the end, Tippett's development as a composer would not let him follow Franks with sufficient commitment and he had to say, 'You be a revolutionary for me.'

The intensity of Tippett's love for Franks, and the torment he suffered when Franks ended the relationship in August 1938, were the making of Tippett as a composer. The trauma sent Tippett spiralling into a breakdown, from which he retrieved himself through Jungian analysis. And out of that came a sequence of fully mature compositions – some of the greatest music written in the 20th century. The first of these was the *Concerto for Double String Orchestra* (1939). The next was *A Child of Our Time* (1944).

David Ayerst was also responsible for introducing Tippett to the poet W. H. Auden and it was through Auden that Tippett then met T. S. Eliot (1888-1965). Tippett had read Eliot's poetry as a student and been impressed; he was also impressed by Eliot's writings as a critic. Eliot wrote that a poet needed to value the cultural tradition, to cultivate a historical sense and to develop the capacity to transmute personal experiences; it was important to belong to the cultural tradition. This idea had a profound effect on Tippett. What Eliot described as 'the dissociation of sensibility' had diminished and corrupted English poetry from the mid-17th century onwards. Tippett was struck by the truth of this and realised that it also explained why English composers of the previous two centuries had failed to live up to the Tudor achievement. So, when the opportunity arose to meet Eliot, Tippett was very pleased. He sensed that there would be a meeting of minds.

Tippett's friendship with Eliot began in 1937. Eliot was a director of the publishing house Faber and Faber. F. V. Morley, one of Eliot's co-directors, had a six-year-old son who was autistic. The boy had a musical gift. The poet W. H. Auden knew about Tippett's interest in the educational value of music, and suggested that Tippett might be able to teach the boy to communicate through music. Tippett lived in a cottage in Oxted, and from there he could easily cycle to the Morleys' house in Surrey. He did this twice a week, partly to help the little boy, partly because he wanted to be part of a family again. And Eliot, for much the same reasons, became a regular visitor there too. That was where Tippett met Eliot. He found the poet-publisher affable and sociable, in spite of his very formal appearance. Together they played endless games of Monopoly with the little boy. Eliot was very good at the game and would have won every time, but both he and Tippett realised that they had to let the boy win, or he became unmanageable. In the end, Tippett felt that he could do nothing significant to help the boy.

Tippett and Eliot agreed to meet subsequently, often at Eliot's office in London, to talk about drama and other more general issues. Eliot became Tippett's artistic godfather, just as Tippett was to become an artistic godfather to a later generation of composers. Tippett respected Eliot's intelligence, but was not particularly interested in Eliot's musical interests. Music was Eliot's 'second art', as Tippett called it; Tippett saw his own second art as theatre. What Tippett wanted was to learn from Eliot about literature. He asked Eliot's advice on what to read, and Eliot introduced him to the poetry of Yeats. Yeats was then still alive, though Tippett was never to meet him. Eliot was full of enthusiasm for Yeats.

Eliot had at the time of their first meeting just completed his drama *Murder in the Cathedral*, and he was still absorbed with the nature of poetry, drama and music and their relative values in the mixed arts, ballet and opera. Tippett was fascinated by Eliot's views on this. Then Tippett set about constructing the outline for his own major work *A Child of Our Time* in 1939, the year of Yeats's death, and asked Eliot to look at his draft of the text. What Tippett was hoping for was a collaboration, that Eliot would offer to write a poetic text that Tippett could then set to music. He was startled by Eliot's reaction. When he read the text, he said Tippett did not need him; with a bit of revision the text would work well as it stood.

This was a turning point for Tippett, as it meant that the new piece, generally acknowledged to be one of his finest, had his words as well as his music. The piece was entirely in his voice and it is the greater for that. Given this confidence by Eliot, Tippett went on to write several operas, all with his own texts, such as *The Midsummer Marriage* (1955) and *King Priam* (1962). Critics for a long time condemned Tippett's *libretti* as clumsy and banal, but there is now an increasing recognition that they have a refreshing directness and aptness. Tippett – and Eliot – were right after all.

IV
ENCOUNTERS WITH LOVE

ANTONY AND
CLEOPATRA

(42 BC)

CLEOPATRA, QUEEN OF Egypt and last of the Macedonian (Hellenistic) dynasty of the Ptolemies, was born in 69 BC. She led a turbulent life, struggling to hang on to her throne and to her kingdom's independence at the fringe of the Roman Empire. Her father's will was that she should share the Egyptian throne with her younger brother, Ptolemy. She was deposed and exiled by Ptolemy's guardians and was about to launch a campaign to assert her right to half the throne when, in the autumn of 48 BC, Pompey fled from the forces of Julius Caesar to Alexandria, seeking sanctuary. Ptolemy was only fifteen years old, but ruthless. He had his throne set up on the shore at Alexandria and from there he cold-bloodedly watched as Pompey was murdered and beheaded on a small boat in front of him. Ptolemy had ordered Pompey's death with the idea of pleasing Julius Caesar; he hoped to ally himself with Rome.

This was a bad miscalculation on Ptolemy's part. When Caesar arrived in Egypt two days later, and Ptolemy presented him with Pompey's severed head, Caesar was upset and angry. Pompey had been a major political adversary, but he was also the widower of Caesar's only daughter, Julia: he was family.

In his anger, Caesar seized Alexandria and set himself up as arbiter between the rival claims of Ptolemy and Cleopatra; he was now pre-disposed to favour Cleopatra. Cleopatra returned from exile and had herself presented to Caesar rolled up in a carpet. Caesar was taken with this gesture, and charmed by Cleopatra herself. In spite of the age difference of thirty years, he (at fifty-two) and Cleopatra (just twenty-one) became lovers. Nine months later, she gave birth to his son,

Caesarion. Julius Caesar gave up his plans to annex Egypt; instead he supported Cleopatra's claim to the throne. Her brother, Ptolemy XIII, resisted this and there was a brief civil war. This ended when Ptolemy XIII was drowned in the Nile. Then Cleopatra was restored to the throne of Egypt, with her younger brother Ptolemy XIV installed as her co-ruler.

Cleopatra pressed Caesar to make her son Caesarion his heir, but he would not; he decided to name his grand-nephew Octavian instead. Cleopatra visited Rome between 47 and 44 BC with her infant son. She may even have been in Rome at the time when Julius Caesar was assassinated in March 44 BC. Ptolemy XIV died, apparently of natural causes, and Cleopatra then made Caesarion her co-ruler and successor.

In the power vacuum that followed Caesar's assassination, a triumvirate was set up, a team of three Roman leaders. Mark Antony, who had been Caesar's friend, was one of the triumvirs. In 42 BC, the forty-one-year-old Mark Antony summoned Cleopatra, who was then aged twenty-seven, to Tarsus; he wanted to meet her and test her loyalty to Rome. She arrived in great style, dazzling Antony. He was so charmed by her, just as Caesar had been, that he travelled to Alexandria with her. In December 40 BC, Cleopatra gave birth to two more children, apparently (though not necessarily) fathered by Antony – Cleopatra Selene II and Alexander Helios.

Three years later, Antony visited Alexandria again, this time on his way to make war on the Parthians. His relationship with Cleopatra was renewed, marrying Cleopatra according to the Egyptian rite, and from then on Alexandria was his home. It seems Antony had become so infatuated with Cleopatra that he overlooked the fact that he was already married. He had a wife back in Rome, Octavia. This was a significant political blunder, because the very publicly jilted and humiliated wife was the sister of Octavian, his fellow triumvir. Though young, Octavian was already an accomplished political operator, and he put this snub to good use. Antony piled one offence on another; soon Cleopatra was producing another child allegedly fathered by him, Ptolemy Philadelphus.

Antony was meanwhile waging wars in the east. His army conquered Armenia. Following this success, in 34 BC Antony announced what was in effect the formation of a new eastern empire ruled by himself and his new Egyptian family. He had Cleopatra and Caesarion crowned co-rulers of Egypt and Cyprus, and Alexander Helios ruler of Parthia, Media and Armenia. Cleopatra Selene was crowned ruler of Cyrenaica and Libya, while Ptolemy Philadelphus became ruler of Syria, Phoenicia and Cilicia. Cleopatra was also given the rather flashy title Queen of Kings. In fact the whole episode looks like a piece of foolish play-acting. It was as if Antony was suffering from too much sun, or too much eastern magic.

In Rome, there was general astonishment at Antony's behaviour. The new personal empire emerging in the east was a clear threat to the power of Rome. It was believed that Cleopatra was planning to set herself up in Rome as Empress of the World. The formal coronations organised in Alexandria gave Octavian the excuse he needed to take military action against Antony and Egypt. Octavian successfully persuaded the Senate to declare war against Egypt. This marked the beginning of the end of Antony and Cleopatra's fantasy empire.

In 31 BC the Roman fleet met Antony's and Cleopatra's fleets off Actium. Tradition has it that when she saw Antony's poorly equipped ships losing to the Romans' superior fleet she withdrew her ships and fled from the scene. It was later said that Antony left the battle to go after her, but this was not based on contemporary reports. Either way, the sea battle was a total defeat for Antony and Cleopatra, and a turning point in the career of Octavian. Octavian was able to invade Egypt, and as he did so Antony's armies deserted, changing sides to join Octavian in August 30 BC.

This incident marked the end of Antony's political career, and the end of his spectacular dalliance with the Egyptian queen. Fantastic stories were told in antiquity about her extravagance, her wild behaviour, her lasciviousness, her promiscuity, and it is now almost impossible to know where history ends and legend begins. But the story about the asp seems to be true; the ancient sources all agree that Cleopatra committed suicide by allowing herself to be bitten by an asp.

When Antony's armies deserted, he cried out that Cleopatra had betrayed him. He was evidently by now distraught and lashing out blindly and irrationally. Cleopatra was justifiably frightened. Not knowing what he might do, she shut herself up in her monument with her two handmaidens and had a message sent to Antony, to tell him that she was dead. This was perhaps to stop him from making any attempt to find her. Antony believed the message and sank into despair. He stabbed himself in the stomach with his sword and slumped onto his couch to die. But the bleeding stopped and he called on someone – anyone around him – to kill him there and then.

Then Cleopatra relented, perhaps sensing that her first message might cause Antony to despair altogether. She sent him another message asking him to go to her. He was relieved and delighted that Cleopatra was still alive and he ordered his supporters to take him to Cleopatra. She was still too fearful (of Octavian?) to open the door of the monument, but threw ropes down from a window. Antony was tied up into a bag and hauled up by Cleopatra and her two handmaidens. They dragged him in through the window, laid him on a couch. In a histrionic display of grief, Cleopatra tore her clothes off and laid them over her dying lover, raving, crying, beating her breasts and cutting herself. Antony told her to stop it, asked for a glass of wine, drank it and then died. This left Octavian the uncontested ruler of the Roman world; Antony's mad adventure in the East had led to the end of the Roman Republic.

Plutarch wrote his account of the deaths of Antony and Cleopatra just over 100 years after they happened, and it is probably historically accurate. He said that Cleopatra was found dead, with her handmaiden Iras dying at her feet and another handmaiden, Charmian, adjusting the queen's crown before she too fell to the ground. She had been provided with the asp or asps secretly, hidden either in a basket of figs or a vase. The queen committed suicide rather than submit to being taken back to Rome in chains. The custom was to put captured kings in cages and parade them through the streets of Rome in triumphal procession – before execution by garrotting. Suicide was preferable to that. Octavian had indeed intended a Roman triumph for Cleopatra, knowing how much the people of Rome hated and despised her. As it was he had to content himself with parading an effigy of Cleopatra, complete with clinging asp. Incidentally, Cleopatra was bitten on the arm; the breast was an invention of Shakespeare's – a poetically appropriate location for the fatal wound given his emphasis on the tragic love story.

Antony and Cleopatra's three children were spared by Octavian. They were taken back to Rome where they were put into the care of Antony's wife Octavia. Octavian arranged for Cleopatra Selene to be married to Juba II of Mauretania.

As for Caesarion, Cleopatra's appointed successor – when Cleopatra's death became known, the Egyptians proclaimed him pharaoh. But Octavian was in charge in Egypt now, and he was reported to say, 'Two Caesars are one too many.' He had Caesarion executed. This brought the Hellenistic dynasty of Egyptian pharaohs to an end. Cleopatra was in effect the last pharaoh – and very largely because of her reckless love affair with Mark Antony, which clouded her political judgement and his equally.

PETER ABELARD AND HÉLOÏSE

(1120)

PETER ABELARD (1079-1142) was born in a village called Le Pallet near Nantes in north-west France. He was the eldest son in an upper-class Breton family and when young was known as Pierre Le Pallet. He was an intelligent and quick student who excelled in the art of dialectic, a branch of philosophy focusing on Aristotelian logic. Instead of pursuing a military career like his father, Abelard became a scholar. He wandered round France, debating and learning as he went. While still in his teens, he reached Paris, where he was taught by William of Champeaux at the cathedral school of Notre-Dame. At this time he changed his name to Abelard. He was soon able to defeat his teacher in argument, and this led to a philosophical dialogue that ended with the fall of Realism, up to that time the main philosophical theory, and its replacement by Nominalism, its main rival, or by Abelard's own Conceptualism.

When Abelard was still only twenty-two, he set up a school of his own at Melun. Then, in order to compete more directly with his opponents in Paris, he moved to Corbeil. His teaching was conspicuously successful, but the strain began to tell and he had to withdraw from it for a while. When his health recovered, after 1108, he found that William, his former teacher, was lecturing at Saint-Victor in Paris. Once again they became rivals. William tried to stop Peter Abelard from teaching in Paris, but in the end could not prevent him from doing so. Abelard set up his school on the Montagne Sainte Geneviève, overlooking Notre-Dame.

Abelard turned from dialectic to theology, and went to hear Anselm lecture at Laon. Abelard was at the peak of his powers, able to lecture

147

without previous training or any special programme of study. He became professor at Notre-Dame in about 1115. He had also become an intellectual celebrity. He was good-looking, well-mannered, charismatic and was always surrounded by crowds of students – thousands, it was said – who flocked from all over Europe to hear him lecture. He was deluged with admiration and praise, and started to think of himself as the only undefeated philosopher in the world.

But a dramatic change in his fortunes was just round the corner. Until this moment, he had steeped himself in scholarly study and debate. But now he fell in love. Héloïse (1101–1164) was the object of his love. She lived in the cathedral precinct of Notre-Dame in the guardianship of her uncle, Canon Fulbert. She was a beautiful and unusually well-educated girl, remarkably knowledgeable in the Classics, and able to read Latin, Greek and Hebrew. Attracted by this lovely and talented seventeen-year-old, Abelard insinuated himself into Fulbert's household first as Héloïse's tutor, then as lodger; and then he seduced her. Abelard could not keep the escapade to himself. He boasted about it.

When Fulbert discovered what had happened, he threw Abelard out of his house, but Abelard and Héloïse went on meeting in secret. Héloïse became pregnant and Abelard sent her to Brittany, where she gave birth to a son. She named the boy Astrolabe. Abelard meanwhile had to appease the angry Fulbert. He asked for Fulbert's forgiveness and proposed a secret marriage, secret so that it did not impinge on his career prospects. Héloïse was opposed to the idea, but went along with it. When Fulbert revealed the marriage in public, Héloïse denied it.

Abelard's response to this was to urge Héloïse to go to the convent at Argenteuil. Fulbert mistakenly interpreted this as Abelard's public denial of the marriage, and an indication that in spite of offering to marry Héloïse he really wanted to get rid of her. Fulbert was furious and in his fury he castrated Abelard. Abelard later wrote about the traumatic incident; 'Violently incensed, they laid a plot against me, and one night while I all unsuspecting was asleep in a secret room in my lodgings, they broke in with the help of one of my servants whom they had bribed. There they had vengeance on me with a most cruel and most shameful punishment, such as astounded the whole world; for they cut off those parts of my body with which I had done that which was the cause of their sorrow.'

Forced now into becoming a nun, Héloïse wrote to Abelard, asking why she had to submit to a religious life: it was not what she wanted for herself. 'While I am denied your presence, give me at least through your words – of which you have enough and to spare – some sweet semblance of yourself . . . I beg you, think what you owe me, give ear to my pleas, and I will finish a long letter with a brief ending: farewell, my only love.'

Abelard's glamorous public life and his romance were over. He sought refuge at the Abbey of St-Denis. He was unable to find any peace in the monastic life, and turned back to academic study. Responding to requests, he reopened his school at an unidentified priory. Huge numbers of students flocked there to hear him lecture and some of his old influence began to return. But he now had many academic enemies, and after the Héloïse scandal he was not able to mount such vigorous defences. He published his lectures, *Theologia Summi Boni*, and his opponents seized upon his rationalist interpretation of the Trinity with accusations of heresy.

In a synod at Soissons in 1121, Abelard's enemies succeeded in getting an official condemnation of his 'heretical' teaching. He was forced to burn his book and was then shut up in a convent at Soissons. It was a bitter experience, not least because Abelard amused himself by goading the monks with perverse academic squibs. He used Bede as a source to argue that Dionysius the Areopagite had been Bishop of Corinth, when the monks thought, using another source, that he had been Bishop of Athens. This was an historical heresy and it led to a new demand that he justify himself. The monastic life did not suit him and he was in the end allowed to leave.

He built himself a hermitage out of reeds on the River Seine. When this became known, students flocked out from Paris to hear him; they covered the landscape round his cabin with their tents and huts. He built an Oratory of the Paraclete. The renewed popularity made him fear renewed persecution, so Abelard left the oratory, accepting an invitation to preside over the Abbey of St Gildas in Brittany.

One glimmer of light in the darkness was that, when Héloïse's convent at Argenteuil was closed, he was able to set her up as the head of a new religious house at the deserted oratory. As its spiritual director, he was able to revisit the oratory, but the unhappy pair still lived apart.

Abelard wrote his *Historia Calamitatum* (The Story of My Troubles). This inspired Héloïse to write her first letter to Abelard, a statement of great passion and devotion in which she showed that she was resigned to their brother-sister relationship. By 1136 Abelard had returned to lecturing on Mt St Genevieve. But Abelard had made an enemy of Bernard of Clairvaux, who set great store by unquestioning faith and who detested Abelard's reasoned approach. Bernard now moved to crush the offender.

At Bernard's instigation a council was called at Sens in 1141. Before it Abelard faced several charges of heresy. Bernard opened the proceedings, then Abelard appealed to Rome. But it was no use. Bernard was very powerful, and he managed to secure a condemnation at Sens and a second condemnation from Rome the next year. Abelard set off for Rome to argue his case, but on the way he collapsed at Cluny and died at a priory near Châlon. Peter Abelard's remains were secretly taken to the Oratory of the Paraclete at Héloïse's request. When in 1163 she in her turn died, she was buried beside Abelard.

Peter Abelard's sexual misbehaviour provided his scholarly enemies with a lever that they could use against him. But it was not centrally the indiscretion with Héloïse that made other scholars regard him with such intense hatred. It was his confrontation with the accepted philosophical stance of the early middle ages that made him hated. Before Abelard, the orthodox philosophical position was Realism, based on the authority of Plato. What Abelard was offering was the alternative philosophical authority of Aristotle. This was to become firmly established as the orthodoxy in the Christian Church during the decades after his death – and endure for centuries.

Beside and behind this very public struggle of ideas lay the private anguish of the thwarted love affair and the broken marriage. It was the archetypal tragic love affair. In a letter Abelard wrote to Héloïse, 'You know, beloved, as the whole world knows, how much I have lost in you, how at one wretched stroke of fortune that supreme act of flagrant treachery robbed me of my very self in robbing me of you; and how my sorrow for my loss is nothing compared with what I feel for the manner in which I lost you.'

DANTE AND BEATRICE

(1274)

DANTE ALIGHIERI WAS born in Florence in 1265. Like other aristocratic Florentine boys, Dante was educated in both Christian and classical literature, though he was taught only Latin, not Greek. This meant, significantly, that he could read Vergil's *Aeneid* – but he could not read Homer's *Iliad* or *Odyssey*. Most people assume, because of the wanderings involved in *The Divine Comedy*, that Dante must have read the *Odyssey*, but it seems he would have been incapable of doing so. All he knew about Homer's world seems to have come from Vergil.

At the age of twelve he was promised to his future wife, Gemma Donati. But by then Dante had already fallen in love with another girl whom he called Beatrice. Dante was nine years old and Beatrice was eight when he first saw her, just once, and fell in love with her immediately. Her real name was Bice Portinari and she was the daughter of Folco di Ricovero Portinari. Dante met her when his father took him to the Portinari house for a May Day party. She was dressed, he tells us, in a soft crimson cloth and wore a girdle about her waist. Dante was instantly taken with her and remained devoted to her for the rest of her life. Years later Dante met Beatrice for a second time – and that, apparently, was all.

The second meeting took place in a Florence street. She was walking along dressed in virginal white and flanked by two older women. She turned and greeted him. This direct address overwhelmed him with such happiness that he had to return to his room, to think about the Lady of the Salutation. As he meditated, he fell asleep and had a dream – and that dream became the subject of the first sonnet of *La Vita Nuova*.

In 1287 she married a banker and died three years later, in June 1290, at the age of only twenty-four. After her death, Dante continued to nurse his love and admiration for 'Beatrice' and this infatuation continued alongside his marriage to Gemma Donati. After Beatrice died, Dante withdrew into himself. He began a period of intense study and started writing poems about her. These and some poems written during Beatrice's lifetime became *La Vita Nuova*, his first book (1292), dedicated to the poet Guido Cavalcanti. Dante had sent one of his early sonnets to Cavalcanti, marking the beginning of their friendship. *La Vita Nuova* was a celebration of his love for Beatrice. He never mentioned his wife Gemma in any of his poems, and one wonders what she made of her husband's outpourings to and about another woman.

Dante's fixation with Beatrice and his love-at-a-distance for her had its roots firmly in the medieval tradition of courtly love. This entailed a rarefied non-sexual admiration of a woman, who might well be someone else's wife. In this type of secret and unrequited relationship the woman was impossibly idealised, held up as an icon of beauty, virtue and chastity. What is unusual is that this particular courtly love affair was publicised and immortalised in the writings of a great poet. One theory is that Dante was turning Beatrice into a more specific symbol, the symbol of Santa Sapienza, which was a focus of secret societies at the time.

Whether Beatrice had any more specific symbolic meaning to Dante will probably never be known. She was certainly Dante's greatest muse, his inspiration. She became a leading theme in his work. It is also strange to think that he immortalised her, for as long as literature is read, without her having the slightest suspicion of it. She died in 1290 without knowing that someone else in Florence was already turning her into an icon of western literature.

In 1310–14 Dante produced his epic poem, *The Divine Comedy*. This huge sprawling panoramic picture of the universe as conceived in the medieval mind is one of the master works of Western literature. Beatrice appears in that, almost transformed into a goddess or an angel. The pagan Virgil cannot be Dante's guide in Heaven. It is Beatrice who acts as Dante's guide through the nine circles of Heaven. He describes her as 'maternal, radiant and comforting'. She has by this point become almost a divinity herself, the ultimate idealisation.

Are we to take what Dante says about Beatrice at face value? There are good reasons for being suspicious. Dante and Beatrice belonged to the same social circle in Florence, so it seems highly unlikely that he only saw her twice in twenty-four years. The numbers invoked are also suspicious. Dante was preoccupied with numerology. He was obsessed with the number three, representing the Holy Trinity, and multiples of three. The number nine (three times three) was especially significant to him. So Beatrice's appearance to him when he reached the age of nine seems too good to be true. It would be nine years before the second meeting, when Dante was eighteen. Whatever the historical reality, Beatrice was certainly his muse, 'the glorious lady of my mind', as Dante himself says.

QUEEN ISABELLA AND ROGER MORTIMER

(1324)

ROGER MORTIMER'S CAREER was one of the most remarkable of any medieval ruler. He started as a near-nobody, a very minor baron, became the lover of a queen, murderer of a king and ruler of England; he also died on the gallows as a convicted traitor. He was born at Wigmore Castle in Herefordshire and was probably fostered in the household of his uncle, Roger Mortimer of Chirk. This uncle, significantly, had taken the head of Llywelyn to King Edward I in 1282. Roger was married in 1301 to Joan de Geneville, the daughter of a neighbouring lord, and by this marriage he acquired extensive lands and properties, including Ludlow Castle, which became the main Mortimer stronghold.

Mortimer's childhood came to a sudden end when Lord Wigmore was killed in a skirmish in 1304. As Roger was still under age, he was placed by Edward I under the guardianship of Piers Gaveston; King Edward knighted him in 1306. That year Roger also came into his inheritance, including the title Baron Wigmore. When Gaveston was appointed Lord-Lieutenant of Ireland, it was natural for Roger to accompany him to Ireland from 1308 to 1312. After that he may have served in Aquitaine. In 1314 he was back in England, where he was required to supply 300 infantry for Edward II's campaign against the Scots. At the Battle of Bannockburn he was captured by the Scots but released without ransom, because he was a cousin of Robert the Bruce. He was given the task of returning King Edward's privy seal and shield, which the king had evidently dropped on the battlefield.

After military service in Wales, in 1316 Roger was appointed Edward II's Lieutenant of Ireland, and he worked hard to block an attempt by Edward Bruce, Robert the Bruce's brother, to destabilise Ireland. Roger was given a £4,000 reward for his part in suppressing the rebellion, but was then re-appointed with the less prestigious title of Justiciar.

The Despenser and Mortimer families were sworn enemies. Hugh Despenser the Younger swore he would take revenge on the Mortimers for the death of his grandfather. For his own survival, Mortimer had to oppose Hugh Despenser. The only way to do this was to change sides; to join the opposition to Edward II, the Contrarians (Humphrey de Bohun, the Earl of Hereford and other Marcher Lords). Initially the Contrarian revolt was successful, forcing Edward II to banish the Despensers. But soon the Despensers were back. A royal army moved against the Contrarian strongholds. Roger had to surrender to the King at Shrewsbury in 1322.

Now Roger Mortimer found himself condemned to death for treason, though this was commuted to life imprisonment. He was confined to the Tower of London. He was still not safe, though, as the Despensers would be working on the king to carry out the execution. News came that an order for Roger's execution was on its way, and this was what prompted Roger to escape from the Tower in August 1324. Not only did he get out of the Tower; he succeeded in crossing the Channel. In France he went to the court of the French king, where he tried in vain to gain support for an invasion of England.

But then Queen Isabella arrived, the French wife of Edward II. She had persuaded Edward II to let her travel to France on a peace mission; she was very anxious to get away from her husband and his favourites. She and Roger Mortimer were both equally, in their different ways, dissatisfied with Edward II. She hated her husband's Despenser favourites; so too did Roger Mortimer. The two became lovers, but like the relationship between Antony and Cleopatra it was as much a political alliance as a love affair – a double bond. Their relationship caused a scandal at the French court and they were obliged to move to the Netherlands, where they found William the Good was eager to supply them with the men and the ships to launch an invasion. The invasion fleet landed in September 1326 and within a few weeks the king's régime had imploded through lack of any real conviction among its supporters. Edward II was captured on 16 November and forced to abdicate in favour of his son, who became Edward III.

But Edward III was still a boy, and the real power lay in the hands of Roger Mortimer, who ruled England unobtrusively from the wings. Mortimer recognised that he would have to honour his pre-invasion promise to Robert the Bruce to end the war against Scotland. This was perhaps enlightened and imaginative, but giving in to the Scots lost him a lot of support in England at a critical moment. The Treaty of Northampton, which recognised the independence of Scotland, was unpopular among some of the barons. The Earl of Lancaster in particular was strongly opposed to this development.

Mortimer excited jealousy when he was created Earl of March in 1328. Then the seizure and judicial murder of Edmund of Woodstock the following year generated widespread fear, especially as it was accompanied by the naming of alleged conspirators against the new régime. There was no real plot, but the fear of being named was real enough. These were major political gaffes. Then, at a Round Table tournament, Mortimer appeared dressed as King Arthur. He was parading his descent from the ancient kings of Gwynedd. He was, many thought, preparing England for his own coronation. The situation looked extremely dangerous. The Earl of Lancaster persuaded the young King Edward III that he needed to act against Roger before Roger had him murdered, too.

In October 1330 a Parliament was called at Nottingham Castle, and there Roger Mortimer was seized and put in chains. Queen Isabella begged for him to be treated well. 'Have pity! Have pity on the gentle Mortimer!' The young king, Edward III, wanted to see Mortimer slaughtered on the spot, but Lancaster persuaded him to have Mortimer taken to London and put on trial. In November, Mortimer faced fourteen serious charges, including procuring the death of Edmund of Woodstock, illegally removing Edward II from Kenilworth Castle and ordering his murder at Berkeley Castle. Other charges related to self-enrichment and usurping the authority of the king. This was a show trial: Mortimer was not allowed to speak. From the point of view of history this is unfortunate. It would be interesting to know how he would have answered the main accusations, especially since so little is known about his thoughts and motives. He left very little in the way of evidence. There are no letters, no documents bearing his stamp. Even from the time of his great power, he seems to have preferred to stay in the shadows, giving orders by word of mouth. Perhaps it was safer that way, and one might suspect that his motives were dark.

There can be little doubt that he did order the horrible and cruel murder of Edward II, carried out by Sir Thomas Gourney, William Ogle and Lord Maltravers, even if there is no paperwork to prove it; who else could have ordered it? But the murder of Edmund of Woodstock and the naming of names look more like the actions of a man who is seriously frightened and insecure. Was he perhaps a man who was completely out of his depth? A man who had risen too far too fast?

As it was, Mortimer said nothing in response to any of these accusations; he could say nothing at his trial because he was bound and gagged, and his accusers had dressed him in a cloak bearing the contemptuous legend, 'Where is your glory?' The verdict, a foregone conclusion, was that Mortimer was a traitor, an enemy of the king and the realm. He was sentenced to be 'drawn and hanged'.

On 29 November, Roger Mortimer was dressed in the same black tunic that he had hypocritically worn to Edward II's funeral three years earlier, and then dragged on an oxhide pulled by two horses through the streets of London from the Tower to Tyburn Hill. On the scaffold he was allowed to make a short speech, in which he admitted that the Earl of Kent had died as a result of a conspiracy. Psalm 52 was read aloud to him: 'Why do you glory in mischief?' Then he was hanged. He was spared the disembowelling, possibly in exchange for publicly confessing to at least one of the charges. The body was left hanging on Tyburn Tree for two days. A document was recently discovered in which Joan, Mortimer's widow, petitioned Edward III for the return of her husband's body so that she could bury it at Wigmore Abbey. Edward III's cold and clever reply was, 'Let his body rest in peace.'

It is interesting to speculate what might have happened if, after

158

Mortimer's escape to France, he had not met Queen Isabella. He might have lived quietly in exile, dying in comfortable obscurity on the fringe of the French court. If the encounter with Isabella had not happened, the love affair, the invasion; then the deposition of Edward II would not have happened either, and the course of British history would have been different.

HENRY VIII AND ANNE BOLEYN

(1526)

LIKE ROGER MORTIMER, Anne Boleyn rose from obscurity to dizzy heights, had three years on or close to the English throne, and then fell, disgraced and charged with treason. But Anne was no murderer or conspirator. She was just extremely unlucky, twice over: once, in catching the lustful eye of Henry VIII, and twice, in failing to produce him a male heir. Her beginnings are so obscure that even when and where she was born are uncertain, though it is likely that she was born at Blickling in Norfolk between 1500 and 1507.

She spent part of her childhood at the court of the Archduchess Margaret. It was the custom in England, and had been for centuries, to place upper class young men and women in the households of other aristocrats in order to learn independence, civilised manners and etiquette; the English public schools developed out of this tradition. Anne was schooled in this way as a 'maid of honour'. At the age of perhaps thirteen, she was moved to the household of Henry VIII's sister Mary, who was married to the French king Louis XII. Anne's older sister Mary was already there, in attendance on the French queen. When Louis died, Mary Boleyn came back to England with Mary Tudor, while Anne stayed in France where she attended the new French queen for six years.

During her long stay in France, Anne Boleyn learnt to speak French fluently and acquired a taste for French music, clothes and poetry. She may well have been at the Field of Cloth of Gold, the great state occasion where the new French king Francis I met Henry VIII.

It is hard to believe all that has been said about Anne's appearance.

When Henry VIII could have his pick of the women in England, is it really likely that he would have chosen one who was not pretty, had six fingers on one hand instead of the usual five, and a large mole or goitre on her neck? One courtier described her as 'not one of the handsomest women in the world', but these words may mean only that she did not conform to the standard idea of the English rose, with pale skin, fair hair and blue eyes. Anne was of average height, with small breasts and a long graceful neck; she had olive-coloured skin, thick dark brown hair and very dark brown eyes that could appear black. It was the large dark eyes that people noticed most, and she deployed them skilfully to manipulate people.

It was in 1521 that Anne fatefully returned to England. Her marriage to the heir of Ormonde was being arranged. While this was happening, she went to attend Queen Catherine, Catherine of Aragon. She is known to have attended a masque at the English royal court on 1 March 1522. The planned marriage fell through and she started an affair with another rich heir, Henry Percy. Cardinal Wolsey intervened, stopping the romance, and it has been suggested that he did so because the King had noticed Anne and wanted to keep his options open. Wolsey was in effect reserving Anne for the King. On the other hand, some historians believe that the King did not notice Anne until 1526, while the Percy affair ended four years earlier.

At about the same time, Anne had an affair with Sir Thomas Wyatt, the poet. He was married in 1520; although he then separated from his wife there could be no question of marrying Anne, so their affair – whether carnal or courtly – could lead nowhere.

As soon as Henry VIII noticed Anne Boleyn, he wanted to have sex with her. He naturally assumed *droit de seigneur*, and had already had sex with her sister some years earlier, so he was taken aback when Anne refused him. Anne may have remembered that Elizabeth Woodville, Edward IV's wife, had told the king that she would only be his wife, not his mistress; she was following a precedent. There was a presumption at court that Anne would end up as one of the long sequence of royal mistresses, but in 1527 Henry moved towards annulling his marriage to Queen Catherine, and that could only mean that he intended to remarry.

The King was intent on creating a dynasty. He needed to have sons, and this provided a major drive to changing wives. Catherine had produced no male heir – maybe Anne would oblige. But Henry also became infatuated with Anne. He disliked writing letters or documents of any kind and there are very few surviving documents in his handwriting. But of those, seventeen are love letters to Anne Boleyn. They are undated, but the following letter is probably one of the earlier ones.

My mistress and friend: I and my heart put ourselves in your hands, begging you to have them suitors for your good favour, and that your affection for them should not grow less through absence. For it would be a great pity to increase their sorrow since absence does it sufficiently, and more than ever I could have thought possible reminding us of a point in astronomy, which is, that the longer the days are the farther off is the sun, and yet the more fierce. So it is with our love, for by absence we are parted, yet nevertheless it keeps its fervour, at least on my side, and I hope on yours also: assuring you that on my side the ennui of absence is already too much for me: and when I think of the increase of what I must needs suffer it would be well nigh unbearable for me were it not for the firm hope I have and as I cannot be with you in person, I am sending you the nearest possible thing to that, namely, my picture set in a bracelet, with the whole device which you already know. Wishing myself in their place when it shall please you. This by the hand of Your loyal servant and friend
H. Rex

Henry's subsequent letters are more informal and they show clearly that he had genuinely fallen for Anne.

No more to you at this present mine own darling for lack of time but that I would you were in my arms or I in yours for I think it long since I kissed you. Written after the killing of an hart at a xi. of the clock minding with God's grace tomorrow mightily timely to kill another: by the hand of him which I trust shortly shall be yours.   *Henry R.*

Mine own sweetheart, these shall be to advertise you of the great loneliness that I find here since your departing, for I ensure you methinketh the time longer since your departing now last than I was wont to do a whole fortnight: I think your kindness and my fervents of love causeth it, for otherwise I would not have thought it possible that for so little a while it should have grieved me, but now that I am coming toward you methinketh my pains been half released . . . Wishing myself (specially an evening) in my sweetheart's arms, whose pretty duckies [breasts] I trust shortly to kiss. Written with the hand of him that was, is, and shall be yours by his will.   *H.R.*

By 1528, Anne Boleyn had started to become a significant figure at court. She revealed an interest in religious reforms. By introducing and advocating some of the current ideas for reform to the King, Anne made powerful enemies at court. Some of these enemies would soon bring about her downfall. Behind the glitter, the Tudor court was seething with dangerous jealousies and intrigues; Anne may well have believed that she was immune to the danger because of the King's infatuation with her.

But the legal complications surrounding the annulment of Henry's marriage to Catherine of Aragon caused endless delays. Anne became frustrated, irritable, tetchy. Her famous quick temper flared up, even in front of the entire court, and she and Henry quarrelled openly. Henry continued showering her with presents, but Anne was afraid that he might tire of the delay, go back to Catherine and leave her stranded. Then she would not only have wasted a lot of time failing to acquire a husband, but too many prospective husbands would know too much about her. How many eligible aristocrats would want to marry the King's most famous cast-off?

Anne was also becoming very unpopular with the English people. At the Christmas celebrations, she was given precedence over the Duchess of Norfolk and the Duchess of Suffolk, who was the King's sister. This was generally seen as inappropriate. She was made Marquess of Pembroke. Anne finally gave in to Henry near the end of 1532; she became pregnant. An illegitimate son was no use to Henry at all. He had to have a legitimate heir and this forced him to take desperate action. Towards the end of January in 1533, Henry and Anne were secretly married. The marriage to Catherine of Aragon had not been dissolved, but Henry had by now persuaded himself that it was invalid in the first place and this left him free to marry. This was an argumentative sleight of hand; the fact that he was seeking annulment meant that he was currently bound to Catherine; he had committed bigamy. This tricky situation was resolved four months later, when Archbishop Cranmer proclaimed that the marriage to Catherine was invalid.

Now Anne's coronation could take place. She was taken by river from Greenwich up to the Tower of London dressed in cloth of gold and followed by a procession of barges. Then, on 1 June, she left the Tower in procession to Westminster Abbey, where Cranmer crowned her queen.

In August, preparations were under way for the birth of Henry's heir. Whether he was going to be Henry IX or given some other name was being discussed; a proclamation announcing the birth of the royal prince was drafted. Henry had already decided that the baby must be a boy, because it was what he wanted, and he was used to getting his own way.

On 7 September the baby was born. It was a girl, the future Queen Elizabeth I, and Henry was acutely disappointed. Anne knew she had to produce a son. By January 1534 she was pregnant again, but she miscarried. In 1535 the same thing happened again, and what made it worse was that the child had been a boy. Anne was extremely upset, knowing now that her failure to produce a male heir threatened her own life. Somehow, Henry would replace her with a new wife. She could even see who that new wife would be: one of her own ladies-in-waiting, Jane Seymour. How cruelly apt that phrase must have seemed to the distressed Anne – lady in waiting.

Anne's enemies also saw the King's interest in Jane Seymour, and they scented blood. They closed in on the Queen, plotting her downfall. Cromwell took some of the court gossip to the King and persuaded him to instigate an investigation into the Queen's behaviour. In April 1536, Mark Smeaton, who was Anne's musician, was arrested and under torture he gave the evidence needed to launch a treason charge. Then Sir Henry Norris was arrested and taken to the Tower for questioning. Then the Queen's brother George, Lord Rochford, was arrested. An extraordinary scenario was cooked up in which the Queen was guilty not only of adultery, which because of her position was treasonable, but of incest with her brother. She was supposed also to have plotted the King's death.

On 2 May, Anne Boleyn was arrested at Greenwich, told of the charges against her and conveyed to the Tower - the same journey by water that she had travelled for her coronation, and was taken to the same apartment. To ensure Anne's condemnation, her enemies lined up some more adulteries, with Sir Francis Weston and William Brereton. Sir Thomas Wyatt was arrested too, though later released. On 12 May 1536, all the accused men were tried at Westminster Hall, found guilty and sentenced to death.

Three days later, the Queen and her brother were tried at the Tower. They denied any wrongdoing, but Lady Rochford testified against her husband and they were found guilty. They were either to be burnt at the stake, the punishment for incest, or beheaded: the King himself would decide the penalty. The men were all beheaded, which implies that the incest charge was a pretext and Henry did not really believe it. Truth mattered little; it was the result that counted. Anne's request for a French swordsman was granted and she was also given the dignity of a private execution inside the Tower. The swordsman took off her head with one swift stroke.

Curiously, shortly before Anne's execution, her marriage to Henry was annulled on grounds of invalidity. Henry had, after all, he now decided, at the time of his marriage to Anne, still been married to Catherine of Aragon. In the topsy-turvy world of Tudor tyrant politics, the reasoning shifted with the strategic needs of the moment. If Anne had not really been married to Henry it is hard to see how she could have been guilty of adultery; there had been no offence against Henry at all. But it did not matter. Anne was in the way of the King's next marriage, in the way of a male heir, and she had to go.

CATHERINE THE GREAT AND GRIGORI POTEMKIN

(1762)

CATHERINE THE GREAT achieved her greatness by marrying well. She married the prospective Tsar of Russia, Duke Peter. To do so she moved to Russia, converted to Eastern Orthodoxy and changed her name from Sophia to Catherine. This was in 1744. The long-planned marriage took place in 1745. This became an open marriage, with Peter taking Elizabeth Vorontsova as his mistress and Catherine taking a series of lovers, including Sergei Saltykov, Grigori Grigoryevich Orlov, Stanislaw Poniatowski and Alexander Vassilchikov. Catherine was extremely astute politically and very aware of the significance of events in Russia and in the world outside. She developed friendships with her husband's political opponents, which was an ominous hint of what was to come. Peter meanwhile was elected King of Sweden and King of Finland, but when he became Tsar, in 1762, he was only to reign for six months.

Catherine became Empress Consort of Russia and the couple, if they can be called that, moved into the Winter Palace in St Petersburg. Catherine accepted her husband's liaison with the Countess Elizabeth and was not at all shocked when the countess moved into the palace with them. The new tsar was an incompetent ruler. He quickly alienated the whole of Russia with his undiplomatic praise of all things Prussian, including the Prussian king. His offences against the Orthodox Church also made him unpopular. It was relatively easy for Catherine to organise a palace coup (9 July 1762), which marked the end of Peter's reign and the start of hers. A few days later, Peter was murdered by

Alexei Orlov and others with Catherine's full complicity.

Now a usurper and a murderess, Catherine set to work extending the borders of the Russian Empire. She added an area the size of France to Russian territory. She was well served by her foreign minister, Nikita Panin, who set up the Northern Accord, a power bloc consisting of Russia, Poland and Sweden. But as soon as it became clear that his scheme was not succeeding, Catherine replaced him with someone else: Alexander Bezborodko.

Catherine led a remarkable love life. She had a string of lovers. She put them into promoted positions while she was interested in them, then, when she got tired of them, pensioned them off with golden handshakes consisting of large estates. Grigori Potemkin was not only her lover, he was her very capable adviser. After she ended her affair with him in 1776, she went on seeking his advice – even on her lovers. Potemkin went so far as lining up possible candidates for the position of Empress's lover. They had to be extremely good-looking but also have well-developed minds in order to hold her interest. The last in the long sequence of lovers was Prince Zubov, who was forty years younger than the empress.

Catherine had offspring and she seems to have been confused as to their parentage. She wrote in her memoirs that her son Paul was fathered by her first lover Sergei Saltykov. This seems unlikely, as Paul bore a resemblance to her husband Peter. Perhaps she had a motive for this 'mistake', as she wanted to exclude Paul from the succession; she wanted her eldest grandson Alexander to succeed her; he became Tsar Alexander I. She may have distrusted Paul because of his character or because she saw him as a potential threat to her authority. For whatever reason, she kept him in semi-captivity at Catchina and Pavlovsk. Another son, Alexis, was fathered by Grigori Orlov. She kept him away from court, at Tula, but he was later created Count Bobrinskoy.

In 1764, Catherine placed one of her former lovers, Stanislaw Poniatowski, on the Polish throne. But perhaps the greatest of her lovers was Prince Grigori Potemkin (1739-91), a field marshal and statesman. One of his greatest achievements was the colonisation of the empty steppes of southern Ukraine after they passed into Russian hands in 1774.

Catherine made war against the Ottoman Empire (1768–74) and with Potemkin's help inflicted some devastating defeats on the Turks. The idea was to gain access to the Black Sea. The great military victories enabled her to do this, and Potemkin founded new cities there: Odessa, Nikolayev, Yekaterinoslav and Kherson. In 1783 Potemkin achieved the annexation of Crimea to Russia. For this he was awarded a grandiose victory title, His Serene Highness the Prince of Tauris, which was the ancient name of Crimea. The Ottomans resumed hostilities (the Second Russo-Turkish Was of 1787–92) and were catastrophically defeated. The Russians were now securely in control of much of the Black Sea coast, including the Crimea.

It was Potemkin who founded the new towns. It was Potemkin who created the Black Sea Fleet. Potemkin was a career soldier, who participated in the palace coup that ousted Peter III and brought Catherine to the throne. Potemkin's precise role in the coup may never be known. Many apocryphal stories were told about him, including some that connect him to the assassination of Tsar Peter, but the truth of these is uncertain. He was promoted to second lieutenant of the Guards. After the coup, Catherine needed reliable people around her and she quickly recognised Potemkin's huge potential, his energy and his ability to organise.

By 1774 Potemkin had become a favourite of the Tsarina. She showered him with awards and positions. In 1776, Catherine persuaded Emperor Joseph II to make Potemkin a prince of the Holy Roman Empire. It seemed there was nothing the Empress would not do to advance her favourite.

For seventeen years he was the most powerful man in Russia – a kind of undeclared Tsar. Potemkin loved his new position, loved the wealth and the ostentation, loved the absolute power. But, like Catherine, he was also attracted to many of the ideals of the Enlightenment. He believed in religious tolerance. He believed in tolerating and protecting ethnic and national minorities. He also adopted a more humane approach to army discipline; when he became commander-in-chief of the Russian army in 1784, he required officers to take care of the men under them in a more paternal way.

Potemkin's period of ultimate glory, in the Empress's bedchamber, was quite short. As early as 1775 he was superseded as her lover by Zavadovsky. But this led to no diminution of his political power or indeed of the friendly relations that existed between them. He might not be her lover any more, but Catherine still wanted his friendship and his advice. For another ten years there was an uninterrupted flow of correspondence between them. There were rumours in Russia at the time that Catherine and Potemkin secretly married. Perhaps they did, but there is no evidence either way.

Potemkin died in 1791 out on the open steppe, after eating a whole goose while in a high fever. He died as he had lived, extravagantly. Catherine had him buried at the cathedral in Kherson, the city he founded.

LOUIS XVI AND MARIE ANTOINETTE

(1770)

Marie Antoinette had a privileged upbringing in the Austrian royal family, yet it was also an educationally deprived upbringing. Her native language was German, yet at the age of twelve she could neither read nor write German properly. Her family launched a series of arranged marriages for Antoine, as she was then known, and her sisters, to seal the various alliances that Maria Theresa had agreed in the 1750s as a result of the Seven Years War. But for that war, the marriage between Antoine and the French Dauphin Louis-Auguste would never have been organised: France was Austria's traditional enemy.

Smallpox hit the Austrian royal family in 1767. The Emperor Joseph's wife, Maria Josepha, was the first to die. Maria Theresa's daughter Josepha caught it from the imperfectly sealed tomb of her sister-in-law, and also died. Maria Elizabeth, another older sister, caught the disease and though she survived she was too badly disfigured to be considered eligible for marriage. Antoine was immune as she had had smallpox when very young. The reduction in the number of sisters meant that there was only Antoine available to marry the French Dauphin. She was twelve; he was fourteen. Portraits were exchanged and she was restyled Marie Antoinette. She was taken as far as the Rhine and handed over to her French retinue, who conveyed her to Versailles to meet Louis XV and Louis Auguste, her new husband. On the way she met her new brothers-in-law, the Comte de Provence and the Comte d'Artois. The wedding took place on 16 May 1770, and the couple went to bed together afterwards, but the palace gossip was that they had not had sex. The non-consummation of the marriage was a major problem to them – it turned out that the sixteen-year-old Louis just did not know

what to do – and it severely damaged their reputation through the
eight years.

Initially, Marie Antoinette made a favourable impression in Paris
was attractive in appearance and charming in manner. There were
'Princess Diana' moments, when she performed unexpected ac
charity, personally attending a dying man and arranging for his fa
to be looked after financially, and on another occasion picking
homeless boy and finding him somewhere to live. To begin with
was more popular with the French people than with the court, w
long-standing tensions between France and Austria were still rem
bered. Some old courtiers contemptuously called her 'the Aus
woman'. As the hated grew, the French word 'Autrichienne'
mutated, and Marie Antoinette rather tactlessly asked the mistres
her household who 'that woman', a certain imposing great lady,
She was told, 'That woman is here to give pleasure to the King.'
woman was Madame Du Barry, the mistress of Louis XV. Undaun
Antoinette commented, 'Well, I am also here to give pleasure to
King.' There was quite a lot of smoothing over to be done befor
partial reconciliation could be achieved. Antoinette managed thro
gritted teeth to say to Madame Du Barry, 'There are a lot of peopl
Versailles today.' Du Barry heard in this an apology of sorts and
satisfied, and so was the King. Versailles was a minefield for a hi
profile incomer like Marie Antoinette.

Antoinette was also being badgered by streams of letters from
dominating mother, who was scrutinising and criticising her behavi
from afar. Her mother constantly criticised her for losing her looks and
her failure to 'inspire passion' in her husband. The absence of sex in
marriage was still the talk of court circles. Louis did not sleep with her a
showed no interest in doing so. He was more interested in his hobbi
such as lock-making. Marie Antoinette began to look for diversio
clothes, shopping trips, gambling on cards and horses. The later image
the extravagant pleasure-loving queen was in its formative stage. She w
expected by everyone at court to outshine all the other ladies there, to
the queen of fashion; that was not really a matter of personal choice f

her. She made friends with various women at court, and with the composer Gluck. The first performance of Gluck's opera Iphigenia in Aulis showed Antoinette emerging as a major patroness of the arts.

Then, six days after sending Du Barry away from Versailles, Louis XV died of smallpox. On 11 June 1775 Louis Auguste was crowned King Louis XVI; Marie Antoinette accompanied him, but was not crowned.

Marie Antoinette was later accused in slanderous publications of a range of improprieties, including lesbian affairs with her lady friends at court and meddling in state affairs. She clearly had no influence over politics. Her husband Louis in fact went out of his way to block candidates whom she supported; he was strongly influenced by his anti-Austrian upbringing and ready to override any pro-Austrian influence his wife might wish to introduce. He was supported in this by his Chief Minister Maurepas and his Foreign Minister Vergennes, both of whom were anti-Austrian and well aware of the potential dangers of allowing the Queen any say in policy.

So Marie Antoinette was already in these early years seen as a potential problem by her husband as well as his principal ministers. Her situation was made more precarious when her sister-in-law gave birth to a son, the Duc d'Angouleme, who became heir presumptive after his father and uncles. The failure of Louis to consummate the marriage was now having an effect on the succession. Satirical pamphlets appeared, making fun of the King's impotence and the Queen's (imagined) quest for sexual relief elsewhere.

Marie Antoinette's escape from these pressures was to hurl herself with abandon into her gambling and dress-buying. On one occasion she played with Parisian card players for three days solidly. She was given the Petit Trianon by her husband, which she was free to renovate; she concentrated on redesigning the garden in English style. The Petit Trianon was built by Louis XV, but it became associated (unfairly) with Marie Antoinette's extravagances.

In 1777 Emperor Joseph arrived with the aim of finding out why the marriage had not been consummated. The Emperor talked frankly to Louis, and got frank enough answers. It turned out that Louis was not

impotent; he simply did not know what to do with his erection. The Emperor told him in forthright terms what to do, and from that time on there was no problem. Marie Antoinette became pregnant almost straight away.

Marie Therese Charlotte, or Madame Royale, was born in December 1778. This happy event was marred by the Comte de Provence, who claimed that the King could not be the father of the child. The Comte was always open about his wish to replace his brother on the throne; this was another way of trying to discredit him. In 1781, the Queen gave birth to a boy, Louis, who took the title Duc de Bretagne. This was a great delight and relief to Louis, who amused himself by practising remarks that he could make that would include the phrase 'my son the Dauphin'.

Louis continued to exclude his wife from any conversation about politics, because of his entrenched anti-Austrian position. She felt embarrassed about her ignorance and found herself pretending to his ministers to know more than she did. By pretending to have Louis' full confidence she was able to get the information she wanted. The effect of this, though, was to make her courtiers believe she was deeply involved in political decision-making when she wasn't.

Distressed by a miscarriage, Marie Antoinette occupied herself with the building of a model village at the Petit Trianon – a mill and twelve cottages. This was used against her by her critics, who exaggerated the cost. In fact other French aristocrats had built much larger and grander model villages. She was intrigued by Rousseau's philosophy of a return to nature and tried to escape from the artificiality of life at Versailles by trying to lead a simple life at her village. This too was used against her; her critics said she was mocking the poor. Allegations about the Queen's extravagance were becoming a French obsession. She bought the Chateau de Saint-Cloud, a mansion she had always loved, with a view to leaving it as a legacy to her children. This too was interpreted as extravagance and it made her very unpopular, particularly at a time when the country was deeply in debt. There was a cultural objection too, as the people of France thought it inappropriate for the Queen to own property independently of her husband.

In 1785, Marie Antoinette had a second son, Louis Charles, the Duc de Normandie, and a year later a second daughter.

As France's financial situation worsened, so did the reputation of Marie Antoinette. Perhaps if Louis XVI had discussed political and economic affairs with his wife, she might have seen some of the implications of her actions. As it was, she was frustrated, bored, ignorant and almost bound to make mistakes. The situation was a tragedy in the making, and they would both pay the price in ten short years. Louis began to show signs of strain as the country's financial plight worsened. He became depressed. He tried to distance himself from politics. At this moment, his wife decided to involve herself, acting as a mediator with the King. But her appearance as a political figure at this moment was disastrous. She was seen by the public generally as single-handedly ruined France – Madame Déficit.

By 1787, France was spiralling out of control. In desperation, the King announced that he wanted to recall the Estates General, the traditional elected legislature of France, which had not been called since 1614. The ailing Dauphin died of tuberculosis in June 1789, but the event was ignored by the people of France, now gripped by the onset of revolution. At the Estates General, the Third Estate declared itself a National Assembly – the first phase of the French Revolution – while the Queen went into mourning for her much-loved son.

The King and Queen and their family were forced to move to Paris, though they were not yet under arrest. Marie Antoinette told her friends she would do nothing more in politics, as she would only be blamed for the outcome. When the French Constitution was drafted in 1791, which greatly reduced Louis' authority, she kept scrupulously clear of it. Now it was her husband's turn to make a huge political gaffe. He committed himself to a plan to escape in disguise. Marie Antoinette's objection to it was not that the whole idea was foolish and dangerous, only that it allowed her to escape only with her surviving son. Louis was forced to reconsider his plan, and wasted a lot of time deciding which family members could go. When the escape attempt was made, on 21 June 1791, it was a disaster. The whole family was stopped at Varennes and taken back to Paris. From that moment, Louis and Marie Antoinette were doomed. They had shown that they were not to be trusted. The Queen hoped that Austria might mount some kind of military rescue, but that is exactly what the French people hated about Marie Antoinette – that she was a foreigner and had loyalties and dangerous friends and allies elsewhere.

They were deposed, imprisoned, given show trials, and then beheaded. Louis was executed first, on 21 January 1793, and it was not until October that Marie Antoinette followed. In those few months she was in deep mourning, refusing to eat properly or exercise. Her health deteriorated markedly. She was probably suffering from both uterine cancer and tuberculosis, and would not in any case have lived very much longer.

NAPOLEON BONAPARTE AND JOSÉPHINE DE BEAUHARNAIS

(1795)

NAPOLEON'S EMPRESS JOSÉPHINE (1763-1814) was born with an entirely different but equally impressive name: Marie Joséphe Rose de Tascher de la Pagerie. Rose, as she was known until she was thirty-two years old, grew up in a white Creole family which owned a sugar plantation on Martinique. In 1766, a hurricane destroyed the plantation and the family's fortunes were in peril. Rose's aunt Edmée had been the mistress of a French aristocrat, François, Vicomte de Beauharnais. Edmée was able to use this contact to negotiate a marriage between her niece Catherine and François' son Alexandre. This would have been a very advantageous marriage as far as the Tascher family was concerned. Unfortunately Catherine died in 1777, before she even left Martinique. To ensure that de Beauharnais money still came into the Tascher family, Rose was substituted.

In 1779 Rose went to France accompanied by her father and was duly married to Alexandre. The marriage was not a happy one, though it produced two children, Eugene and Hortense; the latter married Napoleon's brother Louis in 1802. In 1794, at the height of the Reign of Terror, Alexandre was arrested and imprisoned. The Committee of Public Safety ordered Rose's arrest too. A great many aristocrats were being rounded up and guillotined, so Rose, with her vicomtesse title was in great danger of losing her head. The vicomte himself was guillotined in July 1794 along with his brother Augustin. Five days afterwards, Rose was released, thanks to the timely death of Robespierre, and the following year she was able to recover Alexandre's possessions.

After that, Rose de Beauharnais became the mistress of several leading political figures, including Barras. She met Napoleon Bonaparte, then a general and six years younger than herself, in 1795. A full-scale romance began. It has been suggested that Barras may have fostered this relationship as Rose's extravagant spending habits were becoming a liability. But Napoleon seems to have needed no encouragement. Her hair was silky and dark chestnut in colour; her voice was low, silvery and beautifully modulated. They were married in March 1796 and Napoleon went off only two days later to lead the campaign in Italy. Napoleon's passionate infatuation with his new wife is evident from his letters. Here is one that he wrote to her on 3 April 1796, just a month after they were married.

I have received all your letters, but none has made such an impression on me as the last. My beloved, how can you write to me like that? Don't you think my position is cruel enough without adding to my sorrows and crushing my spirit? What a way to write! What feelings you show! They are fire, and they burn my poor heart.

My one and only Josephine, apart from you there is no joy; away from you, the world is a desert where I am alone and cannot open my heart. You have taken more than my soul; you are the one thought of my life. . .

By what art have you captivated all my faculties and concentrated my whole being in you? . . . How long before you will read these words, this feeble expression of a captive soul where you are queen?

Oh, my adorable wife! I don't know what fate has in store for me, but if it keeps me apart from you any longer, it will be unbearable! My courage is not enough for that.

Once I was proud of my courage, and sometimes I would think of the evil that destiny might bring me and consider the most terrible horrors without blinking or feeling shaken. But, today the thought that my Josephine might be in trouble, that she might be ill - above all the cruel, awful thought that she may love me less - blights my soul, stills my blood and makes me sad and depressed, without even the courage of rage and despair. To die not loved by you, to die without knowing, would be the torment of Hell, utter desolation. I feel I am suffocating.

My only companion, you whom fate has destined to travel the sad road of life beside me, the day I lose your heart will be the day Nature loses warmth and life for me. I must cease, sweet friend; my soul is sad, my body tired, my spirit oppressed.

I am at Port Maurice, near Ognelia; tomorrow I reach Albenga. The two armies are moving, trying to outwit each other. Victory to the cleverer! I am pleased with Beaulieu; he manoeuvres well and is stronger than his predecessor. I will beat him soundly, I hope.

Don't be frightened. Love me as you love your eyes; but no, that is not enough: love me as you love yourself, more than yourself, than your thoughts, your life, all of you.

Forgive me, dear love, I am raving; Nature is frail when one feels deeply, when one is loved by you.

Bonaparte

Sincere friendship to Barras, Sucy, Madame Tallien; respects to Madame Chateau-Renard; true love to Eugene, to Hortense. Goodbye, goodbye! I shall go to bed without you, sleep without you. Let me sleep, I beg you. For several nights I have felt you in my arms; a happy dream, but it is not you.   *B.*

The one thing that Napoleon disliked about Rose was her name. He took one of her other forenames, Joseph, and gave it a feminine ending; 'Joséphine' was really Napoleon's pet name for his wife, just as the explorer Colonel Fawcett called his wife 'Cheeky', but she adopted it as her proper name from then on. Napoleon sent her a stream of passionate letters, but this did not stop Joséphine launching straight into a new affair in his absence, with a handsome lieutenant, Hippolyte Charles. Napoleon inevitably heard about it and was furious. One effect of this betrayal was to make Napoleon retaliate and launch into a string of affairs of his own. On the Egyptian campaign of 1798, he began an affair with Pauline Bellisle Foures, a junior officer's wife. Because of the location, she became known as Napoleon's Cleopatra.

After this, Napoleon's letters to his wife were less affectionate, less passionate. He took on mistress after mistress.

Napoleon was crowned Emperor in Notre Dame Cathedral in Paris. Just beforehand, there was a scene at the Chateau de Saint-Cloud which nearly ended the marriage. Napoleon was in the bedroom of her lady-in-waiting, Elisabeth de Vaudey. Joséphine caught him there. Seeing attack as the best form of defence, Napoleon threatened her with divorce as she had failed to produce an heir. Joséphine was infertile, could never produce children. It is not known precisely why, but it may have been that the stress of imprisonment and the fear of impending execution during the Terror precipitated an early menopause – or it may have been connected with her fall from a collapsing balcony in 1798. The situation was tense, but there was a reconciliation and Joséphine went through the coronation ceremony with Napoleon in 1804; they became Emperor and Empress of the French. But when it became clear that she could never have a child, she agreed to a divorce. Napoleon needed an heir. He did not just want to be an emperor, like Augustus he wanted to found a dynasty. To do that he needed to divorce Joséphine and remarry.

Joséphine and Napoleon were divorced on 10 January 1810. Three months later, on 1 April, Napoleon married Marie Louise of Austria. They had one child, Napoleon II, who was born in 1811. Following her divorce, Joséphine lived at the Chateau de Malmaison outside Paris. She and Napoleon remained friends. He once said about her that the only thing that came between them was her debts. She died in 1814 and was buried at the Church of St Peter and St Paul in Rueil. In 1815, after his disastrous defeat at Waterloo and his voyage into exile, Napoleon was able to reflect on his past life; he reminisced to a friend about Joséphine, 'I truly loved my Joséphine, but I did not respect her.' And it seems that when he lay dying on St Helena her name was the last word he spoke.

JOHN KEATS AND FANNY BRAWNE

(1818)

LIKE DANTE, THE English Romantic poet John Keats had a female muse, a love that inspired and fuelled his poetry. The difference with Keats was that this was not a courtly love but a full-blooded romantic love affair. Whether it was consummated is uncertain, but there are hints that it was. Keats had already had a 'Dante moment' when he fleetingly met a woman in Hastings. She was beautiful, fashionable, striking. Over a year later he passed her in the street in Holborn. On impulse he turned back and introduced himself, asking if he might walk her home. His boldness was rewarded when she led him to a large panelled apartment in Bloomsbury. The lady was Isabella Jones. She was intelligent and a great talker. She knew Taylor, Keats' publisher. When the moment came to leave, Keats wondered if he might kiss her. He hesitated, she read his mind and said, 'You would please me much more if you would only press my hand and then go away.' He went, wondering whether he had fallen in love with Isabella. But then he met Fanny.

Keats first met Fanny Brawne in November 1818, probably when they were both visiting the Dilkes' house, Wentworth Place in Hampstead, at a time when Keats was distracted by his anxiety over his brother Tom's health. Tom was dying of tuberculosis. The Keats brothers were then living in Hampstead; so were Mrs Brawne, her eighteen-year-old daughter Fanny and two younger children, Sam and Margaret – they lived at Elm Cottage at the top of Downshire Hill. Keats made an impression on Fanny. 'His conversation was in the highest degree interesting and his spirits good, excepting at moments when anxiety regarding his brother's health dejected them.' He seems not to have mentioned the meeting to anyone in letters at that time, but he was emotionally stirred. The *Bright Star* sonnet he was moved to write at that moment seems to have something to do with her.

During that November an intimacy sprang up between the two of them. As with many such encounters, the opening manoeuvres were fitful and patchy. Fanny later reproached Keats for having taken 'an age' to show his feelings. Like many a young man overwhelmed by love, he was terrified of frightening Fanny off by declaring himself too strongly too early. The closeness of his brother's death meant that he was unlikely to play about with flirtation and love-games. Fanny was younger and not menaced by death; she had time to flirt, or so she then believed. Keats often saw her in the company of his artist friend Joseph Severn, and Fanny went out of her way to flirt with Severn, who was not her real target at all. This was another common game – then as now - to tease, test and flush out the real lover. Later she assured Keats, 'You must be satisfied in knowing I admired you much more than your friend'.

On 18 November John Keats's brother Tom was nineteen. On 1 December Tom died. Keats's friends saw that he was close to nervous collapse and they resorted to a hearty Regency remedy. They took him on a whirl of social engagements, visiting friends, watching a bare-fist boxing match, going to the theatre to see Edmund Kean acting in a new tragedy. It seemed to work. Soon he was back visiting Fanny at her family's house. He described her to his friends as 'small, delicate-featured, lively, unsentimental, with good figure and movements'. He was fascinated by the fact that her personality was in the process of formation, and she was the breath of fresh air and innocence that he desperately needed. 'She is not seventeen – but she is ignorant – monstrous in her behaviour, flying out in all directions, calling people such names – that I was forced lately to make use of the term Minx – this is I think not from any innate vice but from a penchant she has for acting stylishly.' He had in fact underestimated her age – she was eighteen, not sixteen – but that is an indication of her liveliness. She seemed very young.

In one way they were unsuited. Fanny read intelligently, but she was as she admitted 'not a great poetry reader'. But 'comedy of all sorts pleases me', and there she had something very important in common with her lover. Keats had a strong sense of humour.

After Tom's death, Keats became a more or less permanent house-guest at Wentworth Place; Mrs Dilke was kind and understanding. When a visit to Chichester was being arranged for January 1819, she prepared her parents-in-law for a young London poet: 'You will find him a very odd young man, but good-tempered and very clever indeed.' Mrs Dilke in effect gave him a home with a substitute family life. But he also spent a lot of time that winter at Mrs Brawne's house. Keats thought Mrs Brawne a very nice woman, and he spent Christmas Day 1818, 'the happiest day', with the Brawne family.

Then he set off with his friend Brown on an expedition to Sussex. In Chichester he walked around the wintry cathedral cloisters and picked up some background for his poem *The Eve of St Agnes*. When he returned to Hampstead, he was irritated to find the Dilkes full of talk about their spoilt son Charley. Mr Dilkes decided that Charley must go to Westminster School, and that they therefore had to move to Westminster. Off went the Dilkes, letting their part of the house to Mrs Brawne and her family. Then it must have seemed as though fate was throwing Keats and Fanny together. He saw Fanny every day then, or heard her voice, singing 'singularly sweetly' through the wall.

One day, while walking on the heath he met the poet Coleridge, a legendary talker, and had a long conversation with him about a huge range of subjects. Once Coleridge was started, he seized his listener by a coat button (like his own *Ancient Mariner*) and went on oblivious of his surroundings; Charles Lamb claimed that once when caught like this he had cut off his coat button and made his escape without Coleridge noticing. It was around this time that he heard the nightingale among the woods on the heath and wrote his *Ode to the Nightingale*. His happiness with Fanny was unleashing a tide of great poems. But Keats's lodgings were shared. He was now in effect dependent on Brown for accommodation. Brown decided, like many other Hampstead residents, that he was going to let his part of Wentworth Place for the summer months, so Keats, the paying guest, would have to find somewhere else to live for the summer. He decided to establish himself as a poet by writing another book. He would do it while on a modest holiday. He would go to Shanklin on the Isle of Wight and take lodgings with his friend Rice.

In June 1819 Keats wrote to Fanny from Shanklin, but he realised the first letter was too passionate to send and he had to send another. That drew a teasing reply from Fanny, who told him he was dwelling too much on her physical attractions. He wrote back earnestly insisting that her beauty was central as far as he was concerned; 'I cannot conceive any beginning of such love as I have for you but Beauty.' It was a genuine and deep-seated belief that he had already expressed in his most famous line, 'A thing of beauty is a joy for ever.' The long-distance love affair was putting him under pressure, but he was getting reassurance from Fanny that her feelings for him were strong too. She sent him a copy of Dante's *Inferno* into which she had copied in her own hand his *Bright Star* sonnet; she obviously understood that it was all about her, and accepted that their relationship was strongly sexual.

> *. . . Pillow'd upon my fair Love's ripening breast*
> *To feel for ever its soft fall and swell,*
> *Awake for ever in a sweet unrest;*
> *Still, still to hear her tender-taken breath,*
> *And so live ever,– or else swoon to death.*

A new problem was that Keats sensed that he was doomed to die like his brother Tom, and that he had not long to live. Could he, under these circumstances, propose marriage? So the understanding he had with Fanny did not amount to a formal engagement. And because they were not engaged, Fanny was free while he was away to enjoy the company of other young men. She teased him with an account of a dance she had been to at the Royal Artillery Mess at Woolwich, and it made Keats furious with indignation and jealousy. But all of this – the sexual attraction, the sexual frustration – was fuelling his poetry, and what magnificent poetry Keats wrote in his final year. Some of the poems were indirectly inspired by her, others were directly addressed to her.

The most moving poem of all is the sonnet *When I have fears*;

> *When I have fears that I may cease to be*
> *Before my pen has glean'd my teeming brain,*
> *Before high-piled books, in charact'ry,*
> *Hold like rich garners the full-ripen'd grain;*
> *When I behold upon the night's starr'd face*
> *Huge cloudy symbols of a high romance,*
> *And feel that I may never live to trace*
> *Their shadows, with the magic hand of chance;*
> *And when I feel, fair creature of an hour!*
> *That I shall never look upon thee more,*
> *Never have relish in the faery power*
> *Of unreflecting love; - then on the shore*
> *Of the wide world I stand alone, and think,*
> *Till Love and Fame to nothingness do sink.*

Fanny, of course, was the fair creature of an hour.

In October 1820, Keats stayed at Wentworth Place for three days, in the house next door to Fanny, who was chaperoned by her watchful mother. Keats was dizzy with happiness to be so close to her. Finally there was a decision on a formal engagement, and Keats gave Fanny a garnet ring. She did not wear it, as the engagement was to be semi-secret. One of Keats's friends wrote, 'It is quite a settled thing between John Keats and Miss Brawne. God help them. It's a bad thing for them. The mother says she cannot prevent it and that her only hope is that it will go off.'

In the end, the only hope left for a cure for Keats was to go to Italy. Friends spoke optimistically to try to make the leave-taking less painful. Only Fanny, who had nursed him while he was ill, knew and seemed ready to face up to the truth. She was unsentimental, as Keats himself said. She said to her mother, 'I believe he must soon die. When you hear of his death, tell me immediately. I am not a fool!' With Keats' sister, also called Fanny, she took the same line, trying to prepare her too for the worst: 'I shall never see him again.'

Keats took lodgings by the Spanish Steps in Rome, and was nursed through his final weeks by Severn. He lay on his bed looking up at a high raftered ceiling and listening to the sound of the fountain outside. In his fever he clutched in his hands a big white cornelian stone, restlessly handling it, never putting it down. Severn commented that it seemed his only consolation; he had been given it by Fanny.

When the news did come to Hampstead, three weeks afterwards, that Keats had died on 23 February 1821, Fanny was overwhelmed with grief. She had loved Keats as much as he loved her. Her rich brown hair seemed to fade. She wore widow's weeds, which may be taken as an indication that she regarded herself as Keats' wife. She took to walking late at night across Hampstead Heath. She went for a month's stay with Mrs Dilke at Westminster, and there was an expectation among her friends that she would quickly recover. They had, after all, thought her relationship with Keats was no more than a passing flirtation. But she insisted, 'I have not got over it and never shall.'

Fanny Brawne went on wearing black in Keats' memory. She and Keats's sister became firm friends. Then, in 1833, Fanny Keats married a young Spaniard who had seen Keats three days before he died; they married, left for Spain and never returned. Just a few months later, Fanny Brawne also married. She married a Sephardic Jew eleven years younger than herself. His name was Louis Lindo, though he changed it to Lindon. She died as Mrs Lindon in 1865.

Long after John Keats had died and entered literary legend, Fanny Brawne was asked what she thought of his state of mind in that last year. It was put to her that he 'might be judged insane'. Fanny's answer was revealing.

That his sensibility was most acute, is true, and his passions were very strong, but not violent, if by that term violence of temper is implied. His anger seemed rather to turn on himself . . . only by a sort of savage despondency he sometimes grieved and wounded his friends. Violence was quite foreign to his nature. For more than a twelvemonth before quitting England, I saw him every day, often witnessed his sufferings both mental and bodily. . . He never addressed an unkind expression to any human being.

We know what Fanny Brawne looked like, thanks to an early photograph taken of her in the 1850s, which came to light in 1979. This is the only known photographic likeness of Fanny Brawne. By the time it was taken she was a middle-aged woman, married to someone else. But her face has an extraordinary soulful beauty, and she looks exactly as Keats described her, 'Beautiful and elegant, graceful, fashionable and strange.' She does indeed look exotic, almost Spanish. With her hand delicately touching her chin, she seems lost in a profoundly sad reverie and her large dark eyes gaze into the distance, remembering. Perhaps the most striking thing of all, though, and it is something that has never been commented on before, is that she has the face of – John Keats. Is that, perhaps, why Keats found her so irresistible? Did he see himself in Fanny Brawne?

QUEEN VICTORIA AND PRINCE ALBERT

(1840)

QUEEN VICTORIA'S ACCESSION to the throne of England in 1837 was surrounded by difficulties. She was only eighteen years old, and she had had a very secluded and oppressive upbringing. Her father, the Duke of Kent, was the fourth son of George III, which was how Victoria came into the line of succession. He died when Victoria was less than a year old, so she never knew him. She was brought up by her mother, the German-born Duchess of Kent, and the duchess's lover, Sir John Conroy, who treated Victoria as if he was her father.

When William IV came to the throne in 1830, Victoria became the Heir Apparent because the king had no surviving legitimate children. William IV was well aware of the strange dynamics of the young princess's household – she was more or less held captive by her mother and Conroy – and he feared that when on his own death Victoria became queen Conroy would have too much power. He feared that Conroy would act as if he was an unofficial regent, especially if Victoria became queen before her eighteenth birthday.

William managed to stay alive just long enough for Victoria to reach that birthday: he died twenty-seven days later. He need not have worried about Victoria. She had kept her thoughts to herself, but she detested Sir John Conroy, and one of the first things she did when she became queen was to banish him from her court. She also shook off her mother's oppressive controlling influence. From the moment of her accession, she insisted on seeing her ministers alone, without her mother; she made a point of emphasising this in her diary.

Having lost her father virtually at birth, then banished her surrogate father and side-lined her mother, the young Queen might have been alone. But she was rescued. Repeatedly in her life, Victoria was rescued by knights in shining armour, and Lord Melbourne was the first of them. It was, for the young queen, a very lucky chance that Melbourne was prime minister at the time of her accession. Melbourne was fifty-eight years old, a widower, and his only child had died. He took to the young queen as if she were a favourite niece, and she to him as if he were her uncle. She became dependent on him for advice and became very fond of him; 'He is such an honest, good, kind-hearted man and is my friend, I know it . . . Such stories of knowledge; such a wonderful memory; he knows about everybody and everything. He has such a kind and agreeable manner.'

Victoria gave Melbourne a suite at Windsor Castle, so that he could easily spend time with her. Some said he spent as much as six hours a day with the queen, and this gave rise to malicious gossip. What was the young, single queen doing, spending so much time with an old widower? The editor of *The Times* wrote, 'Is it becoming? Is it commonly decent?' People in the streets derisively called out 'Mrs Melbourne!' as she passed. There was even speculation that she would marry Melbourne.

But within two years, Melbourne's intimacy seemed to have come to an abrupt end. He was defeated in the House of Commons and resigned. The Tory Sir Robert Peel became prime minister. By tradition the ladies of the Queen's bedchamber were of the same party as the prime minister of the day. Sir Robert accordingly asked the queen to replace her Whig ladies with Tory ladies. The queen refused, and Peel resigned, allowing Melbourne to return to office.

But Melbourne was really a father-figure, not a husband-to-be. In 1839 her first cousin Prince Albert of Saxe-Coburg paid a visit to London. Victoria fell in love instantly. Prince Albert had initial reservations, but these were overcome and the couple were married in February 1840 at St James's Palace in London.

One result of this marriage was the production of nine children. This proliferation of royals had significant dynastic implications all over

Europe, as they married into other royal families. Another result was the replacement of Lord Melbourne's political influence by Prince Albert's. Lord Melbourne did his best to shelter Victoria from the harsh realities of poverty in Britain, even advising her not to read *Oliver Twist*. He did not want her to think about social problems. Prince Albert took the opposite view, that his wife had a duty to learn about what was going on in her country. He even invited the social reformer Lord Ashley to Buckingham Palace to tell them about child labour. It was Prince Albert who stirred Victoria's social conscience and in that way contributed incalculably to her popularity. When the Irish potato famine struck in the 1840s, Queen Victoria gave £2,000 of her own money, a huge sum in those days, to the starving poor in Ireland.

Prince Albert trod a careful path, taking on duties that would not encroach on his wife's authority as the ruling monarch. It was a difficult task, but he showed that it was possible for a husband to hold the title and play the part of Prince Consort to a reigning queen, a model that Prince Philip has ably imitated. Perhaps Albert's greatest contribution as an administrator was his leading role in organising the Great Exhibition of 1851.

In December 1861 Prince Albert died of typhoid. Victoria was grief-stricken – almost theatrically so. She went on carrying out her constitutional duties, reading all the diplomatic papers that were presented to her, but she made a complete withdrawal from public life and wore black until her life ended in 1901. She declined to open Parliament and retreated to Osborne House, Windsor Castle and Balmoral. She even withdrew from England, as she spent increasing amounts of time at Balmoral. The political fall-out from this extravagant display of grief was severe. Queen Victoria's popularity declined; she acquired the nickname 'the Widow of Windsor'. Politicians began to question whether the queen was earning her Civil List allowance.

It was during this extended period of mourning, dragging on for many years, that Queen Victoria fell in love again. The precise nature of her relationship with John Brown has never been established, but she seems to have developed a deep emotional attachment to him that was as strong as her attachment to Albert. Brown was a Scot, a servant at Balmoral. Just as with Melbourne, rumours began to circulate that the queen was on the brink of marrying. Some even believed that the queen and her servant had secretly married. This new scandal caused Victoria's popularity to sink even lower. There were now some MPs who spoke in favour of abolishing the monarchy.

Later, Victoria developed a strong affection for her prime minister Benjamin Disraeli. He was charming and swamped her with flattery. When Disraeli died in 1881, the queen wrote to his secretary to say that she was devastated by the news and could not stop crying.

There is no doubting the sincerity or the depth of Victoria's feelings. She was an intensely emotional woman who reacted very strongly to the men in her life. She could not get on with Lord Palmerston and William Gladstone at all. She detested Sir John Conroy. She liked Lord Melbourne and Disraeli; and she loved Prince Albert and John Brown. When Queen Victoria was buried, she requested that two sets of mementoes were to be placed with her. One was a dressing gown belonging to Albert; the other consisted of a lock of John Brown's hair together with a picture of Brown. And on her finger, the dead queen wears a wedding ring that had belonged to John Brown's mother. This recent discovery has revived rumours that Queen Victoria did secretly marry Brown.

ROBERT BROWNING AND ELIZABETH BARRETT

(1845)

ELIZABETH BARRETT WAS born in 1806 at Coxhoe Hall in County Durham. Three years later, her father, who had made a fortune from sugar plantations in Jamaica, bought a 500-acre estate near the Malverns. Elizabeth was the eldest of twelve children and educated at home by her brother's tutor; she was well-educated by the standards of the time. Her earliest surviving poem was written when she was about seven. When she was fourteen she wrote a long Homeric poem called *The Battle of Marathon*, which her father paid to have printed.

She learned languages and in her teens she was reading Greek and Latin authors and Dante's *Inferno* – all in their original languages. But writing poetry was her main interest. In 1826, when she was twenty, she published her first collection of poetry, with the solemn title *An Essay on Mind and Other Poems*. The appearance of this book attracted the attention of a blind scholar of Greek, Hugh Stuart Boyd, and another Greek scholar called Uvedale Price. They wrote letters to her and this started a correspondence. Boyd suggested that she should translate *Prometheus Bound* by Aeschylus, which she did. *Prometheus* was published in 1833, and she had another go at it in 1850. The correspondence led to Elizabeth Barrett exploring a huge amount of ancient Greek literature, from Homer to Aristophanes. But her enthusiasm for this – and for Boyd – faded. By 1822, her interests were more in scholarship and poetry.

There was a clash of interests within the Barrett family. The family's wealth was made on the back of slave labour in the plantations, while

191

Elizabeth supported the abolition of slavery. As the effects of the abolition of slavery were gradually felt in the mid-1830s, Mr Barrett's income was reduced. In fact his losses forced him to sell Hope End, the estate near the Malvern Hills, and move to a smaller property. The family ended up in the late 1830s at 50 Wimpole Street in London.

After this move to London, Elizabeth Barrett continued writing and sending her poems to various periodicals for publication. She was also exchanging letters with other literary figures. She gained that certain notoriety that 'forward' women, women of talent, initiative and ambition, were inclined to gain in the 19th century. Her tyrannical father was a stereotypical Victorian patriarch and the emergence of a talented and independent-minded poetess in the household made for an uncomfortable atmosphere. Mr Barrett started shipping off Elizabeth's siblings to Jamaica to help on the family's plantations; he treated even his children like slaves. Elizabeth hated the dependence of the plantations on slavery, of which she disapproved, and in any case did not want to lose her siblings. There was a great deal of tension in the house.

In 1838, she published *The Seraphim*, the first volume to carry her own name. Her health was a major problem, and now it prompted a move to the seaside. She went to Torquay with her favourite brother Edward, whom she called 'Bro'. Edward was drowned in a sailing accident at Torquay in 1840, and this trauma had a profound effect on her weak constitution. She went back to London an emotional and physical wreck and she became a reclusive invalid. She spent most of her time for the next five years shut in her bedroom in Wimpole Street, seeing only her immediate family and one or two other people.

After that she regained her strength, while her fame as a poet also steadily increased. In 1843 *The Cry of the Children* was published and the following year two volumes of poems which included *A Vision of Poets* and *Lady Geraldine's Courtship*. The volume of Poems published in 1844 made a huge impression; she was now one of the most popular writers in England. She received an unexpected fan letter from another prominent poet of the day, Robert Browning.

Browning came from a very different background. Born in

Camberwell in 1812, he was the son of bank clerk and a pianist. But his father was no ordinary bank clerk: he was a scholar, an antiquarian and a collector of books. In fact he owned over six thousand books in a variety of languages. A great deal of Robert Browning's education came from his unusually well-read father. Browning was bright, eager, anxious to learn. In 1825, when he was thirteen, he developed a craze for the poet Shelley, who had died in a mysterious boating accident in the Mediterranean just three years earlier. He decided he was a vegetarian and an atheist – just like Shelley. Rather surprisingly, this teenage infatuation with Shelley did not lead him to write any poetry; he did not start writing poetry until he reached the age of twenty. Browning published his first important piece, *Pauline*, in 1833. He tried to write drama. His play *Strafford* ran for five nights in 1837.

While Elizabeth was confined to her room in Wimpole Street, one of the few outsiders she saw was John Kenyon, who was sociable and interested in the arts. Kenyon acquired a copy of Elizabeth's brand-new *Poems* and gave it to Robert Browning's family. When Browning himself returned from a trip to Italy, he picked up the book and read it. He dashed off a letter to Elizabeth on 10 January 1845. 'I love your verses with all my heart, dear Miss Barrett . . . I do, as I say, love these books with all my heart – and I love you too: do you know I was once not very far from seeing – really seeing you? Mr Kenyon said to me one morning, "Would you like to see Miss Barrett?" – then he went to announce me – then he returned – you were too unwell.' But Mr Kenyon the matchmaker was as good as his word and he arranged for Robert Browning to meet Elizabeth in her sick room on 20 May.

This meeting in May was the beginning of one of the most famous courtships in the history of literature, though it is interesting that Browning had decided that he loved her four months before he even set eyes on her. What sort of person was this Elizabeth Barrett? She was noble and charming. As a young woman she was slight and delicate, with a cascade of dark curls falling down on each side of her expressive face; she had big sensitive eyes and her smile was described as 'like a sunbeam'. It was not surprising that Robert Browning fell in love with her, though one of her friends euphemistically described her mouth as 'over-generous'. The family had lived for a long time in the West Indies and was part-Creole. This could account for Elizabeth's unusual facial features, including her dark complexion. Both Elizabeth and Robert were career writers and they wrote an extraordinary volume of words to each other; they wrote 574 letters to each other in the course of just one-and-a-half years. She kept his letters in a collapsible binder. He kept hers in an inlaid box.

Elizabeth's father, Mr Barrett, was bitterly opposed to the courtship. He produced objections to the marriage of any of his children, and Elizabeth and Robert knew from the start that he would disapprove of both their courtship and their marriage. As a result their courtship was conducted as far as possible in secret. Another (perceived) problem was her age: she was six years older than Robert. A greater problem was her delicate health. Elizabeth could not believe that Robert could possibly be serious in his protestations of affection for her: she was old, a hermit and an invalid, while he was young, worldly, healthy and vigorous. She expressed her doubts in a sequence of sonnets written over the next two years. But Browning was sincere, and they were married at St Marylebone parish church: she was then forty and he was thirty-four. After the wedding, they eloped, to get away from the furious Barrett. Browning whisked his new wife away to Italy (in August 1846), and she spent most of the rest of her life there. Elizabeth took her loyal nurse with her. Predictably, Elizabeth's father, whose full name was appropriately bombastic - Mr Edward Barrett Moulton Barrett – never spoke to her again and disinherited her. In fact, he disinherited all of his children who married, but Elizabeth had some money of her own, inherited from someone else, and the newly-married couple were fairly well-off.

The Brownings lived first in Pisa, then in Florence. Marriage and Italy suited Elizabeth Barrett Browning and her health improved accordingly. In 1849, when she was forty-three, she was able to give birth to a son, named Robert Wiedeman Barrett Browning but known as Pen. Robert published his *Collected Poems* in the same year. There is a photograph of Elizabeth with her son Pen in 1860. The boy has shoulder-length curly hair and is wearing an extraordinarily elaborate jacket with huge striped cuffs and calf-length white knickerbockers; he looks like Charles I. Pen in due course became an artist. He married but had no children, so the Brownings have no direct descendants.

When the time came for a second edition of her *Poems* to be published, Browning insisted that she include her love sonnets. These further added to her popularity and confirmed her position as the leading English poetess. When Wordsworth died in 1850, Elizabeth Barrett Browning's name was one of those considered for the position of Poet Laureate, but it was given to Tennyson instead.

The Browning family settled in Florence. Both Elizabeth and Robert sympathised with the Tuscan struggle for freedom, and this inspired Elizabeth to write *Casa Guidi Windows* (1851). There were other British ex-pats in Florence, including the poetesses Isabella Blagden and Theodosia Trollope, and Elizabeth became close friends with them. Elizabeth was the inspiration for Robert's collection of poems entitled *Men and Women* (1855), which was dedicated to her. It is considered to be one of his best works, but at the time he was almost totally eclipsed by his wife's reputation; when the book's author was mentioned, it was as the husband of Elizabeth Barrett. Browning had to be content to live for the time being in his wife's shadow.

In 1856, Elizabeth Barrett Browning published *Aurora Leigh*. This was her most ambitious long poem and one of the most popular, a semi-autobiographical tale of a woman writer making her way through life, balancing the twin needs of love and work and fighting male domination. Among her best known poems are *Sonnets from the Portuguese* (1850). 'Portuguese' was Robert's pet name for her, and ambiguously describing the poems as 'from the Portuguese' strongly implies that they are translations of someone else's sonnets. In fact they were her own poems, but she wanted to hide her personal life to some extent. As part of this clever and innocent deception, Elizabeth used rhyme schemes that were typical of genuine Portuguese sonnets. This is one of the best known collections of love lyrics in the English language, and is thought to be her finest work.

In 1860, Elizabeth Barrett Browning's health began to deteriorate.

She became gradually weaker and died in Florence on 29 June 1861. Exactly what was wrong with her is not known for certain. Her last illness may have been brought on by long-standing problems with her lungs, which began when she was fourteen. These were probably aggravated by the morphine which she took all her life. She also suffered a spinal injury at the age of fifteen, acquired while she was saddling a pony. But her early collapse looks as though it may have been a psychosomatic illness produced in response to her brother's death.

Elizabeth died in their bedroom at the Casa Guidi while Robert was attempting to feed her. Their clasped hands, both then and now a powerful symbol of their relationship, were sculpted by their American friend Harriet Hosmer six years earlier; now they were clasped in bronze for ever. Robert then cut off Pen's long flowing curls in readiness for their return to England and he commissioned an artist, George Mignaty, to paint a picture of the green salone at the Casa Guidi just as it was when Elizabeth was alive. The Florentines put a plaque on the house, saying that Elizabeth's verse was a golden ring, marrying England and Italy. Robert later used the compliment for the opening of his great work, *The Ring and the Book*.

After Elizabeth's death, Robert returned with Pen to London to live and never visited Italy again. Browning published Dramatis Personae in 1863. *The Ring and the Book,* published in 1868, was based on a seventeenth century murder trial and it earned Browning wide acclaim. At last he had moved out of Elizabeth's shadow and into the sun. In his later years, Browning became the grand old man of English letters, a respected and venerable figure with a snow-white beard. He was awarded honorary degrees by the Universities of Oxford and Edinburgh in 1882 and 1884. He also lived long enough to see The Browning Society founded in his honour in 1881. His final volume of poetry, *Asolando*, was published in 1889; he died on publication day.

The relationship between Elizabeth Barrett and Robert Browning was one of the greatest, happiest and most productive literary partnerships in history. The encounter between them in 1845 was turned into a stage play by Rudolf Besier in 1930, *The Barretts of Wimpole Street*. This in turn was made into a classic film four years later, with Norma Shearer as Elizabeth Barrett, Fredric March as Robert Browning and Charles Laughton as Edward Barrett Moulton Barrett. It was remade (in colour) in 1957, using the same screenplay, with Jennifer Jones as Elizabeth Barrett, Bill Travers as Robert Browning and John Gielgud as Mr Barrett.

OSCAR WILDE AND LORD ALFRED DOUGLAS

(1891)

OSCAR WILDE'S NOVEL *The Picture of Dorian Grey* was a huge success when it was first published in April 1891. No other novel had attracted so much attention for many years. The bookseller W. H. Smith refused to stock it on the grounds that it was 'filthy', but Wilde's circle of admiring young men loved it. One of his friends, Lionel Johnson, wrote Wilde a witty Latin poem in praise of it, then lent his copy from the author to his young cousin at Magdalen College, Oxford. The cousin was soon passionately absorbed in it, and claiming to his friends that he had read it fourteen times running. The undergraduate was keen to meet the famous author and got Johnson to introduce him at the earliest opportunity. That fateful meeting came in June 1891, when he went with Lionel Johnson to Wilde's place in Tite Street.

The young man was Lord Alfred Douglas, and this was his first encounter with Oscar Wilde. Lord Alfred was rather short, thin, very pale, with blond hair and no talent, but he was thought by his friends to be very charming. He was the youngest son of the Marquess of Queensberry. His temperament was, from Oscar Wilde's point of view, to prove disastrous. The youth was spoilt, reckless, insolent, and when he did not get his own way he was extremely vindictive. But Wilde only saw his beauty, and he was of course delighted by his praise of *Dorian Grey*. When Wilde heard that Lord Alfred was reading Classics at Oxford, he enthusiastically offered him coaching. But Wilde was a busy man, and he quickly turned to various writing tasks and the coaching never materialised.

Oscar Wilde wanted a consuming passion, and he seems to have applied this to Lord Alfred without much thought of where it would lead either of them. Lord Alfred later said that Wilde pursued him, but Wilde was not quite doing that. Their acquaintance was slight until early in 1892, when Douglas wrote to Wilde for help. Douglas it seems had sent an indiscreet letter and was being blackmailed over it. Wilde went to Oxford, and stayed in Douglas's rooms in the High Street while he listened to the young man's problem. He resolved it simply enough by putting his solicitor George Lewis onto it. Lewis's method in such cases was a simple one; he offered the blackmailer £100 for the document. But the mini-crisis, set up by Lord Alfred, was just what was needed to trigger a love affair.

Until this moment, Wilde had been most attracted to another young man, John Gray. Now Lord Alfred began to take his place. In June, Wilde gave Lord Alfred a copy of his *Poems*, which he inscribed, 'From Oscar/To the Gilt-mailed/Boy/at Oxford.' It was, given what had just happened, almost incredibly indiscreet of Wilde to write a dedication like that. But there was a recklessness about Wilde, almost a death-wish. He started talking and writing about Lord Alfred in a foppishly affectionate way that was bound to get him into trouble sooner rather than later. He wrote about him in the following terms in a letter to his friend Robert Ross:

My dearest Bobbie, Bosie [Lord Alfred Douglas] has insisted on stopping here for sandwiches. He is quite like a narcissus – so white and gold. I will come either Wednesday or Thursday night to your rooms. Send me a line. Bosie is so tired: he lies like a hyacinth on the sofa, and I worship him.
Your dear boy. Ever yours
Oscar.

It was silly stuff in itself, but sillier still when one knows that homosexuality could lead, through the courts, to a stiff prison sentence. And here was Wilde putting incriminating evidence on paper, for anyone to read and later produce against him.

Lord Alfred talked to his mother, Lady Queensberry, about the new friend. She was beside herself with worry about Bosie's difficulties at Oxford, where he was not coping with academic work, so in desperation she invited the Wildes out to her house at Bracknell. She hoped Oscar Wilde was going to be able to give her good advice about putting her son back on the rails. This visit, which had the makings of a scene from one of Wilde's plays, took place in October 1892. This was about the time when Wilde and Lord Alfred declared their love for each other. Douglas sent the first of a series of love poems to Wilde, *De Profundis,* which contains a teasing mixture of declaration and concealment, the sort of thing that Wilde's *Dorian Gray* had made popular. Not long after came Douglas's poem *The Two Loves.* This contained the notorious line, 'I am the love that dare not speak its name.' It would be held against them, and against Wilde in particular, in court. But Lord Alfred Douglas was far from coy and discreet. He was boasting about his conquest, and keen to flaunt his success with Wilde in front of other young men.

For a year from November 1892 until December 1893 the two men were inseparable. Wilde came to realise that Douglas could be un-manageable when crossed and almost mad when he lost his temper. Another quirk was financial dependency. He wanted to be loved, and the way Wilde was to show him that he loved him was to give him money. Lord Alfred had a difficult relationship with his even more unhinged father. When the Marquess of Queensberry threatened to cut off Lord Alfred's allowance in 1894, the young man egged him on, so that he could throw himself upon Wilde's flagging generosity.

Douglas became editor of an Oxford student magazine called the *Spirit Lamp,* and used this as a medium for the publication for more of the *De Profundis* type of poetry. His idea was to win acceptance for homosexuality. Now he was not just exchanging poems privately, but publishing them – gay love poems by Ross, Symonds and Wilde. He boasted about his intention of 'making Oxford homosexual'.

It was very dangerous stuff. In 1885, the Criminal Law Amendment Act had been passed. This for the first time clearly made illegal sexual acts between consenting adult males in Britain. Not only did it criminalise the activities of people like Oscar Wilde and Lord Alfred Douglas, it exposed such men to predation by blackmailers. Wilde was indiscreet enough, but he had now put himself in the hands of someone even more indiscreet.

But Wilde seems not to have been worried about this; he was more worried about all the money the young man was taking from him. Yet somehow he managed to go on writing – and writing some of his best work. The fifteen months starting in December 1893 were his most productive period. And Wilde carried on being sociable and kindly too. He was fundamentally soft-hearted. When Oswald Sickert died, Wilde called to see his widow. Mrs Sickert was too upset to see anyone, she said, through Nelly, the mediating daughter, but Wilde insisted on seeing her. She tried again to get rid of him, but he still insisted on speaking to her. Eventually she went to him. She was crying. He led her to a chair and sat her down. Nelly Sickert left the room. 'He stayed a long time, and before he went I heard my mother laughing. She was transformed. He had made her talk, asked her questions about my father's last illness, and allowed her to unburden. Then, she didn't know how, he had begun to tell her all sorts of things, which he made amusing. "And then I laughed," she said. "when I thought I should never laugh again." '

The Marquess of Queensberry was not happy about his son's relationship with Oscar Wilde. Wilde and Douglas were having lunch at the Café Royal on 1 April 1894, when they were spotted by the Marquess. He was angry. He understood the nature of their relationship and hated it. But then they invited him to their table, and he was instantly won over by Wilde's charm. He said to his son, 'I don't wonder you are so fond of him. He is a wonderful man.' After this incongruous encounter, the Marquess went home and changed his mind again, writing his son a letter. In it he rebuked Lord Alfred for giving up on Oxford and for messing about regarding a career. He had been assured by his son that he would be going into the Civil Service, or the Foreign Office, or the law. Then he went on to the more painful matter of his 'loathsome and disgusting relationship' with 'this man Wilde'. He must either stop seeing Wilde or be disowned. The letter was signed, 'Your disgusted so-called father, Queensberry'. Bosie's typically silly response was to send a telegram back: 'WHAT A FUNNY LITTLE MAN YOU ARE.'

Wilde did not want to get tangled up in this unseemly fight between father and son and took himself off to Paris and then Florence, but accompanied by Bosie. The idea was that they should travel incognito, but Wilde was instantly recognisable everywhere he went; he was huge, eccentrically and foppishly dressed, and he behaved in a theatrical manner. He was unmistakable. The French writer André Gide met and recognised the pair of them in a café, but was queasy about being seen with them. The relationship between Wilde and Douglas was by now notorious halfway across Europe.

Running out of money, Wilde went back to London, where he was confronted by the Marquess at his house in Tite Street. The Marquess released a torrent of obscenities at Wilde, who eventually managed to make him leave. Wilde's friend Frank Harris warned Wilde that Lord Alfred was using him as a weapon in a long war against his father. Wilde tried to get a lawyer to press the Marquess to withdraw his libellous allegations, but the Marquess said he hadn't made any.

Wilde and Douglas went to stay at the Grand Hotel in Brighton, at Douglas's insistence. Douglas caught influenza and had to stay in bed. Wilde acted as nurse until Bosie recovered. Then, after they moved to lodgings, Wilde fell ill. Bosie had no intention of returning the favour, and abandoned him, returning to the Grand Hotel on his own. Then Bosie wrote Wilde a nasty letter boasting that he had run up a bill at the hotel for Wilde to pay. 'When you are not on your pedestal you are not interesting. The next time you are ill I shall go away at once.' Wilde was never able to forget this particular unkindness of Bosie's.

In 1895 *The Importance of Being Earnest* had its première. But the clouds were gathering. Several compromising letters from Wilde to Lord Alfred were now in the Marquess of Queensberry's hands. Queensberry's solicitor advised him that they were not in themselves evidence of homosexual acts. In his anger and frustration, Queensberry had gone to the opening night of *The Importance* with the intention of embarrassing Wilde at the theatre. He was denied access, so he left a bouquet of vegetables for Wilde at the stage door. He also left a card at Wilde's club. The writing was hard to decipher, but it was read – in court – as 'To Oscar Wilde posing as a somdomite' [sic]. Wilde was deeply offended and wanted to stop the Marquess from going on any further. He asked his lawyer Lewis for advice, but Lewis told him he was now acting for the Marquess and therefore could not act for Wilde. Lewis later said that if he had been free to advise Wilde, he would have told him to tear up the card and ignore it. But Wilde consulted another lawyer, Humphreys, who sensed that this would be a big, high-profile case, as indeed it was. Wilde had Queensberry charged with publishing a libel against him. It was one of the biggest mistakes of his life.

The case against the Marquess of Queensberry inevitably opened the door to Queensberry's evidence that Oscar Wilde was homosexual. The evidence of his and Lord Alfred's writings was enough to suggest that their relationship was homosexual. Lord Alfred arranged to be out of the country, so that he would not be called as a witness. Wilde knew even before Queensberry's trial opened that Queensberry's defence lawyer had a list of ten named boys with whom Wilde was alleged to have had sex. Several of Wilde's friends, including Frank Harris and George Bernard Shaw, advised Wilde to drop the case at once. Settling out of court would be far safer than allowing these accusations to be aired. But Wilde's death wish prevailed and the trial opened on 3 April 1895 at the Old Bailey. It ended in disaster for Wilde. As the trial collapsed, the lawyers made a gentlemen's agreement to keep it going long enough for Wilde to catch the boat train and get away to France. But Wilde declined to run away.

Oscar Wilde stayed in England for his own trial in late April 1895. The same evidence used in the Marquess's defence at the earlier trial was now used in the prosecution case against Wilde. The jury could not reach a verdict. A new trial was ordered, which opened on 22 May. This time there was a Guilty verdict and Wilde was sentenced to two years' hard labour. Wilde was overcome. He wailed, 'My God, my God! And

I?' May I say nothing, my lord?' Outside, the poet W. B. Yeats said, the harlots danced on the pavement.

Wilde would, after all, not be joining Bosie in Paris next week, as he had hoped. Instead he would be visiting Pentonville, Wandsworth and Reading Gaol. Lord Alfred rented a yacht in Le Havre and hired a cabin boy; the cabin boy brought with him another boy. The local paper published an editorial condemning the young English lord who was corrupting the youth of Le Havre. Douglas made a spirited reply, to the effect that the paper was attacking and insulting him for being the friend of Oscar Wilde. But a day or two later he left for Sorrento.

After prison, which came to an end in May 1897, Wilde understandably felt bitter about Bosie's behaviour. He had abandoned Wilde. Wilde unloaded some of his reflections about Bosie in his own great piece *De Profundis*. It is an elegy for a lost love, a repudiation of Lord Alfred. But after he had written it, he felt ready for a reconciliation. As the reconciliation approached, Lord Alfred played with Wilde's emotions as always, sometimes excusing himself, sometimes accusing Wilde, sometimes hurting. There was an exchange of letters, and suddenly out of the blue Douglas was begging Wilde to live with him for the rest of his life, promising to atone for the disaster he and his family had brought down on Wilde. But the rest of Wilde's life consisted of only three more years. He was to die wretchedly in Paris on 30 November 1900, cared for by his old friend Robert Ross.

MARIE SKLODOWSKA AND PIERRE CURIE

(1894)

MARIA SKLODOWSKA WAS born in 1867 in Warsaw, into a family of teachers. When her mother and sister died, she lost her Catholic faith and became an agnostic. Maria first took a position as a governess and while working for the Zorawski family she fell in love with the son of the family, Kazimierz Zorawski, who would later become an eminent mathematician. Zorawski reciprocated her feelings, but his parents refused to consider his marriage to Maria, who was penniless. Maria lost Zorawski, and lost her job too. She decided to join her sister in France. Zorawski gained academic qualifications and eventually became a professor and Rector of Krakow University. But he was never fully reconciled to the parentally-enforced break with Maria. As an old man, he used to sit and gaze at the statue of Maria that was raised in front of the Radium Institute she founded in Warsaw.

In Paris, Maria studied physics, chemistry and mathematics at the Sorbonne. In 1894, when she graduated in mathematics, she met Pierre Curie. He was an instructor in the School of Physics and Chemistry. Their shared interest in magnetism drew them together. Initially, Maria thought she would be returning to Poland, but she found that she was unable to get a post at Krakow University because she was a woman, which threw her back on Paris – and Pierre. In 1895 they were married. From that moment on, their lives revolved not only round each other but round their shared research interests. Their only recreational activities were long cycling holidays and trips abroad.

When Henri Becquerel discovered that uranium emitted rays, Maria (now Marie) decided to explore this discovery, using a device that Pierre and his brother invented. She showed that the radiation came from the uranium atoms themselves, which was her single most important contribution to science. She discussed her ideas with Pierre, but was keen to establish that they were her own. Presumably after her experience of being excluded from an academic career in Poland by being a woman she was keen to make sure she was taken seriously in France. She knew that there were many scientists around who would be reluctant to believe that a woman could undertake serious original science at this level. When she came to write her husband's biography, she was careful to record – twice over – that the idea was hers alone. There was a great need to publish and claim scientific findings promptly. If Becquerel had not published his discovery the day after he had made it, then the credit for discovering radioactivity would probably have gone to Silvanus Thompson. Marie Curie realised that she was in similar danger and published immediately, through the Académie des Sciences. She was beaten to the discovery of thorium by Gerhard Schmidt, by two months.

Then Marie Curie noticed that pitchblende and chalcolite were even more radioactive than uranium. Pierre was so impressed by this that he dropped his research on crystals to help her in 1898. They jointly published a paper announcing the existence of a new element that they called polonium, after Poland, and a few months later they announced a second new radioactive element, radium.

In 1903, Pierre and Marie Curie were awarded the Nobel Prize in Physics, jointly with Henry Becquerel, for their research on radiation. Suddenly they were world-famous. Pierre was given a professorship at the Sorbonne, and he was allowed to set up a laboratory in which Marie was the research director.

While the Curies were working towards separating samples of the newly discovered elements, Pierre was accidentally killed. It happened in April 1906. He was out in the Paris streets in heavy rain when he was hit by a horse-drawn vehicle. He fell under the wheels and broke his skull.

But the loss of her husband and collaborator did not stop Marie from continuing her work. In 1910, she succeeded in isolating a pure sample of radium. The next year she received the Nobel Prize in Chemistry. She had been the first woman to be awarded a Nobel Prize, and now she had two – she was the first person to win two Nobel Prizes. She should have been euphoric, yet she was in hospital the next year suffering from acute depression. She had been devastated by Pierre's death. From that moment she was 'an incurably and wretchedly lonely person'. The Sorbonne decided to transfer Pierre's professorship to her, making her the first female professor at the university.

Unfortunately, the French press discovered that in 1910-11 Marie had an affair with Paul Langevin. He was a physicist, a married man, though separated from his wife. The press made much of this, turning it into a scandal, mainly because Marie Curie was a foreigner by birth; there was a strongly xenophobic attitude in France at the time. It was even falsely alleged that Marie was Jewish, in order to generate additional hostility. The scandal was a strange storm in a teacup. Curiously, many years later, Marie's granddaughter married Paul Langevin's grandson.

After the First World War, Marie toured America twice to raise funding for further research on radium. These tours earned enough funding to equip the Warsaw Radium Institute. But working with radioactive materials all her life carried a penalty. The dangers of radiation were then unknown, so few precautions were taken. It was exposure to radiation over a long period that led to the anaemia that killed her in July 1934. She had carried test tubes containing radioactive isotopes in her pocket, and even commented on the pretty blue-green glow they gave off in the dark. She had exposed herself to mortal danger without any awareness of it. She was buried alongside her husband Pierre, but later, in 1995, both were transferred to the Pantheon in Paris.

Marie's relationship with Pierre Curie was a remarkable one: a love affair, a marriage, a working partnership, a creative alliance at the forefront of scientific research. Together they made ground-breaking discoveries. They found, for instance, that the radioactivity of radium conflicted with the established principle of the conservation of energy; this meant that the foundations of physics had to be reviewed. The discovery of radium gave Ernest Rutherford information about the sources of radioactivity that enabled him and other scientists to explore the structure of the atom. Radium's radioactivity opened up the possibility of a new kind of cancer treatment. It was a love affair with extraordinary repercussions.

KING EDWARD VIII AND WALLIS SIMPSON

(1930)

WALLIS SIMPSON IS one of those historical figures who is almost impossible to see or portray fairly and without bias. She was the subject of so much vitriolic press treatment during her lifetime that an objective view is almost beyond reach. She was (and still is) portrayed by some commentators as a voraciously greedy social climber or as an unscrupulous sexual predator; but others have portrayed her relationship with the Prince of Wales as the greatest romance of the twentieth century. The truth is that she was a complex person, strong-willed certainly, and trying hard to make her own way in the world after a difficult start. In the end she found herself in a situation that she could not control, and her disappointment was acute.

She was born in 1896 as Bessie Wallis Warfield. When Wallis was twenty she married an airman called Earl Spencer, but she left him after a few years. Spencer was a violent alcoholic, and she had to leave him for her own safety. Her family was scandalised by her behaviour. After being separated from Spencer for three years, in 1928 Wallis plunged into her second marriage. This time she married a banker called Ernest Simpson. The Simpsons moved to London, where Wallis became a society hostess.

In London, Wallis made friends with Thelma Furness, who was married to an elderly shipping magnate and having an affair with the Prince of Wales. The prince, who was the elder son of George V and therefore the Heir Apparent to the English throne, was thirty-six and still single. He had had a string of love affairs. The first was with Freda Dudley Ward; he had been devoted to her and abjectly dependent on her, but her passion had quickly waned and the relationship subsided into a confiding friendship. The Prince's equerry commented that what the Prince liked was to be mothered.

By 1933, Thelma Furness had become the Prince's mistress. She planned to go to America to visit her sister and arranged for her friend Wallis to stand in for her while she was away. Thelma left for the States in January 1934 and when she came back she found that her friend had completely supplanted her; now it was Wallis the Prince wanted.

The Prince of Wales was known to be a womaniser, and there was general tolerance of his behaviour, but the relationship with Wallis Simpson was different. Wallis Simpson was not only American but seen, both by the general public in Britain and by the high society circle she moved in, as ruthlessly ambitious and grasping. As a result, Wallis was an unpopular figure. The situation was made worse by the Prince's habit of descending into servile devotion when he fell in love: and this time it was worse. His equerry John Aird commented that the Prince 'has lost all confidence in himself and follows W around like a dog.'

In November Prince Edward invited Mr and Mrs Simpson to a function at Buckingham Palace, in order to present her to his mother, Queen Mary. His father, King George V, was angry that 'that woman' was in his 'own house' and told the prince that his mistress was unwelcome at court. The prince denied that Wallis was his mistress, which nobody believed, but it is just possible that it was at that moment true. It is possible that Wallis may have been withholding sexual favours in the hope of pushing Edward to the point of marriage, much in the way that Anne Boleyn had done 400 years earlier, and Elizabeth Woodville before her – and both successfully.

The love affair between Edward and Wallis was pushed into crisis in January 1936 when George V died. At the moment of his death, Edward automatically became king. There was an agreement between the establishment and the two leading press barons, Beaverbrook and Rothermere, that the new king's relationship with Mrs Simpson would be kept out of the British newspapers. Wallis could see that she would not be accepted as queen – American, twice married – and offered to 'steal quietly away'. But the king was determined to have her, and in

October the Simpsons began divorce proceedings. But even the free, twice-divorced Wallis was going to be unacceptable to the court and the government. The prime minister pressed the king to make his choice – Wallis or the throne – and the king chose Wallis. He was forced to abdicate in December 1936, eleven months after his accession, and before his coronation. Wallis's divorce became absolute in May 1937. She changed her name back to Wallis Warfield, in an attempt to erase the memory of both her marriages, and married Edward, now an ex-king, in June. No longer Prince of Wales, no longer king, Edward had to be given a new title, and this was to be HRH the Duke of Windsor. Wallis Warfield or Simpson (or Spencer) was still regarded with contempt and hatred by the British establishment, and there was a determination to deny her the accolade of calling her 'Her Royal Highness'. So she became the Duchess of Windsor, but not HRH the Duchess of Windsor. It was, perhaps, petty and certainly indicates the level of personal animosity Wallis aroused.

One major repercussion was that instead of Edward VIII being crowned king of England in 1937 it was his younger brother the Duke of York – as George VI. Because of this, the next monarch was George's elder daughter, Elizabeth II. What would have happened if Edward VIII had remained on the throne is hard to guess. He was a shallow man with very poor political judgement and strong right-wing sympathies, and it is likely that during the course of the Second World War he would have created a serious problem. Some historians have speculated that he might have been forced to abdicate anyway, and that the Wallis Simpson affair was greeted by the government as a heaven-sent opportunity to get rid of him.

The lives of the Duke and Duchess of Windsor took them into a strange twilight world, far from the glittering high society life they had enjoyed in London. The Duke found himself living in exile in France, totally dominated by his wife, who seemed to revel in the hold she had over him. In front of dinner guests she banged the table, forbidding him to tell the servants what to do 'in my house'.

The Duke's wayward political views were entirely his own; Wallis cannot be blamed for his miscalculated liaison with the Nazis. It was his idea to visit Germany in 1937 and to meet Hitler; in fact she later complained that she had been excluded from the meeting with Hitler. Whether the Duke hoped that Hitler would invade England and re-install him as king is not known; he may have entertained some such hope, with a view to making Wallis queen in spite of everything that had happened. Whatever his motive, the outreach to Hitler was a serious gaffe. When France fell to the Germans, Edward and Wallis fled to Spain. The Germans planned to kidnap him, but the British authorities did not know this. All the British were conscious of was that it was an embarrassment to have him living in Europe.

The Duke's 'war job' was decided. He was to be Governor of the Bahamas and he remained there with Wallis until the Second World War ended. But even there he could not be trusted. He mixed socially with a strange assortment of people, including Nazi sympathisers.

The couple had done nothing to rehabilitate themselves in the eyes of the British court or government by their behaviour, so in the post-war world they were still out on a limb. They drifted from Paris to the south of France to Florida to New York and back to Paris. The Duke died in 1972. Whether he ever regretted abdicating in order to marry Wallis is not known. Maybe he did. After the Duke's death there was a formal gesture of friendship from the Queen, who invited Wallis to stay at Buckingham Palace for the funeral. After that, she lived the life of a recluse in their mansion in Paris. She ended up, confused, bedridden, dying in 1986 at the age of eighty-nine.

Whether Wallis was simply the victim of circumstances is hard to judge. She may have harboured the secret ambition to be queen of England. If so, she was bitterly disappointed. She may just have fallen in love with Edward, and being with him was all that mattered. If so, she was a happy woman. But they did not appear to be happy. They seem never to have adjusted to the idea of spending the rest of their lives in exile from England, out of the limelight.

SYLVIA PLATH AND TED HUGHES

(1955)

SYLVIA PLATH WAS born in Massachusetts in 1932. She published her first poem at the time her father died, when she was eight. Otto Plath died following the amputation of a foot. The amputation had become necessary as a result of a treatable form of diabetes, after Otto had made an incorrect self-diagnosis. After this harrowing incident, in Plath's mind poetry and death seemed to go together. Later she attended Smith College, where she went out with Dick Norton. Norton contracted tuberculosis and was hospitalised at the Ray Brook Sanatorium. While she was visiting Norton, Sylvia took herself on what seems to have been a suicidal ski run, which ended with her breaking a leg. It was in that same year that Sylvia Plath made her first medically documented suicide attempt. She crawled under her house and took an overdose of sleeping pills. After that, she was sent to a mental institution where she was given electric shock treatment.

After her third year at college, Sylvia Plath was given a position as guest editor at Mademoiselle magazine in New York. She did not enjoy it, partly because of her negative psychological state. She graduated in 1955, winning a scholarship to Cambridge University in England. There she carried on writing poetry, and publishing some of it. There, at a party, she met the English poet Ted Hughes. They fell in love and were married in June 1956. Sylvia Plath and Ted Hughes spent a couple of years living and working in America. When Sylvia realised she was pregnant, they returned to Britain, settling in Devon. In 1961 she had a miscarriage.

The relationship between Sylvia Plath and Ted Hughes was turbulent and fiery. They stimulated one another's poetry and encouraged one another to write in a very immediate way. Plath wanted to write a book that amazed and appalled the world, and she wrote poems that were full of power and fatality, poems that showed her on the brink of insanity and suicide. When Plath was stuck for subjects, Hughes would set her problems. He made suggestions for subjects, and this technique seemed to jolt Plath out of some of her psychological problems, however briefly. It is thought that some of Plath's best poems, such as *The Moon* and *The Yew Tree*, were composed in this way.

The marriage was fraught with problems. They were two enormously talented and creative people, and they were constantly at war with one another. Hughes had an affair with Assia Wevill and Hughes and Plath separated in late 1962. She went back to London with their two children, Frieda and Nicholas, to live in a flat in Fitzroy Road, in a house where the poet W. B. Yeats once lived. This connection with another poet pleased Plath; it seemed auspicious.

On the morning of 11 February 1963, Sylvia Plath set out bread and milk for the children, sealed the rooms between herself and her sleeping children with wet towels, and then gassed herself. She put her head in the oven, and turned on the gas. There has been much discussion about whether this suicide was a genuine attempt to kill herself or a cry for help. She had previously asked her downstairs neighbour Mr Thomas when he would be leaving in the morning, and left a note saying 'Call Dr Horder' and giving his phone number. Plath turned on the gas at the time when she thought Mr Thomas would be waking up and starting his day. An au pair was due to arrive at nine o'clock to help with the children. When she arrived, she was let in by painters who had a door key. The leaving of bread and milk for the children's breakfast could be seen as a piece of theatre, a successful attempt at adding pathos to the scene.

The circumstantial evidence implies that Sylvia Plath intended to be found in time for her life to be saved. On the other hand, the Coroner's Officer noted that her head was well inside the oven, which implies that she intended to die. Controversy surrounds Sylvia Plath's death and her suicidal frame of mind. Sylvia Plath was taken up as a cause by feminists in the 1970s, and some Plath supporters wanted to pin the blame for her death onto Ted Hughes. This campaign intensified after the suicide of Assia Wevill, the woman Ted Hughes lived with after the separation from Sylvia Plath. Claims were made that Hughes was an abusive partner.

For the rest of his life as a prominent poet, Ted Hughes had to bear the silent, sometimes not so silent, accusation that he had been responsible for Sylvia's death. Books were written, poems were written, directly accusing Hughes of causing her death. Sylvia Plath was a conscientious keeper of diaries from the age of eleven. Her adult diaries, starting in her first year at Smith College in 1950, were published in 1980 as *The Journals of Sylvia Plath*. In 1982, when Smith College acquired the remaining journals, Ted Hughes sealed two of them with instructions that they should remain unopened until 2013, the fiftieth anniversary of Plath's death. In 1998, shortly before his own death, Hughes unsealed the two journals and two years later *The Unabridged Journals of Sylvia Plath* were published.

But Ted Hughes' involvement in the editing and handling of the journals has led to further criticism of his behaviour. He claimed to have destroyed the final journal, 'because I did not want her children to have to read it (in those days I regarded forgetfulness as an essential part of survival)'. The suspicion remains that he destroyed it because it showed Hughes himself in a bad light. Some of his critics think it was inappropriate for him to act as Plath's personal and literary executor, on the grounds that she may have begun divorce proceedings against him. In letters to relatives, she said she had. But Hughes later claimed that they were discussing a reconciliation only days before she died. Some of Plath's supporters claimed that Hughes was controlling her publications for personal gain, but the royalties went into a trust account for their children.

In the three decades that followed Sylvia Plath's death at the age of thirty, Ted Hughes stoically refused to respond to the repeated accusation that he was to blame. The case against Ted Hughes has been unfairly overstated. Sylvia Plath had made at least one and very possibly more than one attempt to commit suicide well before she met Ted Hughes. She had a suicidal personality and would probably have made further attempts at suicide whoever her partner happened to be. Hughes kept silent about Sylvia Plath's death for a long time. Then, suddenly, he published a book entitled *Birthday Letters*, a collection of poems reflecting on Sylvia each year on her birthday. He had decided to break his silence, to try to complete the story. Because of the lapse of time, though, the book is more an old man's reflection on his younger self, on his memories of a long-dead romance. But it is also a tribute to his long-dead wife's legacy to him.

V
ENCOUNTERS BY CHANCE

MARCO POLO AND KUBLAI KHAN

(1274)

MARCO POLO WAS born in 1254 into a noble Venetian family. His father and his uncle were energetic and resourceful merchants who travelled ambitiously long distances east along the Silk Road. When Marco was born, his father Nicolo and his uncle Maffeo were not in Venice; they were away on an expedition to Bokhara and Cathay (China). Their trading operation had taken them from Venice to Constantinople, then on across the Black Sea to the Crimea, and from there eastwards to Bokhara. There they encountered envoys from Kublai Khan and travelled with them into Cathay.

Maffeo and Nicolo Polo were received by the great emperor, Kublai Khan, who, it was said, had never seen Europeans before. He was delighted with the Polos and commissioned them to act as his ambassadors to the Pope. He wanted the Polos to ask the Pope to send a hundred well-educated Europeans who were learned in the sciences and the arts. The Polos returned to Europe with good intentions of carrying out the great Khan's epoch-making mission in 1269. But they found when they reached Acre in Palestine that Pope Clement IV had died the previous year and no new pope had been elected. Frustrated, Nicolo and Maffeo Polo returned to Venice, but with the intention of going back to Cathay.

In 1271, the two brothers set off again, this time taking Nicolo's son Marco with them. He was then seventeen years old. They travelled through Mosul and Baghdad and the Pamirs to the Gobi Desert and arrived at the court of Kublai Khan in 1275. The Khan was again very pleased to see them and he took a special interest in young Marco, who was sent off as an envoy to various distant lands, including Burma, Cochin China and southern India. Marco Polo was taught the languages of the Khan's subjects. Kublai Khan was reluctant to let these useful Westerners leave his court. But the Khan was an old man, and the Polos were anxious about what might happen to them when he died, which could not lie far in the future. For their own safety, they wanted to be out of Cathay before he died. An opportunity to escape arose by chance. The Polos were commissioned to escort a young noblewoman on a long voyage. After delays in Sumatra and India, they succeeded in sailing to Persia. Finally they reached Venice in 1295, bringing with them the great wealth they had acquired along the way.

After Marco Polo commanded a galley in the Battle of Curzola, he was taken prisoner by the Genoese. He had his notes sent across from Venice and while in prison he made a continuous prose account of his adventure. His account caused a sensation throughout Europe, raising awareness of the geography and customs of eastern Asia. Map-makers tried to incorporate Marco Polo's geographical information on their maps. They were unable to do this with any accuracy, but at least huge areas that had been empty were filled in.

Marco Polo did not introduce the idea of block printing from China to Europe. Indeed it is rather odd that he did not mention at all the distinctive method of printing used by the Chinese. Discrepancies and oddities like this have led some modern commentators to question whether Marco Polo's book was a traveller's tale in the worst sense of the phrase – a tall story with little truth in it. One aspect of the story remains puzzling. Why would the great Khan have wanted to use as envoys foreigners with little or no understanding of the languages spoken in China? Perhaps the Polos wanted to exaggerate their importance in Cathay in order to improve the story.

The impact of the Polos' travels was profound. Europeans had to come to terms with the reality that there was a great civilisation in eastern Asia which was in many ways more advanced than the great European civilisation. It encouraged the development of a mental outreach in Europe that would bear fruit in the physical outreach of the Columbus voyage and other major voyages of discovery.

SIR CLOUDESLEY
SHOVEL AND THE
SCILLY ISLES

(1707)

IN THE EARLY days of navigation at sea, people usually kept within sight of land. It was easy, with a little practice, to recognise the coastline of your own home territory and the coastlines of your neighbours' territories. By learning lists of landmarks, it was possible to memorise long itineraries and find your way, coastwise, round long distances of the shores of Europe. This is what happened in the prehistoric period, and what went on happening to a great extent in the middle ages too.

The problems started when sailors lost sight of land. One significant clue to a ship's position was the altitude of the sun in the sky. On 21 March and 21 September, the equinoxes, the sun is overhead at midday on the equator. The angle the sun makes with the horizon is known as the sun's altitude. If the observer was on the equator, latitude nought degrees, the sun's altitude was ninety degrees. If the observer was at the North or South Pole, latitude ninety degrees, the sun's altitude was nought degrees. It was therefore possible for people to calculate their latitude very easily from the sun's altitude (latitude = 90 − altitude).

Latitude told navigators how far north or south they were, but not how far east or west. To pinpoint their position exactly, which is what they needed to be able to do, they needed this second co-ordinate. They needed to fix their longitude. This could not be read from the sun's position or the position of any other heavenly body either.

This uncertainty about longitude was one reason why early maps were very inaccurate. It was also a reason why ships went aground on reefs, and it was one such incident that brought the situation to a head.

Sir Cloudesley Shovel (about 1650-1707) was an English admiral with a distinguished naval career. He had destroyed pirate ships at Tripoli in 1674. His conduct in the fight at Bantry Bay led to his knighthood. He fought at the Battle of Beachy Head in 1690. He was put in joint command of the fleet with Admiral Killigrew and Sir Ralph Delaval and in 1702 he brought home to England the spoils of the French and Spanish fleets after their capture by Sir George Rooke. In 1704 Shovel was promoted to commander-in-chief of the British fleets. He took part in the capture of Barcelona in 1705 and commanded an unsuccessful attack on Toulon in October 1707.

In October 1707 Sir Cloudesley was returning home to England in command of a squadron of ships. He was on board his flagship, the *Association*, sailing north under full sail when he ran into rocks near the Isles of Scilly on 22 October 1707. The ship made impact at eight o'clock at night. The *Association* was badly holed and those on board the *St George*, one of the other ships in the squadron, watched helplessly as the flagship sank in less than four minutes. The ship sank so quickly that everyone on board, 800 men in all, perished.

The *Association* and four other ships in the squadron were wrecked on the Gilstone Reef. When the Scilly islanders picked over the bodies on the beaches for the sake of any valuables, a woman found the admiral's body on the beach at Porthellick Cove, then realised that he was still alive. She cut his throat for the sake of the gold rings on his fingers.

The wreck of the *Association* was one of the biggest peacetime disasters in British history and rightly regarded as a national catastrophe. Up to 2,000 men, five ships and the commander-in-chief were lost. The *Association* was also carrying a vast amount of treasure. There were chests of gold and silver coin and plate that were put on at Gibraltar by British merchants. There were chests containing British government funds for the war in France. There were chests containing Sir Cloudesley's own cash and still others containing regimental funds and silverware. The financial loss alone was colossal.

The squadron had sailed northwards onto a known reef and therefore Sir Cloudesley must have mis-navigated. The visibility was very poor that day and he and his officers had been unable to navigate by eye. He was either further to the east or west than he had believed, or the maps were inaccurate and had misled him. In other words he had not been aware of his own longitude or the longitude of the reef.

The outcome of the wreck of the *Association* was the offer of a huge cash prize by the British government for the invention of an instrument that could measure longitude accurately on a ship at sea. The prize was offered by way of an Act of Parliament in 1714, and the award of the prize was to be administered by a newly created Board of Longitude. A British Parliamentary committee consulted scientists, Sir Isaac Newton among them, and they advised that a seaworthy clock that could be trusted to keep accurate time would supply the information needed – a chronometer. The level of accuracy the committee required was the calculation of the longitude of the port of arrival in the West Indies at the end of a voyage from England; this meant that the chronometer had to keep accurate time for at least six weeks.

After a very long struggle, this prize was eventually won by John Harrison, who invented the ship's chronometer. In fact Harrison manufactured several clocks that were so accurate that they lost no more than one second per month, which was more than accurate enough for the purpose. The main problems Harrison had to overcome were those of making the chronometer seaworthy. Because ships swayed and pitched so much, it was impossible to use a conventional pendulum clock. The chronometer had to carry on working regardless of big changes in temperature and humidity too.

In 1730, Harrison met Edmond Halley, who was the *Astronomer* Royal and also a member of the Board of Longitude. Halley looked at Harrison's plans and saw that, if the chronometer worked, it would solve the longitude problem. Harrison was encouraged to build his chronometer with a view to a trial, and he completed the first one, H1, in 1735. It was given a successful sea trial to Lisbon. The Board was favourably impressed and awarded Harrison £500 to enable him to build an improved model that would take up less deck space. H2, which was completed in 1739, was narrower and taller than H1. H2 did not have a sea trial, and Harrison went on refining and redesigning until he produced H4. This was Harrison's most famous invention. It was a great advance on the earlier chronometers because it was much smaller. It was just over five inches in diameter, like a large pocket watch. It was technologically very impressive, and a beautifully intricate piece of craftsmanship.

Harrison's H4 chronometer was given its transatlantic sea trial in 1761. On arrival in Jamaica it proved to have lost just five seconds, which amounted to an error of one minute of longitude. With this triumph, John Harrison qualified for the award, but the Board of Longitude failed to pay up. George III himself intervened when he saw Harrison's final version, H5, in 1772, and forced the Board to pay Harrison his prize money.

The rigorous testing of Harrison's chronometer had proved its worth, yet almost incredibly Captain Cook set off on his earlier voyages without it. In July 1771, though, James Cook set sail from Plymouth with the *Resolution* and the *Adventure* with a copy of Harrison's H4 chronometer on board. This enabled Cook to make far more accurate charts of his discoveries than were ever previously possible. It also accurately fixed John Harrison's place in history.

John Harrison's invention enabled navigators and explorers to pinpoint locations with far greater accuracy than ever before. As a result, the regional and world maps produced in the later 18th and 19th centuries were far more accurate than the charts Sir Cloudesley Shovel had been using in 1707. It also became possible for ships' captains to navigate their courses more accurately – and safely. The chronometers were difficult to manufacture, and not susceptible to mass production, so their use spread slowly, but by 1850 every vessel in the British navy was carrying three Harrison chronometers. Harrison himself did well out of his invention, making a total of £23,065 in prize money.

WILLIAM WILBERFORCE AND JOHN NEWTON

(1785)

JOHN NEWTON WAS born in 1725, the son of a ship's captain. He was sent to boarding school for a couple of years and then, at the age of eleven, he was taken to sea on several voyages by his father, who planned for him to become a slave master on a Jamaican sugar plantation. After his father retired, John Newton became a captain of a slave ship. In 1743, he was pressed into naval service and became a midshipman on HMS *Harwich*. The eighteen-year-old Newton tried to escape and he was court martialed. The captain of the *Harwich* decided to make an example of him and he was given ninety-six lashes in front of the assembled crew.

After this terrible physical and psychological ordeal, Newton thought of killing himself. But then he asked to be put into service on a slave ship headed for Africa. This took him to Sierra Leone. He became the servant of a slave trader who subjected him to abuse. He later remembered the sense of degradation, of feeling that he was leading the life of 'an infidel and libertine, a servant of slaves.' Newton's father was aware that he had disappeared and he asked a sea captain to keep a lookout for him, and in 1748 Newton was rescued. He was returning to England on the slave-ship *Greyhound* when he encountered a great storm. Newton woke up in the night to find the ship filling with water. In desperation he prayed to be saved. It was a turning point in his life, a moment that led to his conversion to evangelical Christianity. By the time the *Greyhound* reached England, on 21 March 1748, he was a

fostering was born. Some of Barnardo's schemes were too adventurous, and because of the lack of proper monitoring some of the boarding-out placements exposed the children to further abuse and suffering. But the main work, setting up the Barnardo Homes, was a huge success, rescuing many children from a wretched childhood on the streets, sleeping out in all weather and exposed to all kinds of danger.

ALGERNON SWINBURNE AND GUY DE MAUPASSANT AT ETRETAT

(1868)

IN THE 19TH century, the British started to explore Normandy. The Channel crossing between Brighton and Dieppe was longer than between Dover and Calais, and the British presence there was less conspicuous; the French seemed even more French. The quaint local costumes and culture were attractions, as were the sea-bathing and casino-gambling. The opening of a railway from London to Brighton, and then Newhaven, along with the commissioning of steam-packets, made the journey quicker and easier.

Painters started arriving as soon as the Napoleonic Wars were over; John Sell Cotman, then Turner, then Richard Bonington. At the end of the century the French Impressionists took over the Normandy coast, but the British had been there already.

The British smart set discreetly installed themselves in summer retreats. The Prince of Wales kept a mistress and maybe an illegitimate child in Dieppe. The prime minister, Lord Salisbury, had a chalet built for himself outside Dieppe and found that he was able to keep in touch with London by telegraph via Beachy Head. And there were many other visitors, both fashionable and unfashionable, including Percy Grainger, Max Beerbohm, Aubrey Beardsley, Walter Sickert. One night in 1897, the Channel packet brought Oscar Wilde, just released from Reading Gaol, and adopting the attention-seeking pseudonym Sebastian Melmoth.

Just along the coast from Dieppe at Etretat, there was another, smaller colony of British artists, mixing with the summer residents. Among the summer residents in 1868 were the eighteen-year-old Guy de Maupassant and his mother. The young French aristocrat was a muscular heterosexual, keen on rowing and swimming. At Etretat he was to encounter the slight, fragile, homosexual English poet, Algernon Swinburne.

The thirty-one-year-old Swinburne was staying in a cottage belonging to his friend George Powell. Because he led such a bizarre and solitary existence the local people decided that Powell was an alias, and that he was secretly an English lord; in fact he was George Powell. Swinburne decided to go for a swim one day in September from the beach at Etretat. He got into difficulties. Swinburne was sure he was going to die and reflected that he was exactly the same age as Shelley when he drowned. But this was a delusion; Swinburne always lied to himself about his age, believing that he was a couple of years younger than he really was.

Powell later said that dangerous undercurrents had swept the auburn-haired poet out to sea 'through a rocky archway'. The natural arch in the chalk cliffs was, and still is, a major local feature. Powell heard shouts from the cliffs. A man was drowning. But a few minutes later he heard that Swinburne had been picked up by some fishermen in a boat and was being taken along the coast to be put ashore. The boat was the *Marie-Marthe*, and she was headed for the harbour at Yport. Once hauled out of the sea, the fishermen rubbed him dry and wrapped him in a sail. He started reciting the poetry of Victor Hugo to them almost at once, while his mop of wet red hair was fanned out on the sail to dry. Swinburne himself wrote to his mother that he had been swept two miles out to sea. 'Luckily I was all right but very tired, and the result was that I made immense friends with all the fishermen and sailors about – who are quite the nicest people I ever knew.' Swinburne kept the oversized garments the fishermen dressed him in for the rest of his life.

Guy de Maupassant was on the scene and claimed that Swinburne was drunk, even though the incident happened at ten o'clock in the morning. Because of Swinburne's wild and hysterical manner, it would have been quite difficult to assess whether he was drunk or not.

Maupassant also claimed that he had gone out in one of the boats to rescue Swinburne. He seems to have been involved in the rescue in some way, as he was invited to lunch the next day by Powell, who had meanwhile collected Swinburne from Yport.

Maupassant described the visit to Powell's cottage three times, first orally in 1875, then in print in 1882 and 1891. The story he tells is consistently racy, though it varies in its detail in the three versions. He describes Powell's house. There were bizarre paintings and displays of bones; there was the flayed hand of a parricide. Powell himself was short and fat, Swinburne was short and thin, trembling and 'talking incessantly like a madman.' Lunch consisted of a type of meat which Maupassant could not place and Powell, his host, refused to identify. Instead of wine, there were spirits.

After lunch, things got worse for poor Maupassant. Powell and Swinburne showed him gay pornographic photographs, presumably in a misguided attempt to seduce him. Powell was drunk, and sucked the fingers of the flayed hand. Yet somehow the conversation surged along on a high level, with Swinburne translating some of his poems into French for Maupassant and waxing lyrical about Victor Hugo, and Powell telling of the old songs and legends he had brought back from Iceland and translated. Maupassant was greatly impressed – how could he not have been? – by the peculiarity of these two men. He described them as 'singularly original, remarkable and bizarre.' He thought they were like fictional characters out of Poe or E. T. A. Hoffmann.

The young Maupassant was self-assured enough to go back for a second lunch a few days afterwards. He was not to be put off by a few pornographic pictures, a misbehaving monkey or a flayed hand. The second lunch was more peaceful, as the large pet monkey that had caused such a disturbance at the first was now dead, apparently hanged from a tree by a black servant boy who had tired of cleaning up after it. The servant boy was threatened by Powell and ran off. The boy later found employment selling barley-sugar in the streets, but when he nearly strangled a dissatisfied customer he was run out of Etretat. Powell ordered a large block of granite to make a tomb for the monkey. At the end of the lunch Powell and Swinburne gave Maupassant some alcohol that almost knocked him out. After that he escaped to the safety of his hotel.

Yet Maupassant ventured back to Powell's weird cottage once more. On the earlier visits he had noticed an inscription above the door, but thought nothing of it. This time he drew Powell's and Swinburne's attention to it. It said 'Chaumière de Dolmancé', the Cottage of Dolmancé. The young Frenchman asked them if they knew who Dolmancé was. Maupassant did; he was the homosexual seducer in one of de Sade's books. Oh yes, they knew. Maupassant asked them if that was the sign of the house. They answered, 'If you like!' Maupassant commented that the expressions on their faces were terrifying.

Maupassant went back to the safety of his hotel and never returned to Powell's cottage. It was probably wise, as he was clearly in some moral danger from the two older men. Powell had relays of servant boys of fourteen or fifteen sent out to him from England every few months, 'little boys of exquisite cleanness and freshness', Maupassant commented. He also understood that the two men were real anti-heroes straight out of the pages of de Sade, men who would not have held back from crime.

But one can't help wondering if Maupassant was exaggerating. He was, after all, a novelist, and his different versions of what happened suggest a certain amount of invention. One of his accounts of the Etretat episode ends, 'Then this house, so full of living mystery, was suddenly silent, suddenly empty. Powell just disappeared, and no one knew how he had got away. No carriage was ever called for him, and no one had met him on the roads.' It reads like the ending of a short story by Edgar Allan Poe. And there is a certain roguish knowingness in the older Maupassant teasing his readers with the tale of his innocent younger self falling into the hands of English reprobates. But behind all this, Maupassant had huge admiration for Powell and Swinburne. He admired their passion for art and literature. He admired their rejection of accepted middle-class values. He revelled in their recklessness, their bravado, their sheer originality. They were – in spite of everything – role models for a young creative writer.

And that strange encounter in the sea at Etretat, between the athletic youth in the rescue boat and the decadent red-haired English poet floundering in the water, led eventually to a French prose edition of Swinburne's poems with an introductory essay – written by Guy de Maupassant.

HENRY MORTON STANLEY AND DAVID LIVINGSTONE

(1871)

DAVID LIVINGSTONE WAS born in Scotland in 1813. After taking a degree in medicine he became a missionary. The London Missionary Society sent him to Africa. He wanted to convert Africans to Christianity and put an end to the slave trade. But as he travelled into central Africa he became an explorer. He tried to establish which rivers might be navigable by missionaries trying to reach the interior; he had a practical reason for finding out the physical geography of the continent. In the 1850s he became the first white man to travel right across Africa, and on that journey he also became the first white man to see the huge waterfall that he named after Queen Victoria.

After returning to England to find that he had become a celebrity, Livingstone led a major new expedition across central Africa, starting in 1859. Then in the late 1860s he started exploring the area round Lake Tanganyika. It was then that he disappeared from view as far as the outside world was concerned. It turned out later that he was in fact writing despatches, but nearly all of them failed to reach their destination. So, without realising it himself, David Livingstone had disappeared from view. By 1871 he had been in central Africa and out of touch with the outside world for five years. In Europe and America it was widely feared that Livingstone was dead. In November 1871 Henry Morton Stanley, an American journalist, mounted an expedition to find him.

Stanley was born in 1841 in Denbigh in Wales, with the name John Rowlands. He had a very poor upbringing, spending his boyhood in a workhouse for orphans. At seventeen he became a cabin boy on a ship sailing for New Orleans. Once in America, he joined up as a Confederate soldier in the Civil War, was captured by Unionists, changed sides, and then was discharged through ill health. The violence and harshness of these early years may go some way towards explaining, though not excusing, his unusually harsh treatment of African porters. After this turbulent start he became a journalist, a reporter for the *New York Times*. This led to travel, and to his most famous assignment – to find Livingstone.

Stanley trekked across from Zanzibar on the east coast towards Ujiji on Lake Tanganyika. He travelled with a huge party of 200 porters, and gained a reputation for his harsh treatment of bearers. He did not see the huge lake until the last moment because of the hills. It was only as he and his party passed over the crest of the last hill that he saw the lake and the port of Ujiji only 500 yards from him.

Our hearts and our feelings are with our eyes as we peer into the palms and try to make out in which hut lives the white man with the grey beard we heard about on the Malagarazi. We were now about three hundred yards from the village and the crowds are dense about me. Suddenly I hear a voice on my right side.

Good morning, sir!'

Startled at hearing this greeting in the midst of such a crowd of black people, I turn sharply round in search of the man and see him at my side, with the blackest of faces, but animated and joyous – a man dressed in a long white shirt, with a turban of American sheeting around his head, and I ask, 'Who the mischief are you?'

'I am Susi, the servant of Dr Livingstone,' said he, smiling.

'What! Dr Livingstone is here?'

'Yes, sir.'

'Are you sure?'

'Sure, sir. Why, I leave him just now –'

'Now, run, Susi and tell the Doctor I am coming.'

'Yes, sir,' and off he darted like a madman. Soon Susi came running back and asked my name. He had told the Doctor I was coming, but the Doctor was too surprised to believe him.'

Stanley pushed his way through a great crowd of people and saw Livingstone, looking pale and weary. He wanted to run to him and throw his arms round him, but because Livingstone was British Stanley controlled himself. He walked purposefully towards Livingstone, took off his hat and said, 'Dr Livingstone, I presume?'

Livingstone simply replied 'Yes', smiled and raised his cap a little.

In reality, the famous greeting line may not have been uttered. Livingstone did not mention it, and Stanley tore the relevant page out of his diary, presumably to cover his tracks. The line was probably an invention for the newspaper, though it has subsequently been quoted without question. What happened next is that Stanley told Livingstone the European and American news of the last few years. Among other things, Stanley told Livingstone that the presidential election campaign had started in America and that the Democrats had nominated Horace Greeley. Livingstone is supposed to have stopped Stanley there, saying, 'You have told me curious things and wonderful, but there is a limit. When you tell me the Democrats have nominated Greeley for President I am hanged if I will believe it!' But this may well be apocryphal, geared more to the American newspaper readers than to historical accuracy.

The result of Stanley's finding of Livingstone was a major news story round the world. Stanley was a journalist and that was why he had done it. The incident became a legendary moment in the history of 19th century adventure, and of course it greatly benefited Stanley's career.

Stanley was under instructions from his employer, the *New York Times*, to return as soon as he had found Livingstone. Instead he lingered with Livingstone, who was frail and needed help. The two men became firm friends. Livingstone was striving to find the source of the Nile to the south of Lake Victoria; Stanley stayed with him until March 1872 before returning to America.

Livingstone died a year later and Stanley decided he himself would continue Livingstone's exploration work. Stanley's great achievement was following the entire course of the River Congo from source to mouth, which filled in a huge area of the map of central Africa. He reached the mouth of the Congo in 1877. But the expedition had been difficult and dangerous; he had had to abandon two-thirds of his party, originally 350 strong.

Stanley wrote up his remarkable expedition in a book called *Through the Dark Continent,* parading his exploration as if it were a military conquest. One of his readers was the Belgian King, Leopold II. Following directly on from this, Stanley was commissioned by the ambitious king to assist in the setting up of a large Belgian colony. In 1876, King Leopold organised a private holding company disguised as a scientific and humanitarian society, and called the International African Society. The King spoke in terms of introducing Western civilisation and Christianity to the area, but did not make clear that he wanted to claim the land as, in effect, a private kingdom. Stanley went back to the Congo to organise treaties with the tribal chiefs, and build roads to improve communication, though these merely helped to make the slave trade more efficient.

When Stanley realised that King Leopold intended to develop the Congo as a wealth-generating estate for his own personal gain he did not resign. He stayed on and went on working for him.

This was the shadiest part of Stanley's career, because of the sheer cruelty of the régime King Leopold set up there – with Stanley's help. In later years, Stanley found himself forced to defend his behaviour in the Congo, where the native workforce had been treated with abominable violence; many people were mutilated for minor offences. The truth was that Stanley, like a great many unenlightened white people in the nineteenth century, thought of black people as no better than ignorant beasts. He said, 'the savage only respects force, power, boldness and decision.' Stanley was himself responsible for a number of deaths in the Congo.

The entirely worthy and honourable Livingstone had died alone and in obscurity in Africa. Henry Morton Stanley, however, became a British MP at the end of the 19th century, acquiring a knighthood in 1899. He died in 1904.

DR CRIPPEN, CHIEF INSPECTOR DREW AND CAPTAIN KENDALL

(1910)

HAWLEY HARVEY CRIPPEN was an American by birth, born in Michigan in 1862, though the spectacularly newsworthy murder he committed took place in London. He gained his medical qualifications at Cleveland, London and New York. It was after that, while he was working as a doctor's assistant in New York, that he encountered Cora Turner. She was seventeen, lively and attractive, but also pregnant and the mistress of a stove manufacturer. She had a miscarriage. In spite of the very obvious disadvantages of the liaison, Crippen, who was by now a thirty-one-year-old widower, fell in love with her.

It was a misalliance. Love is blind, they say, and Hawley Harvey Crippen was blind to the flaws in Cora's personality, blind to her total unsuitability as a partner. He found that she was not really Cora Turner but Kunigunde Mackamotzki, of Russian-Polish and German parentage. He also discovered that she hoped to become an opera singer. Crippen indulged this pipe-dream, paying for her singing lessons. Cora and Hawley were married in 1893. It was a big mistake for both of them.

In 1900, Crippen moved to London to be the manager of the head office of Munyon's, a mail-order medicine company. Cora followed him across the Atlantic later that year. In London, she decided to lower her sights a little; here she would be a music-hall star. She changed her name a second time, to Belle Elmore. For reasons unknown, Crippen too changed his name, from Hawley Harvey to Peter. Their new life consisted of a riot of Bohemian parties with the gay, outgoing Belle at their centre and the insignificant and slightly lugubrious Peter, with his big sandy moustache and small spectacles, looking dolefully on. Occasionally he treated her to a lavish present – a fur or some jewellery - but life behind the scenes was far from glamorous. Neither of them wanted to do any housework, and they lived in a squalid back kitchen in a tangle of unwashed clothes and heaps of unwashed crockery.

Then things started to go badly wrong. Crippen had to return to America on business and while he was away Cora had an affair with an American music hall entertainer called Bruce Miller. In 1905, the Crippens moved up-market to 39 Hilldrop Crescent in Camden Town, but the move did nothing to heal the damaged relationship. Crippen said, 'There were very frequent occasions when she got into the most violent tempers . . . She went in and out just as she liked . . . I was a rather lonely man and rather miserable.'

Cora worked for the Music Hall Ladies Guild, where she was able to pretend to be a great star helping out less fortunate members of the profession. Cora lived in a world of illusion; one of her fantasies was that her father was titled. Crippen even used his father-in-law's imaginary title in one of his firm's quack remedies, calling it Baron Mackamotzki's Cure for Deafness. She was bored and frustrated with Crippen. She had a string of lovers. Then Crippen formed a new relationship of his own, with one of the secretaries at Munyon's offices in New Oxford Street. She was much more like Crippen than Cora had ever been, and a much better match; she was quiet, demure, lady-like, respectable. She was just the sort of woman Crippen should have married. But for Ethel Le Neve, this encounter with Peter Crippen was to become the defining tragedy of her life. At Hilldrop Crescent the situation got progressively worse. Cora started taking in paying guests, for whom Peter was expected to fetch coal, polish boots and do general cleaning. He was close to breaking point by now.

Then Crippen lost his job as manager at Munyon's and was paid only on commission. Cora chose this moment to give the bank notice that she was withdrawing £600 from their joint account. It was a punishment for Peter's philandering, and a kind of threat. Cora's fate was sealed.

On 17 January 1910, Crippen went to a chemist near his office and ordered hyoscine, a strong depressant. The chemist had none in stock and delivered it two days later. On 31 January, Cora and Peter Crippen were 'at home' to two retired music hall friends, Clara and Paul Martinetti. Paul was a retired mime artist. There was dinner followed by whist, then death, for Cora. Clara Martinetti recalled that it was 'quite a nice evening and Belle was very jolly'. They left for home at 1.30 in the morning. Clara's last words to Cora were, 'Don't come down, Belle. You'll catch your death.' After the Martinettis had gone Cora picked a fight with Peter. Within hours she was dead. Crippen never owned up to killing her, and it is by no means clear how Cora Crippen died. The neighbours later claimed that they heard a woman screaming, pleas for mercy and a pistol shot, or perhaps a door being slammed. It must be assumed that he somehow administered a huge dose of hyoscine, waited for her to die, shot her when he tired of waiting, and then set about dismembering her body.

Two days later, Crippen pawned some of his wife's jewellery for £80. He also sent a letter to the Music Hall Ladies Guild to explain that Cora would be missing the next few of their meetings. She had gone to America to attend to a sick relative. Crippen released increasingly alarming bulletins about Cora. She was out of reach in the mountains of California. She was ill with pneumonia. She was dead. Her body, Crippen put it about, had been cremated in America.

Then Crippen had a piece of really bad luck. A couple of Cora's friends, Lil and John Edward Nash, returned from an American theatre tour and told Crippen they had heard nothing of Cora's death in California. They asked him some leading questions. Where had Cora died? 'Some little town near San Francisco, with a Spanish name I think,' was all he seemed to be able to come up with, then 'Los Angeles'. They were suspicious of the answers Crippen gave them and decided to go to the police; by chance they had a friend who was a senior officer at Scotland Yard. On 30 June they took the decisive step, and visited the CID at New Scotland Yard.

Chief Inspector Walter Dew wrote a report on the situation as reported to him by the Nashes. 'It will be gathered from the foregoing that there are the most extraordinary contradictions in the story told by Crippen, who is an American citizen, as is Mrs Crippen, otherwise known as Belle Elmore . . . without adopting the suggestion made by her friends as to foul play, I do think that the time has now arrived when 'Doctor' Crippen should be seen by us and asked to give an explanation as to when and how Mrs Crippen left this country, and the circumstances under which she died.'

On 8 July, Chief Inspector Walter Dew called at Crippen's office with Sergeant Mitchell to ask him some questions about Cora. It was another key encounter, this meeting between Dew and Crippen. Crippen admitted straight away that he had told a lot of lies about Cora's disappearance. 'I suppose I had better tell the truth. All my stories about her illness and death are untrue. So far as I know she is not dead at all.' She had not died. She had left him, run off to America with another man. He made the mistake of mentioning Bruce Miller, but Miller had by this time married and wanted to present a respectable image of himself to his wife. Crippen had lied to everybody in order to protect her reputation and because he felt too ashamed to own up to what had happened.

The interview was amicable and the three men went off to have lunch together before Dew asked Crippen if it would be all right for him and his sergeant to have a look at the house. Crippen agreed to this and went with them to Hilldrop Crescent. Dew was concerned by the fact that Cora had left all her finest clothes behind, but on the whole he was satisfied with Peter Crippen's version of what had happened.

It was then that Crippen made his biggest mistake, after killing Cora, that is. If he had sat it out, the police might well have lost interest, seeing him as an unfortunate husband who had been deserted by his wife. But after Dew had gone he panicked, and persuaded his lover, Ethel, that they should emigrate at once; they must leave the next day for America. He asked his assistant to go out and buy a suit of clothes for a boy and that afternoon the couple left, initially for Europe.

As luck would have it, Dew decided to go back and ask one or two

255

more questions. He found the house empty. He immediately ordered a much more thorough search of the house and the garden, rightly suspecting that Crippen had murdered his wife and that her body was probably buried somewhere in or near the house. It was at the end of the second day that Dew himself found a loose stone in the coal-cellar floor. Underneath, he found an appalling mess of rotting human flesh, but no bones. Crippen had filleted Cora, disposed of the bones in some other way, probably on the kitchen stove, then dumped all her flesh in this pit.

The pathologists, led by Sir Bernard Spilsbury, who had the horrible task of picking through these remains, found that they were those of a fat woman who bleached her hair. There was also skin from the lower abdomen which included an old scar in a position where Cora was known to have one. Most significantly of all, the flesh contained large quantities of hyoscine. On 16 July, there were arrest warrants out for Crippen and Le Neve: wanted for murder and mutilation.

In disposing of the body, Crippen had made several mistakes. He treated the flesh with wet quicklime, whereas quicklime only works as a corrosive when dry. If he had used dry quicklime, the flesh might well have disappeared in the intervening five months. Worse still, he in effect gave the police pathologists a date for the remains by wrapping them in a labelled pyjama jacket, which the manufacturers, Jones Brothers of Holloway, were able to confirm was not made until 1909. There was no possibility that the remains could be older than that.

Peter and Ethel, meanwhile, were in Antwerp, boarding the SS *Montrose* for Quebec, blissfully unaware that they were so soon to be run to earth. They noticed the British policemen watching the gangway as they boarded the ship, but thought they had got away with it once the ship set sail. Crippen had shaved off his moustache, removed his glasses and become Mr John Robinson. Ethel was rather unconvincingly wearing the boy's suit, posing as Crippen's sixteen-year-old son.

The captain of the *Montrose*, Captain Kendall, was suspicious of them. He had read about the gruesome murder at Hilldrop Crescent in the papers, and watched the odd couple carefully. Kendall slipped into their cabin on the first day and saw a piece of flannel torn from a woman's fostering was born. Some of Barnardo's schemes were too adventurous, and because of the lack of proper monitoring some of the boarding-out placements exposed the children to further abuse and suffering. But the main work, setting up the Barnardo Homes, was a huge success, rescuing many children from a wretched childhood on the streets, sleeping out in all weather and exposed to all kinds of danger.

ALGERNON SWINBURNE AND GUY DE MAUPASSANT AT ETRETAT

(1868)

In the 19th century, the British started to explore Normandy. The Channel crossing between Brighton and Dieppe was longer than between Dover and Calais, and the British presence there was less conspicuous; the French seemed even more French. The quaint local costumes and culture were attractions, as were the sea-bathing and casino-gambling. The opening of a railway from London to Brighton, and then Newhaven, along with the commissioning of steam-packets, made the journey quicker and easier.

Painters started arriving as soon as the Napoleonic Wars were over; John Sell Cotman, then Turner, then Richard Bonington. At the end of the century the French Impressionists took over the Normandy coast, but the British had been there already.

The British smart set discreetly installed themselves in summer retreats. The Prince of Wales kept a mistress and maybe an illegitimate child in Dieppe. The prime minister, Lord Salisbury, had a chalet built for himself outside Dieppe and found that he was able to keep in touch with London by telegraph via Beachy Head. And there were many other visitors, both fashionable and unfashionable, including Percy Grainger, Max Beerbohm, Aubrey Beardsley, Walter Sickert. One night in 1897, the Channel packet brought Oscar Wilde, just released from Reading Gaol, and adopting the attention-seeking pseudonym Sebastian Melmoth.

Just along the coast from Dieppe at Etretat, there was another, smaller colony of British artists, mixing with the summer residents. Among the summer residents in 1868 were the eighteen-year-old Guy de Maupassant and his mother. The young French aristocrat was a muscular heterosexual, keen on rowing and swimming. At Etretat he was to encounter the slight, fragile, homosexual English poet, Algernon Swinburne.

The thirty-one-year-old Swinburne was staying in a cottage belonging to his friend George Powell. Because he led such a bizarre and solitary existence the local people decided that Powell was an alias, and that he was secretly an English lord; in fact he was George Powell. Swinburne decided to go for a swim one day in September from the beach at Etretat. He got into difficulties. Swinburne was sure he was going to die and reflected that he was exactly the same age as Shelley when he drowned. But this was a delusion; Swinburne always lied to himself about his age, believing that he was a couple of years younger than he really was.

Powell later said that dangerous undercurrents had swept the auburn-haired poet out to sea 'through a rocky archway'. The natural arch in the chalk cliffs was, and still is, a major local feature. Powell heard shouts from the cliffs. A man was drowning. But a few minutes later he heard that Swinburne had been picked up by some fishermen in a boat and was being taken along the coast to be put ashore. The boat was the *Marie-Marthe*, and she was headed for the harbour at Yport. Once hauled out of the sea, the fishermen rubbed him dry and wrapped him in a sail. He started reciting the poetry of Victor Hugo to them almost at once, while his mop of wet red hair was fanned out on the sail to dry. Swinburne himself wrote to his mother that he had been swept two miles out to sea. 'Luckily I was all right but very tired, and the result was that I made immense friends with all the fishermen and sailors about – who are quite the nicest people I ever knew.' Swinburne kept the oversized garments the fishermen dressed him in for the rest of his life.

Guy de Maupassant was on the scene and claimed that Swinburne was drunk, even though the incident happened at ten o'clock in the morning. Because of Swinburne's wild and hysterical manner, it would have been quite difficult to assess whether he was drunk or not.

Maupassant also claimed that he had gone out in one of the boats to rescue Swinburne. He seems to have been involved in the rescue in some way, as he was invited to lunch the next day by Powell, who had meanwhile collected Swinburne from Yport.

Maupassant described the visit to Powell's cottage three times, first orally in 1875, then in print in 1882 and 1891. The story he tells is consistently racy, though it varies in its detail in the three versions. He describes Powell's house. There were bizarre paintings and displays of bones; there was the flayed hand of a parricide. Powell himself was short and fat, Swinburne was short and thin, trembling and 'talking incessantly like a madman.' Lunch consisted of a type of meat which Maupassant could not place and Powell, his host, refused to identify. Instead of wine, there were spirits.

After lunch, things got worse for poor Maupassant. Powell and Swinburne showed him gay pornographic photographs, presumably in a misguided attempt to seduce him. Powell was drunk, and sucked the fingers of the flayed hand. Yet somehow the conversation surged along on a high level, with Swinburne translating some of his poems into French for Maupassant and waxing lyrical about Victor Hugo, and Powell telling of the old songs and legends he had brought back from Iceland and translated. Maupassant was greatly impressed – how could he not have been? – by the peculiarity of these two men. He described them as 'singularly original, remarkable and bizarre.' He thought they were like fictional characters out of Poe or E. T. A. Hoffmann.

The young Maupassant was self-assured enough to go back for a second lunch a few days afterwards. He was not to be put off by a few pornographic pictures, a misbehaving monkey or a flayed hand. The second lunch was more peaceful, as the large pet monkey that had caused such a disturbance at the first was now dead, apparently hanged from a tree by a black servant boy who had tired of cleaning up after it. The servant boy was threatened by Powell and ran off. The boy later found employment selling barley-sugar in the streets, but when he nearly strangled a dissatisfied customer he was run out of Etretat. Powell ordered a large block of granite to make a tomb for the monkey. At the end of the lunch Powell and Swinburne gave Maupassant some alcohol that almost knocked him out. After that he escaped to the safety of his hotel.

Yet Maupassant ventured back to Powell's weird cottage once more. On the earlier visits he had noticed an inscription above the door, but thought nothing of it. This time he drew Powell's and Swinburne's attention to it. It said 'Chaumière de Dolmancé', the Cottage of Dolmancé. The young Frenchman asked them if they knew who Dolmancé was. Maupassant did; he was the homosexual seducer in one of de Sade's books. Oh yes, they knew. Maupassant asked them if that was the sign of the house. They answered, 'If you like!' Maupassant commented that the expressions on their faces were terrifying.

Maupassant went back to the safety of his hotel and never returned to Powell's cottage. It was probably wise, as he was clearly in some moral danger from the two older men. Powell had relays of servant boys of fourteen or fifteen sent out to him from England every few months, 'little boys of exquisite cleanness and freshness', Maupassant commented. He also understood that the two men were real anti-heroes straight out of the pages of de Sade, men who would not have held back from crime.

But one can't help wondering if Maupassant was exaggerating. He was, after all, a novelist, and his different versions of what happened suggest a certain amount of invention. One of his accounts of the Etretat episode ends, 'Then this house, so full of living mystery, was suddenly silent, suddenly empty. Powell just disappeared, and no one knew how he had got away. No carriage was ever called for him, and no one had met him on the roads.' It reads like the ending of a short story by Edgar Allan Poe. And there is a certain roguish knowingness in the older Maupassant teasing his readers with the tale of his innocent younger self falling into the hands of English reprobates. But behind all this, Maupassant had huge admiration for Powell and Swinburne. He admired their passion for art and literature. He admired their rejection of accepted middle-class values. He revelled in their recklessness, their bravado, their sheer originality. They were – in spite of everything – role models for a young creative writer.

And that strange encounter in the sea at Etretat, between the athletic youth in the rescue boat and the decadent red-haired English poet floundering in the water, led eventually to a French prose edition of Swinburne's poems with an introductory essay – written by Guy de Maupassant.

HENRY MORTON STANLEY AND DAVID LIVINGSTONE

(1871)

DAVID LIVINGSTONE WAS born in Scotland in 1813. After taking a degr
in medicine he became a missionary. The London Missionary Soci
sent him to Africa. He wanted to convert Africans to Christianity a
put an end to the slave trade. But as he travelled into central Africa
became an explorer. He tried to establish which rivers might
navigable by missionaries trying to reach the interior; he had a practi
reason for finding out the physical geography of the continent. In
1850s he became the first white man to travel right across Africa, ;
on that journey he also became the first white man to see the h
waterfall that he named after Queen Victoria.

After returning to England to find that he had become a celeb;
Livingstone led a major new expedition across central Africa, startin
1859. Then in the late 1860s he started exploring the area round L
Tanganyika. It was then that he disappeared from view as far as
outside world was concerned. It turned out later that he was in
writing despatches, but nearly all of them failed to reach 1
destination. So, without realising it himself, David Livingstone
disappeared from view. By 1871 he had been in central Africa and
of touch with the outside world for five years. In Europe and Am
it was widely feared that Livingstone was dead. In November
Henry Morton Stanley, an American journalist, mounted an exped
to find him.

Stanley was born in 1841 in Denbigh in Wales, with the name John Rowlands. He had a very poor upbringing, spending his boyhood in a workhouse for orphans. At seventeen he became a cabin boy on a ship sailing for New Orleans. Once in America, he joined up as a Confederate soldier in the Civil War, was captured by Unionists, changed sides, and then was discharged through ill health. The violence and harshness of these early years may go some way towards explaining, though not excusing, his unusually harsh treatment of African porters. After this turbulent start he became a journalist, a reporter for the *New York Times*. This led to travel, and to his most famous assignment – to find Livingstone.

Stanley trekked across from Zanzibar on the east coast towards Ujiji on Lake Tanganyika. He travelled with a huge party of 200 porters, and gained a reputation for his harsh treatment of bearers. He did not see the huge lake until the last moment because of the hills. It was only as he and his party passed over the crest of the last hill that he saw the lake and the port of Ujiji only 500 yards from him.

Our hearts and our feelings are with our eyes as we peer into the palms and try to make out in which hut lives the white man with the grey beard we heard about on the Malagarazi. We were now about three hundred yards from the village and the crowds are dense about me. Suddenly I hear a voice on my right side.

Good morning, sir!'

Startled at hearing this greeting in the midst of such a crowd of black people, I turn sharply round in search of the man and see him at my side, with the blackest of faces, but animated and joyous – a man dressed in a long white shirt, with a turban of American sheeting around his head, and I ask, 'Who the mischief are you?'

'I am Susi, the servant of Dr Livingstone,' said he, smiling.

'What! Dr Livingstone is here?'

'Yes, sir.'

Are you sure?'

'Sure, sir. Why, I leave him just now -'

'Now, run, Susi and tell the Doctor I am coming.'

'Yes, sir,' and off he darted like a madman. Soon Susi came running back and asked my name. He had told the Doctor I was coming, but the Doctor was too surprised to believe him.'

Stanley pushed his way through a great crowd of people and saw Livingstone, looking pale and weary. He wanted to run to him and throw his arms round him, but because Livingstone was British Stanley controlled himself. He walked purposefully towards Livingstone, took off his hat and said, 'Dr Livingstone, I presume?'

Livingstone simply replied 'Yes', smiled and raised his cap a little.

In reality, the famous greeting line may not have been uttered. Livingstone did not mention it, and Stanley tore the relevant page out of his diary, presumably to cover his tracks. The line was probably an invention for the newspaper, though it has subsequently been quoted without question. What happened next is that Stanley told Livingstone the European and American news of the last few years. Among other things, Stanley told Livingstone that the presidential election campaign had started in America and that the Democrats had nominated Horace Greeley. Livingstone is supposed to have stopped Stanley there, saying, 'You have told me curious things and wonderful, but there is a limit. When you tell me the Democrats have nominated Greeley for President I am hanged if I will believe it!' But this may well be apocryphal, geared more to the American newspaper readers than to historical accuracy.

The result of Stanley's finding of Livingstone was a major news story round the world. Stanley was a journalist and that was why he had done it. The incident became a legendary moment in the history of 19th century adventure, and of course it greatly benefited Stanley's career.

Stanley was under instructions from his employer, the *New York Times*, to return as soon as he had found Livingstone. Instead he lingered with Livingstone, who was frail and needed help. The two men became firm friends. Livingstone was striving to find the source of the Nile to the south of Lake Victoria; Stanley stayed with him until March 1872 before returning to America.

Livingstone died a year later and Stanley decided he himself would continue Livingstone's exploration work. Stanley's great achievement was following the entire course of the River Congo from source to mouth, which filled in a huge area of the map of central Africa. He reached the mouth of the Congo in 1877. But the expedition had been difficult and dangerous; he had had to abandon two-thirds of his party, originally 350 strong.

Stanley wrote up his remarkable expedition in a book called *Through the Dark Continent,* parading his exploration as if it were a military conquest. One of his readers was the Belgian King, Leopold II. Following directly on from this, Stanley was commissioned by the ambitious king to assist in the setting up of a large Belgian colony. In 1876, King Leopold organised a private holding company disguised as a scientific and humanitarian society, and called the International African Society. The King spoke in terms of introducing Western civilisation and Christianity to the area, but did not make clear that he wanted to claim the land as, in effect, a private kingdom. Stanley went back to the Congo to organise treaties with the tribal chiefs, and build roads to improve communication, though these merely helped to make the slave trade more efficient.

When Stanley realised that King Leopold intended to develop the Congo as a wealth-generating estate for his own personal gain he did not resign. He stayed on and went on working for him.

This was the shadiest part of Stanley's career, because of the sheer cruelty of the régime King Leopold set up there – with Stanley's help. In later years, Stanley found himself forced to defend his behaviour in the Congo, where the native workforce had been treated with abominable violence; many people were mutilated for minor offences. The truth was that Stanley, like a great many unenlightened white people in the nineteenth century, thought of black people as no better than ignorant beasts. He said, 'the savage only respects force, power, boldness and decision.' Stanley was himself responsible for a number of deaths in the Congo.

The entirely worthy and honourable Livingstone had died alone and in obscurity in Africa. Henry Morton Stanley, however, became a British MP at the end of the 19th century, acquiring a knighthood in 1899. He died in 1904.

DR CRIPPEN, CHIEF INSPECTOR DREW AND CAPTAIN KENDALL

(1910)

HAWLEY HARVEY CRIPPEN was an American by birth, born in Michigan in 1862, though the spectacularly newsworthy murder he committed took place in London. He gained his medical qualifications at Cleveland, London and New York. It was after that, while he was working as a doctor's assistant in New York, that he encountered Cora Turner. She was seventeen, lively and attractive, but also pregnant and the mistress of a stove manufacturer. She had a miscarriage. In spite of the very obvious disadvantages of the liaison, Crippen, who was by now a thirty-one-year-old widower, fell in love with her.

It was a misalliance. Love is blind, they say, and Hawley Harvey Crippen was blind to the flaws in Cora's personality, blind to her total unsuitability as a partner. He found that she was not really Cora Turner but Kunigunde Mackamotzki, of Russian-Polish and German parentage. He also discovered that she hoped to become an opera singer. Crippen indulged this pipe-dream, paying for her singing lessons. Cora and Hawley were married in 1893. It was a big mistake for both of them.

In 1900, Crippen moved to London to be the manager of the head office of Munyon's, a mail-order medicine company. Cora followed him across the Atlantic later that year. In London, she decided to lower her sights a little; here she would be a music-hall star. She changed her name a second time, to Belle Elmore. For reasons unknown, Crippen too changed his name, from Hawley Harvey to Peter. Their new life consisted of a riot of Bohemian parties with the gay, outgoing Belle at their centre and the insignificant and slightly lugubrious Peter, with his big sandy moustache and small spectacles, looking dolefully on. Occasionally he treated her to a lavish present – a fur or some jewellery - but life behind the scenes was far from glamorous. Neither of them wanted to do any housework, and they lived in a squalid back kitchen in a tangle of unwashed clothes and heaps of unwashed crockery.

Then things started to go badly wrong. Crippen had to return to America on business and while he was away Cora had an affair with an American music hall entertainer called Bruce Miller. In 1905, the Crippens moved up-market to 39 Hilldrop Crescent in Camden Town, but the move did nothing to heal the damaged relationship. Crippen said, 'There were very frequent occasions when she got into the most violent tempers . . . She went in and out just as she liked . . . I was a rather lonely man and rather miserable.'

Cora worked for the Music Hall Ladies Guild, where she was able to pretend to be a great star helping out less fortunate members of the profession. Cora lived in a world of illusion; one of her fantasies was that her father was titled. Crippen even used his father-in-law's imaginary title in one of his firm's quack remedies, calling it Baron Mackamotzki's Cure for Deafness. She was bored and frustrated with Crippen. She had a string of lovers. Then Crippen formed a new relationship of his own, with one of the secretaries at Munyon's offices in New Oxford Street. She was much more like Crippen than Cora had ever been, and a much better match; she was quiet, demure, lady-like, respectable. She was just the sort of woman Crippen should have married. But for Ethel Le Neve, this encounter with Peter Crippen was to become the defining tragedy of her life. At Hilldrop Crescent the situation got progressively worse. Cora started taking in paying guests, for whom Peter was expected to fetch coal, polish boots and do general cleaning. He was close to breaking point by now.

Then Crippen lost his job as manager at Munyon's and was paid only on commission. Cora chose this moment to give the bank notice that she was withdrawing £600 from their joint account. It was a punishment for Peter's philandering, and a kind of threat. Cora's fate was sealed.

On 17 January 1910, Crippen went to a chemist near his office and ordered hyoscine, a strong depressant. The chemist had none in stock and delivered it two days later. On 31 January, Cora and Peter Crippen were 'at home' to two retired music hall friends, Clara and Paul Martinetti. Paul was a retired mime artist. There was dinner followed by whist, then death, for Cora. Clara Martinetti recalled that it was 'quite a nice evening and Belle was very jolly'. They left for home at 1.30 in the morning. Clara's last words to Cora were, 'Don't come down, Belle. You'll catch your death.' After the Martinettis had gone Cora picked a fight with Peter. Within hours she was dead. Crippen never owned up to killing her, and it is by no means clear how Cora Crippen died. The neighbours later claimed that they heard a woman screaming, pleas for mercy and a pistol shot, or perhaps a door being slammed. It must be assumed that he somehow administered a huge dose of hyoscine, waited for her to die, shot her when he tired of waiting, and then set about dismembering her body.

Two days later, Crippen pawned some of his wife's jewellery for £80. He also sent a letter to the Music Hall Ladies Guild to explain that Cora would be missing the next few of their meetings. She had gone to America to attend to a sick relative. Crippen released increasingly alarming bulletins about Cora. She was out of reach in the mountains of California. She was ill with pneumonia. She was dead. Her body, Crippen put it about, had been cremated in America.

Then Crippen had a piece of really bad luck. A couple of Cora's friends, Lil and John Edward Nash, returned from an American theatre tour and told Crippen they had heard nothing of Cora's death in California. They asked him some leading questions. Where had Cora died? 'Some little town near San Francisco, with a Spanish name I think,' was all he seemed to be able to come up with, then 'Los Angeles'. They were suspicious of the answers Crippen gave them and decided to go to the police; by chance they had a friend who was a senior officer at Scotland Yard. On 30 June they took the decisive step, and visited the CID at New Scotland Yard.

Chief Inspector Walter Dew wrote a report on the situation as reported to him by the Nashes. 'It will be gathered from the foregoing that there are the most extraordinary contradictions in the story told by Crippen, who is an American citizen, as is Mrs Crippen, otherwise known as Belle Elmore . . . without adopting the suggestion made by her friends as to foul play, I do think that the time has now arrived when 'Doctor' Crippen should be seen by us and asked to give an explanation as to when and how Mrs Crippen left this country, and the circumstances under which she died.'

On 8 July, Chief Inspector Walter Dew called at Crippen's office with Sergeant Mitchell to ask him some questions about Cora. It was another key encounter, this meeting between Dew and Crippen. Crippen admitted straight away that he had told a lot of lies about Cora's disappearance. 'I suppose I had better tell the truth. All my stories about her illness and death are untrue. So far as I know she is not dead at all.' She had not died. She had left him, run off to America with another man. He made the mistake of mentioning Bruce Miller, but Miller had by this time married and wanted to present a respectable image of himself to his wife. Crippen had lied to everybody in order to protect her reputation and because he felt too ashamed to own up to what had happened.

The interview was amicable and the three men went off to have lunch together before Dew asked Crippen if it would be all right for him and his sergeant to have a look at the house. Crippen agreed to this and went with them to Hilldrop Crescent. Dew was concerned by the fact that Cora had left all her finest clothes behind, but on the whole he was satisfied with Peter Crippen's version of what had happened.

It was then that Crippen made his biggest mistake, after killing Cora, that is. If he had sat it out, the police might well have lost interest, seeing him as an unfortunate husband who had been deserted by his wife. But after Dew had gone he panicked, and persuaded his lover, Ethel, that they should emigrate at once; they must leave the next day for America. He asked his assistant to go out and buy a suit of clothes for a boy and that afternoon the couple left, initially for Europe.

As luck would have it, Dew decided to go back and ask one or two more questions. He found the house empty. He immediately ordered a much more thorough search of the house and the garden, rightly suspecting that Crippen had murdered his wife and that her body was probably buried somewhere in or near the house. It was at the end of the second day that Dew himself found a loose stone in the coal-cellar floor. Underneath, he found an appalling mess of rotting human flesh, but no bones. Crippen had filleted Cora, disposed of the bones in some other way, probably on the kitchen stove, then dumped all her flesh in this pit.

The pathologists, led by Sir Bernard Spilsbury, who had the horrible task of picking through these remains, found that they were those of a fat woman who bleached her hair. There was also skin from the lower abdomen which included an old scar in a position where Cora was known to have one. Most significantly of all, the flesh contained large quantities of hyoscine. On 16 July, there were arrest warrants out for Crippen and Le Neve: wanted for murder and mutilation.

In disposing of the body, Crippen had made several mistakes. He treated the flesh with wet quicklime, whereas quicklime only works as a corrosive when dry. If he had used dry quicklime, the flesh might well have disappeared in the intervening five months. Worse still, he in effect gave the police pathologists a date for the remains by wrapping them in a labelled pyjama jacket, which the manufacturers, Jones Brothers of Holloway, were able to confirm was not made until 1909. There was no possibility that the remains could be older than that.

Peter and Ethel, meanwhile, were in Antwerp, boarding the SS *Montrose* for Quebec, blissfully unaware that they were so soon to be run to earth. They noticed the British policemen watching the gangway as they boarded the ship, but thought they had got away with it once the ship set sail. Crippen had shaved off his moustache, removed his glasses and become Mr John Robinson. Ethel was rather unconvincingly wearing the boy's suit, posing as Crippen's sixteen-year-old son.

The captain of the *Montrose*, Captain Kendall, was suspicious of them. He had read about the gruesome murder at Hilldrop Crescent in the papers, and watched the odd couple carefully. Kendall slipped into their cabin on the first day and saw a piece of flannel torn from a woman's

JOAN OF ARC

A sixteen-year-old peasant girl by the name of Jeanne d'Arc was quite used to hearing voices while she tended the cattle at Domrémy. She recognised the speakers as St Michael, St Catherine and St Margaret, but it wasn't until the winter of 1428 that they gave her a very specific instruction – to raise the siege of Orléans.

THE ROSWELL INCIDENT

A farmer found some metallic fragments on his farm near Roswell. They were believed to be pieces of a weather balloon, and yet when studied closely, certain portions were seen to be covered with indecipherable writing.

ELIZABETH I AND SIR WALTER RALEIGH

Sir Walter Raleigh became a firm favourite of Queen Elizabeth I, although there is little depth to the story about him spreading his cloak across a puddle as pictured here. He became Captain of the Guard and played an enormous part in foiling the Babington conspiracy which was aimed at replacing Queen Elizabeth I with Mary, Queen of Scots.

OSCAR WILDE

Oscar Wilde met Lord Alfred Douglas (or Bosie as he was more affectionately known) in Chelsea when Bosie was just twenty-two years old. Wilde became enamoured with the young man who, in turn, was thrilled to be favoured by such a literary genius. This resulted in many letters being exchanged, containing words that could be interpreted as expressions of passionate love.

THE 'TITANIC'

This picture shows the luxurious reading and writing room on board the magnificent *Titanic*. The largest ship of its day and with innovative technology, the *Titanic* was believed to be unsinkable, and yet when she set sail on her maiden voyage on 10 April 1912, she was never to return. The story of the *Titanic* and the iceberg has grown into a legend of the sea over the years and yet it took her discovery in 1985 to really find out the truth.

THE BUSH-GORBACHEV SUMMITS

USSR leader Mikhail Gorbachev stands at a podium after arriving at the Malta Summit, where he held an important liaison with US President George W. Bush, shortly after the fall of the Berlin Wall in 1989. The summit ushered in a new era and set the pace for a more united Europe.

BEETHOVEN AND NAPOLEON

Most of us know Beethoven (top) as a composer, but he was also a political campaigner for liberty and justice. The *Eroica Symphony* was to be called the 'Bonaparte Symphone' to show the composer's respect for the man who was making large advances towards reforming Europe, Napoleon Bonaparte (right). However, when Napoleon crowned himself emperor in 1804, Beethoven was so angry that he took a knife to the title page and scratched out the name of Bonaparte so aggressively that he made a hole in the paper. Beethoven simply refused to dedicate one of his pieces to a man he now considered to be a 'tyrant'.

PABLO PICASSO AND DORA MAAR

In the winter of 1935, Pablo Picasso (above) became intimately involved with Dora Maar, a beautiful, passionate and extremely intelligent young woman. Maar's influence over Picasso was to stimulate one of the most innovative periods of his career. Pictured below is one of his numerous paintings resulting from their encounter.

bodice; something was not right about this pair. He noticed that there was more hand-touching between the two than would normally be the case between father and son. The boy ate in a rather too refined and dainty way. Kendall cleverly called to 'Mr Robinson', Crippen's newly adopted pseudonym, and timed the rate of reaction: a little too slow to be the real name. He amiably invited the pair to dine at his table. He cracked lots of jokes to make Mr Robinson bare his teeth. Crippen was described by the police as having false teeth. It turned out that this was wrong information, but it shows how thorough Kendall was in chasing his hunch about the Robinsons. Kendall's last doubts were literally blown away when a gust of wind moved the flap on Ethel's jacket, revealing a safety pin inserted to let out the trousers to accommodate her broad, non-boyish hips.

After a couple of days at sea, Kendall was sure. He used the new wireless telegraph to send a message to the ship's owners, telling them of his conclusions. 'Have strong suspicions that Crippen London cellar murderer and accomplice are among Saloon passengers. Moustache taken off growing beard. Accomplice dressed as boy. Voice manner and build undoubtedly a girl.' On 23 July, Chief Inspector Drew and his sergeant sailed from Liverpool on the *Laurentic*. This was a faster ship than the *Montrose*, and it was following a more northerly Great Circle (shortest distance) route. Dew hoped that by taking the faster ship by the shorter route he might overtake the *Montrose* before she reached Quebec. The last thing he wanted was to have to chase Crippen and Le Neve all over North America.

For eight extraordinary days, Crippen lounged in a deckchair on the deck of the *Montrose*, voicing admiration for the wonderful new invention, little suspecting that the wireless telegraph was preparing the trap that would send him to the gallows and break Ethel's tender and innocent heart. 'What a wonderful invention wireless is!' he said to Kendall. Captain Kendall had carefully collected up all the English newspapers he had found at the start of the voyage, so no-one on the ship except Crippen and himself knew what had happened. The outside world, on the other hand, was being told, almost hour by hour, of the net closing on Dr

257

Crippen. There was great excitement about the case, not just because of the grisly murder and the way Crippen had disposed of his wife's body, but because this was turning out to be the very first manhunt triggered and fuelled by wireless. Policing had entered a new era. After 25 July, Kendall's ship was out of receiving range from land, but he was able to listen to reports via other ships fitted with wireless and use them to bounce messages back across the ocean to Scotland Yard. Even the *Laurentic* was out of direct range when it passed the *Montrose* on 27 July.

The newspapers were full of the chase across the Atlantic, full of Crippen and his accomplice, full of the wireless. The sensational success of the radio-assisted chase was a heaven-sent advertisement for wireless. Marconi could not have wished for more. Within a year, the number of merchant ships equipped with wireless increased enormously, and there was an irresistible demand from the public for wireless to be compulsory for all but the smaller ships. Thanks to Crippen, then, the *Titanic* was fitted with wireless and at least those who took to the boats in 1912 were rescued by the *Carpathia*.

The *Laurentic* ambushed the *Montrose* in the St Lawrence, only sixteen hours from Quebec. Dew boarded the *Montrose*, introduced himself to Captain Kendall and then approached Crippen, to whom he said, 'Good morning, Mr Crippen. I am Chief Inspector Dew'. Later, Crippen said, 'I am not sorry. The anxiety has been too much.' He was quick to exonerate Ethel. He insisted that she knew nothing about Cora's death, which seems likely.

On 20 August, after extradition formalities had been completed, Dew set off home for England with his now-infamous prisoners. Once again, no-one on the ship, the SS *Megantic*, knew who they were. Dew, who had been Mr Dewhurst on the *Laurentic*, had now become Mr Doyle - not the brother of Sir Arthur Conan Doyle, the creator of Sherlock Holmes, surely? - and Crippen alias John Robinson had become Mr Neild. As they travelled from Liverpool to London, they were not only recognised but mobbed by angry crowds. Dew was on the crest of a wave; eventually in 1938 he wrote his memoirs, *I caught Crippen*, though he owed much to the incredible Captain Kendall.

The trial of Dr Crippen, which started on 10 October 1910, was short and the verdict a foregone conclusion. He was guilty and sentenced to death. Crippen was hanged at Pentonville on 23 November 1910. Ethel Le Neve, still only twenty-seven, was tried a week after Crippen. She was found not guilty of being an accessory after the fact, and slid instantly and deliberately into obscurity. It had been an extraordinary saga that developed in the way that it did only because of a sequence of chance encounters made by Crippen – first with Cora, then with Ethel, then with Dew and Kendall.

THE TITANIC AND THE ICEBERG

(1912)

THE STORY OF the sinking of the *Titanic* is well known, and it has been retold many times over since the ship went down in the icy waters of the North Atlantic on 15 April 1912, with the loss of over 1,500 lives. Most of the books that have been written about the sinking focus on blame. Who was responsible for equipping the ship with so few lifeboats – far too few for all the people on board? Who decided that there would be no lifeboat drill? Who decided that the ship would steam at almost top speed through a sea known to be infested with icebergs? Was it the captain, the experienced Captain Smith, or the ship's owner, Bruce Ismay? Who decided that the watertight bulkheads would terminate several decks lower than they should?

But one writer considered a different aspect of the disaster. He viewed it as an encounter, and not only that but a predestined encounter, between the ship and the iceberg. Thomas Hardy wrote his haunting poem, *The Convergence of the Twain*, immediately after the sinking of the *Titanic*.

> *In a solitude of the sea*
> *Deep from human vanity,*
> *And the Pride of Life that planned her, stilly couches she.*
>
> *Steel chambers, late the pyres*
> *Of her salamandrine fires,*
> *Cold currents thrid, and turn to rhythmic tidal lyres.*
> *Over the mirrors meant*
> *To glass the opulent*
> *The sea-worm crawls - grotesque, slimed, dumb, indifferent.*

Jewels in joy designed
To ravish the sensuous mind
Lie lightless, all their sparkles bleared and black and blind.

Dim moon-eyed fishes near
Gaze at the gilded gear
And query: 'What does this vaingloriousness down here?'...

Well: while was fashioning
This creature of cleaving wing,
The Immanent Will that stirs and urges everything

Prepared a sinister mate
For her – so gaily great –
A Shape of Ice, for the time fat and dissociate.

And as the smart ship grew
In stature, grace, and hue
In shadowy silent distance grew the Iceberg too.

Alien they seemed to be:
No mortal eye could see
The intimate welding of their later history.

Or sign that they were bent
By paths coincident
On being anon twin halves of one august event,

Till the Spinner of the Years
Said 'Now!' And each one hears,
And consummation comes, and jars two hemispheres.

Long after Hardy wrote this poem, geographers explored the origin of the icebergs that find their way into the North Atlantic shipping lanes. It is now known that the iceberg that sank the Titanic was born on the west coast of Greenland, that it calved from one of the several outlet glaciers that flow from the Greenland ice sheet. Where these glaciers reach the sea, chunks of them break away from their seaward ends and float away, at first northwards, instead of south towards the shipping lanes. Calculation of the speed of the currents has shown that it was born at the same time that the *Titanic*'s keel was being laid in Belfast. It really is as if the two entities, berg and ship, had parallel existences, parallel destinies.

The nameless, anonymous iceberg was first swept northwards by the coastal sea current, the West Greenland Current, towards the Arctic. Then after circling Baffin Bay it travelled southwards with the Labrador Current along the coast of Labrador. As that long sea journey was completed, the *Titanic* too was completed, launched, fitted. She had undergone her sea trials and was setting off on her maiden voyage on 10 April. The berg carried on south and had reached the Grand Banks as Captain Smith gave his Sunday sermon; by this time they were just 300 miles apart.

At 11.40 pm on 14 April, the iceberg and the ship came within sight of one another – the twin halves of one event, as Hardy described, and about to weld. The ship and the iceberg were 600 kilometres to the south-east of Mistaken Point, Newfoundland. The lookouts on the *Titanic*, Frederick Fleet and Reginald Lee, saw the iceberg dead in front of the ship, which was steaming straight at it. Fleet rang the ship's bell three times and telephoned the officers on the bridge, shouting, 'Iceberg, right ahead!' First Officer Murdoch ordered 'Hard-a-starboard', which caused the ship to swing slowly to port; he also ordered the engines to be thrown into reverse. But the ship was moving fast and its huge weight and momentum meant that it was too slow to respond as the berg and ship closed on each other.

Conceivably, if the lookouts had seen the berg earlier, the avoiding action might have been effective. And if they had seen the berg later, the *Titanic* would have hit the berg head on, the bow crashing straight into the ice. Catastrophic though that might sound, it is possible that the ship would have survived such an impact. The forward two compartments might have been badly damaged, crushed and flooded, but the ship would have stayed afloat. The slight turn to port meant that the iceberg scraped along the starboard side of the ship, snapping the rivets, popping open plate after plate for ninety metres, about one-third of the length of the ship. Five of the watertight compartments were flooded. The *Titanic* could have remained afloat with four of them flooded, but not five.

Two-and-a-half hours later the *Titanic* broke in two and sank, plunging over two miles to the deep ocean floor. Of the 2,222 people on board, over two-thirds were lost. 1,517 people died that night as a result of the encounter with the iceberg.

The consequences of the sinking were enormous. Safety procedures were overhauled. Checks of basic equipment, such as the binoculars that should have been in the crow's nest, became routine. Lifeboat drill became mandatory on all voyages, so that everyone on board knew where they had to go in the event of an emergency, and how to get there. The Board of Trade's regulation regarding lifeboat provision was changed; from then on there had to be enough space in the lifeboats for everyone on board.

After the fateful and fatal brush with the *Titanic*, the iceberg continued drifting on its way eastwards. During the following day, 15 April, the chief steward of the liner *Prinz Adelbert*, saw the iceberg. He was sure it was the very one that had sunk the Titanic because it had a smear of red paint on it, the sort of mark that would have been left by the red anti-fouling paint that the Titanic's hull was coated with below the waterline. The steward's photo shows an iceberg with three peaks. Floating in the water round the berg were bodies and debris from the *Titanic*.

But was it fate or destiny, or the mysterious Spinner of the Years, as Hardy imagined it to be? Or was it just an accident? Just chance? It depends to a great extent on the mindset of the observer, but it is all too easy to see patterns in events with the benefit of hindsight. At this distance of time, the sinking of the *Titanic* looks less like an act of God punishing human pride and more like an unfortunate coincidence of unfavourable factors – and a lot of very human mistakes.

VI
POLITICAL ENCOUNTERS

THE ETONIANS: HAROLD MACMILLAN, BOBBETY CRANBORNE, OLIVER LYTTELTON, HARRY CROOKSHANK

(1914)

FOUR ENGLISHMEN WERE born within a few months of one another at the end of the 19th century: Harry Crookshank, Oliver Lyttelton, Bobbety Cranborne and Harold Macmillan. They were all at Eton at the same time, Cranborne and Lyttelton from patrician families (Cranborne was the son of Lord Salisbury, the prime minister), Crookshank and Macmillan from 'new money'. But any social division that might have separated them was removed by the time the four young men joined the Grenadier Guards, in itself a socially élitist group.

When the First World War broke out and they were sent to the Western Front as junior officers, Lyttelton and Cranborne became cynical about their senior commanders. The general view was that Haig was a fool. During action at the battle of Festubert, in which both Cranborne and Lyttelton fought, Cranborne was deafened by rifle fire close at hand and sent home on extended leave. Then in 1915 Macmillan and Crookshank were to fight in the battle of Loos. After a mine exploded, Crookshank was buried by the earth thrown up in the explosion; it was twenty minutes before he was dug out and rescued, shaken but alive, and ready to return to duty the same evening. Of the four men, Macmillan proved to be the least adaptable to life in the trenches. Of the four he looked at that time and later on the least likely to succeed. He tried to create a reading circle among his fellow officers in an attempt to hang onto some vestiges of the civilised life.

In the battle of Loos, Macmillan was shot in the head, a glancing blow which even so concussed him; then he was shot in the right hand. Macmillan was troubled by his damaged right hand for the rest of his life. The battle of Loos was a failure as far as the Guards Division was concerned. Macmillan said, 'It has been rather awful – most of our officers are hit.'

After Loos, Crookshank was out in mist with a wiring party when he too was shot, in the left leg. He was out of the fighting for the rest of 1915 and, being sent back to a London nursing home, he missed Winston Churchill's arrival at the Front to serve with the 2nd Battalion. Churchill had suffered the humiliation of being thrown out of the Cabinet. The Dardanelles expedition had failed and Churchill was held responsible for it. Lyttelton and his circle had regarded Churchill as a turncoat for several years, ever since he had moved from the Tory to the Liberal Party. But Churchill was undaunted by his unpopularity, holding forth at dinner on the theme of the tank as the weapon that would win the war for the Allies.

The death toll among Guards officers was so high at Loos that it was clear junior officers would see rapid promotion. Lyttelton became adjutant of a Guards battalion, third-in-command in battle.

At Easter in 1916 Macmillan had a bad experience; he was in command of a platoon in an exposed trench near Ypres. He was isolated, cold, frightened, and fell back on reading the story of the sufferings of Jesus in St Luke's Gospel. But then in the summer Crookshank joined him. It was a happy reunion and they immediately became tent-mates. Macmillan was unable to achieve much but made his name by holding an extremely unpromising position. He led two men on a scouting patrol in no man's land, ran into some German soldiers who threw a grenade, and was wounded in the face. He was injured badly enough to have been shipped out but he refused, saying his first duty was to the regiment. This was partly bravado, partly a rejection of Crookshank's determination to win promotion. But he was mentioned in despatches and praised for his bravery. Meanwhile a much larger action was unfolding to the south, on the Somme, and the young officers were thrown into training programmes to prepare for it.

It was not long before Macmillan and Crookshank were in action again, and wounded again, Macmillan wounded in the knee, a wound that became dangerously infected, and Crookshank castrated by a shell. At Christmas 1916 the two men were in London hospital beds. Cranborne meanwhile was in good heart; his wife had given birth to a son who would secure the Cecil succession. Lyttelton was parading a French mistress.

When the First World War ended, the four men had to choose careers. Lyttelton married the daughter of a duke, and this carried expensive social obligations. He went into business as a dealer, working initially for the British Metal Corporation. Macmillan had no pressing need to earn a lot of money, and went quietly into the family publishing business, fully expecting to spend the rest of his life at a desk. He wanted to see the world. So did Cranborne and Crookshank. They chose to become diplomats in the Foreign Office. Cranborne's father was one of the architects of the post-war peace settlement, and Cranborne was there to witness it.

In 1920 Macmillan made a strategic marriage, to Dorothy Cavendish, daughter of the Duke of Devonshire. The duke was deeply involved in politics and found Macmillan an interested disciple; they took to discussing politics, especially in relation to Africa, on a regular basis. By 1923, Macmillan was selected as Conservative candidate for the constituency of Stockton. The opposition was tough and he failed to win the seat, but in the next election, in 1924, he won Stockton and his friend Crookshank won Gainsborough, also for the Conservatives. Their careers as politicians were under way. Cranborne's was not.

Cranborne had committed himself to a career in the City in an effort to diversify the family fortune. Although Crookshank was able to throw in his diplomatic career to chase a parliamentary seat, Cranborne was not in a position to give up his City career yet, as he stood to lose a fortune by doing so. But he was sorely tempted – there was nothing he wanted more than to enter politics like his forebears and in 1929 he slipped quietly into the safe Conservative seat of South Dorset.

Lyttelton was also a businessman, and a far more successful one than Cranborne. By 1929, Lyttelton was emerging as a metal tycoon. At that time, Macmillan's personal and public life went into the doldrums. He was not advancing in politics as fast as he had hoped. His wife Dorothy launched into an affair with his friend Bob Boothby, and without any discretion either. She taunted Macmillan with the fact that the daughter she gave birth to in 1930 was not his but Boothby's and boasted publicly of her infidelity. Macmillan was distraught and humiliated. In 1931 he had a breakdown and went off to a sanatorium in Bavaria to recover.

In the 1930s, each of the four Guardsmen flirted with extreme right-wing politics, wondering if it was a better alternative to Conservatism. Tom Mosley, the fascist leader, repeatedly referred to the 'Great War generation' as the right leaders for the future, and the likes of Captain Macmillan, Captain Crookshank and Captain Lyttelton gained in status as a result. Macmillan was a regular visitor at Mosley's house in Smith Square. The managers of the Conservative Party identified Macmillan, currently without a seat, as the likeliest of their candidates or prospective candidates to defect. In the event, when Mosley formed his New Party in 1931, Macmillan decided to stay with the Conservatives; but the press noted that he was an admirer of Mussolini's 'corporate state'. Breakdown and personal unhappiness dominated his life. A friend went to stay at Macmillan's house, Birch Grove, and was thoroughly depressed; 'The gloom of H. Macmillan is something terrible . . . he is a much disappointed man . . . not a cheering companion even for a weekend.'

Harry Crookshank made the same decision as Macmillan, not to join the New Party, but for different reasons. He thought the addition of a fourth party to the Westminster parliamentary system would be practically unworkable. He was inclined to cynicism and some of his speeches against Ramsay MacDonald were so filled with snobbish contempt that they backfired on him. People noticed Crookshank, but thought him waspish. Cranborne went instead for a tone of patrician seriousness and he argued carefully for the idea of a National government, gaining a reputation as an intelligent loyalist. But Cranborne too had his personal setback when his sixteen-year-old son Michael died suddenly at Eton.

By the mid-1930s, the careers of the four friends had developed in a way that separated them from each other. At this time in their lives they saw less of one another than before or after. Of the four, Macmillan was the least successful, and he must have been aware of it.

Macmillan visited Moscow. So did Cranborne with Antony Eden in 1935. Eden was the first British government minister to visit Russia since the Russian Revolution – and the first to meet Stalin. He praised Stalin's quality of mind, pragmatic approach and knowledge. But after that meeting, Cranborne picked up a far less attractive and more realistic view. Cranborne was looking for George Ardreachin, an acquaintance of Boothby's who had vanished, and came to the conclusion that Ardreachin had disappeared into a labour camp or been murdered by Stalin's secret police. Shortly afterwards Cranborne met the Italian dictator Mussolini, who impressed him as a strutting buffoon, 'quite, quite mad'.

Back in England, Cranborne found himself entangled in the usual business of domestic politics, vying for position against other politicians. He threw in his lot with Eden in the campaign for appeasement, but also worked on an idea – a crucial idea – that a firm political and economic alliance with America would be the ultimate salvation of Britain in the face of an aggressive Germany. The prime minister, Neville Chamberlain, rejected the idea of America determining British foreign policy and decided on an alliance with Italy. Eden and his supporter Cranborne were compromised and Eden, as foreign secretary, was forced to resign; Cranborne resigned too.

When the Second World War ended, there was a Labour government and for a time the career Conservatives were in the wilderness. Then came a Churchill government and its sequel, an Eden government. Salisbury, Crookshank and Macmillan had worked hard to replace Churchill with Eden, who was seen as glamorous, charismatic and likely to win an election victory for the Conservatives. In one way they were right, as in 1955 the Conservative majority in the House of Commons went up from seventeen seats to sixty. But in another way their support for Eden was misplaced. Eden now saw Harry Crookshank as surplus to requirements; his skill as a verbal sniper was useful to a party in opposition but not to a party in power. Crookshank was forced to take a peerage and retire. By way of compensation, he was installed as a Masonic leader (Provincial Grand Master) at Butlin's Holiday Camp at Skegness.

Lord Salisbury (Cranborne had succeeded to the major Cecil family title in 1947) too was marginalised. Macmillan began to emerge. He stood up to Salisbury and was soon followed in this by younger Cabinet members. Eden and Macmillan engineered what they hoped would be a détente between Britain and Russia, culminating in a visit to Britain by the Soviet leaders, Khrushchev and Bulganin. Salisbury hated it and offered to resign, but Eden persuaded him to stay in the government. It was Macmillan's time now. In 1955 he became Foreign Secretary, but did not enjoy Eden's interference in details of Foreign Office work.

Eden eventually made it possible for Macmillan to succeed him as prime minister over the Suez Crisis. Eden made the huge mistake of allowing his personal hatred for the Egyptian leader, Colonel Nasser, to influence his decisions. Eden decided to send in British troops to regain the captured Suez Canal. Salisbury quietly looked up the United Nations Charter and wrote to Macmillan, 'I found very little [in the Charter] that would seem to justify the use of forceful methods by a member state . . . we should be sailing pretty near the wind.' He was giving Eden fair warning.

Then Salisbury and Macmillan had a meeting with Foster Dulles. Dulles, the two Englishmen thought, did not want to offer American help with economic sanctions against Egypt. In fact Dulles did not want to help at all. For some reason, Macmillan portrayed Dulles as wanting the British to 'go it alone', and as 'trying to help us by creating the right atmosphere.' What Macmillan was up to here is not clear. But it is possible that he was setting Eden up for the most spectacular fall, one that would inevitably lead to his resignation and replacement; he was preparing for his own succession in the most unscrupulous way possible. Certainly Eden ordered the armed invasion of Egypt and was astonished when the Americans refused to approve it and demanded a British withdrawal. He went into shock. He had a complete mental breakdown and flew off to convalesce at Ian Fleming's house in Jamaica.

But Macmillan was still up against the heir apparent, Rab Butler. When Butler addressed a meeting of the 1922 Committee, he briefed it in a prosaic and matter-of-fact way. Macmillan was supposed to 'second' the briefing. What he actually did was to upstage Butler by delivering a long speech in Churchillian style, outlining Britain's future greatness and the place of Conservatism in that golden future. One witness, Enoch Powell, commented that 'the sheer devilry of it verged upon the disgusting'. It was a powerfully effective bid for the leadership. Meanwhile, Macmillan had arranged to fly to Washington as Eden's deputy. He secured a meeting with Eisenhower, who made it clear that he was ready to do business with Macmillan. Oliver Lyttelton, writing in the *Sunday Times,* commented that it was plain a deal had to be struck with the Americans, implying that it had been by his old friend Harold Macmillan.

All Macmillan needed now was a powerful establishment voice to secure his position. He found that in another old friend, none other than Lord Salisbury – Bobbety. Salisbury had been waiting and watching to see if Eden, stricken by a mental breakdown, could make a come-back. Salisbury hoped that he could, but in January 1957 he admitted to the Cabinet that he could not, that Eden could no longer remain prime minister. Macmillan was pleased; now he did not have to mount a coup to get rid of Eden. Salisbury had done it for him. And it was Salisbury who would now advise the queen to appoint Harold Macmillan prime minister, and not Butler.

The web of old friendships and loyalties did not go unnoticed at the time. Salisbury and Macmillan were brothers-in-law; their Cavendish wives were cousins; Salisbury had spent the New Year with the Queen. It looked to some observers as if Macmillan's succession had been engineered by Lord Salisbury. But some things went unnoticed – such as the fact that Macmillan's friend Harry Crookshank had many years earlier installed Michael Adeane in the Masonic Bard of Avon Lodge, and Adeane had been responsible for steering the succession at the Palace. So much had been achieved by the old school tie, the camaraderie of the Grenadier Guards, the bond of matrimony, the bond of friendship and the sheer habit of loyalty arising from a great many private encounters in war and peace.

THE YALTA
CONFERENCE – STALIN,
ROOSEVELT AND
CHURCHILL

(1945)

As the Second World War was drawing towards a close in February 1945, the main leaders of the Allies met in the Crimea. Representing Britain, America and the Soviet Union, the political leaders Winston Churchill, Franklin Delano Roosevelt and Joseph Stalin met in the Livadia Palace near Yalta, for what became known as the Yalta Conference. This was the second of a trio of wartime summit conferences; the first was Teheran, the third Potsdam. Roosevelt had proposed meeting in the Mediterranean, but Stalin insisted that his doctors were opposed to such a long journey and proposed the Black Sea resort of Yalta. This put him on home territory, which may have given him a psychological advantage in the negotiations; Churchill and Roosevelt were in effect his house-guests.

Each of the three leaders brought his own agenda item to the negotiating table. Roosevelt wanted Soviet backing in the Americans' Pacific war against Japan; Churchill wanted free elections and democratic governments in the countries of Eastern Europe; Stalin wanted a Soviet sphere of influence in Eastern Europe to safeguard the security of the Soviet Union. In addition, all three wanted to organise a plan for the government of a post-war Germany.

The conference was heavily weighted in Stalin's favour. Soviet troops under Marshal Zhukov were closing in on Hitler in Berlin, so Stalin was in a strong position to dictate terms. The issue of Poland arose immediately and Stalin stated the Soviet position; 'For the Russian people, the question of Poland is not only a question of honour but also a question of security. Throughout history, Poland has been the corridor through which the enemy has passed into Russia. Twice in the last thirty years our enemies, the Germans, have passed through this corridor. It is in Russia's interest that Poland should be strong and powerful, in a position to shut the door of this corridor by her own force. It is necessary that Poland should be free, independent in power. Therefore, it is a question of life and death for the Soviet state.'

As far as Stalin was concerned, some demands relating to Poland were not going to be negotiable. Russia was going to keep the territory it had annexed in eastern Poland, and the Poles were to be compensated for this loss by extending Poland west into Germany. Stalin promised to hold free elections in Poland, but it was obvious that he would not honour this promise; Poland was to become a socialist state, a Soviet satellite.

Roosevelt wanted Stalin to enter the Pacific War against Japan, but Stalin made that conditional on American recognition of Mongolian independence from China. This was agreed at Yalta, among the Big Three, but without any negotiation with the Chinese. Six months later, as agreed at Yalta, the Soviets attacked the Japanese, though without making any formal declaration of war, and seized the northernmost islands in the Japanese island group. This land later became disputed territory. The Russians did not sign the formal peace treaty with Japan at the end of the Second World War – and no peace treaty has been signed subsequently either. The aftermath of Yalta is still being felt today.

Many Americans later saw the Yalta agreements as a sell-out to the Soviet Union. Yalta allowed the Soviet Union to expand to the east into Japan, and to the west into Eastern Europe. The agreements made were then violated by Stalin in the formation of the Soviet bloc. Regions that were supposed to consist of neutral buffer states were transformed into Soviet satellite states. The Soviets were allowed to join the United Nations on the (secret) understanding that they, like other permanent members, would be allowed a veto power on the Security Council.

The truth was that the Soviets had the military power to get their own way. They had three times as many troops in Eastern Europe as the Allied troops had in Western Europe; this meant that Stalin was able to control Eastern Europe and decide what happened by simple superior might. But Roosevelt's poor health was also a factor in bad decision-making on the American side. Lord Moran, who was Churchill's doctor, commented that Roosevelt was 'a very sick man. He has all the symptoms of hardening of the arteries of the brain in an advanced stage, so that I give him only a few months to live.' Roosevelt's aides never admitted that he was in too poor a state to participate in such a crucial conference and far too weak to stand up to Stalin, but he did indeed die of a cerebral haemorrhage just two months after Yalta, which implies that Moran was right.

The three Western leaders ratified agreements previously negotiated regarding the post-war division of Germany. There were to be three zones, each to be policed by one of the three principal Allies. Later, the British and Americans ceded parts of their zones to create an additional French zone. In the same way, the German capital Berlin was to be divided into three sectors. This became a symbol of the folly of Yalta when the Soviets erected the Berlin Wall, which physically hived off East Berlin from the rest of the city in the same way that the Iron Curtain separated and isolated Eastern Europe from Western Europe. Both the Iron Curtain and the Berlin Wall became powerful symbols of the Cold War, the hostile stalemate that existed for half a century after the Second World War ended.

At Yalta, the Big Three agreed that that the pre-war political map of Europe would be reinstated to the extent that the original governments would be restored in invaded countries. But in Romania and Bulgaria, the Soviets had already destroyed the existing governments, and Stalin had no intention of reinstating the Polish government-in-exile. There was agreement that democracies would be set up with free elections.

The Big Three at least agreed that there must be an unconditional surrender of Nazi Germany, and that the post-war Germany would be demilitarised and de-nazified. Nazi war criminals were to be tracked down and brought to justice, so Yalta laid down the international foundations for the Nuremberg War Trials, and indeed for future tribunals for the prosecution of war criminals.

The outcome of the Yalta Conference was a far cry from these stated aims. There were no democracies in Eastern Europe. The Soviet zone in Eastern Europe became a thinly disguised extension of Soviet rule in a series of puppet states. The Western powers were hostile to this development, but powerless to prevent it. Yalta was the springboard into the Cold War. One shameful agreement was the decision that all citizens of the Soviet Union, however displaced, were to be handed back to the Soviet Union. This meant the forced repatriation of large numbers of refugees, many of whom were shot immediately on their return home. Roosevelt and Churchill must have realised that this would be the outcome, but they considered it a price worth paying; it seems they believed they must keep Stalin as an ally, however many innocent lives were lost in the process.

THE BANDUNG
CONFERENCE

(1955)

THE BANDUNG CONFERENCE was the very first large-scale Asian-African Conference to take place. It was a meeting of the leaders of Asian and African states, most of which in 1955 were newly independent colonies. The conference was made necessary by the process of decolonisation which accelerated in the years following the end of the Second World War. While countries like Ceylon (now Sri Lanka) and India were part of the British Empire, their policies and orientations were determined largely by British administrators. Once India became independent in 1947, all sorts of new relationships with other nations became possible. The Bandung Conference was a forum where post-colonial states could look at the possibilities for the future, and share their views with other states in the same situation.

The conference was co-ordinated by the head of the Indonesian Ministry of Foreign Affairs, Roeslan Abdulgani, and organised by the governments of five countries, Indonesia, Burma, Pakistan, Ceylon and India. Representatives of those countries assembled to meet delegates from twenty-four other countries. They included Jordan, Laos, Syria, Lebanon and, rather surprisingly, the non-colonial but non-aligned giant state of China. The might and potential power of this conference can be gauged from the fact that delegates represented half the population of the world.

One specific aim of the conference was to promote economic and cultural co-operation among the countries of Africa and Asia. Another was to combat attempts at colonisation or ne-colonialism by any imperialist nation, including the United States.

277

The delegates gathered in Bandung, Indonesia for a week in April 1955. They expressed concern at the lack of interest shown by the Western powers in the effects the Cold War tensions were having on their countries. There was too little consultation about actions that had effects on them. They expressed concern about the tension that existed between the United States and the People's Republic of China. What was needed was a firm basis for a network of peacetime relationships among the post-colonial states, China and the Western powers.

The first president of the Republic of Indonesia, Achmad Sukarno, proposed himself as the leader of this group of nations and named it NEFOS, Newly Emerging Forces.

Delegates also spoke of their opposition to continuing old-style colonialism, especially in the form of French colonial rule in North Africa and the Dutch control of western New Guinea. They were opposed to American neo-colonialism too, seeing US foreign policy as essentially imperialistic. Then there was a major debate circling round the question whether Soviet activity in Eastern Europe and Central Asia should be opposed or censured. Was Soviet policy neo-colonial in the way that American policy was? There was a consensus that 'colonialism in all of its manifestations' should be condemned. This was a vote of censure against Russia as well as France and America.

At the Bandung Conference, the People's Republic of China had a major role to play, not least because of its enormous population, but because of its enormous potential economic and political power. The Chinese premier Zhou Enlai attended the conference, and on his way to it he survived an attempt by foreign agents to assassinate him. Zhou Enlai adopted a moderate and statesmanlike attitude which allayed the fears of some of the delegates who had been concerned about China's intentions. China too, after all, could have turned out to be a neo-imperialist power. Zhou Enlai even signed an article in the concluding declaration, stating that Chinese people living overseas owed their first loyalty to their host country – not to China. This was a very satisfying and reassuring outcome for the Indonesian conference hosts and for delegates from several other countries in South-East Asia.

The Bandung delegates produced a ten-point declaration on the promotion of world peace. These incorporated principles of the United Nations Charter and principles outlined by the Indian head of state, Jawaharlal Nehru. These included respect for fundamental human rights and the principles of the United Nations Charter, respect for justice, respect for the sovereignty and territorial integrity of all nations, and recognition of racial equality. International disputes were to be settled by peaceful means.

In an ambitious final statement, the delegates emphasised the need for developing countries to reduce their dependence on the richer countries by providing one another with assistance.

The discussions that took place at the Bandung Conference were crucial in mapping out the post-war development of large areas of the world. In particular the conference decided the post-colonial futures of twenty-nine Asian, African and Middle Eastern states. It specifically led to the creation of the Non-Aligned Movement, which was a courageous attempt by Third World states to remain independent in the Cold War and to keep the developing countries as far as possible out of the Cold War rivalries. The impressive achievements at Bandung were consolidated at the Belgrade Conference in 1961, which led to the establishment of the Non-Aligned Movement. It was the clear intention to create a Third World, a world apart from East and West.

CHE GUEVARA AND
FIDEL CASTRO

(1955)

WHEN HE WAS one of the leading men in Cuba in the early 1960s, Che
Guevara was described in a secret British dossier as a charming bearded
Argentinian, cultured, softly spoken, but also with a cold and contemptuous streak. He was extremely competent, said the dossier, and perhaps
the most competent man in the Cuban government. Did that, perhaps,
in the end put one of the world's most famous revolutionaries in danger,
and is that how he came to grief in Bolivia?

In the 1950s, the young Che Guevara, a newly qualified medic,
travelled through Latin America on his motorcycle. What he saw
shocked him: the poverty, the deprivation. He came to the conclusion
that the huge contrasts in wealth across the whole region were the
result of capitalist monopolies and neo-colonialism. He saw revolution
as the answer, and revolution on a large scale.

In January 1954 Guevara was in Guatemala City, where he met Nico
Lopez, a revolutionary. Over the next few months, when he was unable
to find work as a medic, he took a series of odd jobs. Guevara began to
study Marxism and became involved in political activities that were
aimed at social reform, and in doing so he met a number of Cuban
revolutionaries. When in June 1954 President Arbenz of Guatemala was
toppled in a coup assisted by the American CIA, Guevara's tendency to
go for radical solutions was intensified. Revolution was the only answer.
He became gradually more radical.

In September 1954, Guevara arrived in Mexico City. In the following
May, Fidel Castro and other revolutionaries were released from a Cuban
prison. In Mexico City, Lopez arranged for Guevara to meet Raul

Castro. In July 1955, Fidel Castro, Raul's brother, arrived in Mexico from Cuba and within days Che Guevara met him. The two men took to each other at once: they were friends instantly. Castro immediately invited Che to became part of his Cuban revolutionary effort, the so-called 26th of July Movement. Castro's aim was to overthrow the Cuban dictator Fulgencio Batista, who was supported by the US. Fidel Castro was the charismatic leader of the Cuban revolution who went on to be the new Cuba's head of state for several decades afterwards. He and his brother Raul and his new friend Che were unquestionably the revolution's driving force.

In November 1955, Guevara was one of Castro's band of eighty-two revolutionaries – and one of only four non-Cubans – when they set off from the coast of Mexico on board the yacht Granma. On 2 December the Granma made landfall on a beach in western Cuba, where Batista's troops were waiting for them. It was scarcely an invasion. Many of the revolutionaries were killed by Batista's men on the beach or as they dispersed into the woods. Guevara himself was wounded in this fiasco, and only fifteen men remained to fight on. They took to the hills to organise a guerrilla campaign.

It was at this stage that Fidel Castro began to appreciate Guevara's leadership qualities. He promoted Guevara to Comandante and he played a key role in the successful guerrilla campaign that brought Batista and his régime down. He was given the task of directing a military training camp in the Sierra Maestra. From August through to October 1958, Guevara led his troops from one mountain area to another. In December he joined two other groups of revolutionaries to capture a number of towns in Las Villas Province in central Cuba, which in effect divided the island in two.

On 1 January 1959, Batista, his family and his closest associates boarded a plane and flew out of Cuba. On the same day, Castro and his revolutionary forces were able to take control of Havana, the capital. The next day, Guevara arrived in Havana to share Castro's triumph. A few weeks later, Guevara was declared a Cuban citizen.

Che Guevara was a major figure, second only to Fidel Castro, in the success of the Cuban revolution. In its aftermath, he was responsible for reviewing the appeals of the men who were convicted of war crimes in the revolutionary tribunals. He was appointed commander of La Cabana Fortress prison, where he oversaw the trial and execution of perhaps as many as 550 former officials of the Batista régime. Then in October 1959 Castro appointed him minister of industry and shortly after made him president of the national bank. In his new role as a front-ranking politician, Guevara found himself travelling round the world meeting world leaders; his mission was to present Cuban socialism to the world. But the life of a statesman, wearing a tie and being diplomatic behind an office desk, did not really suit him. He was still a revolutionary at heart and in 1965 Che Guevara left Cuba and Castro behind, to foment revolution elsewhere, first in the Congo, then in Bolivia, where he met his death.

As he left Cuba, he wrote Castro a farewell letter.

Fidel –
At this instant I remember many things; when I met you in Maria Antonia's house, when you proposed I come along, all the tensions involved in the preparations. . . Today everything has a less dramatic tone, because we are more mature. I feel I have fulfilled the part of my duty that tied me to the Cuban revolution in its territory and I say farewell to you . . .'

Che Guevara travelled to Europe. Castro tried repeatedly to get him to return to Cuba, but Che would only agree on condition that he was allowed to go off and launch a revolution elsewhere in Latin America.

He was captured by Bolivian army troops in 1967. He handed over his diary to a Bolivian officer, Nino de Guzman. One entry read, 'We make our voices heard for the first time. We have to reach all the corners of this continent with the echo of our cry for rebellion. We rise today having exhausted all possibilities of a peaceful fight.' De Guzman, a helicopter pilot, was sent in to interview Guevara immediately after his capture in a village 400 miles south-east of La Paz. He met him in a room surrounded by Bolivian soldiers. Guevara told him he had wanted to start a revolution in Peru but had been sent to Bolivia instead – by Castro. He complained that he had been inadequately supported from Cuba. More than once he declared, 'Fidel betrayed me.' Nino de Guzman saw Guevara as a man in a state of despair and later remembered, 'Nearly all of Guevara's actions and words amounted to a wish to die.' Guevara said to him, 'I'm worth more dead than alive to you and Fidel.' After that, on the orders of the Bolivian army high command, Guevara was shot.

When he heard the news of Che's death, Castro declared three days of national mourning in Cuba and delivered an emotional eulogy to his friend.

> *It was a day in July or August 1955 when we first met Che. And in one night, as his account tells, he became an expeditionary. Since then, twelve years have gone by, twelve years fraught with struggles and obstructions. Through these years death reaped many valuable lives . . . Tonight we gather here, you and I, to try to express these sentiments in some way about a man who was one of the most familiar, one of the most admired, one of the most beloved and, without any doubt, the most extraordinary of our comrades of revolution. Che was one of those people whom everybody liked immediately because of his simplicity, because of his naturalness, because of his originality, even before his other singular virtues were revealed . . .*

Fidel Castro's eulogy continued at great length. Castro knew how much he owed to Che in bringing about a successful revolution in Cuba; he also knew that Che had become an iconic figure; he knew that together he and Che Guevara had created an imperishable modern legend.

KENNEDY AND NIXON
ON TV

(1960)

THE 1960 US presidential election campaign was a closely fought contest between Richard Nixon and John F. Kennedy. Both candidates had won their party nominations on the first ballot and both left their party conventions with positive party support and a good chance of winning. Kennedy was the first to gain nomination. In the primaries he had impressively beaten his main rival Hubert Humphrey. Although himself a Catholic, Kennedy had shown that he had the ability to overcome any religious prejudice by gaining winning votes in strongly Protestant states like Wisconsin and Virginia. Up to that time some commentators had wondered whether it would be possible for a Catholic to win a presidential election. But after the Wisconsin and Virginia results, the Democrats realised that Kennedy really could overcome that political handicap to win.

Kennedy chose Lyndon Johnson as his running mate. He was an old-style politician, a tough fighter who was ready to hammer at political opposition, and he was likely to help Kennedy to win. Johnson was a good choice. Two weeks later, the Republicans nominated Richard Nixon, the serving vice-president and the deputy of the outgoing president, Dwight Eisenhower.

Kennedy had no experience in foreign affairs and had served little more than a single and rather undistinguished term in the US Senate. Richard Nixon, on the other hand, was a two-term serving vice president of the United States. He had made a successful political career by fighting Communists at home and overseas. He had relentlessly pursued the former State Department official Alger Hiss. He had even handled a confrontation with the Soviet leader, successfully beating Khrushchev in the so-called 'Kitchen Debate' when he argued that the American way of life was superior. At a moment when a major issue of the presidential election was the missile gap, political commentators were joking with each other about the 'stature gap' between the two presidential candidates. From the point of view of experience, of track record, of CV, Richard Nixon was easily the stronger candidate.

Nixon should have won the 1960 election. So what went wrong?

Although Kennedy and Nixon came across as very different people, their political agendas were strikingly similar. Both wanted change and progress. Kennedy wanted to develop new technology, to make advances in space exploration, to confront and annihilate poverty, war and ignorance. He wanted a brighter future for America. Nixon wanted the same, though putting the emphasis on giving scope to private industry and decreasing public spending. The two candidates would use different means, but they aimed for the same goals. They were both equally clear about the threat from Communism and the need for a strong defence strategy.

The public debate in 1960 was therefore not really a debate about policies or principles at all. It was about the two men, their personalities, their experience, their fitness for the job, their appearance. Both Kennedy and Nixon had, as it happened, become congressmen at the same time in 1946. But Kennedy was a young-looking forty-three, and might appear to many to be lacking in experience. Nixon was able to play on this by putting the emphasis on his own experience in foreign and domestic policy as vice president, and here he found the chink in Kennedy's formidable armour; Nixon turned his political experience into his great selling point. Nixon's campaign was strong.

But then Richard Nixon was unexpectedly undermined by a comment from the outgoing president, Eisenhower. Eisenhower was at a press conference that he was keen to bring to a close. He was tired. A reporter asked Eisenhower which major decisions vice-president Nixon had participated in. It was a very good question. Eisenhower's reply was, 'If you give me a week, I might think of one.' Eisenhower was really making a comment on his own mental exhaustion, but it came across as a slight to Nixon. The snub from Eisenhower gave Kennedy and his aides renewed confidence. Kennedy answered charges that he was inexperienced by saying, 'Mr Nixon is experienced – in the policies of retreat, defeat and weakness.' Both Eisenhower's comment and Kennedy's spirited reaction to it were given wide press coverage.

Kennedy appeared on television at the Ministerial Association of Houston, where he assured the audience he was in favour of a separation of church and state. He opposed state funding of church schools, and the American constitution must remain above any possible interference from the church. This was reassuring to Protestant viewers, who might have feared a swing towards Catholic-inspired measures. Kennedy also came across as authoritative. Richard Nixon meanwhile was suffering from a knee infection. He had made a promise to campaign in every state and, instead of taking advice to cut back, he tried to keep his promise. By the end of this gruelling tour, Nixon was tired, and not in the best shape to perform well on the first television debate.

On 26 September 1960, an estimated seventy million Americans watched Kennedy and Nixon in the first televised presidential debate. It was to be the first of four, and the first had domestic issues as its focus. The focus of the second and third debates, on foreign policy, turned out to be US involvement in islands off the Chinese coast. Those took place on 7 and 13 October. The fourth and final debate, which took place on 21 October, homed in on American relations with Fidel Castro's Cuba.

The first debate was held in a television studio in Chicago. Each candidate was given eight minutes to make an opening speech. After that a series of questions was put to them by a panel of correspondents. These included Walter Cronkite of CBS News, John Edwards of ABC News, John Chancellor of NBC News and Frank Singiser of Mutual News. To end the debate, which was hosted by Howard Smith of CBS News, Kennedy and Nixon were allowed three minutes and twenty seconds to make a final statement.

Kennedy opened with the aspiration to see America fulfil its economic potential and sustain the needs of individuals through welfare programmes. 'I think it's time America started moving again.' In his opening statement, Nixon also spoke about moving ahead, but defended the record of the Republicans by saying that they had built more schools, hospitals and roads than the previous Democrat administration.

The questions from the panel ranged widely. The candidates were asked about their experience for the job of president, about agricultural policy, and about the threat from Communism within the USA. The candidates disagreed over farm subsidies and about the way extra spending on education and welfare would be funded. Kennedy argued that steady economic growth would generate the additional tax revenue to pay for his welfare programme. Nixon argued that taxes would need to be raised to pay for additional medical care and education.

Summing up, Richard Nixon said, 'I stand for programmes that will mean growth and progress. But it is also essential that he [Kennedy] not allow a dollar spent that could be better spent by the people themselves.' In his reply, John F. Kennedy said, 'The question before us all is: Can freedom in the next generation conquer, or are the Communists going to be successful? That's the great issue. And if we meet our responsibilities I think freedom will conquer.'

Nixon was a good debater and had looked forward to doing battle with Kennedy on television. But as the broadcast developed, things went against him. Kennedy had already proved that he performed well on television, coming across as assured, well-informed, honest and direct. He prepared himself well for the debate with Nixon, who was not expecting Kennedy to have such a good grasp of the facts. Kennedy's charismatic assurance and command of detail put Nixon on the defensive; he was obviously unnerved to find himself upstaged by Kennedy.

But the major thrust of the television debate was the images of the two men. This was the first time ever that the American electorate had seen presidential candidates close up, face to face, and been able to assess and compare their character from appearance and animation.

There was Kennedy, looking young, fresh, honest, upright, commanding, attractive. And there was Nixon, looking older, less than fresh with his perpetual five o'clock shadow, evasive and tired. Nixon's poor image was partly the result of his poor health in the run-up to the debate, which had resulted in weight loss. Nixon had spent two weeks in hospital with his knee problem and lost twenty pounds in weight. He looked pale. He arrived for the debate in an ill-fitting shirt and refused to allow the TV make-up people to improve his facial colour. The set had a freshly painted backdrop that had dried to a light grey that matched Nixon's suit; this made his body fade into the background. Nixon was also perspiring heavily. While Kennedy took Nixon to task on some issue, the TV cameras cut to Nixon mopping away perspiration, which made him look like a man on the run. Kennedy meanwhile was immaculately dressed, well rested, composed and tanned. He had spent September campaigning in California. Nixon later commented, 'I had never seen him looking so well.'

When the debate was over, television viewers were asked who they thought had won. A large majority believed that Kennedy was the winner. The same debate was broadcast on the radio, and the radio listeners thought that Nixon had performed at least as well as Kennedy, maybe better. The outcome of each of the following debates was closer, but the audiences for them were smaller. It was the initial television debate that really made the difference to public perceptions of the two candidates. The episode made it clear that television audiences made their judgements according to what they saw, not according to what they heard.

Kennedy had found his medium, and he was to use it to great advantage.

There were other media opportunities, which Kennedy exploited to his advantage. He went to the aid of Martin Luther King when Mr King was arrested in Alabama. Nixon, who was still vice-president, found himself trapped between conflicting interests. Because he was actually already in public office, he was unable to speak out in King's favour. As a presidential candidate, though, he needed to state his position. The conflict of interests led to his maintaining silence on the issue, which meant that Kennedy scored on an event that was highly publicised. Kennedy was able to reinforce his charismatic compassionate image.

Eisenhower then damaged Nixon again. Late in the race, the outgoing president stepped up to support Nixon. But this half-hearted gesture, coming late in the day, only served to make Nixon look like a lame duck – a man who couldn't win an election on his own.

All of these events had the effect of weakening the Republican cause. When the election came in November 1969, the result was very close. The popular vote was divided almost exactly 50-50. The electoral margin was more clear-cut, a 303 to 219 win for Kennedy. Some political commentators saw the television debates as confirmation of a swing that was already going in Kennedy's direction, and they held that the debates did not really change the result. But as many as six percent of American voters said that they cast their vote only on the basis of the Great Debates. And since that time across the Western democracies television has played a major role in elections. Shortly after the American Great Debates, Germany, Finland, Sweden, Italy and Japan all mounted televised debates between contenders for national leadership.

The debates also created a precedent in American politics, where it became clear that some formal ground rules were going to be needed. New federal laws came in that required equal air-time to be given to all candidates. This created a problem for programming in situations where there were multiple candidates, and it led to a blocking of debates in the next three elections. With his bruising 1960 experience behind him, Richard Nixon refused to debate in 1968 and 1972. By 1976, both the law and the candidates had changed and, since then, some form of adversarial television debate has been an element in presidential politics. For better or worse, television became a key element in Western democracy.

The importance of the media was to Kennedy obvious, right from the start of his presidency. And Kennedy was astute enough to see that this was going to be a great area of strength for him, provided he played it right. Kennedy continued to develop his media strategy, making sure that every event was as good as possible from the photographic point of view. The whole 'Camelot' image that the Kennedys projected at the White House was the result of a sophisticated advertising campaign. How Kennedy looked was vital to his success. He spent a lot of time organising photoshoots of himself and his family. He was extremely photogenic, and so was his wife, Jackie. They made sure that they both looked as good as they possibly could for the cameras, wherever they were.

The consciousness that appearance was crucial was a factor in his assassination, which came only three years later, on 22 November 1963. That day security in Dallas dictated that he should ride in the motorcade in a closed vehicle. But Kennedy decided he needed to be seen – to be photographed looking relaxed and confident and charismatic – so he decided to ride with the roof off. The result was fatal. If, as the Warren Commission concluded, all the bullets were fired by Lee Harvey Oswald, diagonally downwards from a sixth floor window of the Texas Book Depository, then none of the three fired in rapid succession from there could have hit President Kennedy. He would have been protected by the limousine roof. If there were five shots and the final two came from the grassy knoll, those last two might have hit Kennedy through the car's open window, but taking aim on a target enclosed inside a roofed car would have been much more difficult.

RICHARD NIXON AND CHAIRMAN MAO

(1972)

IN 1969, RICHARD Nixon became president of the United States of America, and was in office at the moment when, in the July of that year, people first set foot on the Moon. They were Americans, and they reached the Moon in what was an entirely American project. Nixon rightly commented on the historic nature of the achievement, but there was another achievement in store for him and his administration, and it was already being planned. His new executive and his national security adviser, Henry Kissinger, were setting up an equivalent giant step for mankind in the field of international relations.

On 21 February 1972, Nixon's aircraft touched down in Beijing and, like Armstrong stepping down onto the dusty surface of the Moon, Nixon stepped onto the airport tarmac. He shook the hand of Zhou Enlai, China's prime minister, and stood to attention as a People's Liberation Army band played *The Star-spangled Banner* in his honour. Just a few hours later, Richard Nixon for the first time met China's legendary head of state, Chairman Mao. They exchanged pleasantries. So began what Nixon himself described as 'the week that changed the world'.

The significance of the meeting was overwhelming. It was the middle of the Cold War, when there were huge tensions between America and the Soviet Union. And China itself had gone unrecognised by America, who still preferred to give diplomatic recognition instead to the 'government in exile' based on the island of Taiwan. Clearly ignoring a country as large and potentially powerful as China was unsustainable. This initiative was designed as the first and most significant step towards ending the international isolation that America had in effect imposed on China. It brought to an end a quarter of a century of bitter hostility.

The Nixon visit was regarded, at the moment before it happened, as inconceivable. Yet almost everyone afterwards regarded it as a perfectly sensible and constructive overture. Nixon has been widely remembered for the shabby Watergate scandal that led to his ejection from office in disgrace. But his initiatives in foreign affairs were statesmanlike and visionary. When he took office, he inherited from the previous administration a war in Vietnam that was costing huge numbers of American lives. Nixon had the courage to withdraw, to bring that war to an end. The strategic arms balance had shifted in the Soviet Union's favour, and the Soviets were able to intervene in Czechoslovakia to crush dissent with impunity. In the USA there were race riots and an emerging culture of youthful rebellion. Nixon feared that the United States looked weak, fragmented and increasingly ungovernable; it looked as if the nation was 'going down the drain as a great power'.

Nixon's gesture in visiting China was an inspired public relations coup, showing that America could still surprise the world, could still change everything. Nixon and Kissinger impressed America's allies, though they were understandably irritated that there had been no prior consultation. Nixon's critics at home were also dazzled and silenced. By making this positive gesture, he was then able to make what would be seen at home as the negative gesture of withdrawing from South Vietnam. Nixon would lose South Vietnam, but gain China – a far greater prize.

Chairman Mao arrived at this moment by a different route. Nixon arrived in office to find all the problems waiting for him. Mao had created most of China's problems himself. His extraordinary initiative, known as the Great Leap Forward, had caused the death by starvation of thirty million of his own people between 1958 and 1961. He had provoked the Soviet Union to the point where China's only powerful ally had turned into an enemy. By his insane policies Mao had turned China into a weakened, exhausted, isolated and unstable state.

In 1969, Soviet diplomats asked American diplomats an alarming question. If Moscow found it necessary to launch a pre-emptive war against China, by implication using nuclear weapons, how would America respond? Apparently Moscow wondered whether Washington would be relieved to see China wiped off the map. The question was passed along the line, and President Nixon's reply surprised the Russians. He said that the United States regarded China's security as vital to its own. American diplomats conveyed this policy statement to Mao, who was naturally very interested and gratified to have found this expression of friendship. Mao was a cunning political operator, and from then on he himself steered a course towards a rapprochement with America, even though his subordinates were uneasy about it.

Mao's personal involvement in this process was evident at each step. He personally authorised a visit by an American table tennis team to Beijing in 1971. That year, Henry Kissinger made a secret trip to Beijing to prepare the way for something more significant in the following year. In spite of his communist doctrine, Mao seemed happier to do business with the Americans than with the Soviets. Mao said, in relation to Nixon, 'I like to deal with rightists. They say what they really think – not like the leftists, who say one thing and mean another.'

With similar inconsistency, the committed right-winger with a life-long hatred for Communism, Richard Nixon, was very excited about meeting Mao. He was touched when Mao shook his hand and would not let go of it, a gesture charged with symbolic meaning. Nixon flattered Mao. 'The Chairman's writings moved a nation and have changed a world.' Of the journalists who travelled with Nixon, there seems to have been only one who was repelled by the amiability of the meeting. William F. Buckley complained that it was as if the prosecutors at Nuremberg had suddenly embraced the defendants and invited them to join in the making of a better world.

One jarring note was struck during the 1972 Nixon visit. That was the contentious issue of America's determination to defend Taiwan against any attempt at an invasion from the Chinese mainland. But the Americans were able to sweeten their Chinese hosts by offering generous gifts of sensitive intelligence relating to Soviet Military deployments. And they even explicitly promised to pull American military personnel out of Taiwan, 'at some time in the future'.

The encounter was a meeting of two heads of state, but it was also a meeting of two very different cultures. The Chinese were puzzled by the cigarette packets carried by Nixon's staff. How was it that they carried the surgeon-general's health warning and also the presidential seal, implying approval? It was also virtually impossible for the Americans to throw anything away without having it conscientiously returned. The Americans found the Chinese hard to talk to; there seemed to be little common ground that could form the basis of small talk. Nixon dredged about for things to say to Zhou Enlai to fill the silences.

In the years since Richard Nixon's visit to China, it has become a benchmark for courageous diplomatic initiatives. Commentators have repeatedly proposed that international problems might be resolved by this head of state or that going to some trouble spot. It was probably with the Nixon precedent in mind that Edward Heath went to Iraq to talk to Saddam Hussein in 1990, a meeting specifically intended to persuade Saddam to release the British hostages that he had been holding for two months. As the situation worsened in Iraq in succeeding years, Heath believed that American political leaders should do the same, following his (and Nixon's) example.

TONY BLAIR AND GORDON BROWN

(1983)

AFTER GRADUATING IN history at Edinburgh University in 1972, Gordon Brown completed a PhD thesis on *The Labour Party and Political Change in Scotland 1918-29*. Meanwhile, he was lecturing in politics at Glasgow College of Technology. His first foray into politics was the 1979 general election, where he lost Edinburgh South to the Conservative candidate, Michael Ancram. After that he worked for Scottish Television, serving as current affairs editor until he was elected to parliament in 1983. Two years later he became opposition spokesman on Trade and Industry. In 1992 he became Shadow Chancellor. As Shadow Chancellor, Brown strove to show that he was a sound and competent chancellor-in-waiting. He was aware that the business world and the moneyed classes needed to be reassured that Labour could be entrusted with running the British economy. The legacy of the 1970s – inflation, unemployment, overspending – would not be made worse under a Labour government with him in charge at the Treasury. He also made a public commitment that he would implement the Conservative administration's spending plans for the first two years after a Labour government took power.

Tony Blair is two years younger than Gordon Brown. He graduated in law at Oxford in 1975, taking his degree three years later than Brown. Tony Blair won the Sedgefield seat in 1983, so they became MPs at the same moment, and were friends from that time onwards.

When they were two young MPs, Tony Blair and Gordon Brown were close friends. According to John Prescott, at that time it was Gordon Brown who was the obvious leader of the two. Blair 'looked up to Gordon . . . hung on his every word.'

Just eleven years later, in 1994, the Labour Party leader John Smith died suddenly and Gordon Brown was widely seen as a candidate for his successor. Once Tony Blair emerged as the party's favourite, Brown did not contest the leadership, though John Prescott believes that Gordon Brown must have been very annoyed when Blair got it. There is an unconfirmed story that the two men struck a deal at the Granita restaurant in Islington. If a deal was struck, the precise nature of their agreement is uncertain, but it is believed that Gordon Brown agreed not to contest Blair's leadership in exchange for taking control of economic policy. There was also speculation that there was an additional agreement that after Blair had held the Labour leadership for a time he would resign in Brown's favour.

Whatever the nature of the agreement, there has been a distinctive political relationship between the two men. Brown did indeed toil away as Chancellor of the Exchequer while Tony Blair held office as Prime Minister for many years. In fact Brown remained as Chancellor of the Exchequer for ten years and two months, making him the longest-serving Chancellor in modern times. And tension did mount as those years passed, with reports of some serious private rifts between them; Brown appeared to be getting increasingly frustrated and dissatisfied as if he was being kept waiting for the top job.

Serious strains came to the surface when Labour was in power. For the first year, in addition to the cabinet meetings there were regular meetings of the 'Big Three', Tony Blair, John Prescott and Gordon Brown. The deputy prime minister, John Prescott, watched the two men working together from close up in these meetings, and witnessed their frequent rows. Sometimes Brown would say nothing, sometimes he would explode, so the Big Three meetings petered out.

Prescott found Gordon Brown 'frustrating, bewildering, prickly'. But according to Prescott's reminiscences, Tony Blair promised to step down to make way for Brown to move up to Number 10 Downing Street, and went back on his promise several times. If so, it is understandable that Brown's feelings ran high. Prescott arbitrated at hundreds of reconciliation meetings. At the time when Blair was complaining that he could not work with Brown, Prescott said that his response was to tell Blair to sack Brown, but he got the impression that Blair was afraid to do so because he knew it would tear the party in two. Blair in any case did not like confrontation. Prescott also says that in a similar conversation with Brown about Blair, when Brown felt he had been misled yet again, he urged Brown to resign and oppose Blair from a position on the back benches. Again, Brown was unwilling to take such a big gamble. It was a stalemate. But it is also clear that John Prescott himself was not easy to deal with. As the highest-ranking representative of Old Labour in Blair's government he sometimes felt left out when the New Labour 'beautiful people' were invited for policy discussions and he was not. There were moments when Prescott too exploded – and with some justification.

In Labour's second term in office, the relationship between Blair and Brown became even more tense. John Prescott was required to devote even more time to his role as conciliator; there would be difficult meetings at which Prescott tried to get them to see one another's point of view, arrange a dinner, restore peace, and then another issue would spark renewed conflict. John Prescott's insight is revealing. He thinks the tension sprang from a deep positive political connection that they felt. Their political views and analyses were deeply shared, and it was this deep connection that fuelled their interaction.

Gordon Brown seemed to have the impression that Tony Blair would be leaving office midway through the second term. Prescott noticed that as the time approached for a possible announcement something else came up. Blair delayed. Whether Tony Blair promised to go and then renegued on the promise is not clear, but an impression was probably given and certainly received. Prescott's view is that promises were made, but they were hedged by conditions.

Whatever their private differences, Blair and Brown remained united in public, each of them acutely aware that that unity was central to the strength of 'New Labour'. One negative aspect of Gordon Brown's long period in office as Chancellor is that, as Britain slides into economic recession with Brown in office as Prime Minister, he cannot escape a

297

major share of the blame; he presided over the long run-up to the recession. There is also disquiet over a number of specific outcomes of his policies. His changes to income tax, for example, have had the effect of further impoverishing the lowest income group, those on incomes below £18,000 a year. And taxation in the UK increased from 39.3% of GDP in 1997 to 42.4% in 2006. This is a higher level than Germany. There has also been criticism of various stealth taxes, such as stamp duty. One, involving a change to the way corporation tax is collected, resulted in dividends on stock investments to be taxed within pension funds. This led to reduced pension returns. This in turn led to the phasing-out of many final-salary pension schemes – a life-changing culture shift for many workers. There is the suspicion that many of the unpleasant 'end result' effects of Brown's financial decision-making were not foreseen.

In October 2004, Tony Blair said publicly that he would not lead the Labour Party into a fourth general election, though he would serve a full third term. Labour won the 2005 election, though with a reduced majority. In public, Blair and Brown campaigned together and supported one another, though there were press reports of private tensions. On 7 September 2006 Blair announced that he would be standing down as Labour leader within twelve months. Other candidates were floated as possibilities, but there was little doubt at Westminster that Gordon Brown was to be the successor. Efforts were made to present Brown as a statesman with a global vision. Tony Blair described Gordon Brown as a 'great clunking fist'. He probably meant it flatteringly, in the sense that he was going to be formidable in power and any opposition party would find him very tough. But some observers have interpreted it as a deliberate signal from Blair that he thought Brown was politically clumsy and lacking in subtlety: in other words, an unsuitable candidate for the top job.

If that second interpretation is correct, it would be consistent with Charles Clarke's comments about Gordon Brown in an interview in September 2006. Clarke thought Brown needed to confront some psychological issues, and enlarged on this by saying that Brown was a control freak and 'totally uncollegiate'. Clarke was outlining the case for Blair's not handing Number 10 to Gordon Brown on a plate, for looking at other candidates. In January 2007, Gordon Brown addressed a Fabian Society conference, covering a wide range of issues in a way that implied he was setting out his prime ministerial stall. Then in March there was a statement from Lord Turnbull, who worked as Permanent Secretary at the Treasury under Brown. He accused Brown of 'Stalinist ruthlessness' in the way that he had run the Treasury and accused him of treating Cabinet colleagues with 'more or less complete contempt'. This attack was the more damaging because it reinforced Charles Clarke's earlier comments.

But, in spite of these warning shots from some experienced co-workers, on 27 June 2007, Gordon Brown became prime minister of the UK. There was a widespread feeling that he should not have acquired the position without having to fight for it. He was, nevertheless, the sixth post-war British prime minister (out of a total of twelve) to have come into office without a general election. When standing down as prime minister, Tony Blair went out of his way to praise his Chancellor, but at the same time he expressed deep frustration with his own time in power. 'Every time I've ever introduced a reform in government, I wish in retrospect I had gone further.' Perhaps buried within this high-profile public statement, Blair's farewell to power, is a clue to the nature of the tension. Was Brown the voice of caution, the voice of moderation that got in Blair's way?

THE REYKJAVIK
SUMMIT

(1986)

IN OCTOBER 1986, two world leaders met in an Icelandic house to discuss ending the Cold War. The tensions between America and Russia had led to an arms race that was financially crippling Russia. The two leaders, Ronald Reagan and Mikhail Gorbachev, came face to face in the house of Hofdi in Reykjavik. They were two men with very different but positive visions for the future; both were ready to discuss the elimination of all ballistic missiles held by their two countries and even the possibility of scrapping all nuclear weapons. Reagan and Gorbachev had met before, at Geneva in 1985, when they had declared that 'a nuclear war cannot be won and must never be fought.'

Reagan was revolted by the idea of a nuclear war between East and West. Reagan opened the path to Reykjavik beginning with the proposals he made in 1981 to eliminate all intermediate-range ballistic missiles and in 1982 to reduce deployed strategic nuclear warheads by at least one-third. He was making a significant departure from arms control thinking as it had been developing since 1960, but it was rooted in a much older and more fundamental idea - disarmament. At Reykjavik he proposed a ban on all ballistic missiles, but he still wanted to continue research on a Strategic Defence Initiative, which might be shared with the Soviets. Reagan's initiative, which had been unhelpfully nicknamed 'Star Wars' by the media, was regarded with deep suspicion by the Russians. If missiles could be spotted, monitored and perhaps even intercepted from specially designed satellites, they might also be launched from them. Gorbachev was right to be sceptical about

Reagan's sincerity. Reagan had at the beginning of his administration worked hard to inflate the American nuclear arsenal, which made his disarmament proposal look like a ruse.

Another problem was the two very different agendas Reagan and Gorbachev brought to the negotiating table. The Reykjavik meeting had been intended as a preliminary meeting only, yet both leaders brought very ambitious and revolutionary proposals. Reagan wanted the Soviets to change their policies on human rights, the emigration of Soviet Jews and dissidents; he wanted Gorbachev to halt the Soviet invasion of Afghanistan. But Gorbachev only wanted to discuss arms limitation.

The timing of the Reykjavik Summit was unfortunate. It followed the unsuccessful Geneva Summit of 1985, and there was the Daniloff-Zakharov espionage affair as well. One thing that was in favour of success was the recent Chernobyl disaster, which showed the continent-wide havoc that could be caused by a nuclear strike, whether deliberate or accidental. Because of this, Gorbachev was prepared to accept that intermediate-range ballistic missiles should be removed from Europe. He was also prepared to go as far as proposing a complete ban on ballistic missiles, including the inter-continental missiles, within ten years. Reagan responded with a proposal in the same direction, which was to eliminate fifty per cent of all the ballistic missiles, but he wanted to link this with continuing research on 'Star Wars' and Gorbachev was not prepared to accept that. Gorbachev was not going to withdraw missiles from Europe while America continued with its plan to put missile or anti-missile bases in space.

Neither side trusted the other enough to relinquish nuclear weapons completely. In an atmosphere of continuing mistrust, the Reykjavik discussions collapsed. They ended without any formal agreement. But they led on to a momentous agreement the following year, the Intermediate-Range Nuclear Forces Treaty (December 1987), an important agreement to limit the arms race.

It was a very significant moment in post-Second World War history, one that signalled the beginning of the end of the Cold War. As Gorbachev said, although in formal terms the Reykjavik meeting failed, it was a success in 'reaffirming the vision of a world without nuclear weapons and paving the way towards concrete agreements on intermediate-range nuclear forces and strategic nuclear weapons.' Although they disagreed, their meeting rightly filled both men with optimism that the future could be very different from the past. It could be better.

THE BUSH-GORBACHEV SUMMITS

(1989-1990)

WHEN THE BERLIN Wall fell, it was obvious to everyone that major and rapid changes were under way not just in Germany but throughout Eastern Europe and Asia. The Iron Curtain was being lifted and the Cold War was coming to a close. It looked as if the Soviet Union itself was fracturing. The leaders of East and West, Gorbachev and Bush, met to discuss how these changes were going to be accommodated, how they were going to be controlled.

The meeting in 1989 took place on board a Soviet cruise ship, the SS *Maxim Gorky*, at anchor off Marsaxlokk, a small port on the south coast of Malta. The idea of a summit meeting on a ship at sea came from President George Bush, who was fascinated by President's Roosevelt's wartime practice of meeting foreign leaders in that way. The precise location in the central Mediterranean was the result of long haggling between Russia and America. What was needed was somewhere neutral, anonymous, and would not involve meeting additional heads of state. The final choice – Malta – turned out to be a poor choice, as the weather there in December was blustery. Bush arrived for the summit on board the USS *Belknap*. The weather was stormy and the sea was rough enough for some of the meetings to be cancelled. The press referred to it as the 'Seasick Summit'. But it was a symbolic location, midway between North and South, midway between East and West, and following the closing of the British naval base it was politically neutral.

Some members of the American administration had low expectations of the Malta Summit, but both the French president, François Mitterrand, and the British prime minister, Margaret Thatcher, among others, exerted pressure on Bush to meet Gorbachev. The Malta Summit of 1989 turned out to be an historic meeting, one in which many of the decisions made at the Yalta Conference of 1945 were put into reverse. No agreements were signed at Malta, but the discussions between Bush and Gorbachev laid out the ground rules for the ending of the Cold War. In fact some commentators regard the Malta Conference as the formal termination of the Cold War.

In the discussions, Bush expressed his support for Gorbachev's great perestroika initiative. Gorbachev said at a shared news conference, 'The world is leaving one epoch and entering another. We are at the start of a long road to a lasting peaceful era. The threat of force, mistrust, psychological and ideological struggle should all be things of the past. I assured the President of the United States that I will never start a hot war against the USA.' By way of response, President Bush said, 'We can realise a lasting peace and transform the East-West relationship to one of enduring co-operation. That is the future that Chairman Gorbachev and I began right here in Malta.'

The Malta Summit led on to another meeting between Gorbachev and Bush and their administrative teams in the following year. At the end of May 1990, Mikhail Gorbachev flew into Washington DC for three days of talks with George Bush. The specific focus of this summit was Germany, and the place Germany was to take in a rapidly changing post-Cold War Europe. But Gorbachev's position at home in the Soviet Union at the time of the Washington Summit was by now very uncertain.

Gorbachev had made valiant attempts at reforms, but the Soviet economy was in crisis and Soviet control over its satellites, such as the Baltic states, was very shaky. Russian republics like Lithuania were overtly campaigning for a new existence as independent republics outside the Soviet Union, and Gorbachev was desperately trying to hang onto them. Gorbachev's behaviour at the Washington Summit may therefore have been strongly influenced by his serious domestic problems, including his own survival as a political leader, back in Moscow. Some American observers believed that in order to strengthen his position at home, Gorbachev tried to win the favour of hard-liners in the Russian Communist Party, and that this made him more aggressive and uncompromising at the Washington Summit.

In East Germany, the Communists were losing their hold on power. The Berlin Wall was down. There were calls within Germany for the reunification of East and West Germany, and for democratic processes to prevail throughout the united Germany. When Gorbachev arrived in Washington in May 1990, the leaders of East and West Germany were already making plans for reunification. So, a key question asked at the Washington Summit was Germany's role in the new Europe. American officials pressed for Germany to become a member of NATO. But Gorbachev was rigidly opposed to this. A reunified and pro-Western Germany could be a direct threat to Russia's security. He snapped, 'The West hasn't done much thinking' and complained that listening to the argument that Germany should join NATO was like listening to a record that had got stuck on the same phrase.

The Washington Summit ended three days later without any clear agreement about the nature of the emerging united Germany. But Gorbachev had even more pressing problems because of the weakness of the Russian economy. He must have been pleasantly surprised by the generosity of the Americans at the negotiating table. In July 1990 Bush promised him a generous aid package and at the same time promised him that the new German army would be a small one. But if anybody needed reassurance, it was the Germans, not the Soviets. The Germans wanted the huge force of 380,000 Soviet troops removed from their territory, ending Soviet occupation. The removal of this army of occupation would scarcely have put the security of the Soviet Union at risk; the Soviet Union had a standing army on its own soil numbering more than five million men.

But he was now under considerable duress from conditions in Moscow, and Gorbachev agreed to allow Germany to become a member of NATO. On this basis, East and West Germany were formally reunified in October 1990. Shortly afterwards Germany joined NATO.

The fate of Lithuania was left unresolved, and nothing was done to stop Soviet military aid to a number of client countries, including Cuba,

Angola and Ethiopia. President Bush seems to have offered Gorbachev rather more than he was promised in return. He had fallen into the trap of measuring progress in American relations with Russia by the development of a personal rapport with the Soviet leader. Because Gorbachev seemed more genial, affable, liberal, progressive and Western than earlier Soviet leaders, Bush and his aides wanted to support and reward him. But Gorbachev was blockading Lithuania, failing to resolve the Soviet economic problems, and stepping up military aid to Angola. Gorbachev was doing little to earn his rewards, yet Bush was rewarding him just the same. One Soviet journalist commented that 'Bush had all the trump cards – and he didn't play them.'

Bush evidently saw Gorbachev as the man who was the key to future reforms in the Soviet Union. In fact, events overtook Gorbachev. Once free elections were held in the Soviet Union, the electorate voted for faster and more radical reform than Gorbachev was offering. It was Boris Yeltsin who was elected to become head of the Russian Republic's Supreme Soviet, and not Vlasov, who was Gorbachev's candidate. In the West, and to President Bush in particular, Gorbachev may have looked like the man of the future in Russia, but that was not how it looked in Russia itself.

THE EARTH SUMMIT
AT RIO

(1992)

THE UNITED NATIONS Conference on Environment and Development held in Rio de Janeiro on 3–14 June 1992, the so-called Earth Summit, was a major landmark in managing the planet. Most summit conferences are about political issues of one sort or another: this one was about environmental issues and their human implications. It was unprecedented in the high level of participation it attracted from countries all over the world. 172 countries sent representatives to the conference, of whom 108 were heads of state. There were also over 2,000 representatives of non-governmental organisations, who attended parallel meetings of a Global Forum.

The output by industry of toxic substances was discussed, including lead, poisonous waste and radioactive waste. So too were alternative sources of energy to replace fossil fuels. Another related issue was the desirability of enhancing public transport systems with a view to reducing vehicle emissions and traffic congestion in cities. Separate issues for discussion included the growing scarcity of water and the need to conserve the environments of indigenous peoples.

A Local Governments Honours Award was given to twelve cities for initiating innovative environmental programmes: they included Sudbury in Ontario, Austin in Texas and Kitakyushu in Japan. There was also agreement on a Convention on Biological Diversity.

Perhaps the most momentous outcome of the summit was an agreement among the politicians on a Framework Convention on Climate Change. This in its turn became the Kyoto Protocol. The Convention on Climate Change was a treaty aimed at stabilising the concentrations of greenhouse gases in the atmosphere at a level that will stop adverse effects on the Earth's climate system. This treaty was based on the assumptions that certain gases, especially carbon dioxide, cause the atmosphere to become warmer and that man-made production of those gases is producing climate change. The conference did not question whether these assumptions were justified, or demand proof that climatic warming was man-made. Given the brevity of the two-week conference, it is hard to see how those issues could have been covered adequately.

The treaty came into force on 21 March 1994, once fifty countries had signed up to it. It did not attempt to set out specific mandatory limits on greenhouse gas emissions, nor did it provide for any enforcement procedures. Instead, it provided for the subsequent publication of 'protocols', which would set mandatory limits. The main protocol is the Kyoto Protocol. The Convention also set up a system of national greenhouse gas inventories; each signatory state became obliged to carry out its own audit of greenhouse gas emissions and removals as a kind of annual budget and submit it for scrutiny. The countries signing up to the agreement were separated into three groups. The Annex I countries were the industrialised countries, including Poland and Estonia; Annex II countries were industrialised, developed countries who were subsidising less economically developed countries, such as the United States and United Kingdom; the third group consisted of the less economically developed countries. Annex I countries were required to reduce their greenhouse gas emissions to levels below those of 1990, though it was possible for industries within their borders to buy emission allowances. At the other end of the scale, the less economically developed countries were not expected to reduce their carbon dioxide emissions unless developed countries helped them to do so. This decision was reached so as not to restrict economic development in the poorest countries.

This aspect of the Convention did not meet with universal approval. Some states claimed that complying with the Convention would put undue stress on their economies. President Bush of the United States gave this as his reason for not forwarding the Kyoto Protocol to the USA for ratification; he would not impose this constraint on the development of his country's economy, even though he had signed the Convention. The governments of 154 countries were prepared to sign up to the Convention.

The Rio Summit was followed by a series of COPs (Conferences of Parties), and the first of these was held in Berlin in 1995. At this meeting, doubts were expressed about the ability of countries to meet the commitments they had agreed to. This led to a 'Berlin Mandate', which set up a two-year assessment phase and exempted countries not on the Annex I list from additional binding obligations. This was decided in spite of the fact that it was understood that the large newly-industrialising countries of the world would become the world's biggest greenhouse gas producers within about fifteen years.

The second Conference of Parties, which met in Geneva in 1996, was notable for its uncritical acceptance of the 1995 report on climate change published by the Intergovernmental Panel on Climate Change (IPCC). This acceptance in itself involved an even greater commitment to preventing further climate change by way of greenhouse emissions. It seems never to have occurred to member states or their representatives to question the objectivity of the IPCC's coverage of climate processes. This was strange, in that the IPCC's remit when set up was explicit; the IPCC was to explore the human impact on climate. Its reports subsequently emphasised the potential human impacts and de-emphasised the natural components of climate change - just as it had been asked to do.

It was COP-3, the third Conference of Parties held in Kyoto in 1997, that yielded the famous Kyoto Protocol. This required most industrialised countries to commit themselves to reduce (by 2008–12) their greenhouse gas emissions to levels 6–8 percent lower than their 1990 levels. The USA was required to reduce its emissions to seven percent below 1990 levels. The response in Washington was negative. Neither President Clinton nor President Bush would send the protocol to US Congress for ratification. In 2001, the Bush administration rejected the Kyoto Protocol outright.

Conference followed conference. From COP-3, the discussions continued through to the most recent, COP-14, which took place in December 2008 in Poznan. These hugely expensive diplomatic encounters revolve around mechanisms for gaining compliance from signatories to the Rio Convention. It is a great pity that more time has not gone into questioning the mechanisms and processes responsible for climate change. If, as some scientists believe, the changes in climate are entirely natural in origin, the whole debate about greenhouse gas emissions could be shelved. Then other key environmental issues, such as the conservation of forests, water, mineral resources and cultural environments, might be discussed more fully – and more usefully, as we know that we can do something about them.

The underlying message of the Rio Summit – that people's attitudes and patterns of behaviour towards the environment needed to change – was timely and constructive. It was good to make the political leaders of the richest countries face up to the fact that they had a responsibility towards the people living in much poorer countries as well as to their own electorates. The summit was highly publicised, with nearly 10,000 journalists in Rio itself reporting the event. As it closed, the conference's secretary-general, Maurice Strong, described the Rio Summit as an 'historic moment for humanity'. And it was. The effect of Rio was to make many governments look again at the possibility of developing alternative, renewable sources of energy, and at improving public transport systems, and at the rights of people to live in a healthy environment. The Rio Summit had a strong influence over all subsequent United Nations conferences. But the assumption that cutting down on fossil fuel burning would bring about a reversal of climate change was ill-founded. The 'science' of climate change ought to have been challenged and investigated thoroughly before national economies all round the world were required to adjust, and adjust at vast expense.

THE CAMP DAVID
SUMMIT
(2000)

On 5 July 2000, US President Bill Clinton announced his invitation to the leaders of the Palestinians and the Israelis, Yasser Arafat and Ehud Barak, to come to his country home, Camp David. The aim was to negotiate a peace settlement for the Middle East. This was to build on the progress made at the earlier Camp David Accords of 1978, in which a peace agreement was brokered by President Jimmy Carter between Egypt and Israel.

Then there had been the Oslo Accords of 1993, in which there was agreement between PLO Chairman Arafat and the Israeli prime minister, Yitzhak Rabin, that all the remaining political issues between Palestinians and Israelis should be resolved within five years. This process had stalled because the expectations of neither Israelis nor Palestinians had been fulfilled. Mr Arafat argued that the summit had been premature.

The Camp David Summit was a determined attempt to resolve the remaining problems and generate a peace settlement. The summit convened on 11 July 2000 and went on for two weeks.

At the end of the negotiations, agreement on a peace settlement had still not been reached, but a statement was issued, called the Trilateral Statement, outlining the principles that had been agreed as guidelines for future negotiations. These were:

1. to put an end to decades of conflict and achieve a just and lasting peace;
2. to continue efforts to conclude an agreement as soon as possible;

3. to avoid taking unilateral actions that prejudge the outcome of negotiations;

4. that the United States remained a vital partner in the search for peace.

Camp David failed to reach agreement on four issues. One was territory. Arafat wanted full Palestinian sovereignty over the West Bank and Gaza Strip; he was prepared to discuss the possibility of land-swapping with the Israelis, though not when the Israelis proposed offering areas of the Negev Desert in exchange for rights in the West Bank. Arafat reminded the summit that Resolution called for a complete Israeli withdrawal from those territories, which had been captured and occupied by Israel during the Six-Day War.

Barak offered to form a Palestinian state on seventy-three percent of what the Palestinians regarded as their West Bank territory, but enlarging to encompass ninety percent of it within twenty-five years. 100 percent of the Gaza Strip would become Palestinian. This entailed Israel withdrawing from sixty-three existing Israeli settlements in Gaza and the West Bank.

A major stumbling block was the status of Jerusalem and the Temple Mount in particular. The Palestinians wanted all of East Jerusalem returned to Palestinian control and sovereignty, with the city given the status of an 'open city' with co-operation on municipal services. The Israelis rejected the idea of Palestinian sovereignty over the Temple Mount, and proposed custodianship instead. They also provocatively demanded Israeli sovereignty over the Islamic sacred sites in east Jerusalem, including the Al-Aqsa Mosque.

A third area of disagreement was refugees and their right of return. Under war conditions, large numbers of Palestinians had either fled or been thrown out of their homes in what had now become Israeli territory. There were 700,000 of these refugees at the time, and the Palestinians wanted them to have the right to return to their homes if they wanted to, or accept compensation instead. The Israelis objected that this influx of Palestinians would fundamentally change the demographics of Israel and jeopardise the country's Jewish character. They also counter-argued that many more Jewish refugees had been forced out of Arab countries in the decades since 1948, and that most of these had taken refuge in Israel. The Palestinians understood the Israeli objection and proposed a mechanism that would channel most refugees towards deciding to accept compensation rather than return; clearly the number returning would have to be limited in some way.

A fourth obstacle to agreement at Camp David was the Israelis' concern regarding security. They wanted control of airspace. They wanted the right to deploy Israeli troops on Palestinian soil in the event of an emergency. They wanted the Palestinian state to be demilitarised.

The initial high hopes for Camp David were dashed. Each side blamed the other for the failure of the talks. The Palestinians were certainly ethically entitled to have expectations from such talks, but it may be that Arafat pushed too hard and too far. For example, he wanted the Israelis to withdraw immediately from the occupied territories, but at the same time undertook to annihilate all the Palestinian terrorist organisations only at some subsequent date. The Israeli negotiators found this unacceptable. Clinton did in fact later blame Arafat for missing his opportunity to bring his nation into being, adding that he prayed 'for the day when the dreams of the Palestinian people for a state and a better life will be realised in a just and lasting peace.' Many European politicians similarly saw the Israelis as more prepared to make concessions than Arafat. In Europe generally there was little sympathy for the Palestinians' later complaints about Israel's refusal to recognise the Palestinian refugees' right of return; a reasonable compromise had been proposed. Arafat was also accused of wrecking the talks by one of his own men, Nabil Amr, a minister in the Palestinian Authority.

President Clinton was once complimented by Arafat: 'You are a great man.' Clinton is said to have replied, 'I am not a great man. I am a failure – and you made me one.'

But some observers see Camp David differently. Professor Norman Finkelstein was one political scientist who saw the Israelis as the more inflexible negotiators. Judged from the perspective of the respective rights of Israelis and Palestinians under international law, he wrote, all the concessions at Camp David came from the Palestinian side, none from the Israeli side. Another observer, Professor Alan Dershowitz, believed that the negotiations failed on one specific issue: Arafat's refusal to give up the right of return.

The fall-out from the Camp David Summit was momentous. The first and most obvious outcome was that there was still no Palestinian state, still no resolution of the fundamental problems. Another was Israeli reaction - the resurgence of right-wing 'Zionist' attitudes towards the Palestinians. Ariel Sharon toured the Temple Mount with a group of Likud politicians in a high-profile demonstration that Jews had and would continue to exert the right to visit the site. It was still the holiest site in Judaism, even though Islamic in its current religious dedication. This was seen by many Palestinians as provocative and a counter-demonstration was mounted the following day. Stones were thrown and Israeli police fired, killing four protesters. The violence escalated. There were street battles in Gaza and the West Bank and many were killed. A Palestinian mob destroyed Joseph's Tomb, a Jewish holy site near the West Bank city of Nablus.

The following year, 2001, an organised campaign by the Palestinians in retaliation for the Israeli killing of civilians got under way with a wave of suicide bombings. This prompted Israel to send in its Defence Force to seal off the Gaza Strip and re-occupy the West Bank. Military rule was established. Clinton tried to halt the bloodshed by writing to Barak and Arafat with proposed ground-rules for future negotiations. Barak accepted at once. Arafat accepted, but only after the deadline had passed and only with what were seen as unacceptable reservations.

The overall outcome was a marked swing to the right in Israeli politics. No further talks could take place because an Israeli election loomed – and Barak lost it. In 2001, Ehud Barak was defeated and replaced by Ariel Sharon. The door that Camp David had seemed to open was now slammed firmly shut; an opportunity for the Palestinians to have their own homeland and have it internationally recognised was lost. And still, years later, the bloodshed continues.

THE PYONGYANG
SUMMIT MEETINGS

(2002 and 2007)

THE PYONGYANG SUMMIT of 2002 was an historic moment in the history of Korea. For fifty years North Korea and South Korea had existed in a state of hostility. Then, in 2002, the leaders of the two countries met for the first time. This summit was preceded by an important September meeting between the North Korean leader, Kim Jong-Il, and the prime minister of Japan, Junichiro Koizumi. It was important not least in marking the re-emergence after the Second World War of Japan as a political power in eastern Asia. North Korea's economy was crippled by its Stalinist regime, and Koizumi was able to exploit the weakness of North Korea by making a series of provocative demands. Koizumi even managed to extort from Kim Jong-Il an admission that between 1977 and 1983 thirteen Japanese people had been abducted to teach Japanese language and culture to North Korean spies. Kim Jong-Il apologised for the abductions, which he said were carried out by over-zealous agents. Most of the abducted Japanese were by then dead, either as a result of accidents or disease. The admission was remarkable, but Koizumi had made it a condition of the continuation of the talks, and the talks were the way to end North Korea's isolation. The North Korean leader also abandoned his country's longstanding demand that Japan must compensate North Korea for the brutal régime imposed during the period of colonial rule from 1910 and 1945. In return, he had to accept a minimal apology for the 'huge damage and suffering'.

Kim Jong-Il also said he was willing to meet the demands from the USA to allow international inspectors into his country to demonstrate that it was not manufacturing weapons of mass destruction.

But these confessions of wrong-doing were not enough. In the 1990s, President Clinton's administration accused North Korea of manufacturing weapons of mass destruction. It used this accusation to maintain the political and economic isolation of a disintegrating North Korea, even though this meant that as many as two million North Koreans starved to death. Some right-wing members of the Bush administration that followed were inclined to be tougher still, advocating a strategy that would bring about the total political and social collapse of North Korea.

Meanwhile, China and the European Union worked towards encouraging a rapprochement between North and South Korea, but the Bush administration asserted what it saw as America's right to have the major say in what happened in the region. America would block any attempts to erode the predominance of America there. Bush worked towards undermining any evolving deal between North and South Korea by being more aggressive with the North, calling it part of the 'axis of evil' along with Iraq and Iran.

The first historic meeting between the political leaders of North and South Korea took place on 13–15 June 2000. The first Pyongyang Summit brought together Kim Jong-Il from North Korea and Kim Dae-jung from South Korea. This was the first time in fifty years that the leaders of the two halves of Korea had met, and the encounter changed the geopolitics of the region. Suddenly it seemed possible that a reunification of Korea might happen. As it turned out, reunification was a very long way off, though it did bring a negotiated settlement closer and the prospect of peaceful coexistence. Regardless of any political differences, the two countries wanted economic improvement, and since the Pyongyang Summit there has been a gradual increase in the economic dependency of North on South.

The benefits were significant. The Summit came at a high cost, though. About $US500 million were given to North Korea as a reward for making the conference possible. Unfortunately this payment has reinforced the impression given to North Korea that international co-operation must be bought, even when co-operation is to North Korea's advantage. But the summit set in motion a dialogue that was to

316

continue. North Korea expressed interest in discussing a peace treaty with the South.

Seven years later, on 2 October 2007, the leaders of North and South Korea met and shook hands in Pyongyang at the opening of what was only the second summit between the two countries. North Korea's leader, Kim Jong-il, wore his usual olive-green tunic and platform shoes as he uneasily greeted the ebullient president of South Korea, Roh Moo-hyun. Crowds of North Koreans dutifully cheered as they shook hands. At the same time, in the South Korean capital, Seoul, a German human rights campaigner was thrown out of a press centre for making a protest against the detention of thousands of political prisoners in North Korea.

The summit took place just one year after North Korea tested its first nuclear weapon. The tension between the two countries had run high for many years, and in fact it had never ceased since the blood-letting of the Korean War of 1950–53. That war had halted in an armistice signed at the border village of Panmunjom, but no peace treaty was ever signed and technically the two halves of Korea had remained at war ever since. The frontier between them remained one of the most heavily militarised in the world. As he crossed the frontier near Panmunjom on his way to the summit, Roh Moo-hyun said, 'This line is the wall that has left our nation divided for half a century. Because of this wall, our nation has suffered so much pain . . . I will make efforts to make my walk across the border an occasion to remove the forbidden wall and move toward peace and prosperity.'

Critics of Mr Roh's initiative accused him of engineering a publicity stunt to improve his party's popularity ahead of the South Korean presidential election that was coming up two months later.

Both Mr Roh and his predecessor crossed the border for summits in North Korea, but the North Korean leader never made the journey south to Seoul. This led some commentators to say that the South Korean leaders were in effect paying homage to the real overlord of Korea, Mr Kim. American officials saw the summit as unlikely to change things in the region. The American view was significant, because the US supplied most of the troops for the defence of South Korea against the North. Mr Roh's position was that any narrowing of the gap in understanding between the two countries would be useful in reducing mistrust; he hoped to bring about a peace settlement that would lead on to economic development.

VII

HOSTILE ENCOUNTERS

CAESAR AND BRUTUS

(47 BC)

JULIUS CAESAR (102-44 BC) was born into an old Roman patrician family. Like other Roman aristocrats, he built his career in public life by working his way through the cursus honorum, collecting public offices of ever-increasing status over the years. Caesar was unusual in collecting so many of these status symbols – to the point where his fellow-Romans became suspicious of his ultimate ambition. He was elected pontifex in 73 BC, pontifex maximus in 63, praetor for 62. In 61 he was governor of the province of Hispania Ulterior and on his return to Rome he was elected consul for 59. He gradually built an impressive portfolio of offices and positions, establishing his place at the forefront of Roman public life. Then he engineered his military career, spending nine years extending the Roman Empire to the west. By 56 BC he was tackling the tribes of Normandy and Brittany and in 54 BC forced a nominal and temporary surrender of south-east England. After returning to northern Italy, Caesar was recalled to Gaul to put down the rebellion of Vercingetorix.

The senate now saw Caesar as uncomfortably powerful and called on him to resign his command and disband his army; the senate preferred to entrust power to Caesar's rival Pompey. Caesar made the critical and dangerous decision to defy the senate. He marched his army into Italy, chasing Pompey to the south of Italy and from there to Greece. Suddenly Julius Caesar was in control in Italy and appointed dictator for a year. In 48 BC Pompey was assassinated in Egypt, not at Caesar's instigation but on the orders of Ptolemy. Either way, the rival had been removed.

In 45 BC, Caesar was at the height of his military and political power. Some Romans, both aristocrats and common people, were alarmed at the emergence of Caesar's personal dictatorship. No-one really knows for certain whether Caesar aspired to further aggrandisement. He certainly claimed that he didn't. Once, while he was travelling from Alba to Rome, some people by the roadside saluted him and addressed him as king. It was a significant step too far. Caesar saw that the rest of the crowd did not like it and he called out that his name was Caesar, not king.

The word had a resonance then that it does not have today. In ancient Rome 'king' could also mean 'tyrant'. Conversely, the title 'dictator' then did not have the unpleasant connotations it has today. Now, we would see 'king' as the inoffensive title, 'dictator' as the offensive one; in ancient Rome it was the other way round.

In the senate, Caesar made rather a show of treating everyone as equals and said he should have honours taken away, not new ones added. But the idea that Julius Caesar was to be made king was circulated, perhaps by his friends, perhaps by his enemies, who wanted to see him fall. He was in a sense caught by the cursus honorum; everyone assumed that when you reached a particular level on the status ladder you would try for the next rung.

Then the plotting began. The instigator of the successful assassination plot was Gaius Cassius Longinus. Cassius had been pardoned by Caesar for earlier disloyalty, but he felt aggrieved that he had not been offered a command in the forthcoming war against Parthia. Cassius persuaded his brother-in-law Marcus Junius Brutus to join the conspiracy. Brutus was fanatical and merciless. He had fought on Pompey's side at Pharsalia, like Cassius, and like Cassius he had been pardoned. Julius Caesar had been more than generous to both of them and they owed him a debt of gratitude. Perhaps that was one of the reasons why they hated him – the unwelcome sense of obligation.

Brutus was well known as a descendant of Lucius Junius Brutus, who lived in about 500 BC and who was thought to have founded republican government in Rome. It was that earlier Brutus who drove an earlier king, Tarquinius, out of Rome for misrule. The later Brutus, in his arrogant, overblown way, came to think of himself as re-enacting that early cleansing of Rome. In killing Julius Caesar, he was destroying the monarchy in Rome for a second time. The idea appealed to his ego.

There was a Lee Harvey Oswald effect: the little man determined to bring down the big man, just to feel bigger. There was a Herostratus effect too: destroying something fine, noble and admirable, like the Temple of Diana at Ephesus, just for the sake of being remembered for it.

Neither Brutus nor Cassius had any real reason to assassinate Julius Caesar, but Cassius's minor feeling of slight combined with Brutus's tendency to fanaticism was enough to do it. It became an obsession.

Brutus was the son of Marcus Junius Brutus the Elder and Servilia Caepionis. His father was one of Pompey's lieutenants. His mother was half-sister of Cato the Younger, and she became Julius Caesar's mistress. Some historians have proposed that Brutus was Caesar's son, but Brutus was a little too old, by about five years, for that to be true; Julius Caesar was only fifteen years older than Brutus. Probably Julius Caesar encountered Brutus when the latter was a boy, when visiting his mistress. As a youth Brutus was adopted by his uncle, Quintus Servilius Caepio, and for a time he was known by his uncle's name. He had enormous respect for his uncle.

Brutus's political career began when he became an assistant to Cato, another uncle, while Cato was governor of Cyprus. Brutus became rich at this time by lending money at high interest rates. Returning to Rome a wealthy man, he was able to marry Claudia Pulchra. When he arrived in the senate, Brutus aligned himself with the Optimates (conservatives) against the First Triumvirate (Crassus, Pompey and Caesar). In 49 BC, civil war broke out between Pompey and Caesar. Brutus allied himself with Pompey, who was the current leader of the Optimates, against Julius Caesar.

At the Battle of Pharsalus, then, Brutus and Julius Caesar were on opposing sides. Julius Caesar seems to have felt some obligation to protect Brutus. This may have been because Brutus was the son of his mistress, or because Caesar had befriended the youth in some other context that has escaped historical documentation. Whatever the nature of the bond, whatever its origin, Julius Caesar gave Brutus special protection on the battlefield. He gave specific orders to his officers at the outset of the battle that they were to take Brutus prisoner if he gave himself up willingly; if he resisted capture, they were to let him alone. Either way, he must come to no harm. After the battle, which Julius Caesar won conclusively, Brutus wrote the victor a repentant letter of apology, and Caesar immediately forgave him.

After that, Caesar did Brutus further favours. He drew him into his inner circle; he offered him friendship. When Caesar left for Africa to pursue Cato, he made Brutus governor of Gaul. In 45 BC, Caesar named Brutus as urban praetor for the following year. In the same year, Brutus caused a scandal by divorcing his wife and giving no other reason than the fact that he wanted to marry Cato's daughter Portia instead, which was not generally regarded as a good enough reason. The remarriage also caused a rift between Brutus and his mother, who disapproved of the new match.

It was at this moment that many senators began to fear the power of Caesar and Brutus was pressed into joining the assassination conspiracy. A new factor in the situation was Brutus' new marriage, which made him more sympathetic to Cato and thus less sympathetic to Caesar. He joined the conspiracy, and his wife Portia was the only woman who had full knowledge of the plot.

On the fateful day, when various omens deterred Caesar from attending the senate, it was Brutus who urged him to attend. When the knives were out and Caesar fell to the marble floor with multiple stab wounds, it was the sight of Brutus, his favourite, among the conspirators that made him cover his face with his toga and resign himself to death.

The events following Caesar's assassination were a bizarre anticlimax. To begin with, nothing much happened. The assassins lay low fearing reprisal attacks from Caesar's supporters; Caesar's supporters lay low fearing that they might be assassinated next. Consequently Rome was very quiet. Brutus was offered a compromise. If Caesar was formally denounced as a tyrant, then all of his acts and senatorial appointments would be declared null and void, and that would include the urban praetorship offered to Brutus by Caesar shortly before he was murdered. It is odd that this should have mattered to Brutus, but it did. On the other hand, if Brutus agreed to recognise Caesar's appointments, he and the other assassins would be granted an amnesty and allowed to keep their positions. Brutus accepted this offer. Caesar was accordingly not declared a tyrant. Another part of the agreement was that Brutus was to leave Rome. He agreed to this too, spending the next two years on Crete, until 42 BC.

But in 43 BC, when Octavian (later to become Augustus) became consul, his first action was to have the men who assassinated Caesar declared enemies of the state. Octavian, like Brutus, had a special relationship with Julius Caesar. His mother Atia was Julius Caesar's niece. Caesar's will declared Octavian to be his adopted son and chosen heir and successor. But Brutus heard that Octavian's and Mark Antony's forces were divided and took the opportunity to rally his own troops – seventeen legions of them - and march on Rome, against Octavian in particular. But this was a miscalculation. When Octavian heard that Brutus was marching against him, he made peace with Antony. Together, they commanded nineteen legions and they marched to meet Brutus and Cassius.

In October 42 BC, these two huge forces met at the Battle of Philippi, really two battles three weeks apart. At the first battle Brutus defeated Octavian but Cassius was defeated by Antony. In the second battle Brutus was defeated. After the defeat, Brutus fled into the hills and committed suicide. Antony ordered Brutus' body to be wrapped in his own most expensive cloak. The cremated remains were sent to Brutus's mother. Portia committed suicide when she heard of Brutus's death.

It was a strange relationship, the relationship between Julius Caesar and Brutus, charged with high and indefinable emotions that we can sense yet scarcely begin to understand. For some reason, the young and volatile Brutus mattered a great deal to Julius Caesar – he felt protective towards him. Finding that Brutus was among his assassins must have been a bewildering shock to the dying man, as he lay bleeding to death at the foot of Pompey's statue.

'You too, Brutus?' Even you.

HAROLD GODWINSON
AND DUKE WILLIAM

(1065)

ALTHOUGH EDWARD THE Confessor now has a safe reputation as a saintly Anglo-Saxon king of England, during his reign there was great uneasiness about his loyalties. Anglo-Saxon he may have been, the son of King Ethelred the Unready, but he had strong pro-Norman sympathies. His mother Emma was a Norman. During the time when England had been ruled by Danes – the Danish King Sven Forkbeard invaded in 1012 and forced Ethelred to flee – the Saxon royal family took refuge in Normandy. Sven died in 1014, but he was succeeded by his son Cnut who ruled over a northern empire that included Denmark and England. It was only when this Danish empire fell apart in 1042 that England reverted to Anglo-Saxon rule. Ethelred's son Edward became king, but he had spent a great deal of time in exile in Normandy. He had Norman habits, and Norman advisers.

It was natural that the Anglo-Saxon lords were suspicious of the strong foreign influence on their king. The leading Anglo-Saxon magnates were Godwin, Earl of Essex, and his son Harold Godwinson. Neither of them wanted any more foreign influence on the English throne. England had had enough of Danish influence, and the Normans were Northmen, descended from Vikings. Edward's mother, Emma, was a Norman and, as it happened, the great-aunt of William of Normandy. William of Normandy was born in 1028 and in his teens when Edward the Confessor became king. William was the son of a wayward Norman knight, Duke Robert of Normandy, sometimes known as Robert the Cruel. Robert died while on pilgrimage to Jerusalem to expiate his sins, and was succeeded by William.

Duke William had a turbulent and dangerous childhood. He had to fight off pretenders to his throne, and defend himself against assassins. On one occasion a plot to kill William was thwarted by his jester, who stole into William's bedroom, woke him up and persuaded him to escape on horseback. William survived, inherited his father's title and power, holding court at Rouen. But for that nocturnal encounter with the jester, William would have been murdered in his bed and the Norman conquest of England would not have happened. The course of history would have been different.

In 1052, Duke William travelled to England to visit King Edward. A chronicler of the time wrote, 'William Earl came from beyond the sea with company of Frenchmen and the King received him, and as many of his comrades as to him seemed good, and let him go again.' Behind this bland account lurks a potentially dangerous conversation. According to William's version of events, during this visit the English king promised him the crown of England. This was later to be one of the props for William's usurpation of the English throne in 1066.

In the autumn of 1064, William had a visitor from England. By chance, a storm drove Harold Godwinson's ship onto Duke William's shore and the encounter between the two men provided William with another prop for his seizure of power.

At that time, Harold Godwinson, now Earl of Essex, was thirty-two years old and in his prime. He was a great warrior, with long and shaggy fair hair and a bushy moustache. Harold and his father had to work and fight hard to maintain their powerful position in England. They had fought King Edward openly in a civil war in the 1050s, a war in which Earl Godwin killed the king's brother Alfred. For this insubordination, Edward exiled both Godwin and Harold for a time, but they were powerful enough to be able to return and oust the Norman advisers to whom they objected so strongly.

Godwin died in 1053, and his estates and title were inherited by Harold. Harold's brother Tostig became Earl of Northumbria. Against all the odds and in spite of past events, Harold and the King were on good terms. Harold achieved this by being Edward's great war-leader;

one notable success was his leadership in a spectacularly successful campaign against the Welsh in 1063. Harold sent the Welsh leader's head, along with the figurehead from his ship, to King Edward.

Edward himself was in physical and mental decline. He spent his time wrapped up in spiritual concerns, in particular in building a great abbey. Edward and Harold became so completely reconciled, according to Harold at least, that Edward promised him the English throne on his death.

The situation was explosive. The reigning monarch, Edward the Confessor, had promised his throne to two people, to the Anglo-Saxon Harold Godwinson and to the Norman Duke William.

In September 1064, accompanied by many retainers, Harold boarded one of two ships at Bosham in Chichester Harbour and set sail into the English Channel. The purpose of this voyage is still a matter for speculation. He may have been on a diplomatic mission to the European mainland. He boarded the ship with a falcon on his wrist and accompanied by hunting dogs, so he may have been bound for Flanders, to holiday at the friendly court of Tostig's brother-in-law. The two longships struck out into the Channel, where a fierce storm struck them and drove them off-course. Harold's ship ran aground near Abbeville, on land owned by Count Guy de Ponthieu. Guy stuck to the letter of his law, which allowed him to hold any traveller shipwrecked on his shore to ransom. This unusually rich traveller was an especially welcome hostage. He seized Harold and his companions, manacled them and threw them into a dungeon.

When Duke William heard about the incident, he sent two of his own men to Guy de Ponthieu's castle to demand the release of Harold. Guy recognised William as more powerful than himself and acquiesced. Guy took a large retinue of French knights and escorted Harold and his companions to William. They met a party led by Duke William on the main road along the way. This encounter took place in open country. Guy rode forward, turning in his saddle to point out Harold Godwinson to Duke William. The two men met each other then for the first time. Both were strongly built warriors, but William was the taller of the two and built very solidly indeed. Harold wore his blond hair long and shaggy, with a full moustache; William was clean-shaven in the Norman fashion. William treated Harold with great kindness and courtesy, ushering him into his palace at Rouen.

This auspicious meeting was followed by the most generous of hospitality. There were tournaments and displays of arms. William even persuaded Harold to accompany him on campaign in Brittany where he was trying to suppress a rebellion. Harold fought with exceptional skill on this campaign. He was no doubt inwardly hankering to return to England, and must have been somewhat uneasy about risking his life for his great rival for the English throne – if indeed he then realised this was the situation. After the Breton campaign, an extraordinary ceremony took place. Harold swore fealty to William in front of the Norman nobles. This scene was later portrayed in the (Norman) Bayeux tapestry. The Norman version of events was that Harold had already in private agreed that William's claim to the English throne was superior to his own. He agreed to give his sister to one of William's barons in marriage. In reciprocation, Harold would marry William's daughter Adeliza.

The fact is that, beneath the surface courtesies and pleasantries, Harold was a hostage, a prisoner in a foreign land. He had no choice but to go along with the marriage arrangements William proposed, no choice but to concede that William had the better claim to the throne of England. If he had not, he would not have been allowed to return; the lavish 'hospitality' would have gone on indefinitely.

A few days after these exchanges of oaths, Harold was allowed to embark for England. Observers noticed that he was deeply troubled.

Within the year, Edward the Confessor died. On his deathbed, Edward named Harold his successor. Whatever promise he had made, years before, to William of Normandy, it was set aside now and Harold Godwinson was to be the next king of England. Harold was anointed king on 6 January 1066. William had his informants in England and through them he heard about the coronation only three days afterwards. His first response was to fire a series of letters at Harold, reminding of his oath, accusing him of perjury, demanding that he give up the crown to him. Harold of course was not going to relinquish his throne in response to a series of letters. William did not expect him to. What William was doing was documenting the moral basis for his invasion of England. The letters might have no effect, but they would, after the event, show that he was not an aggressor. He was striving, like so many war-mongers since, to establish his invasion as a just war. It was the eleventh century equivalent of the paper trail leading to (or rather not leading to) the weapons of mass destruction in Iraq.

William next appealed to Pope Alexander II. William had been generous to the Church in the past and this will have predisposed the pope to side with William in his claim to the English throne. The English church had been independent-minded with regard to Rome and slow to pay its tithes. If William were to invade and take over England, that anomaly could be made good.

Alongside this well-planned correspondence, William carefully prepared his army and equipped his ships, taking all of the spring and summer months, ready to invade England. Harold too tried to prepare, but he was under a huge disadvantage. His brother Tostig chose this moment to rebel against him. Tostig joined forces with Harold Hardrade, the king of Norway, who himself had a claim to the English throne. Throughout the spring and summer of 1066, Harold's messengers rode round England gathering military support, mainly in the form of foot-soldiers.

King Harold marched his army north to deal with Tostig, routing the armies of Tostig and the King of Norway at the Battle of Stamford Bridge. In the battle, both Tostig and Harold Hardrade were killed. But the effort involved in achieving this victory overstrained King Harold and his army. William landed his invasion army at Pevensey on 27 September. Harold heard this terrible news while he was in York on 1 October and set off at once to confront the second invader. On 14 October, after an exhausting march south to Hastings, Harold met William again, but it was under very different circumstances from their first meeting. This time the two men had huge armies at their backs; this time there were no smiles, no civilities; this time it was a fight to the death.

Harold lost the Battle of Hastings mainly because he had won the Battle of Stamford Bridge. He and his army were exhausted. He did not lose because he deserved to lose. The Norman view, the victors' view, was that right prevailed; Harold was a perjurer and a usurper and therefore William's inferior; Duke William deserved the victory. A French chronicler wrote of Harold, 'The Englishman was very tall and handsome, remarkable for his physical strength, his courage, his eloquence, his ready jest and acts of valour. But what were these gifts to him without honour, which is the root of all good?' The French chose to forget that Harold's promise had been made under duress.

THOMAS BECKET AND THE FOUR KNIGHTS

(1170)

THOMAS BECKET, ARCHBISHOP of Canterbury, was born the son of a wealthy London merchant in 1118. He was educated at Merton Priory, then London, Paris and Italy. Like many ambitious young men, he decided that his best chance of progress lay in the Church. He became secretary to Archbishop Theobald of Canterbury, who thought so highly of his administrative abilities that he eventually, in 1154, recommended him to King Henry II as his Chancellor.

Thomas excelled in this new role, the medieval equivalent of prime minister, in spite of his remarkably swift promotion. He worked closely with the King and they became firm friends. Becket appeared to give his absolute support to the King's plan to unify the laws relating to Church and state. In this Henry II misread Thomas's wishes and it led to trouble later. In 1162, Henry decided to select Thomas as the new Archbishop of Canterbury, assuming that Thomas would continue to collaborate from 'the other side'. Thomas warned him not to do this, recognising a clash of interests, but Henry insisted. Given the charge of looking after the interests of the Church in England, Thomas did just that, and steadfastly resisted Henry's attempts to reduce the Church's great power. Within a very short time, the two men were enemies, and Henry wanted to remove Thomas, who was now an obstacle to his reforms.

The men who were to remove this obstacle were four barons: Reginald Fitzurse, Richard le Breton, William de Tracey and Hugh de Morville. These were the men who were demonised as the four 'knights' when Thomas was canonised. Perhaps the most peculiar thing about these men is that in spite of committing the most notorious crime of the middle ages, very little is known about them. They appeared out of nowhere, rode to Canterbury to insult and murder the archbishop, and vanished again. Rather more is known about Reginald Fitzurse than the others.

Reginald Fitzurse was a Norman knight of the 12th century, the eldest son of Richard Fitzurse. He was probably born in about 1130, inheriting the manor of Williton in Somerset when his father died in 1168. He has sometimes been referred to as a baron, because he held his lands from the King. He was certainly a major landowner. In addition to the land he owned in Somerset, he owned the manor of Barham in Kent and lands in Northamptonshire too.

Hugh de Morville was probably the son of the Hugh de Morville who held the barony of Burgh-by-Sands and several other estates in the northern shires. De Morville was attached to Henry II's court from the beginning of his reign, and his name appears as a witness on a string of charters. He married Helwis de Stuteville, and so came into possession of the castle of Knaresborough. After the murder, he was ordered to do a penance of service in the Holy Land by the pope, but he was not punished by Henry II; he had after all loyally done what the king wanted. We know that he was allowed to obtain a licence to hold a weekly market at Kirkoswald. He died shortly after this, certainly before 1203, leaving behind him two daughters and the sword with which he held back the crowd in Canterbury Cathedral: for a long time it was preserved in Carlisle Cathedral – with no intended irony – as a holy relic in its own right.

Richard le Breton eventually retired to the island of Jersey after the murder.

Obscure though these men are – and were, even in their own day – they are remembered for one encounter: their single act of phenomenal brutality and sacrilege, the murder in his own cathedral of Archbishop Thomas Becket, the greatest saint of the middle ages.

They were in attendance at the court of Henry II in northern France late in 1170 when they heard the King's intemperate words, 'Will no-one rid me of this turbulent priest?' Henry II was exasperated with Becket's non-co-operation with the reforms he was trying to introduce, and had already brought him to trial at Northampton Castle in 1164, a confrontation that led to Becket's flight and self-imposed exile to France. Thomas Becket had fled Northampton Castle in the middle of the night in fear of his life. The King's temper was such that he might have ordered his archbishop's execution or mutilation on the spot. Becket decided not to risk staying in England any longer.

In 1170 the exile had lasted six years, while the administration of the see of Canterbury was left in the hands of others. Thomas felt he needed to return to England, even though he knew he risked death from the King or the King's supporters in doing so. Relations with the King were only a little better than they had been at Northampton in 1164.

Whatever he meant by it, Henry II certainly did utter words such as, 'Will no-one rid me of this turbulent priest?' and 'What a set of idle cowards I keep about me who allow me to be mocked so shamefully by a low-born clerk!' and he uttered them more than once, as he admitted afterwards. It sounded to the four knights as if it was an order to get rid of Becket. They certainly took it as such, and together they plotted how to murder the Archbishop. The conspirators left Bures, near Bayeux, where the King was staying and travelled separately, secretly and rapidly by different routes to England. When it was noticed that they had gone, an attempt was made to overtake them and bring them back, but it was too late. The four barons expected the King to change his mind and countermand the order, and they wanted to act, to solve the problem of Thomas before he could do so.

They arranged to meet at Saltwood Castle, which was held by one of the four, Ranulf de Broc, on 28 December 1170. Saltwood Castle was close to the English Channel coast of Kent, and not too far from Canterbury.

The following day, they set off with a small entourage of armed men for Canterbury itself. At St Augustine's Abbey, which stood on the eastern edge of the city, they stopped and gathered further reinforcements from the abbot, who seems to have been glad to assist in Becket's downfall. From there they rode into the cathedral precincts through the gate-house in Palace Street and entered the Archbishop's hall to the north-west of the Cathedral, probably at about three o'clock in the afternoon, and demanded to see Becket.

The four knights' plan was to strike the Archbishop down in his private chamber next to the hall. When they entered the hall, where the servers were eating, they sat awkwardly and silently, not acknowledging the Archbishop – nor he them. At length, Thomas offered them greetings. None of them replied except Fitzurse, who muttered, 'God help you!' Thomas reddened at this insult.

Reginald Fitzurse told Thomas that he bore a message from the King. All four of the knights were there, but it was Reginald Fitzurse who dominated this exchange, and Reginald Fitzurse who was the most aggressive and offensive of the four. Reginald had been one of Thomas's tenants when Thomas had been Chancellor. Thomas reminded him of this, to make him remember his lower status, but this reminder only made Reginald angrier and he called on everyone present who was on the King's side to prevent the Archbishop from escaping. One senses in Reginald's mounting anger that afternoon a self-conscious effort to make the adrenalin flow and get himself to a pitch where he could assassinate the Archbishop; he needed to be angry to carry it through. Reginald Fitzurse accused Thomas of refusing to absolve the people he had excommunicated.

'The sentence was not mine but the Pope's,' Thomas reminded him.

'You were behind it,' Reginald persisted.

'Granted, but the sentence itself was given by one greater than I. Let those concerned go to the Pope for absolution.'

Reginald Fitzurse went on, 'The king's command is that you and yours shall leave this realm. There can be no peace with you after your insolence.'

Thomas told Reginald to stop threatening him.

At this the knights went outside to arm themselves and shut the gate-house doors to prevent any help arriving for the Archbishop. They posted guards on the Archbishop's hall. Reginald Fitzurse forced one of the Archbishop's servants to fasten his armour, then snatched an axe from a carpenter who was working on some repairs.

Out in the Great Court, the knights prepared themselves. The cloaks they had worn to cover their coats of mail were off. Now ready, they charged at the Hall door, but the Archbishop's servants had bolted it. Robert de Broc knew the building well, and took the knights round the kitchen, through some bushes and into the orchard on the south side of the Hall. From here there was a staircase up to the Hall. The stairs were being repaired and the workmen had knocked off for the day and thrown down their tools. Ranulf de Broc climbed a ladder to a shuttered window. The others picked up axes and other tools and with these they smashed their way back into the Hall.

Meanwhile, the noise of the splintering wood and shouts of the servants alerted Thomas and his friends to the imminent danger. The monks tried to get Thomas to move, but he was reluctant. 'Not a bit of it. Don't panic. You monks are always afraid of being hurt!' Eventually, when they told him it was time for Vespers, he allowed himself to be hurried out of his chamber and by way of a private staircase into the north range of the cloisters, and then the east range, which was the normal route into the cathedral via the door into the north transept. The service of Vespers was due to begin. Thomas was reluctant to be hurried, but the monks around him could see that the angry knights were preparing to do murder and thought Thomas would be safe once he was within the sanctuary of the cathedral. How wrong they were! Probably Thomas himself knew there could be no other outcome now but his death, and knew there was no point in hurrying anywhere. His destiny was fixed; these four knights were going to kill him.

Thomas and his small group of monks arrived in the cathedral's dark but crowded north transept just ahead of the knights, who could be heard running heavily along the south range of the cloisters. There were shouts; 'There are armed knights in the cloister!'

Even at this late stage, Thomas could have vanished inside the dark cathedral; had he wished, he could have spirited himself away in the roof or the crypt and the knights would never have found him. But Thomas had no real intention of escaping this time. Thomas was mounting the steps leading up from the north transept towards the choir when Reginald burst in, still taking the lead in every way, shouting, 'King's men!' The four armed knights were there, with their huge swords unsheathed, and a body of men-at-arms, a sight that frightened all of them, though the huge congregation filling the nave saw none of this. With the knights was one of Thomas's monks, a sub-deacon called Hugh - later called Hugh Evil-Clerk because of his part in this historic murder.

Reginald Fitzurse bellowed, 'Come to me here, King's men! Where is Thomas Becket, traitor to the king and the kingdom?' No-one responded; it must have seemed an unnecessary question, though in the twilight the knights may not have been able to see him. 'Where is the Archbishop?'

Thomas gave an oblique answer, 'The righteous will be like a bold lion and free from fear,' and walked back down the steps to meet the knights. He said in a moderate voice, 'Here I am, no traitor to the king but a priest. Why do you seek me? God forbid that I should flee on account of your swords or that I should depart from righteousness.'

Thomas was now standing in the centre of the transept beside the big drum-shaped Norman pillar. He turned to look straight at the altars dedicated to the Virgin Mary and St Benedict. Perhaps he had an idea that he would die in front of these altars. The knights moved towards him demanding, 'Absolve those you excommunicated and return to office those you suspended'.

He refused because no penance had been made.

'Then you will now die and suffer as you deserve.'

At this point, most of Thomas's monks sensed what was about to happen and instinctively ran away and hid, John of Salisbury among them.

Then the knights rushed at Thomas. Reginald laid hands on Thomas and tried to drag him roughly back towards the door, so that he could kill him out in the cloisters. Together they tried to hoist Thomas onto William Tracy's back so that they could carry him outside. Thomas grappled with them and rebuked them. 'Don't touch me, Reginald. You owe me faith and obedience, you who foolishly follow your accomplices. Do you bear a sword against me?'

All the other monks fled for their lives except Edward Grim, who instinctively tried to defend his master with his arm. The moment Thomas ended his prayer, Reginald Fitzurse at once swiped at Thomas with his sword, knocking his fur cap off, cutting the tonsure off the top of his head and slicing into his left shoulder. The same blow cut Grim's arm to the bone. Grim tried to support Thomas, but fell back. Grim reflected on his master's awful death. What a worthy shepherd to his flock he was to set himself against the wolves so that the sheep would not be torn to pieces! He was abandoning the world, the world that was overwhelming and overpowering him now, yet that same world would one day elevate him beyond any of their dreams. . .

A sword blow fell on Thomas's head but somehow he remained standing firm. He put his hand to his head, looked at the blood and said, 'Into thy hands, O Lord, I commit my spirit'. A third sword blow, from William Tracy, brought him on to his knees, and he muttered, 'For the name of Jesus and the protection of the Church I am ready to embrace death.' He fell full length, with his arms stretched out in front of him as if in prayer. Now Richard le Breton, who had not till now used his sword, aimed a blow at Thomas's head, inflicted a terrible wound, cutting the top of the skull right off and spilling Thomas's brains; the energy of the blow broke the sword's point on the stone pavement. By this stage, Thomas was motionless on the ground - and probably dead.

The fourth knight, Hugh de Morville, had been keeping the huge crowd in the nave back with his sword-point. The evil cleric who had come in with the knights, Hugh, placed his foot on Thomas's neck and dug his sword inside the wound on his head and flicked it, scattering the brains across the floor. He shouted to the others, 'We can leave this place, knights. This traitor will not rise again.' Then the knights, once again shouting, 'King's men, King's men!' made their way out of the place that would from that day forward always be called The Martyrdom, into the cloisters and the great court, ransacking the Archbishop's palace before they left.

Thomas was dead. His body lay where it had fallen, face down, with arms outstretched. Edward Grim, who was with him through this nightmare, commented afterwards that Thomas had not cried out or uttered a word, not so much as sighing when struck. He stood or knelt waiting fearlessly for the blows. A martyr had been born. Thomas's body-servant, Osbert, cut off a piece of his own shirt and covered the mutilated head with it. For a few minutes, the dead Archbishop lay all alone in the darkness. Then, gradually, from the shadows, the monks emerged from their hiding places and were occupied with ushering the huge congregation out of the desecrated cathedral. Then they crept into the north transept to see what they most feared. It was obvious to all who were there that something horrible, but also profoundly momentous and historic, had happened. Pieces of cloth were steeped in his blood and kept as sacred souvenirs.

A thunderstorm broke while the monks washed and dressed the body and laid it to rest overnight in front of the high altar. They prayed in silence as no service could be sung in the desecrated church.

The next morning, astonishingly, Robert de Broc arrived and called the monks together. He told them that Thomas's body would be thrown to the dogs unless they buried it secretly. He must have known already that Thomas would be seen as a martyr, that there was a danger of a Thomas-cult developing – and he vainly tried to stop it. The monks obediently buried Thomas in the crypt, keeping the clothing and bloodstained cloths from the pavement as relics. One of the entrances to the crypt was right next to the spot where Thomas fell. A tomb was built between two pillars of shining Purbeck marble, a spot that is now an empty space. Later, much later, there would be a great ceremony of translation, in which the remains of Thomas, by now St Thomas of Canterbury, were carried up and entombed in a spectacular shrine behind the cathedral's high altar. By the early sixteenth century, that shrine would be an Aladdin's cave of gold and precious jewels – too great a prize for Henry II's successor, Henry VIII, to resist. That too is now an empty space.

After the murder had been done, the four knights rode to Saltwood. There are two different versions of their mood afterwards. One account says that they gloried in their deed, but William de Tracy, another of the four, said that they were overwhelmed by a sense of guilt. That may of course have been a revisionist view of things, when it became clear that the world as a whole was revolted by what they had done - not just the murder but the sacrilege. The earlier de Tracy's penitence had begun, the more chance he had of being forgiven. On 31 December, the last day of the year, they rode to South Malling near Lewes, one of the Archbishop's manors. There, it is said, they placed their armour on a table, but the table itself rejected it: it was hurled onto the floor.

They were excommunicated by the Pope. They were not punished by Henry II, who seems to have genuinely regretted giving them the order to kill Becket. They sheltered at Knaresborough, and stayed there for a year, enduring ostracism by the local people. If they were waiting for the dust to settle, waiting for people to forget about Thomas Becket, they were wasting their time.

No-one wanted to have anything to do with Thomas Becket's murderers, who were regarded by everyone as little better than the men who killed Jesus Christ. They were pariahs. They were forced to give themselves up to the King. Henry II did not know what to do with them. Although he himself had quarrelled with Becket over this very issue of benefit of clergy, he had lost, and he now found – thanks to Thomas – that he was not in a position to put four laymen on trial for the murder of a priest. So Henry II sent them to the Pope. The Pope's punishment was fasting and banishment to the Holy Land; that was the limit of his power. It was ironic that Thomas, by opposing Henry II's legal reforms, had in effect put his own murderers beyond the reach of natural justice. Just about everyone wanted to see the four knights hanged, but there was neither secular nor ecclesiastical law that allowed it.

Before leaving for the Holy Land, Reginald Fitzurse gave half of his manor of Williton to his brother and the other half to the Knights of St John. Fitzurse and his companions are said to have done their penance at a place called 'the Black Mountain'. It is not known what or where this was, but it may have been some sort of religious retreat near Jerusalem. They died there, all of them within three years of the assassination, and were buried in Jerusalem outside the door of the Templars' Church.

But there are alternative versions of the fate of the four knights. One of them has Reginald Fitzurse seeking shelter in Ireland, where he founded the McMahon family. If so, it would be quite appropriate; Thomas McMahon was one of those responsible for the assassination of Lord Mountbatten in 1979. William de Tracey founded a chantry at Mortehoe in Devon; his altar-tomb is still there. Hugh de Morville may have lived on into the first decade of the 13th century.

Miracles were claimed at Thomas Becket's tomb. Pilgrims flocked to Canterbury in ever-increasing numbers as the years passed, and St Thomas of Canterbury became the greatest saint, not only in England but in Europe.

Becket's murder hung over the middle ages like a great scarlet banner. His was the greatest shrine of pilgrimage in Europe. His struggle for Church against state was iconic and key to the politics of the middle ages, imitated and re-enacted again and again in country after country. If one man's death gave the European middle ages their distinctive quality and character, it was Becket's death.

From the time of Becket's martyrdom until the Reformation, his shrine in Canterbury Cathedral was visited by thousands of pilgrims, whose offerings brought great wealth into Canterbury. The Canterbury pilgrimages have been immortalised in Chaucer's Canterbury Tales.

At the Dissolution of the monasteries in the sixteenth century, Becket's gilded and jewelled shrine was plundered and demolished, and Henry VIII referred contemptuously to 'Bishop Becket' when he ordered his bones to be scattered. A revisionist biography was constructed, and the holy martyr was brought down to the level of a scheming priest, an upstart and a traitor; his murder, if not actually approved, was presented as come-uppance for his presumption in opposing the authority of a King. This was pure Tudor propaganda. Thomas More found out the hard way what happened if you opposed the authority of Henry VIII. This 'Reformation' view of Becket's character and career prevailed until the twentieth century, when a second revolution in appraisal and opinion took place. Thomas Becket has been presented once more as a worthy man of high principle – a staunch defender of the rights of individuals and a stout resister of feudal tyranny.

But Becket is not an easy man to admire. He was obstinate and headstrong, and it is hard to be sympathetic to his wish to make the church paramount over the state. But his grand gesture opposition to an insatiably power-hungry Plantagenet monarch has irresistible appeal, and the sheer epic theatricality of the self-imposed exile and the return to martyrdom in his own cathedral has a mythic quality that the highly intelligent Becket himself understood perfectly.

EDWARD I OF ENGLAND AND JOHN BALLIOL OF SCOTLAND

(1291)

THIS IS A story of a hostile encounter between two medieval kingdoms, England and Scotland, a dispute about sovereignty and a significant stage in the development of the United Kingdom. It is also about an unequal encounter between two kings.

Little is known about the origins of the Scottish king, John Balliol. He may have been born in 1249, though that is not certain: nor is it known where he was born. He was the son of John, 5th Baron Balliol, lord of Barnard Castle, and his wife Dervorguilla of Galloway. He held many estates by inheritance, including large areas of Galloway as well as estates in England and France.

In 1290, the Maid of Norway was supposed to succeed to the Scottish throne. Following her death, John Balliol was one of the competitors to replace her. His claim was based on the fact that through his mother he was a great-great-great-grandson of King David I. Balliol's main rival was Robert Bruce, 5th Lord of Annandale, who was one generation closer to David I, but who also traced his line through his mother, Isabel. On the face of it, Robert Bruce had the slightly stronger claim. Balliol and Bruce submitted their claims to the Scottish Guardians in a meeting at Berwick-on-Tweed on 6 June 1291, with King Edward I of England as the arbiter. In this remarkable conference Edward I acted as host to the Guardians, who were to discuss and decide on the future king, and to the thirteen claimants to the Scottish throne. The number of claimants was reduced to three, and then to two, Bruce and Balliol. King Edward was no shy bystander. He acceded to the English throne in 1272, while on crusade. By prior arrangement he was acknowledged king from the moment of his father's death, even though he was not to be crowned until August 1274. As in many matters, Edward set the precedent for the future. From his reign on, to avoid a hiatus, English monarchs have been deemed to reign from the moment of their accession, not their coronation. In this way, Edward IV's son became Edward V in 1483, even though he was never crowned.

Edward I was a conqueror. One of his early initiatives was the conquest of Wales. Henry III had tried to take Wales, but the Welsh under Llywelyn ap Gruffydd resisted his invasion. The 1267 Treaty of Montgomery even allowed Llywelyn to extend Welsh territory into what had been estates belonging to English Marcher Lords. Llywelyn also refused to pay homage to the English monarch in the mid-1270s, on the grounds that Edward had given protection to Llywelyn's enemies. Edward launched his first offensive against Wales in 1276 and succeeded in forcing homage; Llywelyn lost all but a small patch of territory in north-west Wales. Then Llywelyn's brother Dafydd took Edward by surprise by organising a new revolt in 1282, but the English king responded immediately and strongly. At first there were English defeats and the Welsh appeared to be winning, but the death of Llywelyn in a skirmish in December 1282 turned the tide. After Dafydd was captured and executed in the spring of 1283, Wales was conquered. Edward conspicuously consolidated his conquest by building a chain of mighty stone castles to encircle Wales.

Wales was incorporated into England in 1284 under the Statute of Rhuddlan. The conquest of Wales was a triumph, but the huge expense damaged Edward's military capabilities in the Scottish campaign that followed. With Wales conquered and assimilated into his kingdom, Edward turned his attention to Scotland. He himself as Duke of Aquitaine had to do homage to the French king, Philippe le Bel, so he well understood the psychological effect of homage. Offering homage to another king meant that you were his vassal. Edward wanted homage from the Scottish king, and control over Scotland.

Edward returned to England in 1289 after a long visit to Gascony, with plans to marry his son, Prince Edward (later to be Edward II), to Margaret, known as the Maid of Norway, who was the successor to the Scottish throne. A dynastic marriage like this would join the two kingdoms into one, without a war. Margaret, the daughter of King Eric II of Norway, was sent to Scotland. The ship was driven off-course in a storm and landed in Orkney. There, the eight-year-old princess died, apparently from the effects of sea-sickness.

Margaret's unexpected death spoilt Edward I's plan to weld England and Scotland peacefully. The Scottish Guardians, unwisely as it turned out, invited Edward to arbitrate the succession; having the matter decided by an outsider would, they thought, prevent a civil war. But before the selection process was under way Edward insisted on being recognised as Scotland's overlord. The Scots were surprised and uneasy, but under pressure they agreed to his temporary overlordship.

Edward had forced the Scots to recognise him as Lord Paramount of Scotland, which meant that any Scottish king had to do him homage. In the Great Hall of Berwick Castle, on 17 November 1292, the Guardians finally decided in favour of Balliol. Bruce had one less generation separating him from King David I, but the weak link in his line was a younger daughter. Balliol had the additional generation, but his weak link was an eldest daughter, so his blood line was deemed stronger.

On St Andrew's Day, at the end of November, John Balliol was formally inaugurated as king of Scotland. But Edward's role as arbiter meant that the new king of Scotland owed his throne to Edward: Balliol was beholden to King Edward. Nor would King Edward allow him to forget it. He did everything possible to remind him that Scotland was a vassal state, repeatedly humiliating John Balliol and undermining his authority. He also made it clear that he had no intention of relinquishing his overlordship.

In 1294, Edward went one step too far, demanding military service from the Scots against the French. Edward I had overdone it. His demands and general high-handedness provoked a reaction. If he had gradually conditioned the Scots to accept English overlordship the strategy might have worked, but he went too far too fast. The Scottish king became known as 'Toom Tabard' (empty jacket), a reference to his lack of authority. He was a stooge, a puppet.

The control of Scotland's affairs was taken over by some of the leading men who at Stirling in July 1295 formed a council of twelve, in effect a panel of advisors to King John. One of their acts was to arrange a treaty of mutual assistance with France. So, by humiliating the Scots excessively, Edward I had driven them into a defensive alliance with England's enemy across the Channel.

Edward provoked the Wars of Scottish Independence. These opened in March 1296 with the Scots crossing the border and attempting to take Carlisle. They failed. A few days later, Edward's huge army made a massive retaliatory strike against Scotland. Edward demanded the surrender of the border town of Berwick. This was refused and Edward ordered a terrifying attack on the town, which resulted in the death of most of its citizens. How many civilians were killed is not known, but estimates range from 7,000 to 60,000. The massacre at Berwick is an indication of Edward I's campaigning style: swift, relentless, unyielding, and extremely brutal.

At Dunbar the Scottish army was defeated. On 27 April 1296 the English troops took Dunbar Castle and just over two months later John Balliol abdicated. In a final humiliation, the royal arms of Scotland were torn from his surcoat. Balliol was taken to London and imprisoned in the Tower, but in July 1299 he was released and allowed to travel to France. Further humiliation was in store for him at Dover, where his baggage was checked before his voyage across the water. In his chests were found the royal seal of Scotland and the royal crown, along with many gold and silver vessels and a quantity of money. Edward I confiscated the crown and the seal, but ordered the money to be given back to John to cover his expenses. Edward was able to be magnanimous in victory. He now after all had what he wanted, which was control over England, Wales and Scotland. In a final symbolic gesture, he took the Stone of Destiny, the ancient stone of inauguration used for

Scottish coronations; the stone was carted to London and installed in Westminster Abbey, where it was mounted under the English Coronation Chair.

John Balliol was released into the custody of the pope, on condition that he lived in a papal residence, but in 1301 he was allowed to retire to one of his French estates, at Hélicourt in Picardy. John Balliol's abdication and retirement were not straightforward, though. There were still many Scots who were angry about King Edward's interference in Scottish affairs and believed that John Balliol was still Scotland's rightful king. A rebellion was mounted in 1297, led by William Wallace and Andrew de Moray, who claimed they were acting on John's behalf. But, as time wore on and John Balliol continued to live under house arrest hundreds of miles from Scotland, his cause became increasingly hopeless. From the time of his retirement to Hélicourt, John Balliol made no further attempt to enlist support. Scotland meanwhile had no monarch other than King Edward, until 1306 and the accession of Robert Bruce, the grandson of the earlier claimant of the same name.

John Balliol died in 1314. About a month afterwards, Edward II wrote to Louis X of France to say that he heard of the death of 'Sir John de Balliol' – a final, posthumous snub to the Scottish king – and that he would like to receive the homage of his son Edward Balliol, at least by proxy. Edward Balliol was later to revive his father's and family's claim to the throne of Scotland.

An agreement with the Scottish people in 1304 seemed to settle the question of Scotland in Edward's favour, so when rebellion flared up again he was furious. The rebels were to be shown no mercy. A great many of Robert Bruce's supporters were hanged. Bruce was forced out of Scotland, but by 1307 he had returned. Now old and ill, but still determined to overpower Scotland, Edward I led his army north to beat down the rebel king. But he died before reaching Scotland, at Burgh-by-Sands on the Scottish border, beaten not by the Scots but by age and infirmity.

THE ENGLISH AND FRENCH ARMIES AT AGINCOURT

(1415)

THE FINAL PHASE of the Hundred Years' War between England and France coincided with the reign of England's most charismatic king, Henry V. Within that final phase came the best-known battle, the Battle of Agincourt. For the English, the confrontation of the two armies in this single battle came to symbolise what it means to be English.

The plans for this campaign had been under preparation in the time of Henry IV, but it was not until the reign of his son that they came to fruition. The Armagnac faction in France offered Henry V a deal in return for his military support. He turned them down. Instead, he bullishly demanded a return to the borders as they stood in the time of Henry II. To press his territorial claim, he set sail for France on 1 August with an army of 12,000 soldiers. He laid siege to the town of Harfleur and took it. He was tempted to march on Paris at once, but instead made an expedition across the north of France. Henry marched his dysentery-reduced army across Normandy, in the hope of reaching Calais without having to do battle with the French. The French army was huge. Its exact size has been disputed, but it seems probable that it was about three times larger than Henry's. It had been mustered by the French king while the Harfleur siege had been going on. It marched along, mirroring the English army's advance along the valley of the Somme, the two armies separated by the river. Then at Agincourt the French army swung across to bar the way forward. Faced with such overwhelming odds, the English should have lost this battle, yet they won and the battle immediately acquired a unique status in English history.

The battlefield had recently been ploughed and was muddy after rain. This made it very unfavourable terrain for the heavily armoured and heavily equipped French knights, some of whom drowned in the mud when they fell into it and were unable to get up again. The ground conditions played a large part in giving the English victory.

Before the battle the French were understandably confident of defeating the much smaller English army. They even cast lots for the king and nobles, who were worth a great deal in ransom money. The English were astonished at the 'innumerable hateful French' but prepared their ground in a highly organised way under Henry V's exceptional leadership. He ordered wedges of archers to be interspersed among the lines of infantry, with lines of stakes in front of them to protect them from cavalry charges. For some reason the French were reluctant to attack. Those present wondered if the French were waiting for the English to break their battle order. In the end, knowing how short of food his army was, Henry V ordered his men forward. Then the French too moved forward. The flanking French cavalry on each side charged the English archers, and they were stopped and pierced either by arrows or stakes. When the English archers had run out of arrows, they picked up axes and swords from the men lying wounded or dead on the ground and used those to beat off the enemy. The battle was so violent and the odds were so heavily against the English that the English took no prisoners. Every French combatant was struck down, regardless of rank.

French dead and wounded soon lay piled up in heaps in front of the English lines. English soldiers climbed onto the heaps and killed those still living underneath their feet. After about three hours the French fell back. The English began to sort out the heaps of French soldiers and separate the living from the dead, but were interrupted by shouts that the French were charging back at them in huge numbers. For their own safety, as they saw it, the English had no alternative but to kill their prisoners. They killed all of them except for a few who were clearly too important to kill, such as the Dukes of Orléans and Bourbon.

Not long after that the French finally withdrew. In spite of the huge apparent advantage the French had at the start of the Battle of Agincourt the French defeat was total and catastrophic, with many of the Armagnac leaders left dead on the field of battle.

After this major victory, Henry V was able to go on to take Caen in 1417 and Rouen in 1419, bringing most of Normandy under English control. He made an alliance with the Duchy of Burgundy, which had taken Paris. In 1420, Henry met Charles VI. They signed the Treaty of Troyes, which arranged the marriage of Charles VI's daughter Catherine with Henry, and the inheritance of the French throne by Henry's heirs. The Dauphin was declared illegitimate.

Back in England, the mythic status of the great encounter with the French at Agincourt was launched by a lavish Victory March through London in November 1415. Henry V began his march by visiting the 'sacred thresholds' of Canterbury Cathedral and St Augustine's Abbey in Canterbury. News of the king's imminent arrival prompted preparations in London, and a crowd of citizens including the mayor and twenty-four aldermen dressed in scarlet went out to meet him at Blackheath. There the king was formally congratulated and accompanied into the city. At the entrance tower to London Bridge a giant had been erected, an enormous figure holding a great axe in one hand and the keys of the city in the other, like a door-keeper. Beside him stood a giantess, dressed in a scarlet cloak. The gigantic couple greeted the king.

There was a great crowd of boys representing a host of angels, dressed in white robes and with gilded faces and shining wings. As the king approached, the boys sang to an organ accompaniment. A tower in Cornhill was draped in scarlet cloth to turn it into a tent. In Cheapside, twelve men were dressed as the apostles, another twelve as kings, and they too sang for the king as he passed by. There was also a beautiful wooden castle, built on arches projecting over the street and painted to look like white marble; over the arches ran the inscription, 'Glorious things of thee are spoken, O city of God.' A bridge from the castle carried a choir of girls dressed in white, playing tambourines and singing, 'Welcome, Henry the Fifth, King of England and of France.' On the castle's turrets were lots of boys dressed in white as angels, with shining wings and gems in their hair; as the king passed underneath they threw down gold coins and laurel leaves while singing, 'We praise thee O God; we acknowledge thee to be the Lord.'

This great ceremonial public occasion ensured that Agincourt and all that it represented would become embedded in the English memory. This is where the idea of plucky little England was born.

HENRY TUDOR AND RICHARD III

(1485)

THE ENCOUNTER BETWEEN Henry Tudor and Richard III was a struggle for the throne of England. King Richard III of England, the incumbent, was the fourth son of Richard Plantagenet, the Duke of York, who had himself been a strong claimant to the throne of Henry VI. This gave his son Richard a place in the succession. When the duke and Richard's older brother were killed at the Battle of Wakefield, Richard, who was then still a boy, was taken into the care of the Earl of Warwick.

When the Lancastrian Henry VI was deposed, Richard's elder brother became king as Edward IV. Richard gave his elder brother loyal service as a military commander and was appropriately rewarded with large estates and given the title Duke of Gloucester. Richard became the richest and most powerful nobleman in England, second only to the king. The third surviving brother, George Duke of Clarence, mounted a rebellion against King Edward and was executed for treason.

Richard had a loyal following in the north of England, which he in effect governed for his brother the king. In April 1483, at the age of only forty, Edward IV died unexpectedly and of unknown causes. The description of his last days suggests that he died of pneumonia, and it is known that he got very cold on a fishing trip immediately before his last illness. He knew that the jealousies and enmities surrounding the Woodville family and its rapid advancement would cause trouble after his death, especially since his heir was so young. On his deathbed, he called on all of them to swear friendship to one another.

Edward IV left his son Edward king at the age of twelve. Richard intervened, imprisoning Lord Rivers (Edward IV's brother-in-law and the young king's guardian) along with other members of the Woodville faction. In his will, Edward explicitly named Richard as Protector and entrusted him, not Lord Rivers, with guardianship of the young king. The queen and her Woodville faction did not inform Richard of this: indeed they did not even inform him of Edward IV's death. Instead, they tried to transfer the new king quickly from Ludlow to London in order to have him crowned as fast as possible and enforce the power of the Woodvilles – and all of this before Richard, the rightful Protector, knew what had happened. It was Lord Hastings who went to Richard in the north to tell him what was happening. Richard was right to interpret what was happening as a grand Woodville conspiracy to flout the dead king's wishes.

Richard intercepted the young king at Stony Stratford, took him into his own care, and charged Lord Rivers and the other Woodvilles with plotting the assassination of the young king; then he had them executed. Richard took the young king and his brother, the Duke of York, to London where they were housed in the Tower.

Richard's motives for these actions are still a matter of debate. Some historians believe that Richard was an unscrupulous usurper, that he captured his nephews and had them murdered in the Tower in order to take the throne for himself. Others believe that he had the boys' safety in mind and that his intention was to have them secretly spirited abroad; something similar had been arranged for him when he was a boy and in similar danger. There is also the possibility that Richard genuinely believed that Edward, the young king, was not a legitimate heir to the throne. This is what he publicly argued. Certainly he was doing his duty in asserting his role as Protector and taking custody of his nephews, as he was fulfilling the terms of Edward IV's will.

On 22 June 1483, a public lecture was given in front of St Paul's Cathedral by a cleric, Dr Shaw, stating Richard's right to take the throne himself. The main reason he gave was that Edward IV's marriage to Elizabeth Woodville was bigamous and therefore invalid. A priest had testified that a troth-plight had been contracted between Edward IV and Lady Eleanor Butler, daughter of the Earl of Shrewsbury, before

Edward's marriage to Elizabeth Woodville – and Lady Eleanor Butler was still living at the time of his marriage to Elizabeth Woodville. In consequence, the young prince Edward was illegitimate and must therefore be removed from the succession. This left Richard himself, the late king's brother, as the legitimate heir. It was a breath-taking revelation.

The troth-plight, the medieval equivalent of engagement, was regarded as every bit as binding as marriage, except when it was dissolved by mutual consent. Troth-plight was held to be binding as it was often used by men as a means of persuading women to have sex; it was susceptible of abuse. This particular troth-plight was sworn before Robert Stillington, a priest who went on to become Bishop of Bath and Wells in 1465 and then Lord Chancellor in 1467. He became ill and either resigned or was dismissed from this high office in 1475, after which he went back to Bath and Wells. Because Eleanor Butler was dead, there was no possibility of finding out if she had agreed to dissolve her troth-plight to King Edward. The Duke of Clarence was the greatest landowner in south-west England, and it may be that the disappointed, possibly disaffected ex-chancellor, won over by the duke's easy charm, told the duke his secret. And Clarence was indiscreet as well as opportunistic. He would use any information against his brother. But Stillington would later regret breaching the king's confidence.

Richard knew, as the rest of the family had always known, that Edward IV was himself illegitimate. He had been conceived when the Duke of York was away campaigning, and it was also common knowledge that the Duchess, Cicely Neville, had taken a lover, a common soldier whose name was Blaybourne. Blaybourne was a big man, and Edward IV was also a big man. The Duke of York's legitimate sons were both slight and small men, like the Duke. Both Richard Duke of Gloucester and George Duke of Clarence knew that their older brother was illegitimate. George was foolish enough to publicise it.

Clarence was headstrong and on several occasions rebelled against Edward. Several times Edward forgave him. Though in other ways he was ruthless, Edward felt strong ties of loyalty towards his brothers.

Even though Clarence betrayed him repeatedly, Edward let him go unpunished – but only until January 1478. Then the Houses of Parliament were summoned to pass an Act of Attainder against Clarence. He had been imprisoned in the Tower and was taken to the bar of the House of Lords. There he faced the king. In an encounter unique in English history, the monarch announced the charge against his own brother, the Duke of Clarence. Edward reminded those present of his magnanimity towards traitors, but this treason of the Duke of Clarence was 'more malicious, more unnatural, more loathly' than the rest. He reminded them that he had forgiven his earlier acts of treachery, showered gifts of goods and possessions on him, and been rewarded with renewed acts of treachery. Clarence had set about destroying the king and his family. He had sent his servants round the country, where, among other things, they had systematically promoted the story that the king was illegitimate 'from the incontinency of his mother'. So, on that semi-public occasion, Edward IV admitted that the rumour of his illegitimacy was abroad, and we know from the chronicle of the trial that Clarence had recklessly encouraged this rumour.

It may seem extraordinary for Edward IV to voice all these charges himself, and it may seem as if it was done out of reckless fury, but it was very astute. By acting as prosecuting counsel he was defying anyone to come forward in Clarence's defence. To speak up on Clarence's behalf now would entail contradicting the king – which everyone knew was a dangerous thing to do. No-one did speak up on Clarence's behalf. The Act of Attainder was passed. Then all that remained to be decided was when, where and how Clarence was to die. According to contemporary chroniclers, on 18 February 1478 Clarence attended mass in the Tower and was then drowned 'in a rondelet of Malvesey', Shakespeare's 'butt of Malmsey' (a barrel of Madeira). That was the price Clarence paid for putting it about that Edward IV was illegitimate.

A month later, Bishop Stillington was arrested and imprisoned in the Tower. The charges against Clarence that reflected on the honour of the royal family had not been made public. The charges against Stillington were not made public either. He was held for three months before the king decided to release him. There was an official exoneration, a declaration that Stillington had proved himself faithful to the king. Presumably the king was content to humiliate and frighten Stillington; that was enough punishment for his indiscretion in talking to Clarence. After his terrifying stay in the Tower, Stillington would be very unlikely to tell his troth-plight story again.

What Richard Duke of Gloucester thought about the execution of his brother Clarence is not known. He seems to have kept his own counsel. He probably already understood the danger of challenging the legitimacy of his own brother the king while he lived; then came the proof, in Clarence's death, of what would happen if he did. But Edward IV was dead now. Richard may have thought that this was an opportunity to rectify a long-term wrong. All the time his older, illegitimate, half-brother had been king it was he, Richard, or his older brother, George, who should have been on the throne – and George's rebellion against Edward had been well-founded. Knowledge of Edward IV's illegitimacy had spread far and wide, though few would have dared to mention it. Charles the Bold of Burgundy was one who did, and he delighted in contemptuously referring to the king of England as 'Blaybourne', long before Dr Shaw's lecture. Dr Shaw's proclamation did no more than suggest that Edward IV had been illegitimate, though now that his powerful and ruthless older half-brother was dead he had nothing to fear from him.

So Richard III had two arguments for challenging the legitimacy of Edward IV, two foundation stones for his own claim. A third reason may have been the knowledge that in pragmatic terms a boy could not rule medieval England. He might have contented himself with the role of Protector, but from the evidence he had it was clear that he, Richard, really was the rightful king.

In July 1483 Richard III was crowned king in Westminster Abbey. The Yorkists held the throne, but there were still Lancastrian followers who wanted their claimant to be king instead. Now, though, there were not many claimants to be seen. When one came forward, they gave him their support, though his claim was a poor one.

Henry Tudor, the unlikely candidate who challenged Richard III for the English throne, was born in 1457, the only son of Edmund Tudor, Earl of Richmond, and Lady Margaret Beaufort. Edmund Tudor died just before his son was born and the boy Henry was brought up by his uncle, Jasper Tudor. When Edward IV became king (again) in 1471, the fourteen-year-old Henry Tudor fled to Brittany, where he remained for fourteen years.

Henry Tudor's mother was meanwhile active in promoting him as the Lancastrian alternative to Richard III. She did this in spite of the fact that her husband, Lord Stanley, was a Yorkist. Encouraged by signs that he had support in England, Henry Tudor tried to mount an expedition to invade England, using money and supplies borrowed from the Duke of Brittany. This plan fell apart and his main co-conspirator in England, the Duke of Buckingham, was executed by Richard. Richard tried to get his hands on Henry Tudor, but a scheme to have him extradited from Brittany failed when Henry escaped into France, where he was welcomed. The French king provided him with troops and gear for a second invasion attempt.

After their rough treatment by Richard III, the Woodvilles were ready to support Henry Tudor, and there were others too who knew they would find no favour with the Yorkist king. With promises of support, Henry Tudor landed with a force of French and Scottish troops in Pembrokeshire, and marched from there into England. He was accompanied by his uncle Jasper and the Earl of Oxford. As he marched he gathered an army of 5,000. Henry knew that the sooner he met Richard in battle, the better were his chances of success; Richard had reinforcements stationed in Nottingham and Leicester, and given time could muster a huge army.

It was a gamble, but Henry engaged Richard at the Battle of Bosworth in August 1485. Henry was outnumbered, and therefore should have expected defeat, but in the chaos of battle anything can happen. What did happen, decisively, was that several of Richard III's key supporters changed sides during the battle. These included the Earl of Northumberland and the Stanley family. This shifted the weight of numbers in Henry Tudor's favour, and the psychological damage to Richard and his loyal troops can only be imagined.

When Richard ordered Northumberland to attack and Northumberland held back, refusing to obey the order, both Richard and Henry were uncertain what was happening. The waiting army of Lord Stanley had also failed to move. At that moment Henry personally took the initiative and rode off with his bodyguard in the direction of Lord Stanley, apparently intending to appeal to him in person to change sides.

King Richard saw this and attempted a charge directly against Henry Tudor. He was able to hack down the small bodyguard of knights. Richard himself killed Henry's standard-bearer, William Brandon, and made for Henry. A direct confrontation, a personal duel between king and would-be king, was narrowly prevented by the arrival of the Stanley army. Stanley saw what was happening and made his decision – in Henry Tudor's favour. Suddenly the situation was reversed. Because of Stanley's split-second decision it was now Richard and his bodyguards who were surrounded and overwhelmed and the final outcome of the Wars of the Roses was decided. First Richard's standard-bearer was cut down, then Richard himself; he died fighting bravely to the very last.

The outcome of this crucial battle was that the Wars of the Roses were over. In a long war of attrition, the Plantagenets (Yorkists) were more or less obliterated. The few surviving high-ranking Yorkists, who might have become claimants, were weeded out during the reign of Henry Tudor and his son, Henry VIII. Indeed some historians have suggested that Henry VII rather than Richard III may have been responsible for the two princes' murder. This sinister cull has been referred to as the 'extirpation of Plantagenet blood'. The fact that the Tudors won the wars meant that they were able to present the official version of what happened; Tudor propagandists successfully promoted two ideas: that Richard III was a murdering usurper with no right at all to the throne, and that Henry Tudor was the rightful heir. The truth is that Richard III had the strongest claim to the throne, superior to that of Edward IV's young sons, and far superior to that of Henry Tudor. Edward III was Richard III's great-great-great-grandfather – four generations separated them, whereas five generations separated Edward III and Henry Tudor. Henry Tudor's ancestry in any case only linked back to Edward III by way of his mother.

In spite of the Tudor version of history, it was Henry Tudor who was the usurper.

GILBERT GIFFORD AND MARY QUEEN OF SCOTS

(1586)

MARY QUEEN OF Scots was brought to her death by her implication in the Babington Plot, a plot to assassinate Queen Elizabeth I and put Mary on the English throne in her place. She was implicated in this plot by her encounters with Gilbert Gifford.

Mary had been deposed by the Scots because of her suspected collusion in the cold-blooded murder of her husband, Lord Darnley, and her subsequent elopement with Bothwell. She had fled for her life across the border into England, where she had sought sanctuary with her cousin, Queen Elizabeth. Elizabeth was embarrassed to have this unwanted house-guest, because Mary was a Catholic and a natural focus for a Catholic rising. Sir Francis Walsingham saw Mary as a dangerous presence and wanted to expose her and bring her down.

To ensure that Mary was unable to win friends and rally support, she was regularly moved from one English mansion to another, always under house-arrest. She had her maids and servants with her and was allowed a certain amount of freedom and exercise, but she was guarded and under observation at all times. She did not realise how closely she was being watched. Walsingham devoted a lot of time to watching her, by proxy. He had agents. In 1586 he discovered she was exchanging letters with a group of Catholic rebels led by Sir Anthony Babington. Then Walsingham sprang into action.

He encouraged one of his agents to insinuate himself into Mary's confidence. The agent also persuaded Mary that he had enlisted the help of a Catholic brewer living in the local village; the brewer would provide a means of smuggling messages in and out of Chartley, Mary's prison at the time. The letters would go in and out, hidden inside a beer barrel. The barrel would travel via the Catholic brewer to a local Catholic gentleman, who in turn would use his servants to take the letters to London. Mary used a fairly straightforward substitution code, so Walsingham was able to decode her messages quickly. The decoded messages were conveyed to Queen Elizabeth to demonstrate Queen Mary's treachery. The secret messages were resealed, and sent on their way to Mary or her friends. The letters went back and forth, the plot progressed, and Walsingham and Queen Elizabeth watched and waited.

Babington and his fellow plotters were inexperienced and astonishingly indiscreet. It was easy for Walsingham to obtain information about their activities and movements. In July 1586 Babington sent Mary a letter outlining his plans to Mary at Chartley. They included the rescue of Mary, the assassination of Elizabeth and the installation of Mary on the English throne; he even mentioned a military expedition by Philip of Spain once Elizabeth was removed. The July letter also mentioned plans to assassinate Sir Francis Walsingham and Lord Burghley, who was Elizabeth's chief minister. All Babington needed was Mary's positive participation; without Mary's agreement there would be no future Catholic monarch to support. This of course was the moment that Sir Francis had been waiting impatiently for – for twenty years. Catching Babington and his co-conspirators was easy. But incriminating the Queen of Scots was something he had ached to achieve.

Mary sent a final letter asking for further details. It was intercepted and Walsingham had a postscript added, forged in Mary's handwriting by Thomas Phelippes, a cipher expert working in his service; it was a request for the names of the gentlemen who were involved in the assassination conspiracy. This would help Walsingham in rounding up the conspirators. The forged postscript also implicitly approved the assassination of Elizabeth. Babington received the letter, but did not get as far as replying. The list of names was not supplied. It would have sealed their fate – the terrible death of a Tudor traitor by hanging, drawing and quartering. Babington tried to get to Spain in order to meet the Spanish king, but he was arrested when he applied for a passport.

Walsingham could not afford to take the risk of letting Babington leave England at this crucial moment.

But Walsingham's spy network was sufficiently effective for him to find out who the six gentlemen were, even without a list from Babington. By this stage, Babington and his friends had realised that something was wrong and they had gone into hiding. Walsingham's agents found them easily enough. Sir Anthony Babington, John Ballard, Chidiock Tichborne, Thomas Salisbury, Robert Barnewell, John Savage and Henry Donn were all captured in early August 1586. They were arrested, charged, tried and given public executions on 20 September. Another seven men were rounded up, tried and convicted soon afterwards. The first executions were so awful – disembowelling while still alive - that Queen Elizabeth relented with the second batch of traitors; they were allowed to hang until they were dead.

By corresponding with these traitors, Mary too had sealed her fate – she had put her head upon the block. She would be executed at Fotheringhay Castle on 8 February 1587. But even if she had not exchanged letters with the plotters she would have been guilty. A new Act of Parliament, passed because of increasing concern for Queen Elizabeth's safety, provided for the execution of anyone who would benefit from the queen's death if a plot against her were uncovered. This cruel Act was directed against Queen Mary. It meant that any Catholic plot would lead to her death, whether she sanctioned it or not, indeed whether she knew about it or not. She was doomed.

The agent Sir Francis Walsingham used to spring his trap was a man called Gilbert Gifford. He was a member of a well-known Catholic family at Chillington in Staffordshire. His father, John Gifford, was imprisoned for his faith. Gilbert was educated at Douai and Rheims. In 1579 he moved on to the English College in Rome. While he was in Rome, he was approached by Solomon Aldred, a Catholic agent who was in the service of Sir Francis Walsingham. Gifford was ready to consider entering the English secret service and to betray his fellow-Catholics. It is hard to understand what was in his mind, but perhaps he was simply motivated, like so many people, by money and the will to power. His teachers at the English College did not know about his career plans, but they complained about his deceitful character; in 1582 they expelled him, for unstated reasons.

In that year, Gifford went back to Rheims to teach theology, apologising to Cardinal Allen for his past misconduct, whatever that was. On 29 March 1583, Cardinal Allen wrote a statement objecting for unstated reasons to Gifford's presence at either the seminary at Rheims or the one at Douai. One can guess that his sincerity was in doubt, but there may have been other reasons. He went back to Rome, and then in April 1585 he was ordained a deacon at St Remigius' Church in Rheims.

By this time, it is known that Gifford was already in Walsingham's service, which may have been why Cardinal Allen wanted nothing further to do with him. At Rheims Gifford met John Savage, who had the idea of murdering Queen Elizabeth, and who became a conspirator in the Babington Plot. When he was in Paris, Gifford met Thomas Morgan, who was a representative of Mary Queen of Scots. Morgan gave Gifford a letter commending him to Queen Mary, who was then held at Chartley; Morgan described him as someone who could be trusted to convey letters from Mary to Chateauneuf, the French ambassador in London and also Mary's main agent in London.

Once in London, Gifford went to see Phelippes, Walsingham's chief spy. He even lived in Phelippes' house for a time while he received further training. In January 1586 he went to Chartley for his first meeting with Mary Queen of Scots. She trusted him implicitly, and readily agreed to let him convey her secret letters to London. Mary's gaoler at Chartley, Sir Amias Paulet, knew perfectly well what Gifford was, an accredited government spy; he initially wondered whether he was a double agent, but he came to trust him. Gifford's local Catholic brewer was fictitious. Gifford kept Mary's letters just long enough to make copies of them, often in collaboration with Sir Amias Paulet, then he sent the originals to Phelippes' house in London. Phelippes decoded them, then had them sent on to their destination. One letter written by the Scottish queen on 31 January was not delivered to the French embassy until 1 March; it had been lying on a table in Phelippes' house for the whole of February. But the French ambassador was not in the least suspicious. He gave Gifford a pile of letters for the past two years, which he had until then had no means of delivering to Queen Mary. Gifford dutifully took all of these to Phelippes, who deciphered them for Walsingham before sending them on to Mary through Gifford. Gifford was back at Chartley in April 1586, with his pile of letters. His duplicity was such that at Chartley he enjoyed the full confidence of both Queen Mary and Sir Amias. In the following months, Gifford made many visits to London and Paris. He got to know Sir Anthony Babington, John Ballard and their fellow-conspirators, and encouraged them in their plotting. In Paris, he met Mendoza, the Spanish ambassador who had been deported from London, and made sure that Mendoza knew about the Babington Plot. Mendoza eagerly promised aid from Spain, no doubt salivating at the prospect of Elizabeth's imminent assassination and the re-conversion of England to Catholicism.

Some historians take the view that Gilbert Gifford developed and arranged the whole conspiracy. He was certainly a major agent provocateur, but it is more likely that the priest John Ballard was the prime mover. Gifford encouraged Ballard and Babington, and Walsingham was happy to see the conspiracy develop to a point where it would positively incriminate the Queen of Scots. By the end of July 1586, Gifford had done his work. All the details of the plot had been fully developed on paper, and brought to Walsingham's notice.

As the arrests approached, Gifford's own position became dangerous, as his role in setting the conspiracy going must soon be suspected, at least, by loyal Catholics. He could alternatively find himself rounded up as a conspirator, if Walsingham was as unscrupulous as he was himself. Gifford left England in a hurry for Paris on 29 July, just before the first arrests. After the conspirators' arrests, he wrote to Walsingham and Phelippes, expressing the hope that his sudden departure would not be interpreted 'sinistrously'.

Early in September, Gilbert Gifford offered his services once more to Sir Francis, but Sir Francis was not interested in him any more. He may have thought that Gifford's cover was well and truly blown by his involvement in uncovering the Babington Plot, and that he could be of no further use to him. Gifford was obviously a totally unscrupulous character, and inevitably both Catholics and Protestants regarded him as treacherous. In 1587 he travelled to Rheims under the assumed name Jacques Colerdin and was ordained a priest. A year later he was allegedly found in a brothel and summoned before the Bishop of Paris, who had him imprisoned, and there he died in November 1590. The Catholics after all took their revenge on Gilbert Gifford. Presumably by way of confession, he wrote to Cardinal Allen before he died to tell him precisely how he had injured the Catholic cause. The Cardinal must have been horrified at what he read – how Gifford had encountered and destroyed the heroine of Catholic Europe, the Queen of Scots.

THE ENGLISH FLEET AND THE SPANISH ARMADA

(1588)

THIS IS A story of England's encounter with not one but several Spanish armadas – a more complex story than is often realised.

The earliest scheme for a Spanish invasion of England was hatched in 1559. It was suggested to Philip of Spain while he was sailing westwards along the English Channel towards Spain that he could make an armed landing on the south coast of England. Philip rejected the idea as too rash, and he went on being cautious about invading for two decades. One reason for his delay was that he had many other obligations and responsibilities, most of which were higher priorities than protecting English Catholics from persecution by a Protestant queen. He was also well aware of the strength of England's navy. But the Enterprise of England, as it was known in Spain, was a continuing project. Spain would invade, and overthrow the upstart Protestant régime of Queen Elizabeth.

Philip of Spain tried to organise the sending of an Armada in 1574, but this project failed before it started. Philip continued to reconsider, never quite bringing his plan to fruition. The plight of the imprisoned Mary Queen of Scots gave him a new reason to invade – the rescue of an imprisoned Catholic queen – and he prepared more plans. In 1583 the English government heard about some of them, and this nudged Elizabeth into ordering an open military intervention in the Spanish-controlled Netherlands in 1585 and a parallel expedition to the West Indies. Philip saw these actions as tantamount to a declaration of war on Spain. He decided that the time to invade and get a quick decisive victory over England had come.

The Armada preparations took two years, starting in 1586. Drake's Cadiz raid set the preparations back, delaying the Armada's sailing for a year. Philip's governor in the Netherlands, the Duke of Parma, was uneasy about mounting an invasion against England from the Dutch coast, because he did not yet have full control over it. Philip's solution was to sail the invasion fleet from Spain, land in Kent, then ferry Parma's army across to England from the Dutch coast. Another element in Philip's plan was to make no attempt to land on the English coast before reaching Kent, and he made no provision for a sea battle with the English or an English attack of any kind in the Channel before making landfall. It was a classic case of a war planned on a map as if it was a board game, a closed system with clear and simple rules. The reality was to be very different.

The 122 ships of the Armada eventually arrived off Land's End in July 1588. The Duke of Parma had by then given up expecting Philip's fleet, and had sent his own ships' crews off inland to work on canals. The English fleet had made a couple of attempts to intercept the Armada but failed because they had been beaten back by storms. The English fleet fell back to Plymouth and was there, taking on new supplies in port, when the Armada unexpectedly appeared off the coast. The English were taken by surprise. Drake, like Parma, had not really believed that Philip's Armada would ever reach English waters.

The sixty-six ships of the English fleet were able to get out of Plymouth, but then had an unrewarding stern chase up the Channel as they followed the Spanish. A lot of ammunition was fired, but to little effect. The Spanish ships held to their formation and only two ships were lost, both by accident. The Spanish admiral, the Duke of Medina Sidonia, unexpectedly decided to drop anchor off Calais on 6 August. This gave the English an equally unexpected opportunity to send in fire-ships which dispersed the Spanish fleet; strong westerly winds blew it into the North Sea. Four Spanish ships were lost there, but most escaped by sailing north along the east coast of England.

The only way home for the Spanish fleet was the long detour round the north coasts of Scotland and Ireland, where another thirty-five ships were lost, either sinking or running aground. There was great relief in England that the invasion plan had failed, but also disappointment that so few Spanish ships had been sunk or captured. Elizabeth's appearance at Tilbury to speak to the troops was an enormously popular event. Above all, she had shown that she was Philip of Spain's most effective and dangerous enemy.

The defeat of the Spanish Armada was by no means decisive. In 1589, an English fleet commanded by Sir Francis Drake and Sir John Norreys succeeded in setting fire to the Spanish Atlantic navy, which had survived the Armada expedition unscathed. The Spanish navy was being repaired and refitted at Santander, Coruna and San Sebastian in northern Spain. The Drake-Norreys expedition was also intended to capture the Spanish treasure fleet when it arrived and eject the Spanish from Portugal. If these latter objectives had been achieved, Philip would almost certainly have had to concede defeat, and the war would have come to an end. But the English fleet was poorly organised and too cautious – a very different situation from the English response to the Spanish Armada. As a result the English fleet was repulsed by the Spanish, who inflicted heavy casualties. The treasure ships were not captured. Lisbon was not taken. The expedition was then hit by illness, and finally the squadron was taken by Drake towards the Azores was dispersed by a storm. It was a major fiasco.

English historians have always made much of the Spanish Armada (which was a Spanish failure) and glossed over, often not mentioned at all, the English Armada (which was an English failure). The result of the failure of the Drake-Norreys expedition was that Elizabeth's treasury made a serious loss; she had been pushed into being a major stock-holder to fund the expedition, and so had to shoulder the loss.

The Spanish refitted their navy, to an extent incorporating modern-ising features learnt from the disastrous Armada experience. The fleet had twelve brand-new galleons, which were enormous; they were called *The Twelve Apostles*. The Spanish navy was now far more effective than before the Armada year. A convoy system was adopted along with new intelligence networks. The result was a much greater resistance to

English privateering in the 1590s. This in turn meant that the expeditions of Hawkins, Frobisher and the Earl of Cumberland to seize Spanish treasure failed. The English squadron that attempted to ambush the treasure fleet off the Azores in 1591 failed; it was in that sea battle that Sir Richard Grenville was killed and his flagship, the Revenge, was captured by the Spanish. The effect on the English treasury was significant, as less money was going into it.

The situation worsened in 1595 and 1596, when the English launched an expedition against Spanish possessions, Panama and Puerto Rico among them. This campaign too was a failure. The English lost many ships and men, including Drake and Hawkins. Not surprisingly, given the provocation and the recovery of the Spanish navy, the Spanish retaliated. A force led by Don Carlos de Amesquita patrolled the English Channel, looking for an opportunity, and landed troops in Cornwall. They seized supplies, sacked Penzance and the surrounding villages, then sailed away before any English force could be mustered to oppose it.

An Anglo-Dutch expedition succeeded in raiding the port of Cadiz again in a repeat performance of Drake's earlier exploit. This left Spanish ships destroyed and the city of Cadiz in ruins. The Spanish commander had nevertheless had the foresight and the vision to scuttle the treasure ships that were in port. This meant that the treasure, twelve million ducats' worth of it, went to the seabed, where it was safe from English hands. Spanish divers got most of it back later, after the raiders had sailed away empty-handed.

Then a new front opened in this long war between Spain and England, the coast of northern France. A substantial Spanish force landed in Brittany, where they ejected the English who were there. The Anglo-French forces successfully held onto the port of Brest, but now there was a clear threat of a Spanish invasion of England launched from the coasts of Brittany and Normandy. Elizabeth sent another 2,000 troops across the Channel when the Spanish took the port of Calais, which was dangerously close to the coast of England. Over the next two years there were further battles.

In 1598, following the conversion of the French king to Catholicism, the French and the Spanish made peace. This left England in a worse state than ever. By then a nine-year-long war in Ireland had started: an attempt by the English to put down a rebellion by the Irish lords. This was not only a distraction for the English, but an opportunity for the Spanish to engage in subversion. The Spanish gave the Irish rebels a certain amount of support. While the English were occupied with containing the Irish problem, the Spanish launched two more Armadas against England.

The 1596 Armada was destroyed when it was hit by a storm off the coast of northern Spain. The 1597 Armada was more successful. It reached the English Channel and came very close to making landfall undetected. It was only adverse weather conditions that stopped this fleet from landing. The following year Philip II died, and then the Spanish determination to invade England petered out. The new king of Spain, Philip III, carried on with the war against England, but less whole-heartedly.

The last Armada was sent against the English in 1601. This was an expedition to deliver Spanish troops in the south of Ireland, to help the rebels in their struggle against the English. The 3,000 Spanish soldiers entered the town of Kinsale, where they were immediately surrounded by English troops. Before the English could annihilate them, Irish rebel forces arrived and surrounded the English. This should have put the English in an impossible position, but because the Irish and Spanish forces acted without co-ordination the English were able to win the Battle of Kinsale. The Spanish could then have opted to stay in Kinsale and hold onto it as a base from which to harass English ships in the area. But instead they surrendered and went home. The Irish rebels, now left unsupported by their fitful allies, were only able to continue for a year or so before they too surrendered, just after the death of Elizabeth in 1603.

When James VI of Scotland travelled south to take the throne of England as James I, the last thing he wanted was to have the Anglo-Spanish War draining his treasury. Consequently, one of the first and wisest things he did was to negotiate a peace with Philip III, which was concluded in the Treaty of London in 1604.

The very real threat of a Spanish invasion of England hung over the greater part of the reign of Elizabeth I. It preoccupied her and her advisers. A successful invasion and occupation by a Catholic nation, and the most powerful one in Europe at that, would certainly have meant a conversion back to Catholicism.

England was run into serious debt by the war. It also had its colonial plans thwarted. The Spanish were able to stop English commercial shipping plying on the Atlantic, and that made colonisation extremely difficult. England wanted to develop colonies in North America, and the war with Spain delayed the establishment of those colonies until the Stuart period. This delay gave Spain the opportunity to consolidate and strengthen its Spanish empire in the New World, which went on for another 200 years.

The English defeat of the Spanish Armada had a major effect on the future conduct of naval warfare. The high seas were also cleared by the 'English Armada' for further privateering, and the English were able to go on supporting the Protestant cause in the Netherlands and France. It is interesting to reflect that the conflict between England and Spain would have vanished overnight if Elizabeth I had converted to Catholicism. The enormous financial and commercial cost of the war with Spain was a direct result of Elizabeth's fierce loyalty to the Protestant cause.

The defeat of the Spanish Armada in 1588 was a major blow to Philip of Spain's reputation. He was well known to be the architect of the project, both in general and in detail, and it was also well known that he had disregarded the advice of experts. He was therefore rightly held to be personally responsible for the failure of the Enterprise. The English defeat of the Spanish Armada was not enough in itself to enable England to replace Spain as Europe's dominant power, nor to clear the Atlantic for an American colonisation programme. But it was an event of great symbolic value and it did an enormous amount to enhance the popularity of Elizabeth I in the closing years of her reign. It was an iconic event which became an important component in England's national myth. As such it remained an inspiration to succeeding generations of English people.

ISAAC NEWTON AND GOTTFRIED LEIBNIZ

(1704)

THE HOSTILITY BETWEEN Isaac Newton and Gottfried Leibniz arose over which of them had been responsible for the invention of calculus. This became one of the most famous academic disputes of all time. Did Newton invent calculus? Or did Leibniz invent it instead?

Newton started working on calculus in 1666, whereas Leibniz started on his version eight years later and published his first paper using calculus in 1684. Like Oughtred before him, Newton delayed. He did not publish his view of calculus until 1693 (partially) and 1704 (fully). These dates suggest that Leibniz was quicker off the mark that Newton, but the water is muddied by the fact that in 1676 Leibniz visited London, where he was shown at least one of Newton's unpublished manuscripts. It is not certain, but maybe Leibniz was given valuable information in these notes, information that enabled him to develop his version of calculus.

Leibniz had made an earlier visit to London in 1673. During this visit he seems not to have met Newton, but he certainly heard about Newton's astonishing intellect from other people. While he was there he was accused of plagiarising the work of Francois Regnaud on a method for the interpolation of series by constructing series of differences. Leibniz was acutely embarrassed and distressed by this accusation and went so far as to display his private notes in public in order to defend his integrity. This episode was a foreshadowing of what was to happen to him over calculus in the years to come.

The murky beginning of a major academic debate about the origins of calculus lay in Leibniz's viewing of Newton's notes during his 1676

London visit. It was in that year that Leibniz and Newton started to correspond with each other about calculus. The letters, which continued until 1704, were amiable and each seemed to accept that the other had made independent discoveries. The controversy was simmering by 1700, and broke out in full fury in 1711.

Leibniz wrote in his notebooks that he made an important breakthrough on 11 November 1675. On that date, he said, he used integral calculus for the first time to find the area under the function y = x. He used a range of notations that are still used today, including an elongated S (for the Latin *summa*) as the integral sign, and d (for the Latin *differentia*) to represent differentials.

Leibniz had a difficult life, and his final years, from 1709 until his death in 1716, were soured by quarrels with John Keill, Isaac Newton and other people about whether he had really invented the calculus independently of Newton. His opponents and detractors accused him of just inventing a different notation for ideas that he had cribbed from Newton.

Newton was a difficult, quarrelsome man and he fuelled and manipulated the controversy. Newton claimed that he had already developed his method of fluxions at the time when Leibniz started working on the calculus. There was no proof of this, and Newton had published nothing that could be produced as evidence, yet curiously no-one ever expressed the slightest doubt that he was telling the truth. The nearest thing to evidence that he had invented something special was a calculation of a tangent which was accompanied by the note, 'This is only a special case of a general method by which I can calculate curves and determine maxima, minima and centres of gravity.' He did not explain this general method until twenty years later, by which time Leibniz had published his version of the calculus, and Newton could have copied that. Newton's notes were found after his death, but they could then no longer be dated, so they shed no light on the matter.

The infinitesimal calculus could be expressed in one of two forms of notation. One was Newton's fluxions. The other was Leibniz's differentials. The earliest use of differentials can be traced to 1675 in

Leibniz's notebooks, and he used this notation when he wrote to Newton in 1677.

There are several arguments in support of Leibniz. He published his method years ahead of Newton. He always referred to calculus as his invention and no-one challenged it for a long time. He always behaved as if he had acted in good faith. His notes show that he developed calculus in a completely different way from Newton. He was ready to work in collaboration with Newton.

Some arguments have even so been levelled against Leibniz. He saw some of Newton's papers on the subject in manuscript. He may have obtained the basic idea of the calculus as a result of seeing those papers.

It is possible, and these things do sometimes happen, that the two men arrived at the calculus coincidentally at the same time. The fact that Leibniz used a different method strongly suggests that he was not merely plagiarising Newton. The situation was complicated by the fact that in addition to the formal publications there were unpublished letters circulating, and there were meetings and conversations – all sorts of informal exchanges of information. By these informal routes, it became clear to both Leibniz and Newton that the other was a long way along the path to the calculus. Leibniz actually mentioned it, but only Leibniz was pushed by the situation into publishing.

When a researcher was going through Leibniz's manuscripts in 1849, he uncovered extracts from one of Newton's papers, copied in Leibniz's handwriting. These notes were probably made in May 1675, when it is known that a copy of Newton's manuscript had been sent for Ehrenfried von Tschirnhaus to look at. As Tschirnhaus was meeting and networking with a great many people at that time, it is very likely that the manuscript was shown to Leibniz; Tschirnhaus was to keep up a life-long correspondence with Leibniz. Other scientists, Collins and Oldenburg, seem to have had access to Newton's manuscript in 1676, and because Leibniz was collaborating with them too he may have had a second opportunity to make notes on the manuscript then. Leibniz mentioned that someone else, Collins, had shown him some of Newton's papers, but implied that they were of little or no use to him.

In 1711 Newton went out of his way to make a case for Leibniz having seen his, Newton's, notes on the calculus, but he by then had a vested interest in arguing this. In 1704, someone published an anonymous review of one of Newton's works in which the reviewer implied that Newton had plagiarised the idea of the fluxional calculus from Leibniz. The reviewer also implied that there was no question that Leibniz had invented the calculus independently of Newton. This was the spark that brought the controversy out into the open, made the integrity of the two great scientists a matter of public debate. The case against Leibniz was published by Newton's friends and supporters in 1712 as Commercium Epistolicum. Newton was behind this attack. Poor Leibniz had no claque of friends and supporters ready to do the same for him. Johann Bernoulli wrote a letter in 1713 making a personal attack on Newton, but the charges he made were false and, when challenged, he weakly denied having written it.

Newton wrote privately to Bernoulli:

I have never grasped at fame among foreign nations, bit I am very desirous to preserve my character for honesty, which the author of that epistle, as if by the authority of a great judge, had endeavoured to wrest from me. Now that I am old, I have little pleasure in mathematical studies, and I have never tried to propagate my opinions over the world, but I have rather taken care not to involve myself on account of them.

In the face of the appalling public controversy, Leibniz retreated into silence. He wrote in a letter in 1716:

In order to respond point by point to all the work published against me, I would have to go into much minutiae that occurred thirty, forty years ago, of which I remember little. I would have to search my old letters, of which many are lost. Moreover, in most cases I did not keep a copy, and when I did, the copy is buried in a great heap of papers, which I could sort through only with time and patience. I have enjoyed

*little leisure, being so weighted down of late with occupations of a
totally different nature.*

Leibniz may not be wholly innocent. He did not actually acknowledge that he had made notes on an unpublished work of Newton's; that
only emerged in the 19th century. In addition, Leibniz more than once
deliberately altered important documents.

While Leibniz's death put a temporary stop to the controversy, the
debate persisted for many years. He altered documents that he quoted
in publications. He also falsified a date on a manuscript, from 1675 to
1673, so that it would seem to be in advance of other publications.

If the world of science had operated in 1700 as it operates today, then
the date of publication would be the decider, and Leibniz would be
regarded as the sole and undisputed inventor of the calculus. But at the
time, the general presumption that Newton must be the inventor of the
calculus prejudiced any real debate. The Royal Society set up a committee
to pronounce on the priority dispute but that committee never invited
Leibniz to give his version of events. It was this committee that published
Commercium Epistolicum in 1713. It came out in favour in Newton. It was
not surprising – the document was written by Newton himself!

Newton was not the pillar of honesty the Royal Society wanted him
to be. John Flamsteed helped Newton with his *Principia*, but
subsequently held back information from him. Newton then seized all
of Flamsteed's work and tried to get it published with the aid of
Flamsteed's enemy, Edmond Halley. Flamsteed had to resort to a court
order to block the publication of his own work, and only just succeeded.
In retaliation, Newton had the acknowledgement of Flamsteed's help
deleted from future editions of his *Principia*.

GEORGE WASHINGTON AND LORD CORNWALLIS

(1781)

AT THE SIEGE of Yorktown in 1781, there was a momentous collision between two enormous military talents: George Washington and George Cornwallis.

George Cornwallis (1738–1805) joined the Grenadier Guards at the age of seventeen and served in the British Army during the Seven Years' War, during which he rose to the rank of Lieutenant-Colonel. After succeeding to his father's title, Lord Cornwallis, he became a politically active Whig in the House of Lords. He was sympathetic to the grievances of the colonists in America. He actively opposed the parliamentary measures that provoked the American Revolution, so it is surprising to find him accepting a command in North America with the rank of Major General.

Cornwallis was a professional soldier, ready to set aside his personal political beliefs in order to carry out his military duties. In August 1776, he helped to produce the British victory at the Battle of Long Island. Later in the year he chased George Washington's army across New Jersey, stopping at New Brunswick on General Howe's orders. After Washington won at Trenton in December 1776, Cornwallis failed to trap the Americans and went into winter quarters.

After a short return to England, Cornwallis was back in America as a Lieutenant General, second-in-command to Sir Henry Clinton. He accompanied the British army on its retreat to New York and successfully beat the Americans under General Charles Lee at the Battle of Monmouth in June 1778. The following summer, Cornwallis joined Clinton and took part in the siege of Charleston. When Charleston fell in May 1780, Clinton went back to New York, and Cornwallis took command of the British forces in the South.

In August 1780, at Camden, South Carolina, Lord Cornwallis and his British army routed General Horatio Gates's army. He went on to pursue the Americans vigorously, but he was defeated by them twice over at King's Mountain and Cowpens. These setbacks sapped Cornwallis's reserves and he entrenched at Yorktown, Virginia. There he and his army were surrounded and trapped by a large combined force of American and French troops led by General George Washington and General Comte de Rochambeau.

When the fighting had broken out early in 1775, George Washington had appeared at the Second Continental Congress in military uniform. It was a signal that he was prepared for war – and prepared to take the lead. Washington had by that time gained the prestige and experience to take the lead; he had the bearing and the charisma for leadership. He never explicitly asked for a position in command, and said he was not equal to it, but there was no-one else. On 15 June 1774 John Adams nominated him Major General and he was elected Commander-in-chief by Congress.

It was Washington who put artillery on the heights overlooking Boston and forced the British to evacuate the city. Then and throughout the war, even the British press unreservedly praised Washington's qualities as a commander; he was skilful, courageous, tough and attentive to his troops' welfare. Washington led the Continental Army as the army of the newly declared independent United States in battle against the British at the Battle of Long Island. This, the largest battle in the whole war, sent Washington scurrying out of New York, leaving the Continental Army's future in doubt. But Washington snatched victory out of defeat when he led a force across the Delaware River to capture several hundred Hessian troops at Trenton. This victory was followed by another at Princeton and the two successes raised his army's morale and secured his position as commander.

Washington was alternately successful and unsuccessful in his engagements with the British army. His loss of Philadelphia even prompted some members of Congress to advocate replacing him as commander-in-chief, but he had enough supporters to keep him in his post. He was helped enormously when General Burgoyne was trapped and forced to surrender his entire army at Saratoga and the French responded to this event by entering the war on America's side. With this help from outside, Washington was able to deliver the final blow in 1781, when he and the joint American and French forces were able to surround the British army under Cornwallis at Yorktown.

Before that happened, Generals Washington and Rochambeau discussed where their joint attack would be most effective. Washington favoured New York as the best option, as there they would easily outnumber the British. Rochambeau had other ideas. He pointed out that a fleet under Admiral de Grasse was heading from the West Indies towards the American coastline, where a convergent attack would be effective. Then Washington proposed an attack on the northern end of Manhattan Island, but both Rochambeau and Washington's own officers disagreed with him. Washington went on, misguidedly, mentally planning an attack on New York until 14 August, when he had a letter from de Grasse telling him that de Grasse's fleet was heading for Virginia with 29 warships. De Grasse actively encouraged Washington to march south and join him in an attack there. It was then that Washington abandoned his plan for an attack on New York.

The march south to Virginia with 4,000 French and 3,000 American troops began. Washington successfully kept the march's destination a secret, even going so far as to send out fake dispatches announcing that it was (still) New York that was going to be attacked. Clinton was convinced by them; he thought Cornwallis was in no danger.

By September, Washington knew that de Grasse's fleet had arrived off the Virginia coast. Clinton sent a fleet to attack de Grasse, not realising how big the French fleet was. The British fleet was defeated by de Grasse's fleet in the Battle of Chesapeake. Then Washington's troops arrived in Williamsburg, leaving from there to surround Yorktown.

Cornwallis had constructed a chain of redoubts and batteries linked by earthworks. On arrival at the end of September, Washington toured the British defences at Yorktown and decided they could be bombarded into submission. The firing started and Cornwallis pulled back immediately from all of his outer defences, which were then occupied and consolidated by French and American troops. Trenches were dug and gun emplacements built, and on 9 October the American bombardment of Yorktown started. Washington ordered it to continue all night, so that the British could not make any repairs. Several British ships were set on fire and sunk in the harbour.

British soldiers began to desert at once. Cornwallis sent word to Clinton that he would not be able to hold out for long. Fired by his success, Washington ordered more trenches dug to enable French and American troops to get closer to the town's two remaining redoubts, which he was determined to take. There was a minor dispute as to which officer should lead the attack on Redoubt No 10. Lafayette wanted his man to do it, but Washington insisted on his own man, Hamilton, and Washington had his way. Both redoubts were captured in this attack.

Cornwallis made a spirited counter-attack, ordering Colonel Abercromby and 350 British soldiers to spike the French and American cannon. He did this in a night attack, and the Americans and their allies were caught sleeping, while Abercromby shouted, 'Skin the bastards!' The British succeeded in disabling six guns before they were forced back into Yorktown. Then the bombardment began again. By 16 October, Cornwallis was attempting to evacuate Yorktown by crossing the York River with a view to escaping to New York. But stormy weather made evacuation impossible. The next day Cornwallis called a meeting of his officers and they agreed that their situation was hopeless. A drummer was sent out accompanying an officer holding up a white handkerchief. The British had surrendered.

Under Articles of Capitulation signed on 19 October 1781, all Cornwallis's soldiers became prisoners of war. The captives walked between the assembled French and American armies, accompanied by

British drummers beating the rhythm of the song *The World Turned Upside Down*, which is exactly how it must have felt to the British troops. Lord Cornwallis himself refused to meet Washington and excused himself from the humiliation of the surrender ceremony by saying he was ill. Instead, Brigadier O'Hara presented Cornwallis's sword to the victors.

After what had been for him a spectacularly successful campaign until Camden, Cornwallis had been suddenly, totally and humiliatingly defeated. Cornwallis was a commander of high ability, but he was hampered and undermined by the stupidity of his superior; now he was defeated by an enemy commander of sheer genius. His surrender on 19 October 1781 brought the war to a virtual end. The siege of Yorktown was the last major land battle of the American War of Independence. George Washington's overwhelming triumph at Yorktown led directly on to his being appointed, in 1789, the first president of the United States.

NAPOLEON AND TSAR ALEXANDER

(1812)

TSAR ALEXANDER I of Russia had two encounters with Napoleon, one at Tilsit in 1807 and one in Moscow in 1812. They were totally different in character. In the first, the tsar was won over to a dream of shared empire with Napoleon but by the second he had grown to hate him.

Alexander succeeded to the Russian throne in March 1801 after the murder of his father. His role in his father's murder is still unclear, but the prevailing view among historians is that Alexander knew about the conspiracy to depose his father but insisted that his father should not be killed. He nevertheless took the throne in the knowledge that his father had lost his life in the process, felt overwhelmingly guilty about it, and carried the remorse and regret with him for the rest of his life. He would eventually, in 1825, relinquish the throne under mysterious circumstances, apparently changing his identity and vanishing completely.

Tsar Alexander was an unusual man, and an unusual tsar. As a young ruler he was determined to introduce reforms to reduce the over-centralised tsarist system of government. He set up a Private Committee consisting of a group of young friends to draw up a scheme of reforms; the idea was to set up a constitutional monarchy and eventually to end serfdom. Two early achievements were to remove censorship of the press and abolish torture. But many of his proposals for reform were ahead of their time, and Russia was not ready for such radical change.

His reign coincided with the Napoleonic Wars that ravaged Europe. Alexander came to oppose Napoleon, whom he described as 'the oppressor of Europe and the disturber of the world's peace'. Napoleon believed that he was the man of destiny, and Tsar Alexander came to

381

see himself in the same way. His public statements regarding the toppling of Napoleon and the establishment of new post-Napoleonic Europe were couched in visionary terms. He wanted to see the universal triumph of 'the sacred rights of humanity', which made him sound like a French Revolutionary. He also wanted to make future war impossible by making the governments of nations incapable of acting in any way other than in the best interests of their subjects; international relations were to be fixed by precise rules. These were ideals that held no appeal to British or other allied politicians in the Europe of the day.

Napoleon was somewhat unnerved by Alexander's ideology, but saw at least that it might be possible to separate him from his coalition allies. With this in view, Napoleon opened negotiations with Alexander in 1805, arguing that there was no real conflict of interests between them; together they might rule the world. That was an idea that might appeal to the idealistic young Tsar. But Alexander wanted to pursue his policy of 'disinteredness', allying himself with Prussia. Napoleon continued working on the idea of a Russian alliance, and stirred up the Poles, Turks and Persians with a view to pushing the Tsar in this direction.

Alexander called Russia to a holy war against Napoleon, this time naming him as the enemy of the Orthodox faith. This ended with the Battle of Friedland in June 1807, in which the Russians were defeated. Napoleon used this defeat as his lever on Alexander. Instead of exacting heavy punitive terms, Napoleon once again offered the defeated Tsar alliance and partnership. It was a psychological master-stroke.

The two emperors met at Tilsit in June 1807. Alexander was dazzled by Napoleon's political and military genius, and of course overwhelmed by his generous offer. He could share Napoleon's limitless glory. Napoleon understood Alexander's psychology well. He offered to divide the world with him; they would be twin-emperors of the East and West; when the time was right, they would drive the Turks out of Europe and then march across Asia to conquer India. Alexander was fired with even greater ambition than before. He had until then thought no further than Russia and Europe. Now Napoleon was extending his horizons.

But within five years, the dream had crumbled and Napoleon sent

Alexander an ultimatum which went unanswered. On 24 June 1812, Napoleon began his invasion. French coalition forces numbering almost 450,000 men entered Poland (Russian territory), encountering very little resistance. Progress was obstructed and slowed mainly by the poor quality of the roads, which were in some places no more than dirt tracks. Foraging too was a problem, as much of the land was barren or forested. Progress was impeded by the onset of bad weather. Torrential rain turned roads into rivers of mud; wagons sank up to their axles, men lost their boots, horses became exhausted. Later, when the sun came out, it turned the roads into rutted and furrowed concrete, which made progress just as difficult. Then, like the biblical plagues of Egypt, influenza and dysentery swept through the army.

The passage of the French army was in itself a disaster. Troops and thousands of deserters plundered and terrorised the local population. Whole areas became depopulated. When Napoleon reached Vilna on 28 June, he imagined Alexander would try to negotiate a peace settlement with him. But in this he was disappointed. Alexander ignored him, just as he had ignored his ultimatum. Absence turned out to be Tsar Alexander's most effective tactic, and he used it against Napoleon more than once, with devastating results. Napoleon's Grande Armée marched slowly but relentlessly towards Moscow, with the Russian army falling back in front of it. Barclay, the Russian commander-in-chief, refused to engage the French in battle, realising the futility of fighting such a huge invasion force. Instead, as the Russian army fell back, it destroyed any supplies that might feed Napoleon's troops.

Russian impatience with Barclay's refusal to fight led to his dismissal as commander-in-chief. He was replaced by Mikhail Kutuzov, who was both boastful and popular, but he behaved exactly as Barclay had, falling back as the French advanced, seeing that meeting them in open battle would lead to a massacre of the Russian army. He nevertheless established a defensive position at Borodino. The Battle of Borodino took place on 7 September 1812; taking the Napoleonic Wars as a whole, this was the day on which most lives were lost. The Russian army was forced to fall back yet again, leaving the road to Moscow open.

Kutuzov ordered the evacuation of Moscow, to avert a civilian massacre, so on 14 September Napoleon entered a city that was deserted. The city's governor, Rostopchin, had removed all supplies. There were few civilians, no troops, no supplies, and there was no tsar either. Napoleon had expected Tsar Alexander to be there to offer his formal surrender, but once again Alexander was ignoring him. The Russian high command would not surrender to Napoleon; there was no intention of surrendering. This left Napoleon in a strange position. He had entered and taken control of the capital city, and yet he did not have the formal acknowledgement of the civil authorities. It was also customary in such situations for the victor, the invader, to demand that the surrendering authority organised billets for officers and arrange for the feeding of soldiers. But now Napoleon and his army had to organise this for themselves. Napoleon was disappointed; he was robbed of his victory.

The French soldiers began looting. In the anarchy, fires started breaking out. These spread and gradually took hold. The French assumed that the Russians were deliberately sabotaging their capital city in order to deprive the French of their prize, but it may be, as Tolstoy described in *War and Peace*, that the fires broke out simply because of the anarchy. Whatever the cause, the spreading fires engulfed about four-fifths of the city, and it was no longer a fit place for the French army to take refuge. And so began Napoleon's disastrous retreat from Moscow, in mid-October, as winter was setting in. Kutuzov harried the retreating army into marching along the same road they had used during the invasion, a road that was already devastated. It was an application of Kutuzov's earlier scorched-earth tactics. Without grazing, many of Napoleon's horses died. Starvation and disease took its toll of the soldiers too. Of the survivors, many deserted, and the deserters were often killed out of hand by peasants. A final disaster was inflicted on the French army as it tried to cross the River Berezina; two Russian armies attacked as the French tried to get away across pontoon bridges. In the end even Napoleon himself deserted his army. He heard that General Matel had tried to overthrow him in his absence, and he needed to return quickly to Paris.

Tsar Alexander's devastatingly effective stand-off in Moscow – a masterful non-encounter – was one of the most powerful defeats Napoleon experienced.

RUDYARD KIPLING, BEATTY BALESTIER AND THE REPORTER

(1892)

THE WRITER RUDYARD Kipling was born in 1865 in Bombay and became a journalist in Lahore. He was a prolific writer, producing six volumes of short stories before leaving India for a world tour that led him to London. He married an American, Carrie Balestier, and for their honeymoon they travelled round the USA, and then stayed on at the Balestier family estate in Vermont. The rural seclusion there made Kipling inventive and prolific, and he settled down to write, from a distant perspective, nostalgically and effectively about India.

In the four years spent there, 1892-96, Kipling wrote *The Jungle Books,* a collection of short stories, a novel and some poetry, including *Mandalay* and *Gunga Din.* Kipling loved the Vermont landscape, especially in the fall, when the maple trees turned blood-red. Rudyard and Carrie Kipling might well have stayed in America for good, but for two things. One was a major political crisis that blew up between Britain and America, which led to a surge of anti-British sentiment in the American press; Kipling strongly resented this attack by fellow-journalists, which he took personally. There was also a family crisis, resulting from friction between his wife and her brother, Beatty Balestier. Drunk and insolvent, Beatty threatened Kipling with violence over a land dispute, and it resulted in a court case, which was also reported in the press.

Kipling had co-written a novel, *The Nauhlaka,* with his agent Wolcott Balestier. After Wolcott died, Kipling married Wolcott's sister Carrie and when they settled in Vermont they named their substantial house there Nauhlaka. The Kiplings' problems started when Rudyard began collaborating with Carrie's brother Beatty, who lived in the area and supplied Rudyard with material for a story about the people of Vermont. The story Kipling produced and published shortly after his arrival angered the local people. They quickly cast the writer as an arrogant and cranky intruder.

A Boston reporter intercepted Kipling while he was out walking and tried to interview him, but Kipling curtly told him he didn't want to be interviewed. The reporter had no more right to hold him up than a highwayman. If the man wanted an interview, he should put his questions on paper and send them to the house. The reporter was encouraged by this. He wrote Kipling a letter telling him he had been unnecessarily rude and boorish; then he crisply asked Kipling what his objection was to being interviewed. He delivered the short letter by hand and waited at the door for an answer.

Ten minutes later, an angry Kipling appeared on the doorstep to tell the reporter that interviews were immoral and criminal, and that journalists were sensationalists. Kipling had momentarily forgotten (though the reporter had not) that he himself had been a journalist in India. 'There isn't a single respectable newspaper in this country. I suppose you want to write me up and put me in some obscure place in your old sheet, though I don't know which one it is.' The reporter assured him that on the contrary he would be getting front-page treatment. His treatise on the American press would certainly guarantee that. What he had to say was valuable. Then, hearing the word 'valuable', Kipling rashly launched into the matter of money. It was another reason why he didn't like interviews; they didn't provide him with any money. He could earn money by writing a piece himself and sending it to an English magazine. An American magazine would steal it; 'American copyright law is damnable . . . English journalism is dignified and respectable. There is no dirty business in it. The English reporter is a gentleman and lets people alone.'

Kipling had lost his temper and in consequence had made several serious mistakes, including confirming that he would not be giving an interview; he was apparently unaware that his angry comments had already given the reporter plenty of copy. The reporter coolly replied that he wouldn't have missed this interview for anything. Kipling retorted, 'You haven't got anything.'

'Oh yes I have,' said the reporter. 'I've got enough.'

With that, as the reporter later triumphantly reported to his newspaper, Rudyard Kipling slammed the door. Mr Kipling had been interviewed. It was one more step towards leaving America for England.

In 1896, after the Balestier family brawl and the relationship with the press became unbearable, the Kiplings packed their bags and set off for England. There, Kipling was able to set himself up as the archetypal English man of letters, living at Batemans, a small country manor house at Burwash, and in 1907 collecting the Nobel Prize for Literature; he was to be the youngest recipient of this prize ever.

VIII

CREATIVE ENCOUNTERS: FROM ANTIQUITY TO 1900

MARTIN BEHAIM AND GEORGE HOLZSCHUHER

(1492)

MARTIN BEHAIM (1459–1507) was a German geographer and navigator who was in the service of the King of Portugal. At the court of King John II he acquired a reputation as a scientist and he was thought to have been a pupil of the astronomer Johann Muller, who was known by the impressive Latin name of Regiomantanus. He may have been, but whatever Behaim's real background, he was appointed by John II to a mathematical council for the furtherance of navigation. One of his contributions in this area was the proposal to introduce to Portugal the cross-staff, a navigation instrument already invented and in use. He made improvements to astrolabes, principally in making them smaller out of brass; the old wooden instruments were cumbersome to use. It is thought that he also worked on producing better navigation tables.

Martin Behaim travelled on one of Diogo Cão's voyages to West Africa in 1484, probably reaching the Bight of Benin. When he returned he was knighted by King John and after that lived mainly at Fayal in the Azores.

While working for the King of Portugal, Behaim had access to all the latest maps. It is thought that he passed on to Magellan a map showing a channel passing through the southern tip of South America. Magellan saw it as a possible route through from the Atlantic into the Pacific. Antonio Pigafetta, who helped Magellan research his circumnavigation voyage, named Behaim as the man who had drawn the original of the map that Magellan took with him. Behaim cannot take credit as the discoverer of this channel, as he almost certainly copied its shape from an existing map.

When Martin Behaim returned to his native city, Nuremberg, in 1492, he was treated like a visiting celebrity, and fêted by the city council. One of the city councillors was a man called George Holzschuher, who was himself a great traveller. Holzschuher formally proposed to the council that Martin Behaim should be invited to build a globe to incorporate everything that was known about the world. The idea was that all the recent discoveries made by the Portuguese and other travellers should be included to give a comprehensive and up-to-date picture of the world's geography.

The globe was to carry lots of labels. One of these, placed inside the still-unvisited Antarctic Circle, recorded that the making of the globe was undertaken on the say-so of three distinguished Nuremberg citizens, Gabriel Nutzel, Paul Volckamer and Nickolaus Groland. The accounts of George Holzschuher have been preserved, and through these it is possible to trace the development of the globe, and even who was paid how much for their various contributions to it; the cost was borne by the city. The accounts indicate how the sphere was prepared by Kalperger, how a vellum covering was applied to it, how the rings and supports were supplied, and how an artist named Glockenthorn transferred the map onto the prepared surface of the sphere; it took him fifteen weeks.

Obviously the biggest undertaking was the preparation of a two-dimensional mappa mundi with all the detailed information on it. This was the task allotted to Martin Behaim himself. Later, this base map was mounted on two panels, framed and varnished, and hung up in the clerk's office in Nuremberg's town hall. In 1532, Johann Schöner was given the task of renovating this map of Behaim's and drawing a new one that incorporated the substantial number of geographical discoveries that had been made in the preceding forty years – including the New World.

It was a great idea, and even though it involved a lot of work and was carried out to the highest specifications, the overall cost to the city was less than fourteen pounds. This great civic undertaking was nicknamed 'the earth-apple'. The layout of the landmasses and the oceans shown on the globe was influenced by Ptolemy, but Martin Behaim made every effort to incorporate all the later discoveries, from the Marco Polo journeys onwards. The timing of the project is significant, in that it falls in the year of the famous Columbus voyage, but just precedes it. So the Behaim globe shows how the most advanced European geographers perceived the world – just before the Columbus voyage, just before the discovery of North and South America.

The age of the globe (it is in fact the oldest surviving globe) and its very specific pre-Columbian date make it an historic artefact of the greatest value and importance.

One thing the Behaim globe shows is that a relatively narrow ocean was believed to separate Europe from eastern Asia. A relatively short voyage west from Portugal would take you to Japan or China, which is what Columbus argued. Behaim and Columbus were therefore presumably drawing their knowledge from the same sources. The two men were apparently in Portugal at the same time, though as far as we know they never met.

As a map, the Behaim creation is uneven. The portolan maps, showing capes, harbours and other landmarks round the coasts of Europe were far more accurate and finely detailed. Continental locations on most contemporary maps of Behaim's time were pretty accurate, accurate to within one degree of latitude: longitude was at that time much harder to pin down. But some of the places Behaim has drawn in are as much as sixteen degrees out.

The Behaim globe is the oldest globe that has survived until today, though others were certainly made. A 13th century mathematician, Giovanni Campano, wrote a treatise entitled a Treatise on solid spheres, which describes making globes out of metal or wood. In 1474, Toscanelli referred to a globe as being the best way of demonstrating that it was in fact quite a long way from western Europe to eastern Asia, which it was if you stuck to Ptolemy's longitudes. Columbus had a globe on board the Santa Maria, which was made before Behaim's globe by

Columbus's brother Bartholomew, who also made charts. So, globes older than Behaim's did exist, but only the Behaim globe and one other survive; the other, the Laon globe, is preserved in Paris and it is smaller than the Behaim globe.

A major implication of the Behaim globe is that, in its very nature, it made a commitment to a specific width for the western ocean that separated Europe from eastern Asia. Behaim gave Eurasia a longitudinal spread of 234 degrees, whereas the correct figure is 131 degrees. The result was to take the eastern shores of Asia much closer to the coast of western Europe: 126 degrees instead of the correct 229 degrees. The real journey from western Europe to China was more than a quarter of a circumnavigation further than he showed – a quarter of a world further. On top of this, Behaim placed the Cape Verde Islands too far west, and this made the voyage west to China look temptingly short.

Unfortunately, the Behaim globe was allowed to deteriorate over the centuries, and was then over-zealously restored in the early 19th century; at that time a lot of inaccuracies were added in because of the illegibility of the original lettering. The globe still belongs to the Behaim family, though in 1907 it was moved by Baron Behaim to the Germanic Museum.

It has a diameter of fifty centimetres, resulting in a scale of about 1:25,000,000. It is crowded with more than 1,000 place names. A major decorative feature of the globe is the addition of more than 100 miniature paintings by Glockenthorn, including forty-eight national flags and portraits of saints and kings. There are ships on the sea, elephants, leopards, camels and ostriches on the land. There are very few mythical beasts, and there is no 'Garden of Eden'. It is a genuine attempt at a secular and scientific portrayal of the world as perceived.

The meeting between George Holzschuher and Martin Behaim in Nuremberg had major ramifications. The 'earth-apple' that resulted from this encounter was so popular that it created a demand for copies. The Behaim globe was the inspiration for something approaching mass production; globe-making became a new industry in Nuremberg. The Behaim globe was regarded as definitive, too, as cartographers making new globes and maps afterwards evidently respected the information given on it. But Behaim himself did not stay to witness all this. He returned to his home in the Azores, where he died in 1507, just two years before Columbus.

MICHELANGELO AND TOMMASO CAVALIERI

(1532)

THE GREAT RENAISSANCE sculptor Michelangelo Buonarroti was a lover of young men. The handsome Gherardo Perini went to work for him in about 1520 as a model and from about 1522 until 1525 they were lovers; their sexual relationship continued until the middle of the 1530s. Michelangelo became dependent on Perini. He was depressed and unable to work properly when the young man was absent from his studio. Michelangelo developed a custom of giving special friends gifts of carefully finished drawings. In 1524, he gave one of these presentation drawings, a picture of Venus, Mars and Cupid, to Gherardo Perini.

Michelangelo had other lovers too, including his servant and companion Francesco Urbino, Bartolommeo Bettini and Andrea Quaratesi. Andrea was an eighteen-year-old boy with whose family Michelangelo lived for several years. Documentary evidence suggests that Andrea was infatuated with Michelangelo. In the early 1530s Michelangelo had an affair with a second model, Febo di Poggio, whom he described as 'that little blackmailer' because of the boy's constant demands for money.

In 1532, the fifty-seven-year-old Michelangelo began his courtship of Tommaso Cavalieri, a handsome and intelligent twenty-three-year-old Roman. Tommaso was the great love of his life, though it was to be an unrequited love. Tommaso came from a distinguished Roman family and expected to lead a conventional life as a married man – he did in fact marry in 1548. He was alarmed by the older man's passion and persistence, and alarmed too by the prospect of gossip. This was a strange relationship, unconsummated, and yet in spite of that long-lasting. Tommaso put up with what may have been rather tiresome repeated declarations of love from Michelangelo, perhaps out of respect for his enormous talent, perhaps because he genuinely valued the friendship. For whatever reason, the relationship lasted until Michelangelo's death in 1564.

The effect of this relationship on Michelangelo was profound. Although he used studio models for his work, he very rarely executed portraits as such. The life-size portrait drawing he made of Tommaso Cavalieri was one of the very few. Tommaso was also the recipient of the largest number of presentation drawings, such as *Cleopatra*. In 1562, when Michelangelo was still alive, Tommaso was obliged to give the *Cleopatra* drawing to Cosimo I de Medici. When he sent the drawing, he also sent a letter to Cosimo saying that giving up the picture caused him as much suffering as the loss of a child. In fact, before he sent it off he had a copy made. In 1614, Cosimo II had the drawing sent back to Casa Buonarroti.

Michelangelo's art was profoundly affected by his relationship with Cavalieri. The sculpture of *Victory* is a thinly disguised depiction of his own erotic desire for subjugation by Tommaso: the proud standing figure is Tommaso, the abject kneeling figure doubled up underneath him is Michelangelo. In the same way all the bound slaves are Michelangelo too. Everything he felt for Tommaso had to be sublimated, converted into art. It is thought that the face of Christ the Judge in the Sistine Chapel is Cavalieri's: Christ offering the heavenly possibility of eternal life in a state of grace.

Perhaps the relationship with Cavalieri was as powerful as it was just because it was unconsummated. Certainly Michelangelo had physical relationships with other men – and boys too. By 1542, when he was sixty-six, he seems to have been having an affair with a boy of thirteen called Francesco de Zenobi Bracci. Just two years later, the boy died. For a year after that Michelangelo composed a series of four-line epitaphs to be inscribed on the boy's tomb, which he designed himself – fifty epitaphs in all. Michelangelo wrote to the boy's uncle, Luigi del Riccio, describing the boy as 'the flame who consumes me'. Riccio encouraged Michelangelo to go on composing and sending him the epitaphs, and Michelangelo became slightly alarmed when Riccio announced that he intended to publish them. Michelangelo proposed to amend some of the more incriminating ones. 'You have the power to disgrace me,' he wrote. It was the end of their friendship, though Riccio relented on the matter of publication.

For Tommaso Cavalieri, Michelangelo wrote his sonnets. One of them ends;

> *. . . If the one loves the other and neither loves himself,*
> *With one pleasure and one delight, to such measure*
> *That one and the other desire to reach a single end:*
> *Thousands and thousands would not make a hundredth*
> *Of such a knot of love, or of such a faith:*
> *And only anger could unravel and untie it.*

Another of the sonnets Michelangelo dedicated to Cavalieri has the following opening lines;

> *You know that I know, my lord, that you know*
> *That I draw close to take pleasure in you,*
> *And you know that I know that you know who I am;*
> *So why do you delay our acknowledging each other?*

GALILEO GALILEI AND HANS LIPPERSHEY'S TELESCOPE

(1609)

WHEN COPERNICUS PUT forward his theory (published in 1543) that it was the Sun and not the Earth that was at the centre of the universe, there was great resistance to it, not least because it contradicted Aristotle. It also seemed to contradict the biblical assertion that the universe had been created for mankind. The idea was heretical. In fact, there was one man who accepted Copernicus' view and argued from it that the stars were spread out through an infinity of space and that there was an infinite number of other inhabited worlds. He was Giordano Bruno – and in 1600 he was burnt at the stake for his heresy. But it was not just established dogma that stood in the way of acceptance of a Sun-centred system; there was also the problem that little could be produced in the way of supporting evidence. It was the invention of the telescope that enabled people to see the nature of the solar system more clearly.

The first known use of a glass lens as magnifier to aid reading was in the 13th century. The English scientist Roger Bacon used lenses in this way. The idea spread through Europe, and before the century ended Italian craftsmen were making reading glasses (with convex lenses) for long-sighted old men. By 1350, reading glasses were being made for short-sighted young men too, and these utilised concave lenses, which were more difficult to make.

It was not until 1608 in the Netherlands that the two sorts of lens were put together to make a telescope. The inventor was a Flemish spectacle-maker named Hans Lippershey. He tried to get his invention patented. In October 1608 the States General (the Dutch parliament) discussed rival patent applications from Hans Lippershey of Middleburg and Jacob Metius of Alkmaar – for the same instrument. It is quite common in the history of inventions for two people to invent the same thing at the same time; it later happened with photography. It seems there was yet another Dutchman who invented the telescope in 1608. Sacharias Janssen, also from Middleburg, developed a telescope; he did not apply for a patent, but went off to the Frankfurt Fair, where he tried to sell it. The States General rejected both of the patent applications because the device was too easy to copy. As a compensation, Metius was given a small financial award, and Lippershey was commissioned to make several binocular versions of his telescope.

Word of the new invention was quickly passed round. In April 1609 it was possible to buy spyglasses with a magnification of three from spectacle-makers' shops on the Pont Neuf in Paris. In the summer of that year, the English astronomer Thomas Harriot was using a six-powered telescope to look at the Moon.

News of the telescope reached the ears of Galileo Galilei, Professor of Mathematics at the University of Padua, in the spring of 1609. Like Harriot, he saw the astronomical potential of the instrument straight away and also saw that its future usefulness would lie in the power of its magnification. He set about improving the Lippershey telescope.

Galileo's first telescope had a magnification of three, which other scientists had already achieved. But Galileo was a born experimenter and he tried out different combinations of lenses to try to improve the magnification. What he discovered was that he needed a weak convex lens and a powerful concave lens. Unfortunately, there was only a limited range of lenses available, so Galileo had to learn to grind his own lenses. In this way, within a few months he produced a telescope with a magnification of eight. This was major progress. Galileo took his improved instrument to show to state officials in Venice. The senators climbed bell towers to look at ships far out at sea and were impressed by the new telescope's power, and its military potential.

Galileo wrote to the Doge of Venice, emphasising the telescope's potential application. He was offering the Doge 'a new contrivance of glasses, which render visible objects so close to the eye and represent them so distinctly that those that are distant, for example, nine miles appear as though they were only one mile distant. This is a thing of inestimable benefit for all transactions and undertakings, maritime or terrestrial, allowing us at sea to discover at a much greater distance than usual the hulls and sails of the enemy, so that for two hours or more we can detect him before he detects us.' Galileo continued with a request for security of tenure in his job, so that he could do the Doge even greater service. The tenure was granted, along with an increased salary, but it was made clear that there would be no further salary increase.

Galileo used a twenty-powered telescope to look at the Moon. He related the story in *The Starry Messenger*. He saw mountains on the Moon, which had not previously been seen. He produced drawings of the Moon's surface under different angles of lighting to show that the changing shadows could only be explained by the presence of mountains. He even estimated the heights of the mountains by observing how far the bright spots (the sunlit peaks) travelled into the darkness and using a little simple geometry. This discovery was sensational, because it implied that the Moon was a world, just like the Earth.

Galileo then turned his telescope on the planets. He saw that Saturn had 'handles'; these were later seen to be rings. He saw that Venus had phases, like the Moon. On 7 January 1610 he spotted three small fixed stars close to Jupiter, and forming a straight line with Jupiter. He watched as on successive nights the positions of the three small points of light changed positions, but always lay on the same straight line. He realised that he was looking at three moons orbiting Jupiter. This discovery caused even more of a furore than the mountains on the Moon. At the time it was believed that there were seven planets in the universe. Seven was a sacred number. The addition of three moons for Jupiter meant that there were now ten bodies. The moons also implied that, after all, not everything in the universe was going round the Earth.

This breakthrough meant that Copernicus's arguments were perhaps not so outrageously far from the truth, that maybe the Moon orbited the Earth, while the Earth orbited the Sun.

Galileo deployed his discoveries with care. He named his new moons after the Medici family, and applied for the position of court mathematician in Tuscany. He also sent the Medicis his latest telescope, with a magnification of twenty, so that they could observe the moons named after them. He also drew attention to the military uses of the telescope.

Then Galileo and other astronomers used their telescopes to discover sunspots, independently of one another. A new age in astronomy had begun, and all because of technology – the invention of the telescope and Galileo's determined efforts to improve its magnification. Not only were many individual discoveries made about the Moon and the Sun and the planets, but enough evidence was amassed to prove that Aristotle's model of the universe, with the Earth at its centre, was wrong. The improved telescope proved that Copernicus was right and that the Earth went round the Sun.

FREDERICK THE GREAT AND JOHANN SEBASTIAN BACH

(1747)

FREDERICK THE GREAT suffered acutely from some appalling childhood experiences at the hands of his half-insane father Frederick William I of Prussia. The young Frederick loved to play the flute, and his father despised him for it. He had to play in secret. There was nothing he loved more than to spend evenings at his mother's palace, where he would dress up in frilly French style and play duets with his sister Wilhelmina. His father by chance caught him doing this once and flew into a rage. It wasn't just the music – it was the Frenchness. Frederick's father hated everything French, which he dismissed as effeminate. Such was Prince Frederick's fear of his father's uncontrolled violence that in 1730, at the age of eighteen, he attempted to escape to England with his friend Hans von Katte. The king caught and imprisoned them, and then, in November, made Frederick watch as his friend was beheaded in front of him.

It was only when his father died, ten years later, that Frederick was free from fear and free to play the flute. The other thing Frederick loved was fighting. After only a few years on the throne, he had greatly expanded his kingdom by masterstrokes of deceitful diplomacy and military force. Voltaire described the extraordinary young king as 'a man who gives battle as readily as he writes an opera. He has written more books than any of his contemporary princes has sired bastards, and he has won more victories than he has written books.'

Frederick quickly became 'Frederick the Great' and his court at Potsdam became one of the most glittering and glamorous in Europe. He was keen to have men like Voltaire at his table and he drew around him celebrities from every branch of the arts and sciences.

In 1747 Frederick the Great had been king for seven years. One evening, as his musicians were gathering for an evening concert, one of his officials brought him the usual list of the day's arrivals in town. Frederick looked down the list and gasped. He announced, with some agitation and awe, 'Gentlemen, old Bach is here.'

By the standards of the day, Bach was indeed old. He was sixty-two and only three years away from his death. He had made the long and arduous journey from Leipzig – and it would be his last journey – under duress. He had been commanded to attend the great king's court. But it was not just the long journey that discomfited old Bach. The Prussian army, Frederick's Prussian army, had stormed through Leipzig little more than a year earlier, and Frederick himself was the sworn enemy of his own patron, the Elector of Saxony. Bach did not want to be there, and did not want to meet the hated invader of his city. But the social obligations of the time meant that he was unable to refuse the command.

In culture generally and in music in particular, Frederick represented all that was new and modish. Bach was seen as representing all that was ancient and reactionary in music; he was even referred to by the slighting nickname 'old periwig'. Bach was seen as backward-looking and he must have suspected that his music would be forgotten after his death. Frederick the Great stood for the modernising forces that would sweep him and his music away into oblivion. Frederick's taste in music was for the French style. He liked ornamented single lines of melody. Bach's taste was for the counterpoint of canons and fugues. They could not have been more different.

But Frederick was a celebrity-hunter, and he must have the famous Kapellmeister Bach at his court. Exhausted by his journey, Bach was almost certainly looking forward to relaxing that evening at his son

Carl's house. Frederick sent for him at once. When Bach arrived at the castle, Frederick greeted him and went at once to the piano and played a theme. Bach was to make it the subject of a fugue, and he duly improvised one on the spot. The court correspondent reported that 'Herr Bach found the theme propounded to him so exceedingly beautiful that he intends to set it down on paper as a regular fugue and have it engraved on copper.'

The press release diplomatically praised both host and guest. But the reality was that Frederick had required the exhausted Bach to improvise a three-part fugue on a very long and complex chromatic musical theme. In fact it looked as if it had been designed to make a fugue impossible to achieve. The twentieth century composer Schoenberg said that it had been cleverly contrived so that it 'did not admit one single canonic imitation'. The Royal Theme, as it became known, was designed to resist counterpoint.

Bach had been set up by the perverse Prussian king, who presumably wanted to see the old man stumble and fall. How many of Frederick's courtiers were party to this practical joke is not known, but the court correspondent reported that 'those present were seized with astonishment'. Frederick the Great was determined to best Bach, though, and asked him straight away if he could try again and this time make the theme into a fugue for six voices. He knew that this could not possibly be improvised. Indeed he probably knew that Bach had never attempted a six-part fugue for keyboard. Bach commented that not every theme was suitable for improvisation in six parts. He would have to work on it on paper and send it to the king later. Bach was very determined and stubborn by nature and it was not in his character to demur, to give in to the absurd challenge – he accepted it. He would write the impossible six-part fugue on the Royal Theme.

Frederick the Great had perhaps invited Bach to Potsdam just to humiliate him. When Schoenberg analysed the Royal Theme he came to the conclusion that it had been assembled with malice aforethought. Whoever wrote it was trying to make Bach fail. He also came to the conclusion that the trap was so well set that Frederick himself, who was not interested in counterpoint, could not have set it up on his own. Someone else must have written the Royal Theme for him. Schoenberg saw Bach's son Carl as the only possible author of the theme. He was the only person at or near Frederick's court with the knowledge of counterpoint that would allow him to write such a theme. Why Carl would do this to his own father can only be a matter for speculation. But we do know that Frederick the Great had a very aggressive and sadistic personality, like his father, and that he was determined to enjoy the pleasure of seeing his distinguished victim squirming in his well-prepared trap. Having visualised the scene and anticipated the outcome – the trouncing of old Bach – he may have applied enormous pressure on Carl to supply the impossible theme.

There is no way of knowing what threats Frederick the Great may have used against Carl. It is possible that Carl too wanted to see his father stumble. He respected and admired his father, but felt that his father did not respect or admire him in return. Carl may have wanted to 'get back' at his father. And maybe old Bach understood that this was where the Royal Theme had its origin.

Bach knew well enough that Frederick wanted him to fail, and his clever choice of title for the finished piece is revealing. He called the piece *Musikalisches Opfer*, a Musical Offering, but the German word 'opfer' means more than just 'offering': it means 'sacrifice' and 'victim' as well. Bach must have seen himself as the Musical Victim. There can be no doubting Frederick's sadism. Voltaire described it. If Frederick described you as his friend he really meant his slave. 'My dear friend means you mean less than nothing to me . . . Come to dinner means I feel like making fun of you tonight.'

After just two days at Frederick's court, Bach was dismissed without payment or reward. According to Carl, his father was thinking about nothing but the Royal Theme and its possibilities as he bumped along in his carriage on the way home. When he returned to Leipzig, Bach worked away continuously at the problem of the Royal Theme and –

astonishingly – finished the six-part fugue in a fortnight. He was determined to meet the challenge, and turn the joke back against Frederick. And to make his point devastatingly clear, Bach gave his sadistic taskmaster much more than a six-part fugue. He gave him a four-movement trio sonata and ten canons on the theme as well as the fugues that start and finish the piece.

He wrote it out, had it printed and sent it off to the Prussian king at once. Not only had he done it, he had done it quickly, and he had created one of the greatest pieces in the history of music. Frederick the Great did not appreciate the joke when it backfired on him. He sent Bach no payment, no reward, no prize, no present, no note of thanks. The king's mind had moved on. Sanssouci was finished. Voltaire would be arriving at any moment. For Frederick the Great, the old Bach joke was over. He gave his copy of the score away. But he never quite forgot the episode. Twenty-seven years later, when he was known as 'old Fritz', he reminisced about it to Baron von Swieten, and even sang for him the Royal Theme. Why did he remember it so well?

But for Bach, the experience was a solemn sacrifice, and the dedication he wrote on the score makes this clear. Not only is there the triple-meaning of 'opfer' as offering, sacrifice and victim, the work is 'consecrated' rather than dedicated. The point Bach was making is that music is serious and holy, a sacred art, and not the stuff of jokes.

SAMUEL TAYLOR COLERIDGE AND WILLIAM WORDSWORTH

(1797)

IT WAS A hot June day in 1797, and the twenty-four-year-old Coleridge was nearing the end of a forty-mile walk from his cottage in the Quantocks to meet the poet William Wordsworth. He stopped at a field gate and looked down across a cornfield. He saw a house, Racedown Lodge, and in its garden two small figures: William Wordsworth and his sister Dorothy. They looked up and saw him on the skyline. They remembered the moment for the rest of their lives. Instead of going on along the curving lane, the long way round to the house, Coleridge jumped over the gate and romped through the cornfield, leaping through the corn to reach his new friends as fast as possible.

Wordsworth and Coleridge had met briefly a few times before, but they knew they needed more time together. Coleridge intended to stay a few days at Racedown, but as the days passed both men felt they needed longer. The stay lasted over three weeks and they still could not bear to separate; there were so many things to discuss. It was agreed that William and Dorothy would move to the Quantocks. There they were to meet virtually every day to discuss the poems they were writing; the young poets were at the peak of their creativity, fizzing with ideas that they wanted to share. It was as if the two men had fallen in love, not a physical love but a love of minds and spirits.

This phase of intense, feverish dialogue lasted sixteen months, and generated the momentum that carried both men through the next ten years of their creative writing.

Wordsworth and Coleridge became a legendary partnership, even while they lived – two names that always went together, like Rodgers and Hammerstein, Lennon and McCartney or Britten and Pears. They shared a belief that poetry could rescue western civilisation. They and many other liberals were disappointed that the French Revolution had turned out badly; now it seemed – to them – that only poetry could change the world. Then Coleridge had a vision of a huge twenty-year project. It was to be a great poem completing the epic work of Milton, the greatest poem ever written, greater even than *Paradise Lost,* and it would contain the sum of human knowledge. It would bring with it, somehow, in its wake the redemption of mankind. But even in his delirious visionary state Coleridge knew he could not write it. He decided that Wordsworth could, and it says much about their relationship that Wordsworth agreed to try to realise his friend's dream and that Coleridge really believed that Wordsworth's genius was that comprehensive. Coleridge described him to a friend as 'The Giant Wordsworth'. Coleridge was wrong in one important particular. His friend was certainly a great and gifted poet, but he was a poet of feeling, not of thought. Wordsworth struggled on with this impossible project, which acquired the name *The Recluse*, for many years before giving up and the two men, perhaps inevitably because they had been so close, had a bitter falling out.

But the *annus mirabilis* that began at Racedown Lodge and continued at Alfoxden, the house in the Quantocks the Wordsworths rented, would never be forgotten. There, Wordsworth and Coleridge spent a lot of their time outside, wandering across the countryside with Dorothy and enjoying the landscape that would feature mightily in their poetry. Coleridge said they were 'three people, but one soul' and he was acutely aware of the unusual closeness that existed between William and his sister. He tried to share it by calling Dorothy 'our sister'. He called the brother 'Wordsworth', after the fashion of the day, and Wordsworth in turn called him 'Coleridge'. The use of surnames did not imply any distance between the two men at all – indeed Coleridge hated both of his forenames and didn't like people using them. Coleridge and Wordsworth admired each other's poetry, and both of them admired Dorothy's keen observant eye and her taste. Dorothy in turn enjoyed Coleridge's company enormously – she was dazzled, in fact – and was very happy to share her brother with him. She would always remember that first sight of him, hurtling down through the cornfield towards her. They were three people uniquely in tune with one another. Really, it was only Coleridge's wife who did not quite fit, and she was excluded from their rambles.

The locals naturally wondered who these strange people might be, and the war with France made them suspicious of anything or anyone unusual. Dr Daniel Lysons took it upon himself to write two letters about the Alfoxden set to the Duke of Portland, the Home Secretary. Lysons said, 'the master of the house has no wife with him, but only a woman who passes for his Sister.' Their sinister activities included excursions, sometimes at night, on which they carried camp-stools and books in which they entered observations. They showed a suspicious level of interest in a river. The clinching details were that they spoke in an unusual accent and spent their Sundays washing and mending clothes. Portland sent an agent down to Alfoxden to investigate. Coleridge was enormously amused when he became aware that his conversations with Wordsworth were being systematically eavesdropped and written down. The agent decided that the Alfoxden gang was not a group of French spies after all, but 'a set of violent Democrats'. The authorities nevertheless decided that these 'rascals' were probably not worth pursuing, but damage had been done, as the local people had become aware of the official interest in Alfoxden and did not want the Wordsworths and their friends there any more. The lease was not renewed.

It was at about this time that Coleridge wrote *Kubla Khan*. He composed it in a state of intoxication, if 'composed' is the right word.

Hazlitt described it as a piece of music. Coleridge thought of it as 'a vision in a dream'. Lamb described the magical effect of it when Coleridge recited it, but feared that if it were read on the printed page it might lose its magic. It was in fact not to be published for twenty years. Coleridge tells us some of the circumstances in which it was written. 'In the summer of the year 1797, the Author, then in ill health, had retired to a lonely farmhouse between Porlock and Lynton.' The poem came to him 'in a sort of Reverie brought on by two grains of Opium, taken to check a dysentery.' He 'continued for about three hours in a profound sleep, during which he had the most vivid confidence that he could not have composed less than from two to three hundred lines; if that indeed can be called composition in which all the images rose up before him as things, without any sensation of consciousness or effort.' When he woke up, Coleridge took a pen and started writing down the lines that were in his mind, until he was famously interrupted 'by a person on business from Porlock', who held him up for over an hour. By the time the unwelcome visitor had gone he found the remaining lines had vanished from his mind, leaving him with only a dim memory of the general vision. He had only fifty-four lines down on paper, but what lines they were! In his sober state, Coleridge was unable ever to complete the poem and *Kubla Khan* remains a wonderful and tantalising fragment.

Kubla Khan was an unusual poem in that it was not the result of any collaboration with Wordsworth. It was purely and simply the result of an encounter with opium.

Nearly all the poems written by Wordsworth and Coleridge at this time were written under the eye of the other poet. Sometimes awareness of the other poet is obvious. In *Tintern Abbey*, Wordsworth borrows a phrase from one of Coleridge's poems, but often the dialogue between the two men was too subtle for any outsider to see. They drew material from the same commonplace books and both used Dorothy's journal, in which she wrote down anything that any of the three friends had noticed. Wordsworth reminisced in later life how he had written

'We are Seven while walking at Alfoxden. When it was all but finished, I came in and recited it to Mr Coleridge and my Sister, and said, "A prefatory stanza must be added, and I should sit down to our little tea-meal with greater pleasure if my task was finished." I mentioned in substance what I wished to be expressed, and Coleridge immediately threw off the stanza.' Then in his own poem *Christabel,* Coleridge included a line from this stanza, a quote from his own contribution to Wordsworth's poem.

They set off on a walk westwards along the West Country coast, hoping to write a poem for the *Monthly Magazine* to pay for it. Coleridge was given to understand that they might earn £5 in this way, and then a friend told him a story about a ghost ship that had appeared in a dream. Coleridge was generally scornful of the ghost stories that were popular at the time, but he needed the money, so a compromise had to be made. Wordsworth meanwhile had been reading George Shelvocke's *Voyage round the World,* which supplied lots of ideas for images and incidents, including the killing of the albatross. Characteristically, Wordsworth and Coleridge started off composing *The Rime of the Ancient Mariner* together, but Wordsworth soon found that their styles did not mesh well. Wordsworth dropped out, but Coleridge dashed ahead with it and within a week he had written half of the poem.

The *Rime of the Ancient Mariner* was an odd creation. It was a haunting, chilling tale, and yet it had its beginning in a very jolly and happy walking party. It was also full of odd archaic expressions, which recalled the forged archaic poems of Thomas Chatterton and 'Ossian' Macpherson. The *Rime* was not a forgery, as Coleridge owned up to being its author, but it has the flavour of a tale from antiquity. The poem had also outgrown its original intention. It was now, when finished, too substantial a piece to fritter away on the *Monthly Magazine.* It had changed from a cheap ghost story into an allegory of human guilt and suffering, of the origin of evil. As Wordsworth said, 'it grew and grew until it became too important for our first object. . . We began to talk of a Volume.' And so was born the idea of a jointly written book of lyrical

411

ballads. It would contain poems featuring the supernatural and poems about everyday life. Coleridge undertook the negotiations with Cottle the publisher. Wordsworth stayed in the background; he knew he was no businessman, and Coleridge in any case knew Cottle already.

Hazlett went to stay with Coleridge at Nether Stowey, walking the 150 miles from Shropshire to Somerset. Hazlett was a great admirer of Coleridge and was happy to walk with him to see Alfoxden and read Wordsworth's poems. Then they walked back to Nether Stowey, discussing Wordsworth as they went. Wordsworth himself arrived at Coleridge's cottage the next day, on his way back from Bristol. Hazlitt was surprised how 'gaunt and Don Quixote-like' Wordsworth looked. 'He was quaintly dressed in a brown fustian jacket and striped pantaloons. There was something of a roll, a lounge in his gait. There was a severe, worn pressure of thought about his temples, a fire in his eye, an intense, high, narrow forehead and a convulsive inclination to laughter about the mouth, a good deal at variance with the solemn, stately expression of the rest of his face.' They walked to Alfoxden the following day, where Wordsworth read them his poem *Peter Bell* outside. Hazlitt commented on 'a chant in the recitation both of Coleridge and Wordsworth, which acts as a spell upon the hearer, and disarms the judgment. Coleridge's manner is more full, animated and varied; Wordsworth's more equable, sustained and internal. The one might be termed more dramatic, the other more lyrical.'

Wordsworth thought Hazlitt was too intellectual, 'too attached to modern books of moral philosophy.' He dramatised their differences in poetry. In *The Tables Turned*, Wordsworth wrote,

> *One impulse from a vernal wood*
> *May teach you more of man,*
> *Of moral evil and of good,*
> *Than all the sages can.*

Sweet is the lore which Nature brings;
Our meddling intellect
Misshapes the beauteous forms of things;
- We murder to dissect.

Enough of science and of art;
Close up those barren leaves;
Come forth, and bring with you a heart
That watches and receives.

Out of that encounter with the young Hazlitt came one of the simplest and most powerful statements of English Romanticism. This was what it was all about – and it sprang almost casually out of the meeting with Hazlitt. After that, the poems were gathered together and published as *Lyrical Ballads*. Slightly more than half of the volume is by Wordsworth, though as Coleridge pointed out that did not mean that Wordsworth did more than half of the work. The publication marked the culmination of an amazing year of friendship. Wordsworth picked up from Coleridge a new type of poem with an intimate conversational autobiographical style. This borrowing yielded the piece that is perhaps Wordsworth's greatest poem, *Lines Written Above Tintern Abbey*. In it, Wordsworth took Coleridge's style to express Coleridge's idea, and making both his own. It was an extraordinary assimilation, a dovetailing of two minds and spirits.

. . . I am still
A lover of the meadows and the woods,
And mountains; and of all that we behold
From this green earth; of all the mighty world
Of eye and ear, both what they half create,
And what perceive; well pleased to recognise
In nature and the language of the sense,

413

The anchor of my purest thoughts, the nurse,
The guide, the guardian of my heart, and soul
Of all my moral being.

BEETHOVEN AND NAPOLEON

(1804)

MOST OF US know the music of Beethoven so well that we often forget that he was an intensely political composer. In a way that is almost unique in Western music, he committed the music he composed to the advancement of noble political causes. He was a campaigner – through music – for liberty and justice, for the ultimate cause underlying the French Revolution, the brotherhood of man.

Beethoven found that he wanted to use music in this way early on in his career. When he was still in Bonn, the city where he was born in 1770, he wrote a cantata that paid tribute to the reforms of Joseph II. Much later he wrote choral extravaganzas to celebrate the Congress of Vienna; although these works are now considered to be musically mediocre, at the time they swept Beethoven to an unsurpassed pinnacle of public adulation. Then, at the end of his career, when he was in Vienna, he wrote his *Ninth Symphony*, with its famous choral finale. As a hymn to universal brotherhood, this *Ode to Joy* is a profoundly political statement, and it has become the anthem of the European Union.

In the intervening years came works that were a direct response to the career of Napoleon – the *Third Symphony* and the opera *Fidelio*, Beethoven's only opera. He also composed assorted patriotic songs and marches, as well as incidental music to highly political plays such as Egmont. Beethoven's output as a composer was to some extent an expression of his utopian ideals, and to a great extent a personal response to the political events of his time. And it was a time of

415

cataclysm. Beethoven was a youth of eighteen when the Bastille fell. Then for a quarter of a century the armies of Napoleon and his allies and adversaries surged backwards and forwards across Europe, locked in mighty battles. Republics came and went. Napoleon himself rose and fell, returned and fell again for ever. The Holy Roman Empire disappeared and a new Europe emerged. All this Beethoven witnessed, and he himself was directly involved when the French twice laid siege to Vienna. This was Beethoven's personal encounter with the continent-wide cataclysm and with Napoleon, whose boundless ambition lay behind it.

Beethoven and Napoleon had much in common. They were men of almost exactly the same age, Napoleon born in 1769, Beethoven in 1770. They both had enormous drive and ambition. They both had humble family origins and the determination to rise far above those origins. Napoleon was winning military campaigns in Italy and Egypt, annexing territories, while Beethoven was taking the concert halls and recital rooms of Europe by storm, annexing all the genres of contemporary music. Both were determined conquerors in their fields. Napoleon captured Beethoven's imagination to the extent that Beethoven identified with Napoleon, and it is not hard to hear an almost military aggression in some of Beethoven's music. There were elements of hero worship, elements of competition too. In the end Beethoven came to hate and demonise his alter ego, but at first he had unlimited admiration for the distant spectacle of Napoleon's sweeping conquests.

Beethoven was initially a great admirer of Napoleon, who seemed to represent the ultimate fulfilment of the ideals of the French Revolution. In 1798, General Bernadotte, who was French ambassador to Austria, suggested to Beethoven that he might write a symphony in honour of Napoleon, and Beethoven readily agreed to this. In particular, Beethoven was impressed by Napoleon as a destroyer of monarchy in Europe. He was profoundly shocked when in May 1804 Napoleon made himself emperor; it was a betrayal of everything Napoleon had seemed to stand for, and a betrayal of the principles of the French

Revolution. He had composed his *Third Symphony* as a tribute to Napoleon and wrote at the head of it his dedication to the great man. Disgusted by the news, he strode to the table where the finished score lay, took a knife to the title-page and scratched out the name of Bonaparte so aggressively that he made a hole in the paper. After striking out the original dedication, he (some time afterwards) changed the symphony's title to *Sinfonia eroica, composta per festeggiare il sovvenire d'un grand'uomo* – Heroic symphony, composed to celebrate the memory of a great man. It was a profound disappointment.

Beethoven's assistant Ferdinand Ries wrote, 'In writing this symphony Beethoven had been thinking of Bonaparte, but Bonaparte while he was First Consul. At that time Beethoven had the highest regard for him and compared him to the greatest consuls of ancient Rome. Not only I, but many of Beethoven's closer friends, saw this symphony on his table, with the word 'Bonaparte' inscribed at the very top of the title page and 'Ludwig van Beethoven' at the very bottom. I was the first to tell him the news that Bonaparte had declared himself emperor, whereupon he broke into a rage and exclaimed, 'So he is no more than a common mortal! Now he will tread under foot all the rights of man, indulge only his ambition, now he will think himself superior to all men, become a tyrant!'

But Beethoven was evidently still torn between admiration and disgust. In the summer of 1804 he was writing to his publisher and telling him that 'the title of the symphony is really *Bonaparte.*' The new title, '*Heroic Symphony*' or as we now call it '*Eroica*', was not actually written down until the orchestral parts were published in October 1806. By 1805 it had become clear that the ideals of the Revolution had been watered down. The French invasion of Austria could not be presented as a liberation; it was a naked war of imperialist conquest and reaction. Beethoven could no longer have any doubts about Napoleon's true nature. He was a conqueror and an oppressor.

When he heard of Napoleon's death in 1821, he revealingly said, 'I wrote the music for this sad event seventeen years ago.' He was referring to the noble slow movement of the *Eroica Symphony*, which sounds like a funeral march – a remarkably powerful piece that towards the end breaks apart under the weight of its own emotion.

The *Eroica* was first performed privately in the summer of 1804 for his patron Prince Lobkowitz. It was first performed publicly at the Theater an der Wien in Vienna on 7 April 1805. The near-simultaneity of the symphony and the coronation (which took place in December 1804) is another parallel between the two great lives of Beethoven and Napoleon. At the same moment, the leader and the composer kicked away the ladder of the past behind them as they claimed absolute power on their own uncompromising terms. Napoleon was not a French Revolutionary. Both he and Beethoven were just a few years too young to have been part of that. Instead they belonged to the post-Revolution generation, products of a revolutionary age when the moulds of tradition and custom had been smashed, and anything seemed to be possible. All that was needed was energy, will, vision, determination. Napoleon's empire was a new departure, a step-change in the revolution. Beethoven's *Eroica* similarly marks a new departure in music. It represents the culmination of classical music and the birth of Romantic music.

Beethoven borrowed music for the final movement of the *Eroica Symphony* from the score of his ballet *The Creatures of Prometheus*. It was no coincidence that Beethoven was fascinated by the Prometheus myth, the story of the hero who stole fire from the gods. It was an idea he returned to again and again, and it takes no leap of imagination to see that Beethoven identified with Prometheus and saw both himself and Napoleon as Promethean. And he was right: they were indeed Promethean in their grasp and their daring.

Napoleon established the most efficient secret police service ever seen in Europe up until that time. Beethoven rightly saw this as a sign of an oppressive regime. A high point at the opening of the French Revolution had been the storming of the Bastille, the great symbol of the old régime's oppression and a place where important political prisoners had been incarcerated. The Bastille had been symbolically demolished stone by stone until there was not a trace of it left; it was attacked rather in the spirit in which Berliners attacked the Berlin Wall in 1989. And yet, under the new regime, Napoleon established at Vincennes, in a fortress that architecturally bore an uncanny resemblance to the Bastille, his own symbol of oppression. Vincennes was used by Napoleon to imprison and execute his political prisoners. Europe was no further forward, after all.

Beethoven's response to this hugely disappointing development – or non-development – was the composition of *Fidelio*, with its profoundly moving Prisoners' Chorus, and the theme of rescue from tyranny, of determination to achieve the ideal in the face of oppression.

The heroine of *Fidelio* is Leonore. Her husband, the Spanish state official Florestan, has been missing for two years. His friends, including the Minister of State Don Fernando, believe he has been murdered by his political enemies. But Leonore is determined to find him. Disguised as a young man called Fidelio, she manages to get inside the prison where she believes he is being held. The gaoler Rocco takes Fidelio on as an assistant and promises him a tour of the dungeons. The prison governor, Don Pizarro, learns that the Minister of State is about to arrive to inspect the prison. He orders a watch to be kept on the road; a trumpet is to sound when the Minister arrives. Pizarro needs to eliminate Florestan and cover all trace of the wrongful imprisonment before Don Fernando enters.

Fidelio persuades Rocco to let the prisoners take some air, with the idea of identifying Florestan, but he is not among the prisoners. The scene where the prisoners come out of their cells and into the light is one of the great moments in Romantic art. The Prisoners' Chorus, *O welche lust*, is one of the most moving pieces Beethoven wrote, and it underlines Beethoven's simple message – all men should be free. Then, in scenes halfway between Romanticism and Gothic horror, we see Florestan languishing in solitary confinement in his dungeon and collapsing in despair, and Fidelio helping Rocco to dig Florestan's grave.

Pizarro enters the dungeon, prepared to kill Florestan. Fidelio rushes forward to protect him. Pizarro is so staggered that he cannot act and Leonore threatens him with a pistol. Then the trumpet sounds; Don Fernando is outside and Florestan is safe. Don Fernando wants to throw Pizarro into Florestan's dungeon, but Leonore and Florestan plead for mercy to be shown. Virtue and determination overcome tyranny.

Beethoven set the prison in Spain, near Seville, but the prison with its secret prisoner could have been in France or anywhere else in Napoleon's Europe. The wicked governor was Spanish, but could as easily have been a Frenchman: the Frenchman, in fact. Pizarro had a superior, the Minister Don Fernando. Napoleon had no superior – unless Beethoven had God in mind. However cunningly Beethoven thought he was covering his tracks, there is no doubt that *Fidelio* was an extremely subversive and courageous statement against the Napoleonic régime. Beethoven was an international celebrity, and this may have provided him with a certain level of immunity from repercussion, but he must have been aware that he was taking a risk.

Fidelio was first produced in a version in three acts in the Theater an der Wien in November 1805 (a month after the spectacular British naval victory at Trafalgar). The three performances were not rapturously received: Vienna was occupied by the French army and most of the audience consisted of French army officers. They were unlikely to approve of Beethoven's sentiments and were baffled by the opera – they could not believe what they were seeing and hearing. But the poor initial reception led to Beethoven's friends persuading him to revise the score significantly, shortening it, recasting it in two acts and providing a new overture.

The new version was performed in March and April 1806, when it got a warmer response. He revised it again for performance in May 1814. Getting *Fidelio* 'right' gave Beethoven a great deal of trouble. The seventeen-year-old composer Franz Schubert saw this 1814 production; he sold his school textbooks to buy a ticket. The opera was conducted by Beethoven himself, but he was so deaf that by now he had to have an assistant, Michael Umlauf, who was doing the real job of conducting. It was Umlauf who conducted the première of the *Ninth Symphony* at Beethoven's side. The role of the villainous prison governor Pizarro was sung by Johann Vogl, who would one day become an important interpreter of Schubert's music.

Pizarro was the oppressor who oversaw the prison where the action of *Fidelio* took place. The prison might be the Bastille, it might be Vincennes – it might be the Europe suffering under the ancient régime or Napoleon's tyrannical rule. It is not too fanciful to see Pizarro as Napoleon himself, as demonised by the mature Beethoven. The fact that Beethoven could not leave *Fidelio* alone, but kept returning to it suggests that it had a profound psychological importance to him.

After Napoleon's final defeat at Waterloo and his humiliating exile to St Helena, Beethoven lived on and wrote on for another twelve years in a post-Napoleonic Europe. There has over the decades been a great deal of comment about Beethoven's creative response to Napoleon, but little has been said about Beethoven's response – or otherwise – after the exile. In a way, Beethoven was an exile in his own mind because of his deafness, which was increasing to totality. The post-Napoleonic world in which he lived was soundless. Even so, his music went on conquering the hearts and minds of his listeners in the *Missa Solemnis* and the *Ninth Symphony*. The late quartets seem so intensely personal and abstracted that it appears Beethoven had withdrawn from the public life of politics and turned his back on the outside world, perhaps disillusioned by the failure of the Enlightenment and the Revolution, disillusioned by the failure of society as a whole to act in a positive and constructive way. He retreated to the personal.

It would have been unsurprising for Beethoven to turn his back on the enfeebled and decadent yet repressive Europe of Metternich and the waltz – the Europe of Rossini. It may be so, but all the elements of Beethoven's late style were in place before 1815, so it cannot be wholly the political situation that made him compose in the way that he did. It is far more likely that the subjective and introspective tone of much of his late work is to be explained by the devastatingly isolating effects of his deafness. He was a man cruelly cut off from the sound of his own music. Like Napoleon stranded among hostile strangers on a lonely island in the South Atlantic, Beethoven was stranded inside his own head, his imagination thrashing about amid a tangle of conservative and revolutionary forces, full of conflict and paradox.

Napoleon died a premature death on St Helena in 1821, of arsenic poisoning. Beethoven survived his former hero by only six years, dying a premature death in 1827 – of lead poisoning.

BENJAMIN HAYDON'S
'IMMORTAL DINNER'

(1817)

BENJAMIN HAYDON WAS a mediocre 19th century English painter who was nevertheless extremely ambitious and convinced of his own genius; he believed God was at his side. Though often gripped by poverty, he was a great striver and self-promoter. There is a pathos about the gap between his actual achievement as an artist and his great aspirations. But Haydon also reached out and befriended a great many writers of his day, bringing them together and exposing them to new ideas and experiences. Not only did he meet them and have high-minded conversations with them about a wide range of issues – he wrote in his diaries what they said and did.

He knew John Keats, Charles Lamb, William Wordsworth and Elizabeth Barrett Browning. It was to Elizabeth Barrett Browning that he entrusted his writings after his death, which came as a despairing suicide; in 1846 he shot himself in his studio. Into his diaries he poured his frustrations at his lack of success as a painter. Haydon was perhaps a manic-depressive, and his phases of exaltation give us enthusiastic reflections on the nature of genius, both his own and other people's. During a phase of success, he said, 'I have been like a man with air balloons under his armpits and ether in his soul.' He also reflects with the same exaltation on his great social triumphs. His description of what he described as 'the Immortal Dinner' was the greatest of these triumphs. 'Wordsworth was in town,' he wrote, 'and as Keats wished to know him I made up a party.'

This was a dinner party that he hosted on 28 December 1817 at his rented home near Regent's Park. He invited three of his famous friends for the afternoon and evening and his eye for character and detail makes his description of the occasion lively and vivid. His writing has often been praised as better than his painting, though there is no denying that his portrait of the older Wordsworth, brooding, arms folded, under a stormy sky, is a very fine character study indeed, and totally convincing. So it was that on a freezing December afternoon the thirty-one-year-old Benjamin Haydon sat waiting for his guests to arrive, eager for tongues to be loosened by claret, for the cut and thrust of brilliant discourse, and for the recitation of brand-new poetry that would become landmarks of literature. He was not to be disappointed.

One of his guests was the rising young poet John Keats. Just twenty-two, Keats was still finding his voice, and as part of that quest he had just completed his long poem *Endymion*. Haydon had taken Keats to see the Elgin Marbles, newly arrived in London from Athens. That experience of seeing the Elgin Marbles was to find its way into Keats's *Ode on a Grecian Urn*.

The dinner party started at three o'clock in Haydon's spacious galleried painting room at the back of his house. He had set up his table directly under the huge unfinished painting of *Christ's Entry into Jerusalem*. The fire in the room lit up the faces in the painting, which included those of Keats, Wordsworth, Hazlitt and Voltaire. Under the picture sat the living presences of Keats and Wordsworth (not yet immortal). The other dinner guests were Tom Monkhouse and Charles Lamb.

Tom Monkhouse was a merchant in the City, a well-read man and the hospitable friend of the other diners.

Lamb the brilliant essayist was forty-two. Behind his light-hearted wit was a sad private life. In a bout of insanity in 1796, his sister Mary had stabbed their mother to death. The authorities accepted Charles's assurances that he would look after Mary from that time on – he was her formal guardian – and he had to devote almost all of his time to caring for her. Charles had fallen in love, but he had been unable to marry because of his responsibility towards his sister. He lived with his sister but her mental state meant that he was in effect living alone. His was a life blighted by duty, poverty and by the long shadow of an unspeakable family tragedy. In 1818, shortly after Haydon's dinner, he collected all his verse and essays into two volumes as the *Works of Charles Lamb*. This gained him some notice, and he was invited onto the staff of the *London Magazine,* which brought him some income at last.

Wordsworth was forty-seven. He was no longer the visionary young firebrand. He had become staid, reactionary, rather dull. But he was the 'big name' at Haydon's party, of that there was no question.

Wordsworth had had an unpleasant encounter with Coleridge the previous day, and welcomed the relaxed, friendly and unchallenging atmosphere of Haydon's dinner; he was unusually relaxed and in very good humour. It was hard not to be in good humour with Haydon around, whose laughs, as Leigh Hunt described, 'sound like the trumpets of Jericho and threaten to have the same effect'.

As the dinner party got under way, the discussion revolved round Homer, Shakespeare, Milton and Virgil. Wordsworth quoted from Milton, 'with an intonation like the funeral bell of St Pauls & the music of Handel mingled'. It was very high-minded and serious stuff.

But then, after a drink or two, Charles Lamb started to get tipsy and deflated Wordsworth a little, taking advantage of their familiarity as old friends. He was able to take the conversation away from these lofty themes by calling him 'a rascally Lake poet'. He also criticised Wordsworth for writing in *The Excursion* that a novel by Voltaire was 'the dull product of a scoffer's pen'. Others at the table defended Wordsworth, agreeing with him that Voltaire could be dull. Lamb relented facetiously: 'Well, let us drink his health. Here's Voltaire, the Messiah of the French nation, and a very fit one.' Looking at the picture hanging above the table, Lamb gleefully attacked Haydon for putting in Newton, who was 'a Fellow who believed nothing unless it was as clear as the three sides of a triangle.'

At this, John Keats was brought into the conversation. Lamb had been to the theatre in Drury Lane to see the great actor Edmund Kean on the stage. He had also read Keats's review of Kean's performances in Riches, an adaptation of Massinger's *City Madam*, and *Richard III* – Keats's first shot at drama criticism. Keats felt a powerful empathy with Edmund Kean, who was small and intensely dynamic like himself. He had seen Kean as Richard III, Hamlet, Macbeth and Othello, and was enthusiastic about all of his roles. Keats saw Kean as demonstrating that principle of deep inner empathy with his subject which Keats too felt when writing poetry. Keats called it 'negative capability'.

Lamb and Keats joined in applying the image of the rainbow to science, agreeing that Newton 'had destroyed all the poetry of the rainbow by reducing it to a prism'. They toasted Newton's health and confusion to mathematics. This met with Wordsworth's approval, as he disapproved of the 'meddling intellect' of scientists; he too had written about rainbows. In fact fifteen years before that he had written,

> *My heart leaps up when I behold*
> *A rainbow in the sky:*
> *So was it when my life began;*
> *So is it now I am a man;*
> *So be it when I shall grow old,*
> *Or let me die!*

And just two years after the Immortal Dinner Keats would write, in *Lamia*:

> *Philosophy will clip an Angel's wings,*
> *Conquer all mysteries by rule and line,*
> *Empty the haunted air, and gnomed mine –*
> *Unweave a rainbow. . .*

But neither Keats nor Wordsworth actually used the word 'scientist'; that was because the word was not invented until 1833 – and by Coleridge, of all people.

Later on, Keats gave a recitation of part of his poem *Endymion*. They moved from the table in the painting room into the front drawing room, where they were to take tea with some more visitors. These included the deaf engraver, John Landseer, and Joseph Ritchie, a young surgeon whom John Keats's brother Tom had met. Ritchie was going off as an explorer to find a new route to the River Niger in Africa. Haydon introduced Ritchie as 'a gentleman going to Africa'. Lamb was by this stage dozing off under the effect of the drink, but woke up with a start. 'Who is the gentleman we are going to lose?' This turned out to be prophetic, as two of those at the table would die shortly of tuberculosis. Ritchie took a liking to Keats, and later spoke of him as likely to be the guiding light of poetry in the future. Keats made Ritchie promise to take a copy of *Endymion* to the Sahara and hurl it into the middle of the desert for him.

It seemed as if Benjamin Haydon had set up this gathering with some sort of climax in mind. When it came it turned out to be like a scene from a farce. Earlier in the day, the deputy comptroller of the Stamp Office, a man called John Kingston, called on Haydon and asked if he might come in the evening. For the last four years, Wordsworth had been taking a salary as a civil servant. With a wife and family to support, Wordsworth needed a reliable income, so he had accepted the position of Distributor of Stamps for Westmorland, Whitehaven and part of Cumberland. Wordsworth had never met Kingston, even though Kingston was his immediate superior in the London office. Wordsworth was therefore very keen not to upset Mr Kingston. Haydon's account continues:

When we retired to tea we found the comptroller. In introducing him to Wordsworth I forgot to say who he was. After a little while the comptroller said to Wordsworth, 'Don't you think, sir, Milton was a great genius?' Keats looked at me, Wordsworth looked at the comptroller. Lamb who was dozing by the fire turned round and said, 'Pray, sir, did you say Milton was a great genius?' 'No, sir: I asked Mr

Wordsworth if he were not.' 'Oh,' said Lamb, 'then you are a silly fellow.' 'Charles! My dear Charles!' said Wordsworth; but Lamb perfectly innocent of the confusion he had created, was off again by the fire.

After an awful pause the comptroller said, 'Don't you think Newton was a great genius?' I could not stand it any longer. Keats put his head into my books. Ritchie squeezed in a laugh. Wordsworth seemed [to be] asking himself, 'Who is this?' Lamb got up and taking a candle said, 'Sir, will you allow me to look at your phrenological development?' He then turned his back on the poor man, and at every question of the comptroller, he chanted –

> *'Diddle diddle dumpling, my son John*
> *Went to bed with his breeches on.'*

[Mr Kingston], finding Wordsworth did not know who he was, said in a spasmodic and half-chuckling anticipation of assured victory, 'I have the honour of some correspondence with you, Mr Wordsworth.' 'With me, sir?' said Wordsworth, 'not that I remember.' 'Don't you, sir? I am comptroller of stamps.' There was a deadly silence – the comptroller evidently thinking that was enough. While we were waiting for Lamb's reply, Lamb sung out . . .

> *'Hey diddle diddle*
> *The cat and the fiddle.'*
> *'My dear Charles!' said Wordsworth –*
> *'Diddle diddle dumpling, my son John.'*

. . . chanted Lamb, and then rising exclaimed, 'Do let me have another look at that gentleman's organs.' Keats and I hurried Lamb into the painting room, shut the door and gave way to inextinguishable laughter. Monkhouse followed and tried to get Lamb away. We went back but the comptroller was irreconcilable. We soothed and smiled

and asked him to supper. He stayed though his dignity was sorely affected. We parted all in good humour and no ill effects followed.

All the while, until Monkhouse succeeded, we could hear Lamb struggling in the painting room, and calling at intervals, 'Who is that fellow? Allow me to see his organs once more.

Haydon was concerned about Wordsworth's financial dependence on such a man as Kingston; 'I felt pain at the slavery of office.'

Keats was less sensitive, at first. He accepted an invitation from Kingston to meet Wordsworth at his, Kingston's, house the following Saturday. Later he cancelled, as he realised he was expected elsewhere. But he did meet Wordsworth again, seemingly by chance, when the two of them were walking in the fog on Hampstead Heath on New Year's Eve – a strange encounter indeed! Keats was keen to see more of Wordsworth, and arranged to call round at Wordsworth's house just before Wordsworth went off to dine with Kingston on Saturday 3 January 1818.

Keats was rather taken aback when he found Wordsworth all dressed up in a frilled shirt front, stiff collar, knee breeches and silk stockings – looking like a court official. He felt that Wordsworth was stooping too low in trying to ingratiate himself with the likes of Kingston. It was not how a great poet should have to behave, he thought, but then Keats was still very young, unworldly and idealistic. Wordsworth for his part was impressed by Keats. In a couple of years' time he would write a letter to Keats expressing his admiration for the *Ode on a Grecian Urn*. He even paid Keats the exceptional compliment of borrowing for a sonnet of his own from Keats's *Ode to a Nightingale*. The ripples from the meeting at Haydon's Immortal Dinner spread wider and wider.

JOSEPH NIÉPCE AND LOUIS DAGUERRE

(1828)

JOSEPH NIÉPCE (1765–1833) started experimenting with permanently fixing optical images as early as 1793. In some of his early experiments, undertaken while the French Revolution was under way, he succeeded in making images, but because they were produced by light continuing exposure to light made them fade. A man of private means, Niépce was also interested in the process of lithography and he worked to develop this process. As he was unable to draw, he depended on his artistic son to draw the images for him. In 1814, the son was conscripted into the army – to fight at the Battle of Waterloo, as it turned out – and Niépce had to manage without him. This meant that he had to look for an alternative way to create images, and he resumed his earlier work on images generated by natural light.

In May 1816, Niépce created his first image of nature, a view out of a window. It was a negative and the image disappeared as continued exposure to light turned the whole of the coated paper black. Niépce called these images 'retinas'. In 1817 he experimented with resin from a conifer. He failed to understand that it was only ultra-violet rays that activated the resin and that they were filtered out by the camera obscura lens, so the technique would not work inside the camera obscura.

The phrase camera obscura means 'dark chamber', which is what it was. It could be a fixed room in a tower, or a portable structure something like a gipsy caravan. Light entered the camera obscura through a tiny hole, and this light was focused through a lens onto a table or onto the wall. There, the projected image of the landscape might be traced, in perfect perspective, and then used by an artist as a basis for a painting or a lithograph.

Then in 1818 Niépce became distracted by another obsession – the bicycle. He developed his own version of the dandy-horse, an ancestor of the bicycle without pedals and became the talk of the neighbourhood as he scooted around on it.

With diversions of this kind, it is not surprising that it took Niépce some years, but he succeeded in producing semi-permanent images by a process he called heliography, meaning 'sun writing'. Until recently the earliest of Niépce's images to have come to light was a picture of a building, a tree and a barn with a sunlit roof, seen from an open window. It was the view across the courtyard of his own house, and it was apparently made in June or July 1826. It is believed that he made the first long-lasting photographic images as early as 1824, when Beethoven was still alive.

Full of excitement, Niépce crossed the Channel and tried to promote his invention by way of the Royal Society, an institution which commanded wide respect. But Niépce wanted to retain the secret of his technique and the Royal Society declined to publicise a discovery if the discoverer was deliberately withholding key information about it. In frustration, Niépce went back to France.

While Niépce was at work, so too was another Frenchman, Louis Daguerre. He had used the camera obscura in the course of his experimenting, and he had also tried out different methods of fixing the light-created images. In particular, he used the tendency for silver salts to darken on exposure to sunlight. When he heard about Niépce's success, he approached him and suggested that they work together. Niépce had reached an impasse and so agreed to a collaboration

Their working partnership began in 1829 and continued until Niépce died, aged sixty-nine, only four years later. Some of Niépce's heliograph pictures have survived, including the barn picture from 1826. Given the eight-hour exposure, and the significant movement of the sun across the sky in that time, the image is surprisingly intelligible. Another photograph by him has come to light. This is an image of an engraving of a boy leading a horse, made in 1825, and recently sold at auction. Niépce did not have a steady enough hand to trace the images projects onto a table by a camera obscura, a popular technique of the time, so he looked for a method to capture images permanently and directly onto paper or metal. He experimented with silver chloride, which darkens on exposure to light. Then he switched to using bitumen and it was this that produced the first successful photographic images. The bitumen was dissolved in lavender oil, a solvent, and coated a sheet of pewter with this light-sensitive mixture. He put the sheet of coated metal inside the camera obscura, removing it after eight hours and washing it with lavender oil to remove the unexposed bitumen. He had in effect turned the camera obscura, until then an aid for drawing landscapes, into a true camera.

By 1829, Niépce had realised that he had taken the process as far as he could, on his own. Then the collaboration with Daguerre began. Together they developed the technique, still using lavender oil, until Niépce died in 1833. After that, Daguerre continued alone. Eventually he developed a technique that was significantly different. He called the new images that he was producing Daguerrotypes. He had more success than Niépce in interesting the authorities in his invention. He managed to persuade the French government to buy his invention for France, for an annual pension of 6,000 francs paid to him, Daguerre, and a pension of 4,000 francs paid to Niépce's heirs. It was an honourable settlement, though Niépce's son did not think so. He felt that Daguerre had gained enormous benefit from the many years of research put in by his father. Louis Daguerre certainly took the limelight as far as his contemporaries were concerned, but the pioneering work and the achievement of Joseph Niépce are well recognised now.

The invention that sprang out of the encounter between Niépce and Daguerre had far-reaching effects. By the end of the nineteenth century, photography was in regular use for the accurate recording of the appearance of people and places, and this released painters from the need to produce likenesses. Photography allows us to see exactly what

Michael Faraday and Abraham Lincoln looked like. The revolutionary art movements of the early twentieth century – expressionism, futurism and cubism – were in a sense permitted by photography. Photography also showed how unglamorous the American Civil War and the Crimean War really were; it made it harder for politicians to deceive people about the nature of war.

JOHN MILLAIS AND WILLIAM HOLMAN HUNT

(1846)

JOHN EVERETT MILLAIS was a born artist. When he was nine years old, his drawing master announced there was no more he could teach the boy. His parents took him to meet the president of the Royal Academy, Sir Martin Archer Shee, who initially did not take the interview very seriously; he suggested the boy might be better employed sweeping chimneys. Then he asked young Millais to draw, there and then, the fight between Hector and Achilles. When he saw the finished drawing, Shee advised the parents that they should 'fit the boy for the vocation for which Nature intended him'. He duly attended the Royal Academy Schools. Millais was blessed with supportive and understanding parents.

In another part of London, Haggerston, another boy was less fortunate. William Holman Hunt was very keen to become an artist, but was undermined by his father. The father had himself once wanted to be an artist, but he was too timid and put aside his dream; he became the manager of a draper's warehouse. He preached to his son on the perils of art, and the virtue of business. When the boy was twelve, his father made him work as a clerk in an office six days a week, though he did allow him to take lessons from a portrait painter called Henry Rogers. Holman Hunt understood that he was locked in a battle with his father over his future. When he was sixteen he told his father plainly that art was his chosen profession, and he decided he wanted to attend the Royal Academy Schools. To enrol he had to submit three finished drawings: an antique figure, an anatomical figure and a drawing of the human skeleton.

In December 1843, Holman Hunt attended the annual prize giving at the Royal Academy Schools. Lots of art students were talking about a prodigy by the name of John Millais, and Holman Hunt wanted to get a glimpse of this young celebrity. Sixty years later, Hunt still remembered that momentous day. The great J. M. W. Turner was there, the distinguished but crotchety old man who dominated the art of landscape painting. But Holman Hunt had eyes only for 'the boy'. Hunt remembered the moment when Millais was called up to be presented with the silver medal. Out of the crowd emerged a slim boy with curly hair, walking down to the arena to bow to great applause. Hunt was not disappointed; 'Millais was exactly what I had pictured, and his work just as accomplished as I had thought.' Holman Hunt had a hero, and Millais had a follower.

Hunt's passage into the Royal Academy Schools was difficult, partly because of his lack of formal training. He was about to apply for a third and last time when he encountered Millais flying along the gallery at the British Museum. Millais stopped behind him, looked at his work and said, 'I say – you ought to be in the Academy. You just send the drawing you are doing now and you'll be in like a shot.' And he did get in. Getting to know Millais would be harder, he thought, because Millais already had lots of admirers, but Millais took the initiative, inviting Hunt to his home. There, Holman Hunt was made even more painfully aware of the difference between Millais' circumstances and his own. The Millais parents' days revolved round the pleasurable task of fostering their son's genius, even playing him music to help him while he painted; Mr Millais built props for the pictures; Mrs Millais researched and made costumes for the models. But Hunt too was lucky. The Millais family liked him and half-adopted him, and the growing friendship with John Millais boosted his self-confidence.

Hunt spent more and more time in Millais' studio, and they talked earnestly about art. English painting was in the shallows at that time. Constable was dead and Turner was a spent force, a frail old man. Their bogeyman was Sir Joshua Reynolds, the Royal Academy's first president;

they nicknamed him 'Sir Sloshua'. The Royal Academy's annual exhibition consisted of tired and formulaic pictures, with every composition based on either an 'S' shape or a triangle. Hunt and Millais longed to revive English art, to paint 'live men', but they also understood that to be revolutionary meant being excluded by the Royal Academy. This was controlled by forty academicians, some of whom had waited decades to gain this position. Hunt and Millais were optimistic that they could be elected and that, once in, they could change things.

The two fervent young artists agreed that nature had to be studied directly; all artifice had to be removed. Art was to be 'a handmaid in the cause of justice and truth'. This was not far removed from the belief of Wordsworth and Coleridge some decades earlier. Hunt found support for what they were thinking in the writings of John Ruskin. Hunt borrowed Ruskin's *Modern Painters* and stayed up all night reading it. Again and again, Ruskin urged painters to trust nature. When he had read it, Hunt rushed round to tell Millais. Ruskin had this effect on a lot of young Victorians. He electrified a whole generation.

Meanwhile, the two young artists were hurrying to finish their pictures for the annual Royal Academy exhibition. They even worked on each other's paintings to get them done in time. Hunt's picture, *The Eve of St Agnes,* was accepted. Millais' *Cymon and Iphigenia* was rejected. Millais was philosophical about it, taking himself off to spend the summer with friends in Oxford. Hunt stayed in London, where he had another important encounter – with Dante Gabriel Rossetti. Rossetti went up to Hunt at the exhibition and told him his *Eve of St Agnes* was the best picture there.

Rossetti was a strange, exotic creature who did not prosper in the conventional and claustrophobic atmosphere of the Royal Academy Schools. He came to see the medieval idea of apprenticeship to an experience painter as the best education, and latched onto Ford Madox Brown. This was an odd choice, as Brown was himself only twenty-six, and he thought Rossetti's fan letter must be a joke. He went round to Rossetti carrying a stick, ready to give him a beating, but was won over by Rossetti's enormous charm. He agreed to give Rossetti lessons for nothing. Rossetti was not initially impressed, as he was made to 'fag at some still life'. The clumsy and leaden result, *Bottles*, survives.

Hunt and Rossetti spent more and more time together. They discovered a mutual passion for the poetry of John Keats. Rossetti introduced Hunt to the poetry of Blake. They realised that they had many interests in common, but Rossetti observed that if they (and Millais) were going to cause a revolution in art they needed to recruit supporters. Rossetti recruited Thomas Woodner, an aspiring sculptor, and James Collinson, another painter. Collinson was a less than lively companion; he had narcolepsy and consequently nodded off in the middle of conversations.

When Millais returned from Oxford he was hurt by the new developments. He felt jealous of Hunt's exciting new friendship, which he saw as excluding him; he also felt excluded from the scheme to create a brotherhood. He was sarcastic. 'Where is your flock? I expected to see them behind you. Tell me all about it. I can't understand so far what you are after.' But the initial pique wore off, and Millais was soon deeply involved in the discussion about the principles of the new brotherhood. They all agreed that a wrong turning had been taken with the painter Raphael. Although Raphael had been a great painter, his disciples had turned his style into a formula. What they needed to do was to return painting to the era of the early Italian artists: people such as Giotto, Fra Angelico and Ghirlandaio. Clarity, simplicity and colour were what they wanted.

Like true revolutionaries, they drew up a manifesto. It incorporated lists of their heroes. There were to be five categories of Immortals. Hunt insisted that Jesus should stand alone at the top of the list, though Rossetti wanted to see Shakespeare there. The second category contained Shakespeare and the author of the *Book of Job*. The third included Homer, Dante, Chaucer, Leonardo da Vinci, Goethe, Shelley, King Alfred, Landor, Thackeray, George Washington and Robert Browning. It is not clear what King Alfred and George Washington were doing in this list. Categories four and five included an even odder assembly of heroes, from Isaac Newton to Edgar Allan Poe. All seven of those present signed the manifesto. They were the Brotherhood. They agreed to sign all their work from that moment on with the initials PRB.

It was no accident that that first great meeting of minds took place in September 1848. It was the year of revolutions all over Europe. Revolution was in the air. It was the year when, in English art, the Pre-Raphaelite Brotherhood was formed.

LEWIS CARROLL AND ALICE LIDDELL

(1856)

THIS IS THE poignant story of a strange, private and ultimately elusive man and his relationship with a ten-year-old girl. Lewis Carroll became famous as the author of Alice's Adventures in Wonderland, and there could have been no *Alice in Wonderland* without Alice. Alice was a real girl, Alice Liddell, and Charles Dodgson, the real man behind Lewis Carroll, first met her in 1856.

Dodgson's father, also called Charles, was an able mathematician and might have become an academic but instead he became a country parson in North Yorkshire, an admirer of Newman and committed to Anglo-Catholicism. Dodgson was uncomfortable with his father's values and with the Anglican church generally. He would not be going into the church. In 1846 he was sent to Rugby School, where he was unhappy. 'I cannot say that any earthly considerations would induce me to go through my three years again.' He wrote of unspecified 'annoyance at night'. He developed a stammer, which had a major negative effect on his social life. He was also, from an early age, a great reader. And he shone at mathematics.

In 1851, Dodgson went up to Oxford, to his father's old college, Christ Church. Inauspiciously, his mother died the moment he arrived there. But his talent as a mathematician carried him forward to a lectureship, which he held for twenty-six years, and he stayed at Christ Church until he died.

Dodgson was a tall, good-looking man with curling brown hair. He was awkward in his movements, which may have been the result of a knee injury, and he had a weak chest as a result of severe whooping cough when young. The stammer too he carried throughout his life. At the same time, he was ready to sing before an audience, tell stories, and was good at charades. Dodgson was easier with children than with adults, but there is no truth in the story that he lost his stammer when talking to children; in fact, with their ear for the unusual they noticed and remembered the stammer more than the adults. His portrayal of himself in Alice as the Dodo may be a reference to the effect of the stammer on his name – Do-Do-Dodgson. He suffered from migraine and possibly a mild form of epilepsy, which may account for some of the strange and alarming experiences he described in *Alice*.

His tendency to reticence did not prevent him from being ambitious. He wanted to make a mark as a writer or an artist. Before *Alice* was published, he was making friends among the Pre-Raphaelites, including Rossetti, Holman Hunt, John Millais and Arthur Hughes. He met the profoundly influential John Ruskin in 1857 and they became friends. He also met George MacDonald, who wrote fairy tales. It was the MacDonald children's enthusiastic response to Alice that persuaded Dodgson to send it off to be published.

Dodgson was writing from a very early age. He contributed to the family's magazine, called *Mischmasch*, and among the early poems there is a version of the *Jabberwocky*. In the mid-1850s, his work appeared in national publications, *The Train and The Comic Times*, as well as some more local magazines. Most of his writing was whimsical, some of it satirical, but he always worked to exacting standards. In 1856, he published the first piece under his pen name, Lewis Carroll. This was developed with characteristic elaborateness from his real name. Lutwidge in Latin was Ludovicus, and Lewis was the anglicised version of Ludovicus. Charles in Latin was Carolus, and Carroll was an anglicised version of Carolus. As it happened, it was in that same year, 1856, that the new Dean arrived at Christ Church with his family. He was Henry Liddell. Dodgson became a close friend of Liddell's wife, Lorina, and the children, especially the three sisters, called Lorina, Edith and Alice.

It was also in 1856 that Dodgson took up photography as a hobby.

He liked to take photographs of the children he befriended – including Alice Liddell. The idea of taking up photography seems to have come from his uncle, Skeffington Lutwidge, and he became very good at it.

The acrostic poem at the end of *Through the Looking Glass*, the second *Alice* book, spells out the name of Alice Liddell, and there are many hidden references to her elsewhere in the text of both books. He had Alice Liddell in mind when he was writing the Alice books, so it is not clear why he denied it. In later years, he repeatedly denied that Alice was Alice Liddell, or that Alice was based on a real girl at all. In his favour, Dodgson included Gertrude Chataway's name in a similar acrostic poem at the start of *The Hunting of the Snark*, and there is no reason to assume that Gertrude is one of the characters in that piece. With characteristic oddity, Dante Gabriel Rossetti became convinced that *The Hunting of the Snark* was about him.

Dodgson kept a diary, but the diaries for the years 1858–1862 are missing. Even so, he was clearly spending a significant amount of time with the Liddell family at that time and his relationship with the family meant a great deal to him. He developed the habit of taking first Harry and then the three girls on rowing trips on the Thames up to Godstow. On one of these boating trips, on 4 July 1862, Dodgson devised the outline of *Alice in Wonderland*. He told the story to the three girls, and Alice begged him to write it down for them. After a long delay, in November 1864 Dodgson presented her with a handwritten copy, complete with illustrations. He gave it the title *Alice's Adventures Under Ground*. Before this, George MacDonald had read through an incomplete draft of the manuscript. The response of both the Liddell children and the MacDonald children encouraged Dodgson to have the book published. The unfinished manuscript was shown to the publisher Macmillan, who liked it straight away. Various working titles were discussed, and the book was eventually published in 1865 as *Alice's Adventures in Wonderland*, under the pen name Lewis Carroll. Dodgson was not confident that his original illustrations were good enough, so John Tenniel was commissioned to produce a new set.

The huge commercial success of *Alice* changed Dodgson's life. He had fan mail to deal with, and he also began earning large sums of money. Oddly, he did not use this opportunity to give up his job at Christ Church, even though he was finding it uncongenial. One of the conditions of his post was that he eventually take holy orders, which he was very unwilling to do. In the early 1860s, he was overwhelmed by a sense that he was a 'vile and worthless sinner', a sense of guilt that has never been explained. Dean Liddell told him he might lose his job if he went on refusing. Liddell eventually granted him special dispensation; he was able to remain in college without becoming a priest, in spite of the college regulations.

The sequel, *Through the Looking Glass*, came out in 1872. This was darker, and it reflects Dodgson's change of mood following his father's death, which brought on a depression that lasted several years.

The nature of Charles Dodgson's relationship with Alice Liddel has been the subject of endless speculation. Whether it was, on Dodgson's side, consciously or unconsciously sexual in nature, has been endlessly debated. He was certainly very interested in young girls, and the subject matter of his photographs indicates this. Just over half of his surviving photographs are of girls, though these images are not by any means dominated by Alice Liddell. His favourite model was Alexandra Kitchin, known as 'Xie'. Between 1869 until 1880 he photographed Xie more than fifty times; he stopped when she was approaching sixteen. Only one-third of Dodgson's 3,000 photographs have survived.

Some of the photographs were of nude children. One of Lewis Carroll's biographers has commented, 'Given his emotional attachment to children as well as his aesthetic appreciation of their forms, his assertion that his interest was strictly artistic is naive. He probably felt more than he dared acknowledge, even to himself.' On the other hand, it may be that Dodgson identified with children and preferred the world the way they saw it; from his writings it is clear he had next to no interest in the adult world. It should also be remembered that in the mid-nineteenth century there was a sentimental cult of the child as total innocent and the nude child was a symbol of that belief. Other photographers, like Julia Margaret Cameron, were also taking photographs of nude children at that time. Nude children appeared even on Christmas cards.

It should not be assumed that Dodgson took up photography when he did in order to find excuses to have the Liddell girls pose for him. Many of his pictures were portraits of notable sitters, and his alter ego as the gentleman-photographer clearly extended his social range. He made portraits of John Millais and his family, Rossetti, Ellen Terry, Julia Margaret Cameron, Michael Faraday and Lord Tennyson. Dodgson abruptly stopped taking photographs in 1880; it is not known why.

An aura of mystery surrounds Dodgson's relationship with Alice Liddell. This is intensified by the disappearance of four volumes of diaries and seven diary pages which have been deliberately cut out. Scholars assume that the diary material was removed and destroyed by members of Dodgson's family with the idea of covering up something untoward. Most of the missing material relates to Dodgson's life between 1853, when he was twenty-two, and 1862, when he was thirty-two (and Alice Liddell was ten). There is some documentary evidence that the suppressed material was indeed about Dodgson's relationship with the Liddell family. A list has survived headed 'Cut pages in Diary'. One entry reads, 'Vol 8 Page 72. Alice not improved by being laid up.' This sounds innocuous, but the next reads, 'Vol 8 Page 92. L. C. learns from Mrs Liddell that he is supposed to be using the children as a means of paying court to the governess – He is also supposed by some to be courting Ina.' Ina was either Lorina, Alice's older sister, or Lorina, the mother. Then there is 'Vol 11 Page 110. [illegible] Does anyone know what "the business with Lord Newey" was which put L. C. out of "Mrs Liddell's good grace".' Although there is potential scandal here, none of it seems to involve little Alice. The break with the Liddell family came shortly afterwards, even so.

Whatever eventually went wrong between Lewis Carroll and the Liddells, the boating trip in 1862 with the three little girls transformed his life, and led to the creation of a unique literary classic.

WAGNER AND
LUDWIG II OF BAVARIA

(1864)

THE NEW YOUNG king of Bavaria, Ludwig II, was psychologically programmed for Richard Wagner long before the two men met. As Crown Prince, Ludwig had haunted the castle of Hohenschwangau, named after the swan on the arms of the castle's previous owners. The swan was also a favourite device of Ludwig's father, Maximilian II, who had a room in the castle decorated with frescoes from the legend of the swan knight. Ludwig grew up with this legend. He was thirteen when he first read the poem *Lohengrin*. And Wagner wrote an opera about Lohengrin. This sparked the connection.

Ludwig listened to Wagner's music whenever he could, and it had an overwhelming effect on him. He also read Wagner's libretti and essays. The first published edition of the poem of *The Ring of the Nibelung* appeared in 1863. Wagner wrote a preface to the text, and in it he wondered where he might find the patron who would support him, enable him to set this huge text to music, then put the completed work on the stage. He asked a grand rhetorical question with biblical reverberations – 'Will this prince be found? – In the beginning was the deed.' When Ludwig read this, he felt that Wagner was addressing him in person. He, Ludwig, would be that prince, and he would find Wagner and make all these things come to pass.

Wagner knew nothing of Ludwig at that time. He was in Vienna and, as usual, on course for trouble. He faced prison for debt – he always lived beyond his means – and he was forced to flee the city. On Good Friday 1864 he was passing through Munich when he saw in a shop

444

window a portrait of the newly crowned king of Bavaria. The image showed a sensitive, aesthetic eighteen-year-old. The youth and grace of the young king moved the fifty-one-year-old Wagner to tears. Wagner moved on. He was offered refuge for a time at Mariafeld near Zurich and from there he wrote to his friend Peter Cornelius, 'Some light must show itself; someone must come forward and help me now with his energetic support . . . Some miracle must now befall me, otherwise it will all be over!'

It was as if the two men, king and composer, separately and independently, felt at that moment that destiny was about to overwhelm them. Six days later, Ludwig sent his cabinet secretary Franz von Pfistermeister to look for Wagner. Pfistermeister went first to Vienna, then Mariafeld, and finally tracked Wagner down at a hotel in Stuttgart, where he presented him with a portrait of the king, a ring and an invitation to Munich. Wagner wrote a letter of gratitude to Ludwig, boarded a train at once and the following day, 4 May 1864, he met the king for the first time. Although once a revolutionary and always and exclusively a lover of women, Wagner was bowled over by the glamour, youth and good looks of the young king. He wrote ecstatically, 'He is so fair of form, so spirited, soulful and sublime that I fear his life must slip away like some celestial dream in this base world of ours.' Wagner was right; Ludwig would not last as a king, he would lose touch with everyday reality altogether, he would be deposed and driven to suicide in 1886.

That first meeting was followed by further meetings and an exchange of letters that demonstrate the extraordinary rapport the two men felt for one another. The choice of language they used was extraordinary too, and not far away from the language of lovers. 'How I worship you!' 'Uniquely beloved!' 'Everything, you are everything to me!' 'Ah, that I might die for you!' 'I am nothing without you!' For Wagner it was a dream come true. The young king would provide him with an income that would make it possible for him to complete *The Ring* – a huge undertaking – and write other new operas too. He would also make the prospect of performances, and good performances, more certain. Wagner's career had appeared to be on the rocks, and now it was suddenly dragged clear and sailing out into open waters. Later, King Ludwig would rightly say, 'It was I who saved him for the world.'

Ludwig provided accommodation for Wagner, Haus Pellet in Kempfenhausen on Lake Starnberg, the lake in which one day Ludwig would drown himself. While there, Wagner wrote a march for Ludwig. A few months later, Ludwig moved Wagner into Munich, into a house in Briennerstrasse, and there, as soon as Ludwig had signed a formal contract for its completion, Wagner resumed work on *The Ring*.

In the following year, Hans von Bulow conducted the première of Wagner's already completed opera Tristan und Isolde. And at the king's request Wagner started to dictate his autobiography, in which he carefully down-played his role in the Dresden rising; the king did not need to know that he was a revolutionary leader. He also wrote a prose draft for the text of what would become his last opera, *Parsifal*.

But even before that first year was up trouble was brewing. Generously treated by King Ludwig, Wagner was still living beyond his means, and his ambitions inflated to match his new prospects. Many in Munich were affronted by Wagner's arrogance and lack of diplomacy. They were also jealous of the king's obsessive interest in Wagner, and concerned about the king's neglect of his official duties. Wagner made a particular enemy of the king's minister of foreign affairs, Ludwig von der Pfordten. Pfordten had once been minister of education in Saxony, and in that capacity had already become the sworn enemy of Wagner in his former roles as Dresden kappelmeister and revolutionary. He saw Wagner as an insurrectionist and thought it would better if no more of Wagner's operas were ever performed. An informal alliance of ministers and other officials formed against Wagner. Wagner was becoming a political force in his own right. When Pfistermeister's position was in danger, he tried to win Wagner as an ally, promising him unlimited credit if he would help him win the king's favour.

The idea for a Festival Theatre came originally from Ludwig, not from Wagner, who was initially unimpressed by it. But the king was set on it, so Wagner had to go along with it, nominating Gottfried Semper as architect. Ludwig's plan was to have this theatre built on the bank of the River Isar and connect it by a bridge to a splendid new boulevard to the centre of Munich. It was going to cost a lot of money and take six years to build. Wagner could not oppose the scheme, but he suggested an interim project, which was a temporary theatre built in one wing of the Crystal Palace. This would have cost only four percent of Ludwig's grand scheme, but it fell foul of the city's planning authority.

By 1867, Ludwig was in difficulties over the annulment of his engagement to his cousin Sophie and did not want to be forever tied to Munich. The theatre project was dropped in favour of a new project, Neuschwanstein, a fake medieval castle which would be 'a worthy temple for my godlike friend'. Ludwig commissioned two theatrical designers to design the castle, parts of which were based on the sets for the first Munich production of Wagner's *Lohengrin*. In time, in Ludwig's mind, Neuschwanstein would become the Grail Castle in *Parsifal*. Either way, Wagner would never go there; it was still unfinished when he died. It seemed that everything Ludwig did revolved round Wagner and his operas. His steamer on the lake was called *Tristan*, and various features at his castle at Linderhof were named after locations in various operas: Hunding's Hut (*Die Walküre*), the Venus Grotto (*Tannhäuser*), Gurnemanz's Hermitage and the Good Friday Meadow (*Parsifal*).

Ludwig's officials worked hard to restrain what was seen as an unwholesome relationship and to reduce Wagner's political influence. In 1865, Wagner was rash enough to advise Ludwig to abolish his standing army, form a national militia, put himself at the head of the German unification movement and declare himself emperor. Wagner sometimes behaved badly enough for Ludwig himself to have doubts. On one occasion Wagner was ill-mannered enough to bang his fist on a table in front of the king, who was not used to this sort of behaviour. There were weeks of cooling off after such incidents, but then reconciliations. Pfordten and his allies saw to it that details of Wagner's spending at the state's expense found their way into the press. Wagner seems not to have seen the danger inherent in the situation, either for himself or for Ludwig. Peter Cornelius saw the danger clearly enough; he wrote to his girlfriend that Wagner's involvement in Bavarian politics was 'the beginning of the end'. In the press, a comparison was drawn between Ludwig II's infatuation with Richard Wagner and Ludwig I's affair with an Irish dancer called Lola Montez.

Wagner retaliated with an anonymous letter to the press, though everyone guessed who its author was. In it he demanded that 'two or three persons be removed who do not enjoy the least respect among the Bavarian people', then the king and his people might be free of vexation. The letter was obviously from Wagner, and it was just what his enemies needed. Ludwig's cabinet insisted on Wagner's ejection from Munich. If not, they would resign. Under this extreme pressure, Ludwig asked Wagner to leave Bavaria 'for a few months'.

Wagner was staggered. He had no idea that this could happen. He left Munich for Switzerland in December 1865. Ludwig was devastated by the separation. He wrote, 'I kneel before your bust and shed bitter tears.' He threatened to abdicate so that he could join Wagner in Switzerland.

The encounter between Wagner and King Ludwig had some remarkable effects. Among other things, it made the completion and performance of *The Ring* possible. It made the writing of *Die Meistersinger* possible. The first performance of *Die Meistersinger* took place in Munich in June 1868; in an unprecedented breach of etiquette, at Ludwig's request Wagner sat with Ludwig in the royal box. Then came performances of *The Ring* tetralogy.

The first performance of *Das Rheingold*, the first part of *The Ring*, took place in September 1869. It was ordered by Ludwig, who felt he had been kept waiting too long to see it. Wagner was very angry and did not hide his feelings from the king. Wagner saw *The Ring* as a special work, a piece that could not be given except under the exceptional conditions of a special festival. Mounting a production in an ordinary opera house under routine conditions was explicitly 'against his wishes'. Wagner tried to delay the production, promising improvements to the piece, but

Ludwig sensed duplicity. 'Never before have I encountered such impudence . . . If W. dares to oppose me again, his salary is to be permanently stopped and no more of his works are to be performed on the Munich stage.' The first performance went ahead, and it led to a deep and lasting division between king and composer.

In 1870, the first performance of *Die Walküre,* the second part of *The Ring,* went ahead in the same way: it was ordered by the king against Wagner's wishes. The situation had by now become intolerable for Wagner, who felt he had lost control of his own greatest work. It pushed him towards an ambitious new plan for an annual opera festival at Bayreuth; it would be in the centre of Germany, outside Bavaria and therefore outside the control of King Ludwig. And so was born the Bayreuth Festival.

It has often been said that Wagner was greedy and rapacious, that he abused Ludwig's generosity, that he took too much. But in all, spread over nineteen years, Wagner took from the king a total 562,914 marks. Although this may sound like a large sum, it amounted to only 0.7 percent of Ludwig's civil list allowance, his personal budget; Ludwig spent sixty times as much money building his castles.

By the time the Bayreuth performances of *The Ring* were mounted, the intense friendship between the two men was over. Ludwig stayed away from the opening performances of *The Ring,* not to snub Wagner but to avoid meeting the Kaiser. But Ludwig also stayed away from the opening performances of *Parsifal* in 1882, which disappointed Wagner. Ludwig wanted to see *Parsifal* mounted in Munich, and Wagner was determined to keep *Parsifal* for the Bayreuth performance alone. When, the following year, Ludwig heard that Wagner had died in Venice at the age of seventy, he said, 'Oh! I'm sorry, but then again not really. Only recently he caused me problems over *Parsifal.*' His cold remark was a measure of how far their friendship had disintegrated – and the extent to which Ludwig's mind had disintegrated too.

VINCENT VAN GOGH
AND PAUL GAUGUIN

(1887)

IN 1888, TWO artists spent nine weeks together, painting at Arles in the south of France. They were Vincent van Gogh and Paul Gauguin.

One morning, when he had sobered up, van Gogh told Gauguin he had a vague memory that he had offended him the previous evening. He had in fact thrown a glass of absinthe at him, that was all, and Gauguin was ready to forgive, but the two-month experiment in living together had not gone smoothly and Gauguin was preparing to leave. The next evening, upset at the prospect of Gauguin's imminent departure, van Gogh ran after him in the street, shouting at him. Gauguin confronted him and van Gogh went back to the house, cut off his left ear lobe with a razor, wrapped it up and presented it to a young woman at the local brothel. Van Gogh was taken to hospital for treatment and Gauguin left for Paris.

This marked the end of one of the most dramatic episodes in art history. Gauguin and van Gogh were friends, but uneasy friends, and they were rival artists. What they produced at Arles in 1888 was a body of work that set the scene for developments in 20th century art.

It was in November 1887 that Vincent van Gogh first met Paul Gauguin, then thirty-nine, at an art gallery in Paris. Van Gogh was thirty-four and had reached the end of a long phase of false starts. He had worked for an art dealer, he had been a teacher of languages, he had been a lay preacher, he had studied theology – all of these before discovering at the age of twenty-seven that he wanted to be an artist. As late as 1886, van Gogh was still painting in the dark and muddy style of

The Potato Eaters. Only then did he experiment with brighter colours and jabbing, pointillist brush strokes.

In some ways, Gauguin had had a similar experience, coming to painting only when he was twenty-five. But he had painted Impressionist pictures since the late 1870s and had worked alongside Camille Pissarro. His 'false starts' had been rather more exciting than van Gogh's. He had been a sailor, he had been a stockbroker who had left his wife and children, he had lived on Martinique. Van Gogh was impressed by Gauguin's worldliness. The two men nevertheless found that they had in common a quest to find a new form of artistic expression. They also had in common respect and admiration for each other's work. Van Gogh liked the poetry of Gauguin's pictures; Gauguin liked the passion in van Gogh's pictures. Gauguin also believed that van Gogh's art dealer brother Theo would be a useful contact in selling work.

In late 1887, they exchanged paintings. Van Gogh gave Gauguin two studies of sunflowers. Gauguin gave van Gogh a painting of a woman, a boy and a cow on a river bank in Martinique. Gauguin then went off to Brittany to paint in an artists' colony. In February 1888, van Gogh went to the south of France, drawn by the clarity and brightness of the light there; it was to revolutionise his style and be the making of him as an artist. He painted everything he saw: haystacks, blossoming trees, landscapes. He tried to describe this visionary time: 'I have a terrible lucidity at moments, when nature is so glorious that I am hardly conscious of myself and the picture comes to me as in a dream.' The colours brightened, strengthened.

But van Gogh was a difficult, uncompromising character who found companionship hard to come by, and his life was a lonely one. He had a dream of a brotherhood of like-minded painters living and working together. He rented a little house in the Place Lamartine in Arles. It had two rooms on each of two floors and was painted canary yellow. He furnished it with some simple rush chairs and two beds. This, the Yellow House, was to be his Studio of the South. Paul Gauguin, the greatly-admired new friend, would be the head of this studio, he decided. In

June, just before Gauguin's fortieth birthday, van Gogh sent him a formal invitation along with fifty francs.

Although Gauguin had no money, he hesitated before accepting. Even after he accepted, he put off travelling to Arles. Van Gogh meanwhile worked to produce paintings to decorate the Yellow House. He painted sunflowers, which were to become something of a trademark. In October 1887 Van Gogh suggested they exchange self-portraits. Van Gogh's picture was stark, gaunt, intense. Gauguin described his own self-portrait as 'the face of an outlaw, like Jean Valjean, with an inner nobility and gentleness; the eyes suggest the volcanic flames that animate the soul of the artist'. But when van Gogh saw Gauguin's portrait he was anxious about the desperation he saw there; 'What Gauguin's portrait tells me above all is that he cannot go on like this.'

By August 1888, Gauguin decided to go to Arles. He wrote to the wife from whom he had separated that he was going to spend 'six months with a painter who will provide me with food and lodging in exchange for drawings'. Over-anxious about Gauguin's arrival, van Gogh worked all day long in order to have as many paintings as possible to show him. He saw himself as to some extent Gauguin's disciple, but he also wanted to show off what he could do without his help; van Gogh was very mixed up. These paintings include *The Yellow House* and *The Bedroom*. Not surprisingly, when Gauguin arrived on 23 October, he found van Gogh in an alarmingly agitated and overwrought state. Gauguin was bohemian by nature, but the untidiness of van Gogh's domesticity irritated him; van Gogh did not even close his paint box properly. 'Everywhere and in everything I found a disorder that shocked me.' Gauguin tried to organise the disorderly common finances, establishing fixed budgets.

Van Gogh's hero worship was still there. When Gauguin started boasting about his adventures, van Gogh was more impressed than ever. But Gauguin sensed early on that there would be trouble between them. He liked to get acclimatised to a place before he started painting it, but van Gogh pushed him into starting painting the very day after his arrival, even pressing one of his own pre-primed linen canvases on him so that he did not need to waste any time buying one. That first day yielded van Gogh's *Old Yew Tree* and Gauguin's *Farmhouse in Arles*.

Gauguin's technique was deliberate and decorative, while van Gogh's was more spontaneous and gestural. Van Gogh was ready to learn something from Gauguin and he experimented with Gauguin's practice of doing studies outdoors and then painting the finished work in the studio. Gauguin also paid a small homage to van Gogh's concern for human suffering by painting a sombre picture of people picking grapes, which he called *Human Miseries*. He tried using van Gogh's thick impasto technique too. But these borrowings were short-term and they quickly reverted to their own personal styles. They painted simultaneous portraits, side by side, of Madame Ginoux, the owner of the Café de la Gare. Van Gogh did his within the hour that she sat for them. Gauguin did only a chalk and charcoal sketch in that time, but then over several days turned the portrait into the foreground of a bar scene, *Night Cafe*. They were two very different artists painting two very different pictures from the same subject.

Van Gogh and Gauguin painted together. They also talked together. They discussed art, literature, religion and history. Van Gogh told his brother about these conversations. 'Our arguments are terribly electric. We come out of them sometimes with our heads as exhausted as an electric battery after it has run down.' In the end Gauguin impatiently dismissed some of what van Gogh was saying about art, putting it down to 'a disordered brain' and an 'absence of reasoned logic'. He came to realise that they would never see eye to eye about art.

But in one important way the encounter with van Gogh was profitable to Gauguin. Vincent's brother Theo sold some of Gauguin's paintings in Paris in November, and Gauguin was better off financially than he had been for years. Gauguin was able to start thinking more ambitiously of setting off for Martinique, where he would found a Studio of the Tropics. Van Gogh sensed that Gauguin was getting restless, and that the experiment in artistic partnership was coming to an end. The two men painted revealing portraits of each other in December. Van

Gogh's picture, *Man in a Red Beret,* shows Gauguin awkwardly, from behind, as if he is being watched secretly, with suspicion. Gauguin's picture, *The Painter of Sunflowers,* gives van Gogh a distorted head and glazed eyes. The pictures show their uneasiness with one another.

The relationship reached its terrible, ear-lopping climax on 23 December 1888. Gauguin left on the night train for Paris and never saw van Gogh again. Four months later, in April 1889, van Gogh was voluntarily admitted to an asylum at Saint-Rémy. There he went on painting, producing masterpieces such as *The Reaper, Cypresses* and *Starry Night.* A year later he went to Auvers to consult Dr Paul Gachet, who was an amateur painter who looked remarkably like van Gogh and suffered from a similar mental disorder. He spent some weeks at Auvers, where he painted his *Portrait of Dr Gachet.* Then, in a state of deep depression, he shot himself.

Gauguin, contrary to van Gogh's prediction, carried on painting for many years in Brittany and the South Pacific. He became increasingly frustrated by van Gogh's growing posthumous reputation and insisted on describing his one-time friend as 'crazy'. Gauguin tried to take the major credit for van Gogh's flowering at Arles. In 1903, he wrote, 'When I arrived in Arles, Vincent was trying to find himself. I undertook the task of enlightening him. From that day on, my van Gogh made astonishing progress.' In order to prove the point, Gauguin argued that the famous sunflower paintings were painted after his arrival in Arles. In fact they were painted before.

But the memories of Arles, of sunflowers, of sun, and of Vincent always stayed with Gauguin. When he was in Tahiti and ill, he asked a Paris friend to send him sunflower seeds. He planted them in his garden and when they grew he did a series of paintings of them.

GUSTAV KLIMT AND EMILIE FLÖGE

(1890)

THE PAINTER GUSTAV Klimt grew up in poverty, the second of seven children of a gold engraver. From 1876 until 1883 he studied at the Vienna School of Arts and Crafts, where he was happy to accept the conservative and academic training of the day, specialising in architectural painting. His brother Ernst enrolled the year after Gustav, and he became a gold engraver like their father. The two brothers and a friend, Franz Matsch, started working together and they took on many joint commissions as The Company of Artists, as they called themselves.

Klimt started his career painting murals and ceilings in public buildings on the Ringstrasse in Vienna. He was extremely successful, and in 1888 he was awarded a Golden Order of Merit by the Emperor Franz Josef for his murals in the Burgtheater in Vienna. Then, in 1892, both his father and his brother Ernst died, events that changed Gustav's life dramatically. The double loss left him as the head of the family, taking the place of both father and brother in pastoral and financial matters. The shock jolted his artistic vision, and he began to develop a more individual, less conservative style. With Ernst dead, Gustav took on the guardianship of Ernst's baby daughter. This naturally brought him closer to Ernst's widow, Helene, and to her sister Emilie, for whom he became a surrogate uncle.

So it was at this emotionally charged time that his relationship with Emilie Flöge began. Whether it became a sexual relationship is not known. Many assumed at the time that it was, and it is certainly true that Klimt was very active sexually; he had many love affairs and fathered fourteen children. Klimt and Emilie were always seen together, and it is tempting to see *The Kiss* as a kind of wordless monument to their undying love. On the other hand, Emilie was a relative, twelve years younger than himself, and a relict of the brother who had died prematurely. It may be that it was simple family friendship that held them together. Certainly they were very close for two decades, until the end of Klimt's life.

Klimt and Emilie corresponded and many of their letters have survived. There is nothing romantic in them at all. Klimt was extremely discreet about his sex life. He kept his mistresses out of the public eye in order to avoid gossip. But he was happy to be seen at the opera or the theatre with Emilie, which in itself implies that their relationship was platonic.

In 1904 the three Flöge sisters, Emilie, Helene and Pauline, opened their fashion salon in the Casa Piccola in Vienna. They needed to earn some money, and as they entered their thirties they had significantly reduced chances of marrying. Klimt was not going to marry Emilie – or anyone else for that matter – though he did joke about the possibility in a poem: 'In weather fair or foul, Every year I tell you true: Rather than ever marry, I shall give a painting to you.'

Between 1894 and 1900, Klimt created three paintings, *Philosophy, Medicine* and *Jurisprudence*, to decorate the ceiling of the University of Vienna's Great Hall. These allegorical images were considered too radical and the content was seen by some as pornographic. The images Klimt was painting now were overtly sexual and there was a general public outcry against them. The three pictures were not displayed on the Great Hall ceiling, and Klimt was never commissioned to paint a work for a public building again. His attitude was summed up in *Nuda Verita*, painted in 1899. It shows a naked woman with red hair holding the mirror of truth; above are the words of Schiller, 'If you cannot please everyone by your deeds and your art, please a few. To please many is bad.'

During the 1890s, Klimt took his summer holidays with the Flöges on the shores of the Attersee, where he painted landscapes in a similar style to his mural figures, showing refined design and reducing surfaces to flat planes.

Then came his golden phase, which produced Klimt's most famous paintings. They show a highly developed sense of pattern and many of them use gold leaf. He may have got the idea for using gold in this way from mosaics seen on his trips to Venice and Ravenna. The best known of these paintings is *The Kiss* (1908). They are in effect the first truly '20th century' pictures, and they show an extraordinary range of cultural influences – Greek, Byzantine, Minoan, Egyptian. They show a fascination with long flowing costumes; he collected many photographs of Emilie modelling clothes that she had designed. Klimt himself often wore sandals and a long robe when he was at home. He spent a great deal of time at home, avoiding café life and tended to avoid other artists too; he was well-known enough to be able to do this. His patrons tended to visit him at his home.

Klimt, who died in 1918, was a private person. He wrote very little about his work, kept no diary, and was discreet about his many love affairs. He once wrote, 'There is nothing special about me. I am a painter who paints day after day from morning to night. Whoever wants to know something about me ought to look carefully at my pictures.' And of course his pictures were sophisticated, highly erotic and full of psychological symbolism.

The precise role of Emilie Flöge in Klimt's life and creativity is hard to define. He was obviously very strongly attracted to women – lots of women – and Emilie was a woman. But she was also a member of his family. When people refer to Emilie as Klimt's mistress of twenty years, they are perhaps making an unwarranted assumption, and forgetting that she was Ernst's sister-in-law, the sister of Ernst's wife Helene: not a blood relative, but a relative by marriage.

One of the commonest themes in his paintings was the *femme fatale*, the woman who dominates a man's life. Was this a projection perhaps of hidden feelings for Emilie? Another recurring motif was exotic costumes and fabrics. Emilie was a fashion designer and she owned, together with her sisters, a salon that catered for a wealthy female clientèle. Was the heavy featuring of exotic clothes in his paintings a calculated homage to Emilie, or had he unconsciously absorbed her interests and tastes into his work? Klimt spent a lot of time with Emilie and painted several portraits of her. Whether she shared his bed or not, Emilie was his muse.

She remained loyal to his memory, even when in Nazi Austria it became dangerous to do so; Hitler hated Klimt's paintings. The Anschluss of 1938 forced the Flöges to close their salon, but Emilie kept a room dedicated to Klimt's memory, even so. His easel was there and the large cupboard containing his ornamental robes, his painter's smocks and hundreds of his drawings. But she was discreet enough always to keep the doors of that room locked – a symbol of their relationship.

J. M. BARRIE AND PETER LLEWELLYN DAVIES

(1897)

J. M. BARRIE WAS the ninth of ten children born to a Scottish Calvinist weaver and his wife. James was a small child and even as a fully grown adult he only reached a height of five feet three inches. To gain attention within the family, he took to telling stories. When he was six, his next-older brother David died in an ice-skating accident at the age of thirteen. David was the mother's favourite, and James tried hard to take David's place in her affections, even to the extent of wearing his clothes. Barrie's mother took comfort from the fact that David would remain a boy for ever; he would never grow up and he would never leave her. It may be that being bereaved, feeling emotionally neglected, and knowing that his mother could only love a boy who would never grow up induced a psychologically-generated dwarfism in Barrie. In other words, his desperate desire to be loved by his mother actually inhibited his growth. He wanted to be David. He wanted to be the boy who would never grow up. The same childhood fixation may lie behind Barrie's lack of a sex life as an adult.

When Barrie went to school, he led a sheltered existence, under the care of two of his siblings who were teachers first at the Glasgow Academy and then at Dumfries Academy. While he was at Dumfries, he and his friends played pirates in a garden, acting out a kind of saga that would eventually become the plot of Peter Pan. The same friends formed a drama club, which performed Barrie's play, *Bandelero the Bandit,* which had the distinction of being denounced by one of the school governors. Barrie was conscious that he was heading for a literary career but his parents were keen for him to go into the church, and with a career in the church in view they persuaded him to go to Edinburgh University.

But writing gripped him. He wrote drama reviews for a newspaper in Edinburgh. He worked as a staff journalist in Nottingham. He wrote a string of sentimental and nostalgic stories of Scottish parochial life, which were popular enough to establish his reputation as a writer. Two novels, *Sentimental Tommy* (1896) and *Tommy and Grizel* (1902) were about a boy who clings to childhood fantasies, leading to an unhappy ending. Barrie turned increasingly to writing plays, including *Ibsen's Ghost* (1891) which was a parody of *Ibsen's Ghosts* and it caused a sensation. Then he had a double success with two successive plays, *Quality Street* (1901) and *The Admirable Crichton* (1902).

Peter Pan made his first appearance as a character in the serialised story *The Little White Bird*, published as a book in 1901. The first stage performance of Barrie's most famous and most enduring work was given on 27 December 1904 – *Peter Pan*. The play's subtitle was revealing enough in terms of its significance to Barrie himself: The Boy Who Wouldn't Grow Up. In a very real sense J. M. Barrie was Peter Pan, the boy who never really became an adult, who wanted to remain a child so that his mother would go on loving him. It was so popular that Barrie developed it into a novel called *Peter Pan and Wendy* (1911), and ever since then the piece has been revived, developed and presented in various forms over and over again. *Peter Pan* is not just a childish fantasy – Barrie was a more interesting writer than that. Unlike Charles Dodgson, Barrie was very interested in commentating on the nature and foibles of modern adult society. In *Peter Pan,* he contrasts the con-strained and well-defined society of late Victorian middle-class Bloomsbury with the chaotic and morally ambivalent child's world of Neverland. George Bernard Shaw spotted that, although presented as a Christmas pantomime, 'ostensibly a holiday entertainment for children', *Peter Pan* was 'really a play for grown-up people'.

Barrie went on to write a lot more plays – the last being *The Boy David* in 1936 – but it is for *Peter Pan* that he will always be remembered.

Barrie was very sociable and knew a lot of people. He met and told stories to the two little daughters of the Duke of York, who would become the Princesses Elizabeth and Margaret. He met Thomas Hardy, corresponded for a long time with Robert Louis Stevenson (then in Samoa), and was a friend of George Bernard Shaw and H. G. Wells for many years. He knew the explorer Captain Scott and was godfather to Scott's son, Peter. He founded a cricket team, the Allakhbarries; its players included H. G. Wells, Conan Doyle, G. K. Chesterton, E. V. Lucas, A. A. Milne, Lord Tennyson's son and P. G. Wodehouse. Not all of Barrie's social contacts were literary. There are photographs of him wearing a long scarf and a trilby hat, in the act of bowling at St Andrew's, and the batsman is none other than Field-Marshal Sir Douglas Haig in full uniform.

Barrie married in 1894 and in 1900 he and his wife found a country retreat at Black Lake Cottage at Farnham, where they would entertain the cricket team and the Llewelyn Davieses. While the Llewelyn Davies boys were there he took photographs of them playing and compiled an album of *The Boy Castaways of Black Lake Island*. There is a fine photograph of Michael Llewelyn Davies dressed as Peter Pan, being attacked by a frighteningly villainous-looking Barrie in the role of Captain Hook. And that was where Barrie wrote *Peter Pan*. The photographs show that Michael and his brother Nico were able to make themselves completely unrecognisable by pulling grotesque faces.

Barrie's encounter with the Llewelyn Davies family was an important element in the creation of *Peter Pan*. The family consisted of Arthur and Sylvia Llewelyn Davies and their five sons, George, Jack, Peter, Michael and Nico. Barrie's first meeting with the family took place in Kensington Gardens. He lived nearby and often walked his dog Porthos in the park. There he met the Llewelyn Davies' nanny, Mary Hodgson, with George and Jack and the baby Peter. They met repeatedly, and Barrie entertained the boys with his ability to waggle his ears and eyebrows –

and of course his ability to tell stories. At a dinner party some months later Barrie, by chance, met the boys' mother, Sylvia, who was the daughter of George du Maurier. After that, Barrie became a constant visitor to the Llewelyn Davies house. Sylvia had a husband and Barrie had a wife, but this seemed not to get in the way of this extra-marital friendship. Arthur Llewelyn Davies was unhappy and uneasy about the diminutive interloper in his family, but he was ill and unable to do much about the situation.

Sylvia's husband died in 1907, and the removal of this obstacle enabled Barrie to become closer still to the family, to the extent of providing financial support. Small wonder that Barrie's wife started an affair shortly after this and divorced him. When Sylvia died in 1910 Barrie claimed that they were engaged to be married. There was no evidence of this; her will stated that she wanted Barrie to be guardian to her boys – but along with three other people: her mother, brother and brother-in-law. She evidently did not trust him enough to be her children's sole guardian.

Barrie's interest in the Llewelyn Davies boys (and other children) aroused later suspicions that he may have been a paedophile, but there was no suggestion of it at the time, from anybody at all, and his active interest in them went on through adolescence into early adulthood – in fact until they left him and Neverland behind. The boys themselves always found his behaviour completely straightforward. The youngest of the brothers, Nico, went so far as to say that he did not believe Barrie ever experienced lust for anyone, man, woman or child. 'He was an innocent – which is why he could write *Peter Pan*.'

The plot of *Peter Pan* emerged from the stories Barrie told the boys as they played their fantasy games about castaways at Black Lake Cottage.

Peter Pan, the character in the play, was drawn partly from Peter, partly from the other boys. To a great extent, Barrie drew on Michael. When the statue in Kensington Gardens was erected in 1912, Barrie intended the sculptor to base the figure on old photographs of Michael.

He was annoyed to find that the sculptor had other ideas and used a different boy as a model: 'It doesn't show the devil in Peter.' Barrie wrote to Michael daily, and was deeply shaken when in 1921 he was drowned at Sandford Lock on the Thames near Oxford in what seems to have been a boating accident. Michael was nineteen when it happened, and he died along with a close friend, Rupert Buxton. In the wake of the double drowning there was speculation about a possible suicide pact, but the pool at Sandford Lock is a notoriously dangerous spot and an accident seems likelier. George had by then already died, a casualty of the Great War in 1915.

Jack served in the navy and died of tuberculosis at the age of sixty-five in 1959.

Peter Llewelyn Davies, the boy who gave his name to Peter Pan and grew up to became a publisher, died in 1960. He had come to believe that he would inherit 'everything' from Barrie and was profoundly disappointed when the money went elsewhere. It is not clear whether Barrie ever made him this promise. Peter hated the fact that everyone identified him as Peter Pan and felt that Barrie owed him something in compensation. In 1960, he threw himself under a train as it came into Sloane Square tube station. It seems he had been going through family papers and it is thought that he had reached some papers relating to Michael's death at Sandford Lock. But he was also depressed that several close family members had inherited Huntington's disease.

Nico lived on until 1980. The Llewelyn Davies family certainly had its share of troubles and tragedies, but there is no reason to see any of these as traceable back to J. M. Barrie. He did not spoil or lead the boys astray. The make-believe games that led to *Peter Pan* were for the Llewelyn Davies boys just an exciting episode in their childhood. But for Barrie, and for the rest of us, the make-believe led to the creation of a literary classic.

IX

CREATIVE ENCOUNTERS: THE 20TH CENTURY

RICHARD RODGERS AND OSCAR HAMMERSTEIN

(1919)

RICHARD RODGERS (1902–1979) was one of the most prolific and influential composers of popular music in the twentieth century. He wrote the music for over 900 songs and forty Broadway musicals. Many of the songs and musicals are still performed and they have a wide and lasting appeal because of their simple and spirited appeal to the emotions. But it was music he wrote, not words, so he needed a creative partnership with someone who could write lyrics for him.

Rodgers went to Columbia University, where he met both of his future collaborators, Lorenz Hart (1895–1943) and Oscar Hammerstein II (1895–1960). For the first part of his career, Rodgers teamed up with Lorenz Hart. It was in 1919 that Richard Rodgers first met Lorenz Hart, and they immediately collaborated in the writing of a song called *Any Old Place With You*. That was their debut song, which was featured in the 1919 musical *A Lonely Romeo*. The first professional production they worked on together was *Poor Little Ritz Girl* in 1920. But it was slow going, and Rodgers seriously considered giving up on show business and composing altogether, to become a salesman.

Hammerstein had been at Columbia University until 1916 and then spent a year at Columbia Law School. Throughout his college career, though, he had been committed to the theatre, both writing and performing in student productions. Eventually he gave up law school in order to pursue a career in show business. He launched into a twenty-year-long collaboration with Otto Harbach; their first musical, *Always*

You, opened on Broadway in 1921. Hammerstein wrote both the book and the song lyrics. During the next forty years Hammerstein was to work with many different composers, including Jerome Kern. It was with Kern that he wrote one of the greatest masterpieces of musical theatre, *Show Boat,* in 1927. He became the most accomplished lyricist, and it is as if he and Rodgers were just waiting for one another to become available for a major collaboration. But that was not to come for some time.

In the early 1920s, Richard Rodgers had been thinking of giving up on music. Then in 1925 Rodgers and Hart had a breakthrough when they wrote the songs for a Theatre Guild benefit show called *The Garrick Gaieties.* The critics liked it and though it was supposed to have only a single performance the response was such that the Guild gave it a run. The most successful number in the show was *Manhattan,* and that was the song that Rodgers believed established him and Hart as a pair of songwriters. Through the twenties they wrote a string of successful Broadway musicals.

In the 1930s the Depression hit New York and Rodgers and Hart took refuge in Hollywood, where they hoped to do better. Rodgers later regretted the move, although he did write several successful film scores while there. At this time, Rodgers wrote a melody, but Hart had trouble in writing a suitable lyric for it. He tried three times and each song failed. Then, on the fourth try, he came up with *Blue Moon,* which became one of their most successful and most famous songs. In 1935 Rodgers and Hart went back to Broadway, where they turned out a string of successful shows including *Pal Joey* and *The Boys From Syracuse.*

Lorenz Hart died in 1943. The working relationship between Richard Rodgers and Lorenz Hart had been deteriorating. The hard-working and self-disciplined Rodgers found Hart unreliable because of his dependency on drink. Then Hart's health had deteriorated. There was both an opportunity and a need to make a fresh start. Rodgers already knew Oscar Hammerstein – they had met way back at college. They had also written several songs together even before Rodgers started working professionally with Hart. Rodgers had been intending in 1943 to work with Hart on a musical adaptation of a play called *Green Grow the Lilacs,* but Hart's alcoholism had by this stage made him too unreliable. Rodgers approached Oscar Hammerstein, who agreed to collaborate.

In a way it was a return to a student relationship – and it was hugely successful. The first musical they wrote together, in 1943, was *Oklahoma!* In spite of its folksy, nostalgic and rather outdated view of rural America, it had a breathtaking freshness which had a universal appeal. It offered one catchy and spirited song after another: *I Cain't Say No, The Surrey With The Fringe On Top* and *Oh, What a Beautiful Mornin'.* But it was also a show that revolutionised the medium. For the first time the plot, lyrics and music were integrated into something that approached opera.

And *Oklahoma!* was not to be the one-off success that it might have easily have been. There were four more that were to rank among the most popular and durable musicals of all time: *Carousel* (1945), *South Pacific* (1949), *The King and I* (1951) and *The Sound of Music* (1959). Rodgers and Hammerstein had their failures, such as *Allegro, Me and Juliet* and *Pipe Dream*, but the huge achievement of their 'big five' musicals easily made up for any disappointment in these lesser pieces.

The songwriting partnership was widely acknowledged to be exceptional, bringing many awards including two Pulitzer Prizes.

Then, in 1960, Oscar Hammerstein died. The prolific and inexhaustible Richard Rodgers worked on alone. He tried writing both words and music for *No Strings* in 1962, though it was only a minor success. He tried working with other lyricists, but could not really find one to replace Hammerstein. A partnership like that came only once in a lifetime – or maybe twice.

PHILIP HESELTINE AND FREDERICK DELIUS

(1911)

LONDON, THE WEEK before Christmas in 1930, was cold with a heavy winter fog. At the end of the evening of Tuesday 16 December, Philip Heseltine had a drink with friends at the Duke of Wellington in Sloane Square and went back to his flat at Number 30 Tite Street, Chelsea. The artist Whistler had once lived at Number 33 and Oscar Wilde at Number 34.

Early the following morning, the neighbours were disturbed by the noise of doors and windows being shut at Number 30 and the piano being played. The piano playing went on until about 7 am. By 8.30 the neighbours noticed a strong smell of gas. Mid-morning, Heseltine's girlfriend Barbara Peache arrived after returning from a dance and found she could not get in. The police were called and they found Heseltine fully clothed on a settee. He had been dead for three hours. Later, Edith Buckley Jones identified the body as that of her son, Philip Heseltine, also known as the composer Peter Warlock.

Philip Heseltine was born at the Savoy Hotel in 1894. He grew up to be a slim, sensitive, charming boy, unhealthily devoted to his mother. In 1904, at the age of nine, he was sent to Stone House, a boarding school in Broadstairs. His letters home show the depth of his affection for his mother. He wrote pathetically, 'Please kiss all your letters.' She often wrote back extorting yet more love by accusing him of writing her letters that were too short, showing he had forgotten her.

At Eton, by the age of thirteen he had become deeply interested in music. He wrote to his mother asking her to book seats for The Ring cycle at Covent Garden. In 1910 he developed a craze for the music of

Frederick Delius, whom he saw as unjustly neglected. He hoped Delius's new opera, *A Village Romeo and Juliet,* was going to succeed. A visiting cello teacher, Edward Mason, was also enthusiastic about Delius, and encouraged the sixteen-year-old's new craze. Philip's interest in Delius, who was then forty-eight, led him to attempt to make a two-piano arrangement of parts of *A Village Romeo and Juliet.* Mason lent him a score of Delius's *Sea Drift,* and Philip was rapidly learning how to read full orchestral scores. He was desperate to hear performances of Delius's music and was thwarted over and over again.

Then suddenly Philip's mother wrote to him at Eton to tell him she would be meeting Delius when he visited London. Delius was then living in France. It is not known how she engineered this meeting. When he heard about it, Philip naturally said how much he too would like to meet the composer but he felt he might not get permission from the school. His mother suggested that Delius might instead be persuaded to visit Philip at Eton. Philip was already working on an arrangement of Brigg Fair for piano and now, if he got it finished in time, he might even be able to play it for the composer. But he was also overawed at the prospect; 'I am afraid my room offers very limited space for so great a man.'

Then Delius's *Songs of Sunset* were given their first London performance by the Thomas Beecham Orchestra and Edward Mason Choir. Philip was able to go, at last, and hear a whole concert programme of Delius's music. He even managed to meet Delius in the interval. The next day he wrote Delius a fan letter, telling him about 'the most glorious evening I have ever spent.' Philip knew that the music of Delius would change his life.

Delius was impressed by the boy's enthusiasm. He must have been flattered to be on the receiving end of so much appreciation and warmth. He commented to Philip's piano teacher later that year, 'Heseltine seems to me to have remarkable musical intelligence and also to be very gifted – I like him very much and find his enthusiasm very refreshing.' It would be hard not to enjoy someone else's unbounded enthusiasm for your work, and it may be that Delius was thinking more about himself than about Philip as he allowed the friendship to develop.

The time came for Delius to leave Eton and it is very revealing about the school values of the day that his final report mentions his English style, his Greek prose, his memory, his intelligence, and nothing at all about what was central to him – his music.

Philip's thoughts turned towards a career in music. He studied at the Cologne Conservatoire, where he failed to build his technique as a pianist; he had no real interest in becoming a good pianist. He heard a performance of *Brigg Fair* at Koblenz and wrote to Delius, criticising the conductor. Delius wrote back at length, returning the boy's piano transcription of *Brigg Fair*. Delius told him there was currently no piano arrangement of *Summer Garden* or the *Dance Rhapsody*; 'Do one of them for two pianos, and I will hear it when I next come to Germany – perhaps in March – Send on the pieces you have orchestrated and I will be very glad to help you – You have great talent for orchestration.' Delius said he would like to see Philip in 'Wild Wales' and that he would try to arrange it for August or September of 1912.

Philip was still struggling with the choice of his life. Would he become a stockbroker, or a civil servant? He wrote to his mother that he was sure he had insufficient musical ability to make a career in music. He also had his first article published early in 1912; significantly, it was not about music. It was called *The Van Railway*; it was about a disused branch line in Wales, and printed in *The Locomotive* magazine. Yet he also tried his hand at composing – for the very first time – at this critical moment. At the back of his mind there was perhaps an anarchic voice telling him to become a composer, not a civil servant or a stockbroker. Roger Quilter, an Old Etonian, had accompanied some of his own songs in a concert at Eton in the previous June, and Philip had been deeply impressed by what he heard; he wanted to write 'English' songs like Quilter's. Years afterwards, Philip sent Quilter a copy of one his own songs with an inscription, 'To R. Q. without whom there could have been no P. W.'

But Philip also knew that his attempts at composition were no good. He said, 'My composition is rather ludicrous; the only way I can produce anything at all is to strum chords at the piano until I light upon one which pleases me, whereupon it is imprisoned in a notebook. When a sufficient number of chords and progressions are congregated, I look for a short and, if possible, appropriate poem to hang them on.' He thought it was likely to be a waste of time. There was a voice of sanity in one part of his mind.

This was perhaps the moment when Philip should have decided between the Stock Exchange and the Civil Service. But the correspondence with Delius continued and blossomed. They became first friends and then firm friends. Delius encouraged Philip to write to him as often as he liked. He was hugely flattered by the young man's adulation and took on the role of father-figure which Philip was pressing on him.

Philip had decided to take the Oxford entrance examinations and that entailed taking some Latin and Greek tuition from the Vicar of Chadlington, the Revd Clarence Rolt. This was under way in March 1912. Rolt picked up Philip's enthusiasm about Delius – who could not, who spent any time with Philip? – and became concerned about it. In the end, he wrote to Philip's mother, expressing his anxiety. He was worried that Philip had learned to dislike Eton and all institutions. It was a loss to him, because he could not thrive on negative reactions. 'Again, Philip's admiration for Delius is not without dangers.' The dangers Rolt was particularly anxious about were Delius's anti-Christian views and his enthusiasm for Nietzsche. Not a good thing for a boy of Philip's age, Rolt thought.

Edith, Philip's mother, decided to go and see Rolt. She told Rolt something confidential about Delius, something about Delius's private life. No-one knows what this was. It may be that Delius had lived with Jelka for six years before they got married. It may be that Delius had led a promiscuous sex life in Paris in the 1890s. It may be that Delius had dabbled in the occult. Whatever it was, it made Rolt even more anxious about Delius's influence on young Phil. There was a Delius concert coming up in Birmingham and it was likely, Rolt thought, that Delius would attend. It was also likely that Philip would want to go. Rolt decided he would 'forbid him to speak to Delius.' It shows a poor understanding of adolescent psychology, as this sort of stricture might have been exactly calculated to throw Philip into the clutches of Delius.

At the Birmingham Festival, Philip and Delius duly met and got to know each other even better. Philip also had the opportunity to hear Elgar conducting *The Music Makers;* Philip commented that Elgar's conducting was sub-standard and that Elgar looked ill – as he was. When Delius and Philip said goodbye in Birmingham, Delius told him to think more of his music than his Latin. This was unhelpful, as Philip was in two months' time to sit his Oxford entrance examination.

Philip was accepted by Christ Church, Charles Dodgson's college, but he was still apprehensive of the course he was taking towards the Civil Service. He wrote a long, anguished letter to Delius expressing his doubts and appealing for advice. Delius's answer was devastatingly simple. 'You ask me for advice in choosing between the civil service – for which you seem to have no interest whatever - & music, which you love – I will give it to you – I think the most stupid thing one can do is to spend ones life doing something one hates or for which one has no interest.' Delius went on to tell him he could become a critic and that he was sufficiently gifted to become a composer. That injudicious letter was the decider.

Philip Heseltine spent just one academic year at Oxford (1913–14). He passed the time there but hankered after a musical career. He left Oxford and did not return. He became a music critic. He struggled to become a composer. He struggled for recognition as a composer. He even tried to leave his old identity behind, becoming Peter Warlock. Warlock was initially just a pen-name, but it gradually became an alternative personality. The gentle, sensitive and charming Philip Heseltine was eventually replaced by the suave and sinister male chauvinist Peter Warlock. Philip was adrift in Bohemian London, and all too often adopting a bohemian way of life has been a cover for artistic mediocrity.

In musical and literary circles, Philip Heseltine's Peter Warlock persona quickly became recognisable as an eccentric figure. In 1916 he had a brief and turbulent friendship with the novelist D. H. Lawrence, who based one of his fictional characters on him: Julius Halliday in *Women in Love* is Philip. This led to a threat of litigation and an out-of-court settlement. Other writers also borrowed Philip's Warlock persona. Warlock appears as Coleman in Aldous Huxley's *Antic Hay* (1923), Roy Hartle in Osbert Sitwell's *Those Were the Days* (1938), Giles Revelstoke in Robertson Davies's *A Mixture of Frailties* (1958) and Maclintick in Anthony Powell's book *Casanova's Chinese Restaurant* (1960).

By 1930 the truth had dawned that he was not succeeding as a composer. He had written some fine pieces, including the *Three Belloc Songs* and the *Capriol Suite*, but he was not making his mark. His songs were not selling. He was running out of ideas as a composer and would have to fall back on music criticism. He had financial problems. He decided to end it all.

When he was a young man, he was given some advice by an older man whom he trusted and to whom he appealed for help. That encounter with Frederick Delius – an encounter with vanity – misled Philip Heseltine, and took him into a maze that led him to 30 Tite Street. Delius could have given more cautious advice, to stick to the Civil Service plan for the time being; a Civil Service career was not incompatible with a good deal of amateur music making and it would have given him financial security, the freedom to compose whatever he liked, and the opportunity to become a full-time composer later if he wished.

Delius and Jelka were devastated by the news of Philip's suicide. Delius told his assistant Eric Fenby that he could think of nothing else. Jelka wrote to Phil's distraught mother, 'We shall always love dear Phil as the best of friends, ever helpful, ever supremely intelligent and lovable, and we shall sorrow for him and miss him with you.'

SALVADOR DALI
AND GALA

(1929)

THE SPANISH SURREALIST painter Salvador Dali was born in 1904. His life was strange from the beginning, as his parents conditioned him to believe that he was the reincarnation of his older brother, who had died nine months before his birth. Dali's father, a lawyer, was strict, while his mother was more indulgent and fostered his artistic leanings. He started drawing, discovered modern art in 1916 and had his first public exhibition in 1919. He studied art at the Fine Arts School in Madrid, where he became noticeable as a tall, thin, eccentric dandy, wearing knee breeches in the style of Oscar Wilde. But he attracted most attention with his paintings, which were experiments in Cubism; there were no Cubist artists in Madrid at that time. Dali also experimented with Dada.

During these student days, Dali developed an intense friendship with the poet Federico Garcia Lorca, but he was seriously frightened when Lorca made sexual advances to him. Dali's career at the School ended abruptly just before his final examinations, when with characteristic arrogance he announced that no-one on the faculty staff was competent to assess his abilities. The faculty response was to expel him. This was in 1926, the year when he painted the *Basket of Bread,* a masterpiece of photographic realism. Dali went to Paris, where he met his idol Pablo Picasso, who in turn had already heard favourable reports of Dali's works through Joan Miró.

Subsequently Dali painted a number of homage works strongly influenced by Picasso and Miró. But he also assimilated influences from a huge range of painters from the past, such as Raphael, Vermeer and

Velazquez, as well the avant-garde. At this time Dali adopted his Velazquez-style handlebar moustache, which became a kind of trademark; it also defied both the art world and the general public to take him seriously. He became the Surrealist buffoon, the clown of the art world. When Dali exhibited his work in Barcelona it attracted a great deal of attention and bewilderment – because it was so eclectic. He was the equivalent in the visual arts of Stravinsky in classical music; Stravinsky also shared Dali's surreal sense of humour and sense of mischief.

In 1929, the year when he collaborated with Luis Bunuel on the script of the film *Un chien andalou* (An Andalusian dog), he met Gala for the first time. She was a Russian immigrant and her real name was Elena Ivanovna Diakonova. She was eleven years older than Dali and she was married to a surrealist poet, Paul Eluard. Dali joined the Surrealist group in the Montparnasse quarter. It was a critical time for Dali. His mother had already died, and his father had reached the point of disowning him. The father was incensed when he read in a newspaper that Dali had exhibited a picture of the Sacred Heart with the caption 'Sometimes, for fun, I spit on my mother's portrait.' Dali's father was extremely angry and demanded a public apology and retraction. Dali refused and was in turn refused further access to the family home; he was also disinherited.

Dali's life was at a watershed. He was disowned by his father in Spain and adopted by the Montparnasse Surrealists in Paris. He found Gala. In the summer of 1930, Dali and Gala rented a fisherman's hut at Port Lligat. Then Dali bought it and gradually enlarged it until it turned into his much-loved seaside villa. Now he had a permanent home and he also had a muse. Gala was frequently to be his model. Gala was also his companion, his lover, his mistress, his soul-mate, his rock. She was the foundation of the rest of his creative life. Almost at once he painted his most famous picture, *The Persistence of Memory*, which has been nicknamed *Melting Clocks*. It introduced the archetypal surreal image of the soft, melting pocket watch. It illustrates Dali's interest in symbolism, and the importance of the unconscious mind, the importance of dreams. The image of the melting watch symbolises the flexibility of time, challenging the everyday assumption that time marches on at a regular rate. Other watches are being devoured by insects to show the impermanence of time. A simple and soft-centred idea, but a slightly subversive one.

Two years after Gala divorced her husband in 1932, Dali and Gala were married in a civil ceremony. Later, in 1959, they were to get married again in a Catholic ceremony; this was made possible by the death in 1952 of Gala's former husband. In the 1930s, Dali became an international celebrity. His appearance in the popular press was guaranteed by his attention-grabbing antics. When he appeared at a New York exhibition he was wearing a bra in a glass case on his chest. When he gave a lecture at a Surrealist exhibition in London, he did so wearing a deep-sea diving suit. When he arrived, he was leading a pair of wolfhounds and carrying a billiard cue. The helmet had to be unscrewed as Dali was suffocating. Even this play-acting was alleged to be symbolic; he wanted to demonstrate that he was diving deep inside the human mind.

This sort of behaviour guaranteed that photographs of him would appear in tabloid newspapers and magazines all over the world. It was excellent self-publicity. But it also got him into difficulties sometimes. He quixotically defended what he called the 'Hitler phenomenon' as irrational, which he made clear he intended as the highest form of praise. Then he realised that he had gone too far and needed to explain that he was not really a supporter of Hitler. But when Franco came to power in Spain after the Civil War Dali supported him and his fascist régime, creating renewed doubts about his Hitler remarks. This led to his ejection from the Surrealist group. One joke at Dali's expense was the coining of an anagram of his name: 'avida dollars', which means 'greedy for dollars'. The inventor of the joke was André Breton, who regarded Dali as nothing less than a traitor to Surrealism.

But Dali was not too damaged. He was a celebrity, he had wealthy patrons like Edward James ready to buy his work, and he could legitimately claim, as he did, that 'I myself am surrealism.'

When the Second World War got under way in Europe, Dali and

Gala moved to America, where they stayed for eight years. They returned to Spain in 1949, a Spain still ruled by Franco, which drew down further criticism on him from other artists. A lot of the criticism of Dali was based more on personal and political hatred than on artistic considerations. Some artists fought to have Dali's work excluded from Surrealist exhibitions.

Dali was very angry when in 1949 his sister Ana Maria wrote a book about him, *Dali as seen by his sister*. What incensed him was her portrayal of his childhood as perfectly normal and happy. Normal was the last thing he wanted people to think he was; he had worked hard to sell the public an image of himself as a bizarre, eccentric genius – possibly mad, but certainly brilliant. His sister had betrayed him. But in recent years Robert Descharnes, who was his secretary for many years, supported Ana Maria's view, describing Dali as 'rather normal'.

In later life he went on experimenting with new media and increasingly incorporated Catholic imagery as he became more embedded in Catholicism. He also spent time creating a personal museum.

From 1965 onwards, Dali and Gala were seen together less frequently and there seems to have been a partial estrangement, but Gala went on managing Dali's business affairs. In 1980, when Gala was becoming senile, she started giving him doses of various unprescribed drugs. These dangerous cocktails permanently impaired his nervous system. Gala had inadvertently poisoned the Dali she loved, and terminated his artistic life. Dali, who was then seventy-six years old and had until then enjoyed very good health, was suddenly a total physical wreck. His right hand now had a Parkinsonian palsy that made it almost impossible for him to paint.

By this time Franco was dead and Spain had a king. In the ultimate surreal gesture, the new king ennobled Dali, bestowing on him the title Marquis of Pubol.

On 10 June 1982, Gala died and Dali lost the will to live. He stopped drinking, apparently hoping that dehydration would bring about his death. But it is also possible that even this act was a bizarre experiment. Possibly he hoped that dehydrating himself would put him into a state of suspended animation; he had read that some micro-organisms were capable of surviving in this way. He moved into the castle at Pubol, which he had acquired for Gala. It was the place where she had died, and he decided it would be the place where he too would die. In 1984, fire broke out in Dali's bedroom. The cause is still not known. It may have been the result of negligence on the part of his staff, or he may have started the fire deliberately himself. But Dali was rescued and lived on for five more years, dying of heart failure in 1989.

He died to the strains of his favourite music, Wagner's *Tristan und Isolde*, with its theme of union in death, another reflection of his undying bond with Gala. She had been the making of Dali, who looked as though he could so easily have descended into insanity, by being the great stabilising influence in his life. She protected him and helped him in a variety of ways, for instance by becoming his business manager; she was the one who mediated the organisation of his major exhibitions in Europe and America in the 1930s, while Dali dressed up and played the fool for the press cameras.

PABLO PICASSO AND DORA MAAR

(1935)

THE GREAT 20TH century painter Pablo Picasso had a long career. Well before the outbreak of the First World War he mixed with a wide spectrum of bohemian writers and artists in Montmartre and Montparnasse. Among them were the Surrealist André Breton, the writer Alfred Jarry and the poet Apollinaire. When Apollinaire was arrested on suspicion of stealing the *Mona Lisa* he implicated Picasso, who was also taken in for questioning. Both were innocent and later exonerated.

Picasso's life style was typical of bohemian Paris at the time – experimental art, wild talk, wild behaviour and free love. In 1918 he married Olga Khokhlova, a ballet dancer. After a honeymoon in Biarritz Olga introduced Picasso to Parisian high society. But Olga's attempt to impose social proprieties on her husband inevitably led to friction between them, and there was constant domestic conflict. Picasso collaborated with Diaghilev and Stravinsky on a production of *Pulcinella* in 1920. Picasso's encounter with Stravinsky gave him the opportunity to produce some fine portrait sketches of the composer.

In 1927 Picasso met Marie-Therèse Walter, a seventeen-year-old girl, and began an affair with her. He separated from Olga. He avoided divorce as French law at that time demanded an equal division of property in divorce cases, and Picasso was anxious not to lose half his wealth to Olga. As a result, Picasso and Olga Khokhlova remained legally married until she died in 1955. The affair with Marie-Therèse lasted many years, produced a daughter called Maya, and she clung to the hope that one day Picasso would marry her. He didn't. Four years after Picasso died, she hanged herself.

In Picasso's succession of lovers, after Marie-Thérèse came Dora Maar, who was a painter and photographer with a Croatian father and a French mother. Picasso met her in the winter of 1935. Dora and Picasso shared many mutual friends in intellectual circles in Paris, including Man Ray, Andre Bréton and the poet Paul Eluard. It was inevitable that they would meet. Picasso noticed Dora on the terrace at the Les Deux Magots café, a Surrealist haunt. Picasso was chatting to his friend, the poet Paul Eluard, when he saw her sitting on her own, stabbing the table between her fingers with a penknife. Sometimes she caught her fingers and blood appeared between the roses embroidered on her gloves. It is easy to understand why Picasso would want to know more about this sad, strange, unusual woman. He asked Paul Eluard to introduce him to her. Later he asked her for the gloves so that he would remember their meeting: he kept them in his flat.

Her unusualness extended to her name. 'Dora Maar' was really made out of two fragments from the middle of her real name, Henriette Theodora Markovitch. The twenty-nine-year-old Dora Maar was beautiful, passionate and very intelligent. She was, moreover, already established as a fashion and publicity photographer – a name in her own right, before she met Picasso. And as well as being a commercial photographer, she was an innovative Surrealist photographer. She was also a political activist. It was very much a meeting of minds and spirits.

Dora's *Portrait of Ubu*, created in 1936, became an icon of the Surrealist movement and was shown in Surrealist exhibitions at Charles Ratton's Gallery and in London. The *Portrait of Ubu* was named after Alfred Jarry's 1896 play. In it, the character of Ubu was based on Jarry's physics teacher who looked like a monstrous sea creature. Dora declined to identify the image, and this only fuelled curiosity about it. Some thought it might be an armadillo foetus. Like her fellow-Surrealists, Dora was exploring the exotic and the grotesque to create disquieting new tensions.

Dora had a great influence on Picasso, stimulating one of the major innovative phases of his artistic career. Above all, she entered his life at a moment when it seemed to be breaking apart. He even felt that he was incapable of painting and instead diverted his creative energy to writing poetry. Thanks to the complex personal and artistic relationship that developed, Picasso was able to resume his work as an artist. Dora possessed one attribute that his other women did not share. She could speak Spanish. She had spent part of her childhood in Argentina, and this enabled her to converse with Picasso in his native language.

Dora became Picasso's mistress and constant companion from the time when they met in 1935, right through the period of great turmoil that embraced the Spanish Civil War and the Second World War.

The artistic collaboration started shortly after that first meeting in the café. Dora took portrait photographs of Picasso at her studio in the Rue d'Astorg. These are important records of Picasso at the beginning of their relationship. Surprisingly, Dora did not make prints from all of the negatives. Perhaps, with her experience as a photographer, she knew by looking at the negatives which ones would make the best prints. Her activity as a photographer and her experiments with technique intrigued Picasso. He started taking his own photographs of her. These became the starting-point for a series of new (Picasso) works which mixed photography and printmaking in an entirely new way.

Picasso used his photographs of Dora as a starting point. He painted portraits on glass and then exposed them over photographic paper to make some surprising photographic impressions. He also scratched the images on glass plates to create different effects. He tried putting lace and other fabrics between the glass plate and the photographic paper, and was able to build up some highly original multi-layered compositions. It is unlikely that Picasso would have experimented in this way with photography if he had not met Dora.

And Picasso used Dora as a model. She was often severely depressed, quite literally a woman in tears, and Picasso painted her in this state.

During the Second World War, Picasso stayed in Paris, in spite of the German occupation. This took a certain amount of courage, as Picasso's style of art was not approved of by the Nazis, but he went on painting in his studio there regardless. The witty Cubist portrait of Dora, *Dora Maar au chat*, was painted in 1941. Bronze casting was outlawed in Paris by the German authorities, but Picasso went on regardless, using bronze smuggled into the city.

After Paris was liberated in 1944, Picasso launched into a new relationship, with Françoise Gilot, who was an art student. Dora's bouts of depression had not been easy to live with. Now that Picasso had a new lover, Dora's depression was naturally accentuated. Picasso and Paul Eluard were concerned about Dora and arranged for her to have psychoanalysis with their psychiatrist friend Jacques Lacan. Picasso gave her a leave-taking present of a drawing. It was not a very cheering image; it was a portrait of his close friend Max Jacob who had just died in a transit camp after being arrested by the Nazis. But he also gave her some still lifes and a house in Provence.

After the huge commitment she had made to Picasso and the nine years spent living with him, Dora Maar found it hard to regain her stability. Her situation was not made easier by the sudden and unexpected death in 1946 of her closest friend, Nusch, the wife of Paul Eluard, and her mother had died in 1941. So when she was abandoned by Picasso she had no-one close to her to support her. Eventually, though, she was able to return to her old social circle.

Picasso and his new mistress Françoise had two children together, Paloma and Claude. Françoise left Picasso in 1953. She was the only one of Picasso's women to take that initiative, and Picasso was surprised and devastated when it happened. She would not put up with his infidelities and with what she saw as abusive treatment. Rejection by Françoise made Picasso realise that he was old. He was now in his seventies, and no longer physically attractive. Some of his drawings from this time explore the idea: a grotesque old dwarf with a beautiful girl.

But Picasso found another girl. This time it was Jacqueline Roque. She worked at the pottery in the south of France where Picasso made and painted his ceramics. Picasso hung onto Jacqueline for the rest of his life, marrying her in 1961. But one reason for marrying her seems to have been spite – directed against Françoise Gilot. Françoise had been trying to find a means of legitimising her two children by Picasso; there would after all be a huge amount of money to inherit when Picasso died as he was very wealthy. Picasso encouraged her to divorce her husband, Luc Simon, apparently allowing her to believe that he would then marry her in order to secure her children's legal rights. But once Françoise had set her divorce proceedings in motion, Picasso secretly married Jacqueline to thwart Françoise' plan. It was a particularly mean-spirited piece of revenge for Françoise Gilot's leaving him eight years earlier.

Picasso died at Mougins in France in 1973, as he and his wife entertained friends for dinner. He said, 'Drink to my health: you know I can't drink any more!' Dora Maar had meanwhile retreated into obscurity. She died in 1997 at the age of eighty-nine. But after her death, more emerged about her relationship with Picasso. The Picasso expert Anne Baldassari was given access to Dora's apartment in the Rue de Savoie in Paris in order to create a photographic record for the Picasso Museum. What emerged was that Dora had kept everything to do with her time with Picasso. Her camera was there, the camera she had used for her own professional work, and which Picasso had also used in his experiments with photography. There was even a piece of stained paper with a label – the blood of Picasso. There was a paper sculpture of her pet dog, made by Picasso out of a napkin.

There were also several paintings of Dora, which she had kept, in spite of the temptation to sell; by the 1990s, Picasso's paintings were selling for record prices. The objects together showed the intimate and creative nature of the relationship. Perhaps Dora Maar's most conspicuous and identifiable contribution to art history was her record of the creation of Guernica. While Picasso painted this great painting in his workshop on the Rue des Grands Augustins, Dora took photographs of the work at different stages in its completion. It makes a unique archive of the creation of a masterpiece.

BENJAMIN BRITTEN
AND PETER PEARS

(1937)

THE CAREER OF the English composer Benjamin Britten was marked by a sequence of important encounters with people – his mother, his two teachers, Frank Bridge and John Ireland, his friends Piers Dunkerley and Michael Tippett, a series of collaborators such as W. H. Auden, Eric Crozier and Ronald Duncan, and his partner for many years, Peter Pears.

Born in 1913, Ben was a child prodigy. At the age of eight he wrote a setting of a poem by Kipling, *Oh, where are you going to, all you big steamers*, and by the age of ten according to his own account he was turning out 'reams and reams' of music. His long prep school day, starting at 7.30 in the morning and going on until 8.00 in the evening, gave him little spare time to compose during the school terms, so he packed all his composition into the holidays. This very early manifestation of time-management gave him a disciplined approach to composing to tight deadlines which he applied right through his life.

While at school he learned to play the viola, and he had his first major formative experience, a real-life encounter with another composer – Frank Bridge. In October 1924, at a festival in Norwich, the ten-year-old Ben Britten heard Bridge conducting his piece, *The Sea*. In his own words, Britten 'was knocked sideways'. Frank Bridge was an isolated figure in English music, an outsider. Born in 1879, the son of a Brighton violin teacher, he studied at the Royal College of Music and then became a freelance teacher and string player. He might have made a success as a conductor, but he lacked diplomacy; if an orchestra was playing badly, he said so and many players disliked him for it. Like Britten, Bridge started composing as a child and by the time Britten heard Bridge's music he was already an accomplished composer. But here again Bridge's progress was limited by his acerbic personality. He gave the impression that he thought everyone else was 'rather a fool', according to those who knew him at that time. *The Sea*, which Bridge wrote before the First World War, was his best-known piece; in the 1920s it was just about the only Bridge piece in the repertoire. Britten loved its lush orchestration and the way it described the different moods of the sea. Britten was strongly influenced by this musical encounter; one day he too would describe the sea using an orchestra in his own, now much more famous, pieces: the four *Sea Interludes* from Peter Grimes.

The young Britten was more firmly committed to music than ever. He was solidly supported in this by his mother, though his father had reservations; he thought the boy spent too much time at the piano. Captain Sewell, Britten's headmaster, tried to push the idea of mathematics as the way to a more secure livelihood than being a genius at music. But Mrs Britten stuck by her son's enthusiasm for music.

In 1927, Bridge was in Norwich again, this time to conduct the piece commissioned the previous year, *Enter Spring*. Britten and his mother were in the audience. A meeting was arranged between the boy and the older composer. Bridge was unenthusiastic; he was always being asked to encourage supposedly gifted children and usually found them far from gifted. But when he met Ben he realised after only a few minutes that here was something and someone quite remarkable. He asked Ben to come back the next day and bring some of his compositions. He did, and Bridge went through them with him. Bridge was impressed by Ben's determination to write in a modern style in spite of his lack of access to modern music. Ben had in fact heard music by Gustav Holst and Ravel, and that had a lasting influence on him. Britten much later told Imogen Holst that a particular harmonic progression *A Ceremony of Carols* was borrowed from her father's music. 'That's one of the things I learnt from your father.'

By the end of his morning with the young Benjamin Britten, Frank Bridge was in no doubt that the boy had the makings of a real composer and should have professional tuition. What he proposed was that his friend Harold Samuel should be his music teacher and that he, Bridge, should give Ben lessons in composition. This was a remarkable offer, as Bridge had no other composition students. There was consternation in the Britten house. Mr Britten was conservative and very sceptical about Frank Bridge, who was the stereotypical bohemian artist with long hair, excitable temperament, and who was excessively talkative. Pop Britten thought that anyone who talked that much must be an empty vessel. A compromise was agreed. Ben would attend public school the next year as had been planned, but make day trips to London for lessons with Samuel and Bridge.

In January 1928, when he was fourteen, Ben had his first lesson with Frank Bridge in Kensington Church Street; his diary innocently (but significantly) noted 'Peter Pan in evening wonderful.' Ben enjoyed the lessons, but they were demanding and sometimes gruelling. One lesson went on for six hours before Mrs Bridge intervened to tell her husband the boy needed a break. Ben would emerge from the lessons blinking and twitching, white with exhaustion. Bridge ruthlessly went through Ben's compositions, often questioning what he had written. He would play them back to him on the piano, repeatedly: 'Now listen to this – is this what you meant?' Bridge taught Britten clarity and ruthless attention to detail; he also taught him a lot about harmony and counterpoint.

After Gresham's School, Britten went to the Royal College of Music. Britten felt that the RCM still suffered from having Sir Hubert Parry as its director from 1894 until 1918; he had stressed the amateur idea, being 'the English Gentleman who generally thinks it rather vulgar to take too much trouble.' Britten took himself and his music very seriously. He admired the music of John Ireland, but found him a demanding teacher. In 1930, when Britten encountered him, Ireland was in his fifties, gloomy and very critical. Britten did not enjoy his lessons at Ireland's house, which was dirty and untidy. When he arrived for his lessons, he sometimes found Ireland still in bed, often with a hangover. It was only in later years, when Britten had become famous, that Ireland began to speak well of him and claimed to have helped him on his way.

At the time when he was teaching Britten he actually regarded another student, Helen Perkin, as his star pupil.

In fact Vaughan Williams made more attempts to help Britten, trying to get his music performed. Britten went into the examination room with a substantial bundle of compositions under his arm. Vaughan Williams asked him genially, 'Is that all?' Britten replied, 'Oh no, I've got two suitcases full outside.' Ireland was not keen to teach Britten composition, perhaps because he knew he had already had lessons with Bridge. Ireland did give him lessons, but made him 'plod through counterpoint'. Later, Britten was grateful for this, and considered that the counterpoint lessons were the most important part of his training.

But Britten still valued Frank Bridge. In the summer of 1931 he went down to stay at the Bridges' weekend cottage at Friston near the Seven Sisters. They explored the South Downs together in Bridge's car. Meanwhile, the sessions with Ireland were getting worse. Ireland was drunk during one lesson and urinated on the carpet. Britten was horrified. Other lessons were cancelled at short notice. Britten even so won the composition prize for the year, in spite of Vaughan Williams' description of his music as 'very clever but beastly'.

It was at this time, at the age of nineteen, that he wrote his *Sinfonietta*, which made one critic write, 'Britten is the most interesting new arrival since Walton.' Sophisticated and advanced though Britten's music was becoming, there was still something very boyish about Britten. He liked Mickey Mouse cartoons. Like Barrie, he was a boy who did not want to grow up and would never grow up properly. And, significantly, as he teetered on the brink of adulthood, he latched onto Barrie's book *The Little White Bird*, which is the forerunner of *Peter Pan*. He met Schoenberg and planned to study with Berg after he left the RCM. His mother said, 'No, dear,' and he accepted that; he was twenty-one and he meekly accepted parental control as if he had been six.

A near-encounter from school days had been Wystan Auden, another pupil at Gresham's, though he was seven years older than Britten. Britten agreed to write soundtrack music for publicity films made by the General Post Office's film unit. Now Auden independently asked to write words for the Film Unit, so Auden and Britten found themselves collaborating. The first of these collaborative films was *Coal Face*. Britten shamelessly plagiarised some pieces by Rossini, and then published them as *Soirées Musicales*. Later came the well-known *Night Mail* (1936), with rapidly chanted words by Auden and an original score by Britten. The collaboration went on, without the Post Office, with Auden writing words for a song cycle, *Our Hunting Fathers*, and eventually an opera, Britten's first opera, *Paul Bunyan*.

Then came the encounter that changed Britten's life. He was, like any young man, looking for love. He found it when he met Peter Pears. It seems possible that Auden may have fallen for Britten, but his feelings were not reciprocated. The second of two poems Auden dedicated to Britten contains these lines near its end;

> *For each love to its aim is true,*
> *And all kinds seek their own;*
> *You love your life and I love you,*
> *So I must lie alone.*

In January 1937, Britten's sixty-three-year-old mother caught pneumonia, apparently while nursing Ben's sister Beth, and unexpectedly died. Britten loved his mother dearly and felt the loss as a disaster, but it also released him and allowed him to take control of his own life. It was not a coincidence that 1937 was the year in which he launched into the first adult relationship of his life.

In March he attended rehearsals of two of his songs with the BBC Singers, and had lunch with some of the singers. One of those singers was Peter Pears, who was three years older than Britten. They both loved music. They both loved sport; for Britten it was tennis, for Pears cricket. Pears too had passed through the Royal College of Music, specialising in opera singing. Pears was tall, imposing, and attracted a lot of women, but he was only attracted to men. By May, Britten and Pears were dining together, going to concerts together, and playing tennis. It would not be many weeks before Britten started writing music for Pears to sing. Peter Pears had one of the most distinctive and instantly recognisable tenor voices of the 20th century – haunting, lyrical, liquid – and Britten was captivated by it.

From then on the life-long friendship between the two men became a life-long professional musical relationship. One composition after another heavily featured the voice of Peter Pears: *Les Illuminations* (1939), *Serenade* (1943), *Peter Grimes* (1945) and *Billy Budd* (1951), on through to *Death in Venice* (1973). It was for Britten stressful to be a closet homosexual in a country where for most of his life homosexuality was criminal, and in a culture where homosexuality was disapproved of and ridiculed. This stress found expression in Britten's music. Under the surface charm and gloss it is taut, nervous and edgy, often dark and savagely disciplined. Robert Tear, another tenor who sang many Britten roles and worked closely with the composer, thought that without that stress Britten might have become another Verdi.

The relationship between Britten and Pears polarised musicians until Britten's death in 1976. There were many gay musicians who supported them and the ambitious festival they founded and organised at Aldeburgh each year. But there was also a backlash from some heterosexual musicians like Charles Mackerras, William Walton, Elisabeth Lutyens, Constant Lambert and Alan Rawsthorne. William Walton in particular was very bitter about what he saw as a gay conspiracy; as Walton confided to Michael Tippett, he felt that his own career had been eclipsed by the meteoric rise of the young Benjamin Britten. Tippett, who was a friend of both Walton and Britten, tried to reassure Walton. He was less concerned about Britten's high profile, believing that in the long term there was room for all of them, including Walton and Tippett. What worried Michael Tippett far more was Britten's musical dependence on Peter Pears' voice. He couldn't understand how a composer of Britten's stature could limit himself to the extent of writing for that same voice, over and over again, and allow it to dominate his creative output. Tippett wished that things could have been different for Britten; but Tippett also had a passionate nature and well understood how Britten had been led by his heart.

There were negative aspects to Benjamin Britten's relationship with Peter Pears, and these were accentuated by Britten's towering dominance of British music in the 1950s and 1960s. But the effect on Britten's output of new and startlingly original compositions was phenomenal. He was prolific before he met Pears, but even more so afterwards, right up to the climax of his creative life, the *War Requiem* of 1961.

ENRICO FERMI AND
LEO SZILARD

(1938)

ENRICO FERMI (1902–1954) was an Italian physicist who played a leading role in developing the world's first nuclear reactor. He could be described as the inventor of the nuclear reactor, but the new technology was really the work of a team of scientists collaborating. His principal collaborator was Leo Szilard. Fermi is regarded as one of the key figures in twentieth century science, an accomplished master of both theory and experiment.

Fermi's interest in mathematics and physics started when he was a boy. They were interests he shared with his older brother, Giulio. When Giulio died unexpectedly of a throat abscess in 1915, the traumatic shock caused Enrico to immerse himself in the pursuit of science as a diversionary activity, an escape from grief. He latched onto an extraordinary book by Andrea Caraffa, *Elementorum physicae mathematicae* (and written in Latin), which covered every aspect of physics, including astronomy and acoustics. He also made friends with another obsessive student, Enrico Persico, and together they worked on projects such as building gyroscopes. When Fermi applied for entry to the Scuola Normale Superiore in Pisa, he wrote an essay on sound. The examiner commented that that essay in itself would have earned Fermi a doctorate. At university, he acquired such an advanced knowledge of quantum mechanics that Professor Puccianti invited him, while he was still an undergraduate, to lead seminars on the subject. In 1921, while still in his third year at university, he started publishing scientific papers.

Fermi explored Einstein's theory of relativity and wrote a paper proving that space continues to behave in a Euclidean way close to the time line. In 1923, in an appendix to a book by Kopff, Fermi became the first person to point out that concealed within Einstein's famous equation $E = mc^2$ there was a huge amount of energy that could be exploited. This was the first intimation of the possibility of exploiting nuclear energy.

While he was still only twenty-four, Fermi became the first Professor in Atomic Physics at Rome University. Founding this new department involved gathering a team of people who included Edoardo Aladi and Fermi's old friend Franco Rasetti. The team of experimenters became known as the Via Panisperna Boys, after the institute's address. Many new breakthroughs in physics were made by the new team, including the discovery of slow neutrons, which became central to the operation of nuclear reactors. The Via Panisperna Boys' experiments systematically bombarded elements with slow neutrons, including uranium, and they narrowly missed observing nuclear fission. Current theory held that nuclear fission was impossible, and at that time Fermi himself thought it was impossible, on the basis of his meticulous calculations.

Enrico Fermi stayed in Rome until 1938, when he won the Nobel Prize in Physics, for demonstrating the existence of new radioactive elements by neutron irradiation and the related discovery of nuclear reactions induced by slow neutrons. After he accepted his Nobel Prize in Stockholm, Fermi and his wife and children emigrated to America, to escape from the anti-semitic laws initiated by Mussolini. In America, Fermi started work at Columbia University with Leo Szilard, who had arrived there from England just before him.

Two German scientists, Hahn and Strassmann, reported detecting the element barium after bombarding uranium with neutrons. The results were seen by Otto Frisch as evidence of nuclear fission, and Frisch confirmed this by experiment in 1939; in 1944, Hahn was awarded the Nobel Prize in Chemistry for discovering nuclear fission. These developments in Europe were taken across the Atlantic by Niels Bohn, who lectured on the discovery at Princeton. A couple of scientists who heard the lecture went back to Columbia to tell Fermi. Then Bohr himself went to Columbia to talk to Fermi, but could not find him.

Instead he went to the cyclotron and talked to whoever would listen. It became clear to a number of the scientists working at Columbia that they should try to detect the energy that was released when uranium was subjected to nuclear fission by neutron bombardment. In January 1939, a team at Columbia University led by Enrico Fermi, carried out the first experiment in nuclear fission in America. At a conference that by chance opened the very next day in Washington DC, the news was disseminated that nuclear fission had been achieved.

After that, Fermi went to the University of Chicago and planned the first nuclear pile. But it also became clear from networking scientists that the Nazis were planning to use the energy from nuclear fission to create an atomic bomb. The research was now leading into extremely dangerous areas.

Fermi's most important collaborator was Leo Szilard, a Hungarian physicist who was four years older than Fermi. He had studied engineering at Budapest Technical University but left Hungary because of intensifying ant-semitism. In Berlin he switched to physics and was taught by some very distinguished teachers, including Max Planck and Albert Einstein. While in Berlin he worked on numerous inventions, including the cyclotron. In 1933 he left Germany for London, again to escape Nazi persecution. He read an article in *The Times* by the distinguished scientist Ernest Rutherford, who rejected even the possibility that atomic energy could ever have any practical application. This annoyed Szilard so much that while he was walking to work at St Bartholomew's Hospital he conceived the idea of the nuclear chain reaction. The idea came to him, he said, as he waited for some traffic lights to change on Southampton Row. His friend Jacob Bronowski didn't quite believe this story, as the Leo Szilard he knew never waited for traffic lights to change. It was in any case an extraordinary insight, given that nuclear fission had not yet been discovered.

Szilard patented the concept and in 1936 assigned it to the British Admiralty to ensure its secrecy. Szilard also became the co-holder of the US patent on the nuclear reactor.

In 1938 Szilard accepted an invitation to continue his research at

Columbia University, where he was soon joined by Enrico Fermi. Once Szilard and Fermi knew about nuclear fission, they concluded that uranium was the likeliest element to sustain a chain reaction. They conducted an experiment, which showed significant neutron multiplication in uranium. It showed that the chain reaction Szilard had envisaged was really possible. It also showed the way to nuclear bombs. After the experiment, Szilard knew what lay ahead: 'That night I knew the world was headed for sorrow.'

In 1939 Leo Szilard drafted a letter warning President Franklin D. Roosevelt about the imminence of a German atomic bomb. Albert Einstein also signed Szilard's letter. There was a delay in delivering the letter to Roosevelt, because of the German invasion of Poland. Roosevelt was concerned about what the scientists were telling him: concerned enough to set up a Uranium Committee. Columbia University was given funding to research atomic energy. But the bureaucrats were nervous about giving money to 'alien' research scientists and there was a delay. Szilard begged Einstein to send a second letter to Roosevelt in the spring of 1940 and this freed the grant money, which was used to create the first nuclear reactor, Chicago Pile-1.

This first reactor was built on a hard squash court under the football stadium at Chicago University. Soviet reports mistranslated this location as a converted pumpkin field. The landmark project was brilliantly planned and carried out by Fermi. The first self-generating nuclear chain reaction was under way. The Chicago reactor served as a pilot plant for the much larger reactors that were then built at Hanford in Washington. They in their turn produced the plutonium needed to make the Hiroshima and Nagasaki bombs. The Chicago reactor work led by Fermi and Szilard was then folded into what became known as the Manhattan Project, which was directed by Szilard.

Fermi moved from Chicago to Los Alamos in the late stages of the Manhattan Project as a consultant and problem solver. He was an indispensable man in a project of this kind. He was able to come up with quick and accurate answers to problems that others could not solve at all. Fermi watched the Trinity atom bomb test on 16 July 1945. He scattered torn-up strips of paper into the air as the shock wave reached him and watched thoughtfully as the paper whirled about. He was estimating the energy yield of this, the first ever nuclear explosion. His estimate was ten kilotons of TNT; in fact it was nearer nineteen kilotons. His way of getting quick approximate answers in this ad hoc way became known among scientists as 'the Fermi method'.

Fermi was a very modest and likeable man, ready to help in any task. He was once invited to do some experiments with the cyclotron at Princeton, and while he was there he thought nothing of helping a student to move a table while another student directed them. He died of stomach cancer at the young age of fifty-three. Two others who worked on the nuclear reactor also died of cancer. He had realised that the work was dangerous, but the outcome of the project was so important that, as far as he was concerned, it outweighed any consideration for personal safety.

JOHN LENNON AND PAUL MCCARTNEY

(1957)

THE POP SINGER and songwriter John Lennon was born in Liverpool in 1940. His father, Alf, was a merchant seaman and, in the Second World War, was often away from home. He sent cheques to his wife, Julia, but these stopped coming in 1943. When he returned the following year, Julia had found another man, by whom she was expecting another child; she did not want Alf back. Julia's sister Mimi contacted Liverpool Social Services about the situation and urged Julia to let her take care of John. Eventually Julia agreed and John went to live with his Aunt Mimi. In the summer of 1946 Alf Lennon visited Mimi's house, ostensibly to take John on a trip to Blackpool, but secretly with the intention of taking the boy with him to New Zealand. Julia followed them, there was a quarrel and the five-year-old was made to choose between his mother and his father. Confused and upset, John chose his mother and did not see his father for many years.

After this disturbed and challenging beginning, the rest of John Lennon's boyhood was more secure. He lived with Aunt Mimi and her husband, George Smith, at 251 Menlove Avenue. The arrangement suited them as they had no children of their own. Julia meanwhile visited her son nearly every day. She taught him to play the banjo and played Elvis Presley records to him. The first song he learned was *Ain't That A Shame* by Fats Domino.

After attending the Dovedale County Primary School, Lennon went in 1952 to the Quarry Bank High School in Liverpool. He acquired a reputation as a carefree student. He drew cartoons and mimicked his teachers. In his last year at school, Julia bought John his first guitar. It was a Gallotone Champion acoustic guitar and she had it delivered to her own house as she knew Mimi wouldn't approve. Mimi hoped John would get tired of pop music. He boasted that he would be famous one day and she was naturally sceptical, believing that he could never make a living out of music. Mimi's anxiety was justified. John failed all his O Level examinations. He was only accepted by Liverpool College of Art after some lobbying by Mimi and John's headmaster.

In July 1958, John's mother Julia was knocked down and killed by a car in Menlove Avenue, close to Mimi's house. Paul McCartney had lost his own mother less than two years earlier (she died as a result of breast cancer). The recent loss of their mothers was to help form a bond between John and Paul.

At Liverpool College of Art, John adopted the persona of a Teddy Boy and met Cynthia Powell, whom he later married. His assertively independent style meant that he was often disruptive in class. He ridiculed and antagonised teachers. Unsurprisingly, he failed when examined and dropped out before completing the course.

While he was still at Quarry Bank, Lennon took guitar lessons but gave up fairly quickly. In March 1957, Lennon formed his own pop group, the Quarrymen. That was before he met Paul McCartney. The fateful first meeting between John Lennon and Paul McCartney happened on 6 July 1957. It was at the Quarrymen's second concert, which was given at a garden fête at St Peter's Church, Woolton. Lennon was seventeen and McCartney was fifteen. McCartney's father was not impressed by the new friendship and told his son that Lennon would get him into a lot of trouble. He later relented and let the Quarrymen rehearse in the McCartney house, 20 Forthlin Road. Aunt Mimi also disapproved of John's befriending Paul McCartney because she thought Paul was working class; she referred to Paul patronisingly as 'John's little friend'.

Paul McCartney was born in 1942, and in 1953 went to the Liverpool Institute. The following year, on the bus on the way to school, he met George Harrison, who lived near him. In October 1956, Paul's mother Mary died following surgery. Paul's father Jim was a musician. He played trumpet and piano and had led Jim Mac's Jazz Band in the 1920s.

He encouraged his two sons, Paul and Michael, to get involved in music. There was a piano in the front room for them to play. Grandfather, Joe McCartney, played tuba and Jim often took the boys to local brass band concerts. Jim McCartney gave Paul a trumpet, but he swapped it for a Zenith acoustic guitar. Paul found the guitar difficult to play because he was left-handed, but when he saw a poster advertising a Slim Whitman concert he spotted that Whitman was a left-handed player; it was just a matter of stringing the guitar the other way round. The problem was solved.

Paul McCartney wrote his first song on his guitar. It was called *I Lost My Little Girl*. It was only later that he started playing the piano. His father suggested taking music lessons, but he preferred to learn and play by ear. In that way he and Lennon were alike.

At Forthlin Road, Lennon and McCartney started writing their own songs. John Lennon's first song, written in 1958, was *Hello, Little Girl*, which, performed by the Fourmost, later became a hit. McCartney persuaded John Lennon to let George Harrison join the group. Lennon thought Harrison was too young, but was persuaded otherwise when he heard George playing *Raunchy* on the top deck of a bus. George was good enough to join the Quarrymen as lead guitarist. Later, a friend of John's from art school, Stuart Sutcliffe, joined them as bass player.

The group changed its name to The Beatles. All the way through, John Lennon was seen as the group's leader, partly because of his age, partly because of his quick-witted personality. But they also needed a manager. Allan Williams became their first manager in 1960, after they played at his Jacaranda Club. Shortly after that he got them a booking at the Indra Club in Hamburg. Aunt Mimi was horrified at this, because she knew it meant that John would not be continuing his course. Jim McCartney was also very reluctant to let Paul go to Hamburg, but Paul told him he would be earning two pounds ten shillings a day. That was more than Jim was earning, so he let him go. Money talks.

After the first stint in Hamburg, Stuart Sutcliffe left The Beatles. He wanted to concentrate on his art; and he wanted to spend time with his girlfriend. Paul McCartney took on the role of bass player. Then the authorities discovered that George Harrison was too young to be there and there were complaints about the group's behaviour. They were asked to leave. They went back to Liverpool. There on 21 March 1961 they played the first of many concerts at the Cavern club. It was Paul McCartney who noticed that other Liverpool bands, their competitors, were all playing the same cover songs – other bands' music – and this prompted him and John Lennon to write more of their own songs.

Once George Harrison passed his eighteenth birthday, The Beatles were able to return to Hamburg. Shuttling back to Liverpool after Hamburg to do more concerts at the Cavern club, in November 1961, they were talent-spotted by Brian Epstein. He signed them up to a management contract. A month later they were driven to London for an audition, but Decca Records rejected them. In 1962 when they arrived at the Star Club in Hamburg they were told that Stuart Sutcliffe had just died. Lennon felt the loss acutely, following the death of his mother and his Uncle George.

Then, in May 1962, came another important encounter, the meeting with George Martin, the record producer and arranger who became known as 'The Fifth Beatle'. He signed The Beatles up for a record deal with Parlophone. George Martin was dissatisfied with the drummer and a replacement was found – Ringo Starr, who was the drummer currently working with Rory Storm and the Hurricanes. It was left to the Beatles' new manager, Brian Epstein, to sack the old drummer and hire the new one. But the result was the production of a strong double-sided single, *Love Me Do*. Ringo Starr did not play the drums on this record, as the delicate negotiations had not been completed; George Martin instead used the services of a session drummer, Andy White.

In February 1963, The Beatles recorded their first album, *Please Please Me*. The songs by John Lennon and Paul McCartney were credited to 'McCartney-Lennon', though this was subsequently to be changed to 'Lennon-McCartney'. The songs were written at incredible speed, often in hotel rooms after concerts, or at Lennon's house or at McCartney's house. The album *Please Please Me* was a huge commercial success. It was offered by EMI to their American subsidiary, Capitol Records, who did not want it. Brian Epstein managed to get the record released through another label, Vee-Jay Records, but it was not nearly as successful in the States as it was in Britain. The Beatles became hugely successful in Britain, but initially there was indifference in America. It was only when *I Want To Hold Your Hand* was released in America that The Beatles suddenly became a big success there too. Their profile was greatly enhanced by their appearances on American television on the *Ed Sullivan Show*.

This was the age of Beatlemania. By 1965, even the British establishment felt that it had to acknowledge The Beatles. They were awarded MBEs. Some members of the group definitely did not want them, but Brian Epstein persuaded them all to accept. The pressure on the four young men was enormous. At live performances, hysterical girls screamed so much that Lennon complained that no-one could hear them playing. Their musicianship was starting to suffer. In 1965, John Lennon significantly wrote a song called *Help!* On his own admission it was a literal cry for help. He could not go on like that.

The change was edged closer when John Lennon gave an interview to a British newspaper. In March 1966 he talked about Christianity being doomed; The Beatles were more popular than Jesus. The quote was picked up in America and repeated. There was a shocked reaction in the Bible Belt; concert venues cancelled Beatles performances; radio stations refused to broadcast Beatles numbers. In August, Lennon attempted a public apology, but it was only half-convincing. 'I never meant it to be a lousy anti-religious thing. I apologise if that will make you happy. I still don't know quite what I've done.'

John Lennon had had enough of the screaming teenaged girls, of being mobbed. Now there was an international press wanting to damage them. The Beatles decided to stop touring. Lennon was relieved. His inadvertently offensive comment about the popularity of the group had resulted in an end to the tours. He later wrote, 'I always remember to thank Jesus for the end of my touring days . . . God bless America. Thank you, Jesus.'

It was suddenly over. People still went on listening to and enjoying

The Beatles' music, but Beatlemania had come to an end. The subsequent influence of The Beatles on popular music, and in particular the influence of Lennon and McCartney, has never ended. The group began to break up. Ringo Starr left, but then came back. George Harrison left in January 1969, during the filming of *Let It Be*, but then came back after a meeting of The Beatles at Ringo's house two days afterwards. John Lennon left The Beatles in September 1969, but agreed not to announce it until the new recording contract had been negotiated. But on 10 April 1970 Paul McCartney issued a statement in the form of a series of questions and answers, in interview format, and in this he said he was no longer a part of The Beatles. This press release came just one week before Paul McCartney released his first solo album, *McCartney*.

It was as if each Beatle wanted to be the one to leave the group, and none of them wanted to be left behind. Lennon was annoyed and bitter that he, the one who had started the band, had not been allowed to be the one to finish it.

In the wake of the break-up, John Lennon felt very bitter. In a 1970 interview, he blamed Paul McCartney for the break-up of the group. When their manager Brian Epstein died, according to Lennon, they 'collapsed'. It was Paul McCartney who took over the leadership of the group, but his leadership led nowhere, as he saw it. But he was able to say, 'I still love those guys. The Beatles are over, but John, Paul, George and Ringo go on.' In August 1971, John Lennon took the decisive step of leaving Britain for New York. Following this, Lennon released an album called *John Lennon/ Plastic Ono Band*, which expresses his pain at losing his mother and losing The Beatles. The album *Imagine* came out in 1971.

Paul McCartney formed a new group called Wings, with his first wife, Linda, and the singer-songwriter Denny Laine, though the make-up of the group changed frequently. The Wings single *Mull of Kintyre* (1977) was to be the first single ever to sell over two million copies in the United Kingdom; it is still the UK's top-selling commercial (non-charity) single. Paul has gone on to produce a long list of songs as a solo artist. He can claim to be regarded as the most successful performer and composer in popular music history, with sales of 100 million singles. His song *Yesterday* has been recorded by more different performers than any other popular song in history – 3,700 artists so far. It has been played more than seven million times on US radio and television.

In the 1970s there was a partial reconciliation between John and Paul. Paul regularly phoned John, but could never be sure what sort of reaction he might get. Paul knew he could not talk to John directly about business, so they often chatted about inoffensive neutral things like cats. Paul McCartney wanted a musical collaboration – he wanted to make music with somebody. If it wasn't going to be John, it would be someone else. In the 1982 album *Tug of War*, Paul McCartney collaborated with Ringo and George Martin. He also sang a duet on a single with Stevie Wonder, *Ebony and Ivory* – a huge commercial success. He sang two highly successful duets with Michael Jackson, *The Girl is Mine* and *Say Say Say*.

In 1980, John Lennon was asked whether John, Paul, George and Ringo were enemies or friends. He said they were neither, but he hadn't seen any of the others for a while. He said the last time he had seen Paul McCartney they had watched *Saturday Night Live*: the television programme in which Lorne Michaels had made an offer of $US3,000 if The Beatles were reunited on the show. They thought of turning up at the television studio just for fun, but they were too tired.

On 9 December 1980, Paul McCartney woke to hear the news that John Lennon was dead. He had been murdered outside the Dakota Building, where he lived in New York. That day, McCartney went to a recording studio in Oxford Street, but as he left he was asked by reporters for a response to Lennon's death. He said it was terrible news, that he had spent the day in the studio listening to some material because he didn't want to sit at home: 'I didn't feel like it.' The next day he spoke to Yoko, John Lennon's partner. She said, 'John was really fond of you.'

Starting from a chance encounter at a church fête, John Lennon and Paul McCartney formed one of the most vibrant and influential songwriting partnerships, one that changed the course of British popular song-writing. They rose to fame and huge commercial success with unprecedented speed. And the unravelling of their partnership was also startlingly swift. For once, using the word 'meteoric' seems appropriate.

TIM RICE AND ANDREW LLOYD WEBBER

(1965)

ANDREW LLOYD WEBBER, the English composer of musicals, was born in 1948. Music was in the family. His father, William Lloyd Webber, was a composer and his brother Julian Lloyd Webber is a distinguished cellist. Andrew was a child prodigy. He started writing music at the age of six and his first published piece appeared when he was nine. He mounted 'productions' with his brother in a toy theatre that he built himself.

Lloyd Webber's music is very popular, and several of his musicals have run for over a decade in London and on Broadway. He has written, among other compositions, thirteen musicals and a Requiem Mass. Several songs have taken on a life of their own, independently of the musicals they come from, such as *Don't cry for me, Argentina* from *Evita* and *Memory* from *Cats*.

Although intensely musical as a boy, he started a degree course in history at Oxford. He was for a time at Magdalen College. But he abandoned Oxford and education when he had the chance to pursue a musical career.

Andrew Lloyd Webber's first collaboration with Tim Rice as lyricist was a musical called *The Likes of Us*. The collaboration started with Tim Rice writing Lloyd Webber a letter. It was dated 21 April 1965 and in it Tim mentioned that he had heard Andrew was looking for a writer of lyrics for his songs. He enjoyed writing the lyrics for pop songs and wondered if they might meet. When they started their collaboration, Andrew was seventeen and Tim twenty-one. *The Likes of Us* was a dramatisation of the life of the philanthropist Thomas Barnado. But it was not performed at the time when it was written. A small-scale student production was available, but Andrew and Tim had their sights set on the West End. It was only in 2005 that it received its first performance, at the Sydmonton Festival. In style, it looks back to the Broadway musicals of the 1940s, with a traditional overture that consists of a medley of tunes from the show. The musical style shows some of the early influences on Lloyd Webber, including Richard Rodgers and Lionel Bart. These characteristics make *The Likes of Us* different from the later pieces, which are more operatic in form.

Tim Rice, born in Amersham in 1944, went to Lancing College and then studied law for a year at the Sorbonne in Paris. Then in 1966 he abandoned law to join EMI Records as a management trainee. The EMI producer Norrie Paramor left EMI to set up his own company in 1968, and Tim Rice went with him to act as assistant producer. Tim Rice has done a wide variety of other things in his career. He was a co-founder of the *Guinness Book of British Hit Singles*, serving as an editor from 1977 until 1996. He also has a career as a media personality, taking part in radio panel games. He is interested in mathematics and cricket. But he is perhaps best known for his early and highly successful collaborations with Andrew Lloyd Webber.

In those early days, Tim Rice and Andrew Lloyd Webber wrote several 'free-standing' pop songs that were recorded as singles. They attempted to write a song for the Eurovision Song Contest. It was, appropriately, called *Try It And See*. It wasn't selected, but Lloyd Webber was able to recycle the music for King Herod's Song in *Jesus Christ, Superstar*.

The major breakthrough into musical theatre came for Andrew Lloyd Webber and Tim Rice in 1968. They were commissioned to write a piece for Colet Court. This became *Joseph and the Amazing Technicolour Dreamcoat* (1967). This is a light-hearted and whimsical re-telling of the biblical story of Joseph. The tone is close to contemporary pop music and it includes parodies of a range of different styles; that range and that eclecticism have become hallmarks of Lloyd Webber's music. Audiences loved *Joseph*. It was an instant success. Lloyd Webber greatly admired Elvis Presley, and the character of Pharaoh was based on Elvis. Elvis in return recorded one of Lloyd Webber's songs, *It's Easy for You*, in his last studio session in late 1976. Joseph was initially cast as a short cantata. After favourable reviews, Rice and Lloyd Webber fleshed it out with additional songs to make it into a two-hour stage work. It was then brought out in the West End after the success of *Jesus Christ, Superstar* (1970).

Jesus Christ, Superstar also had an unusual beginning. It started as a record album, before it had been staged in the West End. It is the antithesis of *Joseph*. Dealing with the last days in the life of Christ, it is dark and unsettling, especially the crucifixion scene. The musical style also contrasts with that of *Joseph*. It was publicised as a rock opera, like The Who's *Tommy*, though some of the music is more conventional pop.

Andrew Lloyd Webber and Tim Rice intended to follow this with a musical based on the Jeeves and Wooster novels of P. G. Wodehouse. But Tim Rice was less confident about this project. He knew Andrew Lloyd Webber admired Wodehouse's writing and was concerned that his book might not meet Andrew's expectations. Rice withdrew and Lloyd Webber subsequently wrote *Jeeves* with Alan Ayckbourn supplying the book and lyrics, though this was fairly unsuccessful, running for only three weeks. In 1996, Lloyd Webber and Ayckbourn thoroughly reworked it as *By Jeeves,* which was more successful.

Andrew Lloyd Webber went back to Tim Rice again to create *Evita* (1976), based on the life of Eva Peron. As with *Superstar*, the music was released as an album before the musical itself was staged. The musical style for *Evita* was more classical than earlier musicals, but there is still a range. It was a huge box office success. In 1980, Andrew Lloyd Webber wanted their next musical to be *Aspects of Love,* based on the book by David Garnett, but Tim Rice declined. After *Evita*, Tim decided that they needed time to recharge their batteries; they needed some time apart. The period of their major creative collaboration turned out to be over. So Andrew shelved the idea for the time being.

In *Cats* (1981), Lloyd Webber managed without Tim Rice by writing a dance musical. He used the poetry of T. S. Eliot for the lyrics. The one conspicuous exception is the most famous song in the musical, *Memory*, and the lyric for that was written by Trevor Nunn, who used the Eliot poem *Rhapsody on a Windy Night* as a starting point. Lloyd Webber uses a huge range of musical styles in this piece. Though perhaps unpromising in concept, *Cats* became the longest running musical in London, going on for twenty-one years.

Tim Rice, meanwhile, was writing *Blondel* (1983) with Stephen Oliver and *Chess* (1984) with Benny Andersson and Bjorn Alvaeus. He collaborated with Lloyd Webber once again for the 'half-act operetta' *Cricket* (1986).

Lloyd Webber's next conventional musical was to be *The Phantom of the Opera* (1986). For this, he did not return to Tim Rice for book and lyrics but went to Charles Hart with Richard Stilgoe for the lyrics, and then co-wrote the book in collaboration with Stilgoe. The form is still that of a musical, but in many places the style of the music is operatic, with references to Mozart, Puccini and Gilbert and Sullivan. Lloyd Webber returned to *Aspects of Love* (1989) using lyrics supplied by Don Black and Charles Hart. *Sunset Boulevard* (1993) has a book by Christopher Hampton and Don Black.

The creative collaboration between Andrew Lloyd Webber and Tim Rice worked extremely well from the time of their first encounter in 1965 until *Evita* in 1976. Since they parted company, there has been a reconciliation of their friendship, but Rice has made it clear that there are no plans to write any more musicals together. He has commented that that would be like trying to get married again. Rice also senses that they would not have been able to sustain the quality of the work they were doing; and if the quality fell, people would say, 'Ah well, we always knew they were never any good.'

BILL GATES AND PAUL ALLEN

(1970)

BILL GATES, WHO was born in 1955, is well-known as the founder of Microsoft, the software company he founded in 1975 with Paul Allen. For a long time he was Microsoft's full-time Chairman. He has now stood down from this role but remains the company's largest individual shareholder. In June 2008, he transferred his responsibilities to Ray Ozzie, Microsoft's chief software architect, and Craig Mundie, the company's chief research and strategy officer. Bill Gates stays on at Microsoft as a part-time, non-executive Chairman.

One of the world's great innovators, Gates was a leader in the personal computer revolution. Many admire him and his achievement, though inevitably there are those in the IT industry who criticise Microsoft's business tactics, which they consider anti-competitive.

Microsoft is a huge firm, generating huge wealth. For fifteen consecutive years, Gates was named the richest person in the world. He is still very wealthy and has turned his attention increasingly to philanthropic work, through the Bill & Melinda Gates Foundation, which Gates and his wife set up in 2000. Large amounts of money have been given to charitable organisations and scientific research programmes.

Bill Gates and Paul Allen were school friends at Lakeside School in Seattle. Allen was born in 1953. The staff at Lakeside made the momentous decision to familiarise their students with the world of computers. At that time, around 1970, computers were extremely expensive. The school organised fundraising in order to buy computer time on a computer owned by General Electric. It was on this computer that Paul Allen, Bill Gates and a few other students from Lakeside

School began to explore what computing could do. Soon Allen and Gates were exploring computer programming too. It was inevitable that the boys used all the computer time Lakeside bought, and they started to get behind with their conventional schoolwork.

As luck would have it, the Computer Center Corporation opened. Lakeside School was able to strike a deal with this company to use the CCC computer at a discounted price. The company was impressed with what the boys were able to do. When problems began to surface with the Corporation computers, they were hired to find the bugs in the system and as a trade-off the boys were given unlimited computer time.

After experimenting with some small-scale business ventures, they started their own company, which they called Traf-O-Data. They were both Basic programmers. They built a computer based on an Intel 8008 chip, using it to analyse traffic data for the Washington state highway department. It earned in the region of twenty thousand dollars for them – a significant sum. After launching this Traf-O-Data project with Gates, Allen went off to work for Honeywell in Cambridge, Massachusetts. Gates meanwhile went to Harvard, not far away in Boston.

Bill Gates and Paul Allen stayed in touch with each other. Allen was keen that they should start a software company together, but Gates was uncertain. Then, in 1974, Allen showed gates a copy of the magazine Popular Electronics. On its cover was a picture of the very first personal computer kit, the Altair 8800. The caption read, 'World's first microcomputer kit to rival commercial models'. This was exciting news, and gave a hint at a colossal home computer market in the near future. Gates and Allen felt sure that they could enhance its performance by applying Basic to it. The manufacturer of Altair was a company called Micro Instrumentation and Telemetry Systems (MITS). Paul Allen had a discussion with Ed Roberts, the president of MITS, and succeeded in selling him the idea of a version of Basic that would work on the Altair. Then Paul Allen and Bill Gates had to work day and night to finish the first microcomputer Basic. What Allen had told MITS was that he and Gates had already done the work; now they had to work hard to produce what they had promised.

They delivered in eight weeks. When the programme was demonstrated to MITS, it was the first time it had been run. Luckily it worked. MITS were impressed and straight away bought the rights to the Altair Basic. Paul Allen went to Albuquerque in New Mexico early in 1975 to take up a position as director of software for MITS. Bill Gates, still at university, had to make the difficult decision to drop out of Harvard; encouraged by Paul Allen he took the plunge and joined him at Albuquerque. Allen had himself dropped out after two years at Washington State University.

Altair Basic was functioning by March 1975. A lot had happened, yet Paul Allen was twenty-two and Bill Gates was still, incredibly, only nineteen. The partnership that would become Microsoft was sealed in April, though it did not acquire its trade name for several months.

While still in its infancy, the new company created versions of Basic for Radio Shack's TRS-80 and the fast-selling Apple II. Microsoft moved from Albuquerque to Bellevue in Washington in 1979 and then seven years later to a new corporate campus at Redmond, Washington.

Paul Allen was diagnosed with Hodgkin's disease in 1983. He was successfully treated by a long period of radiation therapy and a bone marrow transplant. After this, he decided not to return to Microsoft and he began to distance himself from the firm. He formally resigned from the Microsoft board in 2000, but he was asked to remain available as senior strategy advisor. He sold a large number of his Microsoft shares that year, but it is believed that he still owns 138 million shares.

The friendship between the two boys and their shared obsession with computers led to a determination to make a business success out of computing. That in turn led to the creation of one of the most successful companies of all time. Both men became extremely rich. Bill Gates is now said to be the third or fourth richest person in the world. Paul Allen is believed to be the twelfth richest, with an estimated net worth (in 2008) of sixteen billion dollars. Allen is chairman of Vulcan Inc and Charter Communications; he also has an extensive investment portfolio, including a large stake in DreamWorks Animation SKG. He owns three professional sports teams.

Like his friend and collaborator Bill Gates, Paul Allen is very keen on philanthropy. As early as 1986 he set up a foundation, the Paul G. Allen Family Foundation, to administrate his contributions to charitable causes, and about sixty percent of the Foundation's money goes to non-profit-making organisations in his home town of Seattle and the state of Washington. Paul Allen has so far given nearly a billion dollars to charitable causes that range from music to medicine.

But Paul Allen also likes to enjoy himself. He likes a party. He collects Jimi Hendrix memorabilia. His yacht *Octopus*, launched in 2003, is one of the largest motor yachts in the world. 127m (416 feet) long, it has a music studio and a basketball court on board. The lives of Paul Allen and Bill Gates represent encounters with personal wealth on a scale that most of us can only dream of.